"Evidence-informed education does not sit stil
constantly taking place. Findings are never fixe
invigorated by subsequent exploration. This b
revolution happening in classrooms around the world and marks a new
frontier in its evolution."

Tom Bennett OBE,
Founder of researchED

"This is a terrific collection of some of thought-provoking and actionable
articles about classroom teaching. The selections are sure to inform and
challenge readers, and certainly will help them understand teaching
better. It is also not farfetched to imagine that critical thinking about
these articles will lead to better teaching."

David C. Berliner,
Regents' Professor Emeritus, Arizona State University, US

"This is another great summary of the education research evidence.
If you've ever wondered about the importance of subject knowledge,
whether teachers are born or made, or what it means to be an authentic
teacher, this is the book for you."

Daisy Christodoulou,
Director of Education, No More Marking

"Brilliant! How many educators, cowed by the volume and complexity
of the technical literature on teaching, wished for a group of experts to
hand-pick the most important articles to read? And while they are at it, to
explain their importance and what they mean for practice? *How Teaching
Happens* distills decades of complexity into an easy-to-read volume that
dispenses practical wisdom. Anyone connected with education must
read it!"

Daniel T. Willingham,
Professor of Psychology at the University of Virginia,
and author of *Why Don't Students Like School?*

"It is REALLY a great book and I hope there is more of them. *How Teaching
Happens* mines research gold and will sit with *How Learning Happens* as
bookends of the perfect library for all educators. The 30 seminal articles
about effectiveness, curricula, design, techniques, content knowledge,
and assessment are minimal reading and they open a depth of findings,
ways of thinking, and the foundation of pedagogy reality as opposed to the
delusions that often are spouted about teaching. *How Learning Happens* was
my top pick for 2021, and *How Teaching Happens* is my top pick for 2022."

John Hattie,
Emeritus Professor of Education and author of *Visible Learning*

"*How Teaching Happens* is an exceptional piece of work; a worthy follow-up to *How Learning Happens*. As someone who works with hundreds of school leaders engaged in the business of teacher development, I can see this book being an immense support in a wide range of contexts, making seminal research accessible and actionable, informing the many important debates people across the profession are engaged in. The selection of papers is excellent, skilfully chosen to span the broad scope of everyday teaching issues – classroom practice, curriculum design, assessment and the all-important pedagogical content knowledge. Each paper is summarised and explored in depth with great clarity and enthusiasm, always with a focus on the implications for working teachers. It's a great read for anyone with an intellectual interest in the research base around how teachers function but, more importantly, this book is packed with insights that teachers and leaders can act on to improve their practice. It's a magnificent book that should find a place in every school staffroom or CPD library."

Tom Sherrington
Education Consultant and Author of *Teaching Walkthrus*

"Kirschner, Hendrick, and Heal's book is elegant, scholarly and accessible. They gracefully connect the often mysterious insights of research on teaching with principles and strategies of practice. An important contribution to repairing the painful isolation of wise practice from the work of scholars. Combining their careers both in the United States and in Europe, they also offer readers a valuable international perspective."

Lee S. Shulman
Emeritus Professor of Education
Stanford Graduate School of Education/President Emeritus
Carnegie Foundation for the Advancement of Teaching

How Teaching Happens

Building on their bestselling book *How Learning Happens*, Paul A. Kirschner and Carl Hendrick are joined by Jim Heal to explore how teaching happens. The book seeks to closely examine what makes for effective teaching in the classroom and how research on expert teaching can be used in practice.

Introducing 30 seminal works from the field of education psychology research, the learning sciences, and teaching effectiveness studies, each chapter takes an important work and illustrates clearly and concisely what the research means and how it can be used in daily practice. Divided into six sections the book covers:

- Teacher Effectiveness, Development, and Growth
- Curriculum Development/Instructional Design
- Teaching Techniques
- Pedagogical Content Knowledge
- In the Classroom
- Assessment

The book ends with a final chapter on "What's Missing?" in how teachers *learn* to teach.

Written by three leading experts in the field with illustrations by Oliver Cavigioli, *How Teaching Happens* provides a clear roadmap for classroom teachers, school leaders, and teacher trainers/trainees on what effective teaching looks like in practice.

Paul A. Kirschner is Emeritus Professor Educational Psychology at the Open University of the Netherlands, Guest Professor at the Thomas More University of Applied Science in Belgium and owner of kirschner-ED.

Carl Hendrick holds a PhD in education from King's College London and has taught for several years in both the state and independent sectors. He currently teaches at Wellington College, UK.

Jim Heal works at Deans for Impact, a US-based non-profit organisation committed to the transformation of educator preparation. He holds a Doctorate in Educational Leadership from Harvard University's Graduate School of Education.

How Teaching Happens

Seminal Works in Teaching and
Teacher Effectiveness and What They
Mean in Practice

**Paul A. Kirschner, Carl Hendrick and
Jim Heal**

Illustrated by Oliver Caviglioli

Routledge
Taylor & Francis Group

LONDON AND NEW YORK

Cover image: Oliver Caviglioli

First published 2022
by Routledge
4 Park Square, Milton Park, Abingdon, Oxon OX14 4RN

and by Routledge
605 Third Avenue, New York, NY 10158

Routledge is an imprint of the Taylor & Francis Group, an informa business

British Library Cataloguing-in-Publication Data
A catalogue record for this book is available from the British Library

Library of Congress Cataloging-in-Publication Data
Names: Kirschner, Paul A., 1951– author. | Hendrick, Carl, author. | Heal, Jim, author.
Title: How teaching happens : seminal works in teaching and teacher effectiveness and what they mean in practice / Paul A. Kirschner, Carl Hendrick and Jim Heal ; illustrated by Oliver Caviglioli.
Description: Abingdon, Oxon ; New York, NY : Routledge, 2022. | Includes bibliographical references and index.
Identifiers: LCCN 2022002216 | ISBN 9781032132075 (hardback) | ISBN 9781032132082 (paperback) | ISBN 9781003228165 (ebook)
Subjects: LCSH: Effective teaching. | Curriculum planning. | Instructional systems—Design. | Educational tests and measurements. | Classroom management.
Classification: LCC LB1025.3 .K585 2022 | DDC 371.102—dc23/eng/20220215
LC record available at https://lccn.loc.gov/2022002216

ISBN: 978-1-032-13207-5 (hbk)
ISBN: 978-1-032-13208-2 (pbk)
ISBN: 978-1-003-22816-5 (ebk)

DOI: 10.4324/9781003228165

Typeset in Tisa
by Apex CoVantage, LLC

MIX
Paper from
responsible sources
FSC® C013056
www.fsc.org

Printed and bound in Great Britain by
TJ Books Limited, Padstow, Cornwall

We dedicate this book to the (grand)children in our lives:
    Elsa, Benjamin, and Liselotte
    Gracie and Sadie
    Sam and Nora

As part of the world's future, you deserve the best education and the best teachers that exist. Hopefully this book, along with the previous one, will help that happen.

We also dedicate the book to all teachers around the world. You are members of one of the most difficult, most important, and greatest professions there is. It's our hope that this book will be of some help for you to do your job even better.

Contents

Preface: How Teaching Happens   xiii

SECTION 1
Teacher Effectiveness, Development, and Growth   1

1   An Experienced Teacher ≠ An Expert Teacher:
David Berliner on Teacher Expertise   3

2   Those Who Understand, Teach: Lee Shulman
on Knowledge Growth in Teachers   13

3   Teachers are Made, Not Born: Linda
Darling-Hammond on Teacher Training   23

4   The Death of the Teacher?: Jere Brophy
and Thomas Good on Teacher Behaviour   35

5   I Think, Therefore I Teach: Daniel Muijs
and Colleagues on Teacher Effectiveness   47

6   When Thinking and Acting Become One:
Donald Schön on Reflective Practice   59

SECTION 2
Curriculum Development/Instructional Design   69

7   It's All About Alignment: John Biggs on
Constructive Alignment   71

8   Pebble in the Pond: M. David Merrill and
Jeroen van Merriënboer on Instructional Design   81

9   How to Tell the Story of an Idea: Jerome Bruner
on Representing Knowledge   93

10   If you Don't Know Where You're Going, You Might
Wind Up Someplace Else: Robert
Mager on Lesson Objectives   103

SECTION 3
Teaching Techniques   **115**

11   There's No Such Thing as a Child Who Can't Be
Taught: Siegfried Engelmann on Direct Instruction   117

12   Burning the Strawman: Barak Rosenshine on
Explicit Instruction   129

13   Make Something of What You've Learnt: Logan
Fiorella & Richard Mayer on Ways to Generate
Learning   141

14   Learning: No Pain, No Gain: Robert Bjork on Desirable
Difficulties   151

15   Step for Step: Robert Atkinson and Colleagues
on Examples   163

SECTION 4
Pedagogical Content Knowledge   **175**

16   Why You Can't Teach What You Don't Know:
Lee Schulman on Teacher Knowledge   177

17   Mathematical Knowledge for Teaching: Heather Hill,
Deborah Hall and Colleagues on Mathematics PCK   187

18   The Science of Science Teaching: Jan Van Driel
and Colleagues on Science PCK   197

19   Three Chords and the Truth: Pamela Grossman
and Lee Shulman on PCK and English   207

20   How Should We Teach Reading?: Anne Castles
and Colleagues on the Science of Reading   217

21   Why Technology Should Be the Servant Not the
Master: Matthew Koehler and Punya Mishra
on PCK and Technology   229

SECTION 5
In the Classroom   **239**

22   "To Thine Own Self Be True": The Authentic Teacher:
Pedro De Bruyckere & Paul A. Kirschner on Teacher
Authenticity   24

23   Relationships Matter: Theo Wubbels & Mieke
Brekelmans on the Importance of Relationships   25

24   Why Relationships Matter: Robert Marzano
on Classroom Management   26

25 Teachers as Intelligent Consumers: Berliner
    on Classroom Management   275

SECTION 6
Assessment   **285**

26 The Many Faces and Uses of Assessment:
    Benjamin Bloom and Colleagues on Different
    Types of Evaluation   287

27 When Testing Kills Learning: John Biggs
    on Constructive Alignment   299

28 Don't Ask Questions That Don't Require
    Understanding to Answer: Richard Anderson
    on Test Design   309

29 Why Teaching to the Test Is So Bad: Daniel Koretz
    on Grade Inflation   319

30 Hocus-Pocus Teacher Education: NCTQ on
    What Teachers Don't Learn in School   329

Glossary   343
Index   351

Those who can, do. Those who understand, teach. (Lee Shulman)
If I wanted you to understand, I would have explained it better. (Johan Cruijff)

Preface: How Teaching Happens

The Liston Effect: Why Bad Teaching Often Looks Like Good Teaching

Surgery in the early 19th century was not for the faint-hearted. Amputations, for example, were carried out on unwashed wooden tables stained with the blood of hundreds of patients with sawdust on the floor to soak up the detritus. Hospital theatres were packed with eager onlookers jostling to get a better view of the grisly spectacle with little consideration for hygiene or patient dignity.

Surgeons in those days were performers. They would stride into theatres proudly wearing aprons encrusted in the blood and gore of past operations. These grim garments were never washed either: a stained apron was the mark of a good surgeon. Legend has it that some blood-stiffened frocks could stand up on their own.

Known as "the fastest knife in the West End", famed surgeon Robert Liston could remove a leg in less than thirty seconds, an important skill at a time when such operations were performed without anaesthetic. His speed and dexterity drastically limited the amount of suffering patients had to endure and he was in huge demand, often attending to those turned away by other surgeons who would queue for days to see him. He would often begin an amputation by proclaiming "time me gentlemen, time me" before dazzling onlookers with a flurry of rapid incisions, clasping a bloody scalpel between his teeth and removing the limb in three saw-strokes. Such was his speed that during one operation, it is claimed that he accidentally sliced off three fingers of one of his assistants and slashed the clothes of an onlooker who was so shocked at the sight of so much blood that he had a heart attack and promptly died at the scene. Both the patient and the de-fingered assistant later died of gangrene making this the only operation in history with a 300% mortality rate.

Despite this, Liston was known as a highly skilful practitioner with scores of patients queuing up to be treated by him and even more wanting to witness his proficiency at close quarters. But Liston was

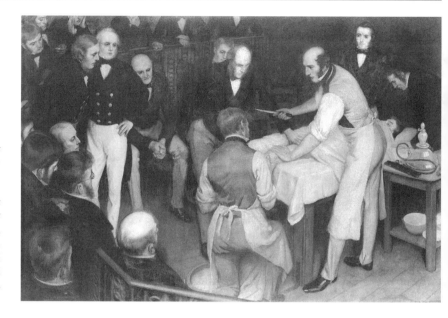

DEPICTION OF ROBERT LISTON PERFORMING AN AMPUTATION IN FRONT OF A CROWD OF SPECTATORS DURING SURGERY IN THE 1800S (SOURCE WIKIMEDIA COMMONS)

working in a time where there was a wilful rejection of evidence and where the virtuosity of the surgeon was seen as the single most important factor. Surgery at this time was particularly uninformed about post-operative infection and the adverse effect of being treated with unwashed hands and instruments. In fact, during the time Liston was working, hospital mortality rates actually went up, giving rise to the term "hospitalism" as a cause of death. As talented a practitioner as Liston was, often he was doing more harm than good.

Certain aspects of modern teaching have a lot in common with early 19th-century surgery in the sense that some teaching practice *looks like* it's effective but in reality, it's making the patient worse. Over the last 50 years a view of teaching has come to dominate the profession that is based not on experimental evidence but on philosophical and often political beliefs where the spectacle of teaching has been privileged over the mystery of learning. The enduring image of John Keating in *Dead Poet's Society* standing on his desk has, for some, come to symbolise what good teaching is where spectacle is privileged above all else. Indeed many teachers will have experienced a lesson observation where they put on a song and dance show with a lot of activities, little teacher talk, lots of student talk only to go back to a simpler form of teaching when the observer has left the room. A pedagogy where the pupils are very busy but learning very little is a debased form of pedagogy, and like Robert Liston's surgery is probably doing more harm than good.

The Pedagogy Delusion

One of the chapters in our last book *How Learning Happens* (henceforth in the rest of this book referred to as *HLH*) is based on a 1989 paper by Richard Clark in which he makes the claim that sometimes, research shows that a certain classroom intervention, no matter how well-intentioned, didn't have the intended effect in comparison to the control condition; usually the "standard" teaching practice. This is an occupational hazard of conducting research in the field, and of course crucially, no harm has been done.

But sometimes something else happens. Sometimes, students who received the new approach actually performed *worse* than those in the control group and/or performed worse after the intervention than before. In educational research we find few publications about these types of results because of the publication bias to publish interventions that worked. Clark calls these effects *mathemathantic* activities (*Greek mathemain*: that which is learned, and *thanatos*: death), in other words when teaching kills learning. Essentially his argument is that often this is due to a mismatch between the method of instruction and the prior knowledge of the student.

This we will refer to as *the pedagogy delusion* which is broadly speaking, a set of beliefs and assumptions about what **should** happen in a classroom that is characterised by a rejection of evidence, an acceptance of the romantic and philosophical, a celebration of the superficial in the form of fads and myths, an assertion that pedagogy is an end in itself, and the creation of an often toxic culture for teachers of unsustainable workload. This delusion is often typified by a domain-general vision of pedagogy so that it ends up generic in nature and is divorced from content. The exaltation of 21st-century skills is a good example of this. Schools often have a whole school training on some aspect of pedagogy and then we go to departments and figure out how to embed that in departments, but should a Physics teacher use the same techniques as a French teacher? In asking teachers to consider generic pedagogy before content we are promoting what Christine Counsell calls "an intransitive pedagogy, a pedagogy without an object".[1] Despite this however, there must be some common principles that we can outline to teachers, particularly those beginning their careers. In that sense, it's helpful to consider teaching in the context of instructional design.

---

[1] COUNSELL, C. (2017). "*GENERICISM'S CHILDREN*" *BLOG*. AVAILABLE VIA HTTPS://THEDIGNITYOF THETHINGBLOG.WORDPRESS.COM/2016/01/11/GENERICISMS-CHILDREN/

WHAT IS TEACHING?

TEACHING METHODS ARE RECURRENT instructional processes, applicable to various subject matters, and usable by more than one teacher. They are *recurrent* in that the activities are repeated over intervals measured in minutes or weeks. They are *instructional processes*, such as patterned teacher behaviour (for example, lecturing, discussion, and recitation); delivery systems for curriculum (for example, printed matter, film, programmed instruction, and computer-assisted instruction); and organisational structures for promoting learning (for example, tutoring, and independent study).

These instructional processes promote student learning of different kinds in various subject matters. The term "teaching method" should not be applied to instructional processes that are useful in teaching only, say, arithmetic (for example, using Cuisenaire rods), or reading (for example, conducting phonics drill). The ways in which the teaching of specific subject matter goes on we call "teaching techniques", which are studied in courses on curriculum and instruction in reading, science, social studies, mathematics, English, and the like. The requirement that a teaching method be *usable by more than one teacher* means that it should not depend upon the talents, traits, or resources unique to an individual teacher. Rather, the use of a teaching method should, in principle, be accessible to any trained teacher.

(Robert Gagne, 1976, p. 5)

One of the central themes of this book is that teaching is inherently counterintuitive and very often, we need to do the opposite of what we **think** we should do. For example, on the surface it would appear that the busier or engaged a student is, then the more they must be learning. On the surface this would seem like a necessary condition for learning however there is some evidence that it may not be a sufficient one.[2] Graham Nuthall explores this dichotomy in his seminal book "The Hidden Lives of Learners":

Our research shows that students can be busiest and most involved with material they already know. In most of the classrooms we have

---

[2]   AND WE MIGHT ADD THAT BEING ENGAGED IS IMPORTANT, BUT THAT'S COGNITIVE ENGAGEMENT AND NOT PHYSICAL ENGAGEMENT. THIS INVOLVES THE TYPES OF ACTIVITIES THAT LOGAN FIORELLA AND RICHARD MAYER CALL GENERATIVE LEARNING (SEE CHAPTER 13).

studied, each student already knows about 40–50% of what the teacher is teaching.

(Nuthall, 2007, p. 24)

Nuthall's work highlights the fact that students are keen to busy themselves doing tasks that *give the appearance* of learning, but which actually might just be disposable activities which do not engender long-lasting and durable learning.

There is also the distinction that learning and performance are not the same thing. According to Nicolas Soderstrom and Robert Bjork (2015) "instruction should endeavor to facilitate learning . . . the relatively permanent changes in behavior or knowledge that support longterm retention and transfer. . . . [This is] distinguished from performance, which refers to the temporary fluctuations in behavior or knowledge that can be observed and measured during or immediately after the acquisition process" (p. 176). In other words, learning is that you know something days, weeks, months and even years later while performance is that you know something for a test directly after you've studied it. The notion that one can enter a classroom and somehow see learning is a misguided one and as Rob Coe (2013) points out, engagement is often a poor proxy for learning. Teachers can be labouring under the delusion that where " 'I have taught it' becomes a proxy for 'they have learned it', without a need for any independent check on what (if anything) has actually been learned" (Coe, 2013, p. xii). So teaching is not only counterintuitive but also deceptive and what seems on the surface to be effective can be anything but.

At an address to the Boston Society for Medical Improvement in February 1843, Dr Oliver Wendell Holmes proclaimed that surgery should take place with hygienic procedures that would prevent infection and disease. This was met with a volley of argument from practitioners at the time where typically "surgeons operated in blood-stiffened frock coats – the stiffer the coat, the prouder the busy surgeon".[3] The weight of evidence in favour of hygiene and the reduction of post-operative infection would eventually come to bear and the image of surgeons like Liston striding around an operating theatre in covered in blood became a thing of the past. The craft of the classroom is at a similar point where we now have a growing body of evidence about how the brain learns and what kind of instruction can best aid that process. It is our wish that this book contribute in some way to a more evidence-informed and less gory future of teaching.

---

3 GORDON, R. (2001). DISASTROUS MOTHERHOOD: TALES FROM THE VIENNA WARDS. IN *GREAT MEDICAL DISASTERS* (PP. 34–36, P. 43 OF PP. 43–46 IN 1983 EDITION). HOUSE OF STRATUS.

This Book

In our first book, *HLH*, we explored the science of learning via expositions on seminal works in the area of cognitive development and how we learn. In that book we invited readers to consider how foundational research in that area might inform how we think about student learning and our planning of instruction. But what about the science of teaching? Is there such a thing and which seminal works would constitute a book on this subject?

As Robin Alexander neatly put it "teaching, in any setting, is the act of using method x to enable students to learn y" (Alexander, 2009, p. 5), and yet we have seemed to complicate the process to the detriment of both teacher and student. Too much pedagogy is focused on teaching and not learning and as John Sweller argues, "without an understanding of human cognitive architecture, instruction is blind" (Sweller, 2017).

This is a book essentially about instructional design in all its complexity which does not argue for a generic pedagogy but instead aspires to furnish educators with a toolbox of techniques and knowledge that they can use in certain situations to help the students in their charge.

Getting evidence from the classroom is hard. It's hard because there are so many variables which make isolating exactly what works in any situation very hard to pinpoint. However, there are many decades of diligent research into what makes for effective teaching and we have selected 30 research articles in several different areas which we feel constitute significant research in the field.

This book is an anthology; a selection of 30 pieces of research that we consider to be key works, or core articles, about teaching plus a final chapter on what's missing in the what we teach aspiring teachers. Like every anthology, this one is far from complete and doesn't pretend to be so. The works included are primarily drawn from the domain of educational (often cognitive) psychology. The selection process also wasn't scientific, although we did look beyond our own bookcases, preferences, and even prejudices. To come up with the list we "threw it in the group" via social media to make use of the wisdom of the crowd. We could easily create a second book with another 30 articles and it would still be incomplete. But as Goethe said: "It is in self-limitation that a master first shows himself".[4]

Each chapter has the same structure. First, we attempt to illustrate why the chosen article is so important. Then we present the article's original abstract. After this we describe the idea behind and the insights from the

---

[4] IN DER BESCHRÄNKUNG ZEIGT SICH ERST DER MEISTER (JOHANN WOLFGANG VON GOETHE, DAS SONETT – KAPITEL 1)

relevant research (i.e., what did the researcher do and find?) and then this is followed by a presentation of how you might use it in your own teaching. Finally, we provide reading suggestions with QR codes (where relevant) that lead you to easily readable articles or useful websites, podcasts, or videos.

Some Final Words Before You Start

We've made the choice for gender neutral language by choosing the plurals *them* and *their* when speaking of the student or the teacher. Also, we've made the choice when discussing the articles spotlighted in the book to often mention that the author used research by others and even name those others, but not to add these secondary references to the chapter. We've done this for two reasons, namely (1) adding these secondary references would make the chapter sound too much like a scientific article which it isn't, and (2) we hope that you, the reader, are stimulated to read the original article where you can then see the original citations and references and follow them up if you wish.

References

ALEXANDER, R. J. (2009). TOWARDS A COMPARATIVE PEDAGOGY. IN R. COWEN & A. M. KASAMIAS (EDS.), *INTERNATIONAL HANDBOOK OF COMPARATIVE EDUCATION* (PP. 911–929). SPRINGER. AVAILABLE VIA HTTP://ROBINALEXANDER.ORG.UK/WP-CONTENT/UPLOADS/2019/12/IHCE-CHAPTER-59-ALEXANDER.PDF

COE, R. (2013). *IMPROVING EDUCATION: A TRIUMPH OF HOPE OVER EXPERIENCE.* AVAILABLE VIA WWW.CEM.ORG/ATTACHMENTS/PUBLICATIONS/IMPROVINGEDUCATION2013.PDF

COUNSELL, C. (2017). *"GENERICISM'S CHILDREN" BLOG.* AVAILABLE VIA HTTPS://THEDIGNITYOFTHETHINGBLOG.WORDPRESS.COM/2016/01/11/GENERICISMS-CHILDREN/

GAGNE, R. M. (1976). THE LEARNING BASIS OF TEACHING METHODS. IN N. L. GAGE (ED.), *THE PSYCHOLOGY OF TEACHING METHODS, SEVENTY-FIFTH YEARBOOK OF THE NATIONAL SOCIETY FOR THE STUDY OF EDUCATION, PART I* (PP. 21–43). UNIVERSITY OF CHICAGO PRESS.

GORDON, R. (2001). DISASTROUS MOTHERHOOD: TALES FROM THE VIENNA WARDS. IN *GREAT MEDICAL DISASTERS* (PP. 34–36, P. 43 OF PP. 43–46 IN 1983 EDITION). HOUSE OF STRATUS.

NUTHALL, G. (2007). *THE HIDDEN LIVES OF LEARNERS.* NZCER PRESS.

SODERSTROM, N. C., & BJORK, R. A. (2015). LEARNING VERSUS PERFORMANCE: AN INTEGRATIVE REVIEW. *PERSPECTIVES ON PSYCHOLOGICAL SCIENCE: A JOURNAL OF THE ASSOCIATION FOR PSYCHOLOGICAL SCIENCE, 10*(2), 176–199.

SWELLER, J. (2017). WITHOUT AN UNDERSTANDING OF HUMAN COGNITIVE ARCHITECTURE, INSTRUCTION IS BLIND. *THE ACE CONFERENCE.* AVAILABLE VIA HTTPS://WWW.YOUTUBE.COM/WATCH?V=GOLPFI9LS-W

SECTION 1

TEACHER EFFECTIVENESS, DEVELOPMENT, AND GROWTH

National Public Radio's "Car Talk" featured the brothers Tom and Ray Magliozzi, affectionately known to their listeners as Click & Clack the Tappet Brothers. First aired in 1977, the deceptively simple formula for their show remained unchanged for over 35 years. Listeners would call in with seemingly insoluble car issues; the brothers would – after joking primarily about themselves, but also about the caller – then offer advice on what was wrong with the vehicle and what to do about it.

What made the show engaging for so many was the way the various symptoms of a troubled car often presented as utterly mysterious at first glance, at least to a novice listener. Chin-scratchers such as, "My car makes a whistling noise when I hit 60mph" would leave most wondering what on earth had happened to bring about such phenomena in the first place. The brothers would then ask a series of questions that didn't seem entirely connected to the problem, at least not on the face of things: "Does it still whistle when you're turning a corner? Does it only happen on a cold day? What colour is the car (when they seemed stumped)? Do you tend to park your car on a sloped driveway at home?" before somehow arriving at an entirely accurate determination of the problem and a suggested solution. By the way: they tested whether they were right by the most vexing problems by calling the original caller back to see if their answer was correct. They called this "Stump the Chumps".

What first seemed like a parlour trick was in reality a product of the expertise Click & Clack had accumulated from the thousands of different car problems they had encountered over time. The brothers were able to ask the right questions and almost always arrive at accurate diagnoses because of their ability to reference vast prior knowledge when confronted with each new problem. The extent of their knowledge meant they could also connect the surface phenomena of the problem to its underlying causes – thus allowing them to get "under the hood" in more ways than one.

DOI: 10.4324/9781003228165-1

This example is very much in keeping with what learning science tells us about anyone who has achieved expertise in a given field. Namely, the honing of an increasingly sophisticated schema representing knowledge items. Anyone who develops sophisticated schema in these ways is able to see more and more how discrete pieces of knowledge in a domain are connected. Rather than seeing isolated facts, they see patterns and connections because they understand the underlying structures of the domain they are exploring. A sure sign that someone is becoming more expert is the ease and automaticity with which they are able to see these networks and transfer old knowledge to new problems. Which is why, for Click & Clack, the whistling of a car at 60mph is much more than just a suspicious sound.

Click & Clack offer us a great example of expertise in the field of car maintenance – but what about the analogous field of human improvement? When it comes to teaching, what does it mean to be an expert and how is this different from being experienced? How might we use a definition of expertise to better prepare and improve teachers over time? This first section of the book deals with such questions by exploring: what it means to be an expert teacher, knowledge growth in teaching, teacher quality's relationship to student achievement, and how to become a reflective practitioner.

Additional Reading

CHISOLM, P. (2019, FEBRUARY 27). "DOES YOUR KNEE MAKE MORE OF A CLICK OR A CLACK?" – TEACHING "CAR TALK" TO NEW DOCS. *SHOTS: HEALTH NEWS FROM NPR.*

Ray and Tom's step-by-step method of diagnosing car trouble can be applied to more than just your broken down old jalopy. A handful of physicians are using the show to teach medical students how to diagnose disease.

AVAILABLE VIA HTTPS://TINYURL.COM/7CESE5UK

SMITH, C. J. (1993). HEALING OUR COLLECTIVE AUTO-ANGST: THE CULTURAL SIGNIFICANCE OF "CAR TALK". *STUDIES IN POPULAR CULTURE, 15(2),* 35–41.

AVAILABLE VIA HTTPS://TINYURL.COM/HNDXAK54

The Andy Scale: How Click & Clack answered the age-old philosophical question: Do two people who don't know what they are talking about know more or less than one person who doesn't know what he's talking about?

AVAILABLE VIA WWW.CARTALK.COM/RADIO/LETTER/ANDY-SCALE-0

AN EXPERIENCED TEACHER ≠ AN EXPERT TEACHER

DAVID BERLINER ON TEACHER EXPERTISE

EXPERTISE

CHESS MASTER

TENNIS PLAYER

PHYSICIST

RESEARCHER

TEACHER

DOI: 10.4324/9781003228165-2

AN EXPERIENCED TEACHER ≠ AN EXPERT TEACHER

ARTICLE Learning about and learning from expert teachers[1]

QUOTE *"Good teaching is judged through reliance on standards applied to the tasks of teaching and related to norms for professional behavior, including moral considerations. Successful teaching is about whether intended learnings were achieved. Judgements of successful teaching are concerned not with the tasks of teaching or professional behavior, but with the achievement of ends."[2]*

Why You Should Read This Article

We all know what an expert chess player, tennis player, physicist, and/or researcher is. And we also know how to spot them. An expert chess player is someone playing at one of the top chess tournaments and has a certain ELO-rating which is a calculation of the relative skill levels of chess players. The higher the rating the better you are with a grandmaster having a rating of 2600 and above. At the time of this writing, Magnus Carlson has a rating of 2875 and is ranked first in the world. He's also world champion. Tennis players also have a ranking system similar to chess, and so there too we have a ranking with number 1 being the best, but we also have specific tournaments such as the four Grand Slam and the eight mandatory ATP Tour Masters 1000 tournaments which we can use. An expert physicist has either won or been nominated for a Nobel prize or has received similar honours. Yes, even researchers have a more or less objective system to determine who is an expert and who isn't, namely the i10-Index, which is the number of publications with at least ten citations, the h-index that measures both the productivity and citation impact of the publications of a scientist or scholar, and of

[1]   BERLINER, D. C. (2001). LEARNING ABOUT AND LEARNING FROM EXPERT TEACHERS. *INTERNATIONAL JOURNAL OF EDUCATIONAL RESEARCH, 35*, 463–482. HTTPS://DOI.ORG/10.1016/S0883-0355(02)00004-6 AVAILABLE VIA HTTPS://TINYURL.COM/YYB65BEK

[2]   IBID., 468.

course the absolute number of citations. The question is this: how can we determine what an expert teacher is and what makes them one?

Abstract of the Article

Studies of expertise in teaching have been informative, despite problems. One problem is determining the relative roles of talent vs. deliberate practice in the acquisition of expertise. When studying teachers, however, a third factor must be considered, that of context. The working conditions of teachers exert a powerful influence on the development of expertise. A second problem is that of definition because expertise in teaching takes different forms in different cultures, and its characteristics change by decade. A distinction is drawn between the good teacher and the successful teacher, characteristics of expertise that are often confused. A prototypical model of expertise is described and found to identify teachers who were both good and successful. Discussed also is the importance of understanding adaptive or fluid expertise, automaticity and flexibility. Finally, the development of teacher expertise is seen as an increase in agency over time.

The Article

Expert teachers

All schools want expert teachers. Research shows that children taught by expert teachers learn more and/or better.[3] Policy makers and governments are even willing to financially reward expert teachers financially and otherwise.[4] But what exactly is an expert teacher? How do we know one when we see one? What determines if a teacher is an expert or just experienced? Is experience enough or is there more? These are questions that David Berliner looked at when he wrote the article "Learning about and learning from expert teachers".

He starts his article with Robert Glaser's (1987, 1990) thoughts on teacher expertise, such as:

- Expertise is domain specific, takes countless hours to achieve, and continues to develop throughout one's career.
- Expertise development is not linear; it makes jumps and stagnates on plateaus.
- Experts' knowledge is better structured than novices'.

---

3   HATTIE, J. A. C. (2003, OCTOBER). *TEACHERS MAKE A DIFFERENCE: WHAT IS THE RESEARCH EVIDENCE?* PAPER PRESENTED AT THE BUILDING TEACHER QUALITY: WHAT DOES THE RESEARCH TELL US ACER RESEARCH CONFERENCE, MELBOURNE, AUSTRALIA. AVAILABLE VIA HTTP://RESEARCH.ACER.EDU.AU/RESEARCH_CONFERENCE_2003/4/

4   CUTLER, T., & WAINE, B. (1999). REWARDING BETTER TEACHERS? PERFORMANCE RELATED PAY IN SCHOOLS. *EDUCATIONAL MANAGEMENT & ADMINISTRATION,* 27(1), 55–70. HTTPS://DOI.ORG/10.1177/0263211X990271005

- Experts' representations of problems are deeper and richer than novices'.
- Experts recognise meaningful patterns faster than novices do.
- Experts are more flexible, more opportunistic planners, and can change representations faster than novices.
- While experts may start solving a problem slower than a novice, they're – in the long run – faster problem solvers.
- Expert have automatised many behaviours allowing easier and quicker processing of more complex information.

The reader who has also read *HLH* will probably recognise many of the things we talked about in Chapter 1 "A novice is not a little expert" in that book.

Talent for teaching

In his article, Berliner first deals with the role of *talent* in the development of expertise. He defines talent as "individual differences in abilities and skills that seem like gifts or innate capacities, and seem to be 'hardwired' into individuals" (p. 494). Using diverse sources running from Anders Ericsson (1996) to Robert Sternberg (1996) to Howard Gardner (1995) and their colleagues/co-authors, he comes to the conclusion that while the debate about the role of talent may be important, it's of little practical interest to when it comes to pedagogical expertise. For him, talent for teaching can better be seen as "an extremely complicated interaction of many human characteristics [including] sociability, persuasiveness, trustworthiness, nurturent [*sic*] style, ability to provide logical and coherent stories and explanations, ability to do more than one thing at a time, physical stamina, the chance to 'play teacher' with a younger sibling or playmate, and so forth" (p. 465).

Power of context

Another reason that the discussion of talent with respect to teaching might be moot, according to Berliner, is because *context* is so powerful. Teachers are more or less productive depending on, for example, workplace conditions, policy of principals, superintendents, and school boards, community expectations of the community, etc. As Rich (1993) determined, expertise isn't simply a characteristic of a person, but rather an interaction of the person and the environment in which they find themselves.

Expertise = Person + Environment

Another important question raised by Berliner is how to define the expert teacher. He notes that though inexperience goes together with being a novice, experience doesn't automatically go hand in hand with expertise. In other words, we could say that all expert teachers are experienced, it's not the case that all experienced teachers are experts.

Teaching culture

One factor which complicates matters is *culture*. While in some fields this isn't the case (e.g., games, sports, natural sciences) in others culture is really important. He notes that an expert shaman in one culture may be an expert by reputational criteria, but will be regarded as a fake by physicians in most Western countries (though alternative practitioners like homeopaths may be highly regarded in certain Western subcultures). In teaching, some countries praise stimulating student participation and see it as a quality that defines an expert teacher (Berliner uses the US here), other countries with different cultures (Berliner uses India here) lauds limiting student participation. The same is true, for example, with respect to lesson planning. In a country with fairly open curricula, this is a laudable quality while in others where the curriculum is mostly fixed (e.g., Taiwan), it isn't at all important.

Teacher authenticity

ARE YOU FOR REAL?

PEDRO DE BRUYCKERE AND PAUL A. KIRSCHNER
(2016) investigated another often spoken of factor, namely authenticity, as perceived by students (see also Chapter 22 of this book). They've concluded that authenticity is a combination of perceived:

Expertise – the professional knowledge that teachers have enabling them to clearly and intelligently explain a topic. These types of expert teachers are able to engage students, spark their interest, motivate them for the topic and collaborate with them to achieve a good result.

Passion (and enthusiasm) for the subject they teach – top teachers are engaged with their subject and with their students. Students believe that passion enables the authentic teacher to invest time and effort in preparing lessons, finding ways and methods to get things across, and making sure that students can keep their attention.

Unicity – allows top teachers to ensure that each lesson has a particular character or, in other words, is unique. Students translate this aspect of authenticity as a teacher who leaves their mark on "being a teacher". Unique teachers stay true to themselves, have their own way of interacting with students, hold on to their own points of view and behave consistently in that role.

Distance – less about teachers themselves and more about the relationship between teacher and student. Top teachers show interest in their students' and their personal life, while, at the same time, keeping a professional distance and keeping their personal lives to themselves.

Achievement

Of course, *achievement* can be offered as a metric of teacher expertise, but here there's also a problem. Outside of the debate now raging in many places about the value of acquiring knowledge and skills versus so-called 21st-century skills, Berliner, based on Fenstermacher and Richardson (2000), speaks of the difference between "good" and "successful" teaching. "Good teaching is judged through reliance on standards applied to the tasks of teaching and related to norms for professional behavior, including moral considerations. Successful teaching is about whether intended learnings were achieved. Judgements of successful teaching are concerned not with the tasks of teaching or professional behavior, but with the achievement of ends" (p. 469).

And what's now the outcome of all of this? For the purposes of separating the wheat from the chaff so to speak (expert teachers from non-expert teachers), Berliner goes to Bond et al. (2000) for the answer.

Prototypic features of expertise

In their study they looked at 13 prototypic features of expertise:

- Better use of knowledge.
- Extensive pedagogical content knowledge, including deep representations of subject matter knowledge.
- Better problem-solving strategies.
- Better adaptation and modification of goals for diverse learners, better skills for improvisation.
- Better decision making.
- More challenging objectives.
- Better classroom climate.
- Better perception of classroom events, better ability to read the cues from students.
- Greater sensitivity to context.
- Better monitoring of learning and providing feedback to students.
- More frequent testing of hypotheses.
- Greater respect for students.
- Display of more passion for teaching.

To this they added outcomes of instruction of expert teachers for students including these:

- Higher motivation to learn and higher feelings of self-efficacy.
- Deeper, rather than surface understanding of the subject matter.
- Higher levels of achievement.

What they found was that "[t]he features with the greatest ability to

Expert teachers

discriminate between expert and nonexpert teachers were the degree of challenge that the curriculum offered, the teachers' ability for deep representations of the subject matter, and the teachers' skilfulness in monitoring and providing feedback to his or her students" (Berliner,

2004, p. 209). John Hattie (2003) reiterated this in a presentation where he posited that expert teachers:

Challenging goals

- set challenging goals for students and give them difficult tasks to challenge them

Knowledge of how people learn

- have a deep conceptual knowledge of the learning content, teaching/ instruction, and how people learn (see Figure 1.1). As a consequence, their knowledge is better organised and they're better able to transfer and explain the connections between new content and students' pre-knowledge. They're also better at connecting learning content with other topics in the curriculum

Monitoring student problems

- are better at monitoring problems that students have and give them more relevant and useful feedback

FIGURE 1.1
THE COMPONENTS OF TEACHER EXPERTS AND KNOWLEDGE OF THE CONTENT, OF THE PEDAGOGY/ INSTRUCTION, AND HOW WE LEARN.

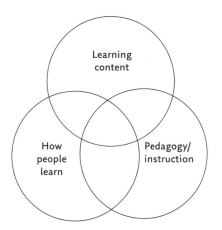

To paraphrase Berliner, the demands of all the ifs, ands, and buts in this area aren't insurmountable barriers when studying teacher expertise, but they're real problems that researchers of expertise in areas like chess, tennis, or physics don't have.

Conclusions

The ideas explored in this chapter make it clear that the relationship between experience and expertise is less closely bound than we might first think. An experienced teacher isn't necessarily an expert teacher. It's much more complicated! Teacher expertise is an interaction between the person (experience, knowledge in different areas, character, . . .) and the environment in which they find themselves (classroom, school, neighbourhood, political system, . . .). Berliner's scrutinising of experience and expertise invites us to question commonly held assumptions about when and how professional development should occur. Many professions already address such questions, offering robust developmental opportunities and requirements over the entire arc of a career. So if it is true that "you're never too experienced to add to your expertise" what steps should we take at the level of systems and individuals to apply these lessons to teaching?

Takeaways

- Teaching expertise isn't easy to define or determine.
- Teaching talent, as such, isn't a "thing", but rather an extremely complicated interaction of many human characteristics.
- Culture (national/ethnic, school) and context are parts of the expertise equation.
- Expertise isn't simply a characteristic of a person, but rather an interaction of the person and the environment in which they find themselves.
- An expert teacher is a successful teacher; it's about the achievement of ends.
- Expert teachers have a deep conceptual knowledge of the learning content, teaching/instruction, and how people learn.

References

BERLINER, D. C. (2001). LEARNING ABOUT AND LEARNING FROM EXPERT TEACHERS. *INTERNATIONAL JOURNAL OF EDUCATIONAL RESEARCH, 35,* 463–482.

BERLINER, D. C. (2004). DESCRIBING THE BEHAVIOR AND DOCUMENTING THE ACCOMPLISHMENTS OF EXPERT TEACHERS. *BULLETIN OF SCIENCE, TECHNOLOGY & SOCIETY, 24*(3), 200–212.

BOND, L., SMITH, T., BAKER, W. K., & HATTIE, J. A. (2000). *THE CERTIFICATION SYSTEM OF THE NATIONAL BOARD FOR PROFESSIONAL TEACHING STANDARDS: A CONSTRUCT AND CONSEQUENTIAL VALIDITY STUDY.* GREENSBORO CENTER FOR EDUCATIONAL RESEARCH AND EVALUATION, UNIVERSITY OF NORTH CAROLINA AT GREENSBORO

DE BRUYCKERE, P., & KIRSCHNER, P. A. (2016). AUTHENTIC TEACHERS: STUDENT CRITERIA FOR PERCEIVING THE AUTHENTICITY OF TEACHERS. *COGENT EDUCATION, 3*(1), 1247609.

ERICSSON, K. A. (1996). THE ACQUISITION OF EXPERT PERFORMANCE: AN INTRODUCTION TO SOME OF THE ISSUES. IN K. A. ERICSSON (ED.), *THE ROAD TO EXCELLENCE: THE ACQUISITION OF EXPERT PERFORMANCE IN THE ARTS AND SCIENCES, SPORTS AND GAMES* (PP. 1–50). LAWRENCE ERLBAUM.

FENSTERMACHER, G. D., & RICHARDSON, V. (2000). *ON MAKING DETERMINATIONS OF QUALITY IN TEACHING.* PAPER PREPARED FOR THE BOARD ON INTERNATIONAL COMPARATIVE STUDIES IN EDUCATION OF THE NATIONAL ACADEMIES OF SCIENCE AND THE NATIONAL RESEARCH COUNCIL, WASHINGTON, DC.

GARDNER, H. (1995). WHY WOULD ANYONE BECOME AN EXPERT. *AMERICAN PSYCHOLOGIST, 50,* 802–803.

GLASER, R. (1987). THOUGHTS ON EXPERTISE. IN C. SCHOOLER & W. SCHAIE (EDS.), *COGNITIVE FUNCTIONING AND SOCIAL STRUCTURE OVER THE LIFE COURSE.* ABLEX.

GLASER, R. (1990). EXPERTISE. IN M. W. EYSENK, A. N. ELLIS, E. HUNT, & P. JOHNSON-LAIRD (EDS.), *THE BLACKWELL DICTIONARY OF COGNITIVE PSYCHOLOGY.* BLACKWELL REFERENCE.

RICH, Y. (1993). STABILITY AND CHANGE IN TEACHER EXPERTISE. *TEACHING AND TEACHER EDUCATION, 9,* 137–146.

STERNBERG, R. J. (1996). COSTS OF EXPERTISE. IN K. A. ERICSSON (ED.), *THE ROAD TO EXCELLENCE: THE ACQUISITION OF EXPERT PERFORMANCE IN THE ARTS AND SCIENCES, SPORTS AND GAMES* (PP. 347–354). LAWRENCE ERLBAUM.

Suggested Readings and Links

COE, R., ALOISI, C., HIGGINS, S., & MAJOR, L. E. (2014). *WHAT MAKES GREAT TEACHING? REVIEW OF THE UNDERPINNING RESEARCH.* PROJECT REPORT. SUTTON TRUST.

AVAILABLE VIA HTTP://DRO.DUR.AC.UK/13747/1/13747.PDF

HATTIE, J. (2003, OCTOBER). *TEACHERS MAKE A DIFFERENCE: WHAT IS THE RESEARCH EVIDENCE?* PAPER PRESENTED AT THE AUSTRALIAN COUNCIL FOR EDUCATIONAL RESEARCH ANNUAL CONFERENCE ON BUILDING TEACHER QUALITY, MELBOURNE, AUSTRALIA.

AVAILABLE VIA WWW.ACER.EDU.AU/DOCUMENTS/RC2003_HATTIE_ TEACHERSMAKEADIFFERENCE.PDF

VIDEO

DAVID BERLINER: EVALUATING TEACHER EDUCATION AND TEACHERS USING STUDENT ASSESSMENTS

This lecture challenges policies requiring the evaluation of teacher education programs and classroom teachers via students' scores on standardised tests. A sensible alternative to the use of student test scores to evaluate teachers and the teacher education programs from which they came is offered.

AVAILABLE VIA WWW.YOUTUBE.COM/WATCH?V=LQKSNPFVBCS &FEATURE=EMB_LOGO

BLOG

WHAT MAKES A TOP TEACHER?

AVAILABLE VIA HTTPS://3STARLEARNINGEXPERIENCES.WORDPRESS. COM/2018/10/02/WHAT-MAKES-A-TOP-TEACHER/

2 THOSE WHO UNDERSTAND, TEACH

LEE SHULMAN ON KNOWLEDGE GROWTH IN TEACHERS

OI: 10.4324/9781003228165-3

2 THOSE WHO UNDERSTAND, TEACH

ARTICLE Those who understand: Knowledge growth in teaching[1]

QUOTE *"Mere content knowledge is likely to be as useless pedagogically as content free skill."*[2]

Why You Should Read This Article

What is a teacher? To really answer this question, we need to take a step back (in history) to when teaching was a highly honoured profession which took many years to join. Originally, at least in the Parisian model (Ong, 1958), becoming a master (in law) or a doctor (in other areas) gave you formal entrance to the guild of teachers. "A physician whom a university faculty certifies as a practitioner of medicine is called a 'doctor' of medicine, as though he [*sic*] were going to teach medicine, just as in some countries, one trained to practice the law is also called 'master' or its equivalent" (pp. 153–154). When you graduated to master or doctor, you did this via a commencement[3] or *inception*.[4] It was, literally, the beginning of a teaching career. The doctoral examination, in the Netherlands called a defence, requires candidates to demonstrate that they possess the highest levels of subject matter competence in the domain AND are able to teach the subject. They present a brief oral synopsis of their thesis and then defend it in dialogue with examiners/ opponents, paralleling two modes of teaching: lecture and disputation. This oral examination is the ultimate test of subject matter expertise; it examines the candidate's ability to teach the subject by employing the

---

1   SHULMAN, L. S. (1986). THOSE WHO UNDERSTAND TEACH: KNOWLEDGE GROWTH IN TEACHING. *EDUCATIONAL RESEARCHER*, 15(2), 4–14. HTTPS://DOI.ORG/10.3102/0013189X015002004
2   IBID., 8
3   LATE 13C., "A BEGINNING, ACT OR FACT OF COMING INTO EXISTENCE," FROM OLD FRENC COMENCEMENT "BEGINNING, START" (MODERN FRENCH COMMENCEMENT), FROM COMENCI "TO BEGIN, TO START" (WWW.ETYMONLINE.COM/)
4   EARLY 15C., "A BEGINNING, A STARTING," FROM OLD FRENCH INCEPTION AND DIRECT FROM LATIN *INCEPTIONEM* (NOMINATIVE *INCEPTIO*) "A BEGINNING; AN UNDERTAKING" (WWW ETYMONLINE.COM/)

dual method of lecture and discussion. Lee Shulman, in his Presidential Address at the 1985 annual meeting of the American Educational Research Association, tried to determine whether anno 1985 teachers still need to meet those standards. Read further for the answer.

Abstract of the Article

"He who can, does.
He who cannot, teaches."

I don't know in what fit of pique George Bernard Shaw wrote that infamous aphorism, words that have plagued members of the teaching profession for nearly a century. They are found in "Maxims for Revolutionists", an appendix to his play Man and Superman. "He who can, does. He who cannot, teaches" is a calamitous insult to our profession, yet one readily repeated even by teachers. More worrisome, its philosophy often appears to underlie the policies concerning the occupation and activities of teaching.

Where did such a demeaning image of the teacher's capacities originate? How long have we been burdened by assumptions of ignorance and ineptitude within the teaching corps? Is Shaw to be treated as the last word on what teachers know and don't know, or do and can't do?

The Article

Lee Shulman, then Professor of Education and Affiliate Professor of Psychology at the School of Education, Stanford University, after lamenting George Bernard Shaw's disparaging characterisation of teachers, began by looking at what was covered in the California State Board examination for elementary school teachers from March 1875. The topics that the exam covered were as follows:

Teacher requirements 1875

1. Written Arithmetic
2. Mental Arithmetic
3. Written Grammar
4. Oral Grammar
5. Geography
6. History of the United States
7. Theory and Practice of Teaching
8. Algebra
9. Physiology
10. Natural Philosophy (Physics)
11. Constitution of the US and California

12. School Law of California
13. Penmanship
14. Natural History (Biology)
15. Composition
16. Reading
17. Orthography
18. Defining (Word Analysis, Vocabulary)
19. Vocal Music
20. Industrial Drawing

Typical questions – and remember that this was for elementary school teachers – on the exam were:

- Find the cost of a draft on New York for $1,400 payable 60 days after sight, exchange being worth 102.5% and interest being reckoned at a rate of 7% per annum. (Written Arithmetic, one of ten items.)
- Divide 88 into two such parts that shall be to each other as 2/3 is to 4/5. (Mental Arithmetic, one of ten items.)
- Name and illustrate five forms of conjugation. Name and give four ways in which the nominative case may be used. (Grammar, two of ten items.)
- What is adhesion? What is capillary attraction? Illustrate each. (2 of 10 items from Natural Philosophy.)
- Name five powers vested in Congress.

And with respect to pedagogy (which was admittedly a little underrepresented in the exam) there were questions like these:

- What course would you pursue to keep up with the progress in teaching?
- How do you succeed in teaching children to spell correctly the words commonly misspelled?
- How do you interest lazy and careless pupils? Answer in full (!).

Teacher requirements 1985

Fast forward to 1985 when Shulman gave his address. The categories for teacher review and evaluation being proposed then were as follows:

- Organisation in preparing and presenting instructional plans.
- Evaluation.
- Recognition of individual differences.
- Cultural awareness.
- Understanding youth.
- Management.
- Educational policies and procedure.

The big question here is this: where did the subject matter go? Shulman muses that anno 1985 perhaps Shaw was correct. The next question is this: how did it happen that content disappeared in favour of an emphasis on procedures? In Shulman's words, policymakers justified this "by referring to the emergent research based on teaching and teaching effectiveness. They regularly define and justify these categories by the extremely powerful phrase 'research-based teacher competencies'. In what sense can it be claimed that such a conception of teaching competence is research based?" (p. 6; question mark is his, not ours). The categories and standards chosen were based on research on teaching relating to teaching effectiveness, process-product studies, or teacher behaviour research, meant to identify patterns of teacher behaviour that led to improved learner performance. He laments that these policy makers grasped at research in which "in their necessary simplification of the complexities of classroom teaching, investigators ignored one central aspect of classroom life: the subject matter" (p. 6) and refers to the educational researchers' neglect of focus on subject matter as the "missing paradigm" problem whose consequences "are serious, both for policy and for research" (p. 6).

Process-product

Shulman goes on to note that the research programs that arose "in response to the dominance of process-product work [researchers] accepted its definition of the problem and continued to treat teaching more or less generically, or at least as if the content of instruction were relatively unimportant" (p. 6). Even when teacher cognition was studied, it looked at teacher planning or interactive decision making neglecting how content knowledge was organised in general, but primarily in the teachers' heads.

SKILLS WITHOUT KNOWLEDGE

AT THIS MOMENT, and arguably for the past 50 years, schools are placing great emphasis on technical reading and comprehension skills. Learners are drilled in skills like "recognising" the main points, discriminating those words or letter types (italics, underlined) which clue the reader to either what's important or relationships between concepts, and so forth. Unfortunately, this emphasis on process/product skills, doesn't help when it comes to understanding what you read. Here's a small clipping we came across:

In the sixth over, Nagesh took the first wicket from the Schiedammers[5] *and ended his game with beautiful numbers: 7 overs – 12 runs – 1 wicket – 3 maidens! Haney, too, noted some important points in the*

(Continued)

---

5   SCHIEDAM IS A CITY IN THE NETHERLANDS.

(Continued)

score book: 4-15-1-0.And in the last overs of the game, Umer showed that he should certainly not be written off as a bowler: 2-7-1-0.

Without knowledge of cricket, it just as well could have read:

Real ale gobsmacked meat and two veg scouser sling one's hook Victoria sponge cake odds and sods pork dripping Northeners, bow ties are cool crumpets have a butcher's at this hadn't done it in donkey's years bossy britches pigeons in Trafalgar Square off-shop.

But content (what is taught) and pedagogy (how it is taught) are part of one indistinguishable body of teachers' understanding! As we saw in Chapter 1, the expert teacher has deep knowledge of and skills in the domain being taught (the subject matter), the intricacies of teaching (the pedagogy), and how learners learn (human cognition).

The Missing Paradigm

This clear dichotomy between knowledge and pedagogy is not historical, but rather, a more recent development from the last third of the 20th century. In Shulman's words,

Missing paradigm

The pendulum has now swung, both in research and in policy circles. The missing paradigm refers to a blind spot with respect to content that now characterizes most research on teaching and, as a consequence, most of our state-level programs of teacher evaluation and teacher certification . . . What we miss are questions about the content of the lessons taught, the questions asked, and the explanations offered. (pp. 7–8)

Ultimately, the question is "What pedagogical prices are paid when the teacher's subject matter competence is itself compromised by deficiencies of prior education or ability?" (p. 8)

A Perspective on Teacher Knowledge

To deal with this missing paradigm/problem, Shulman suggests that in teacher education and training we distinguish between three categories of content knowledge, namely these:

Subject matter content knowledge

- *Subject matter content knowledge*: The amount and organisation of knowledge in the mind of the teacher in their domain of teaching.

This requires going beyond the simple knowledge of a domain towards understanding its intricacies and structures.

Pedagogical content knowledge

- *Pedagogical Content Knowledge*: Knowing and understanding the subject matter for teaching. This includes understanding what makes certain things easy or difficult to learn, knowing the conceptions, preconceptions, and even misconceptions that different learners bring with them to the lessons.

OTHER FORMS OF PEDAGOGICAL CONTENT KNOWLEDGE?

SHULMAN adds in an endnote that there is also a type of pedagogical knowledge which relates to teaching itself: in other words, teaching as distinct from subject matter – which is also terribly important. He defines this as "the knowledge of generic principles of classroom organization and management and the like that has quite appropriately been the focus of study in most recent research on teaching" (p. 14).

Curricular knowledge

- *Curricular knowledge*: Knowledge of the full range of how to teach the content at a certain level, the instructional materials available, and when, why, and how to use or not use certain things in certain circumstances. Shulman distinguishes here between *lateral curricular knowledge*: what is being taught at that point in the year in other subject areas and how what you're doing now relates to those other subjects and *vertical curricular knowledge*: what has been taught and what will be taught in your own subject area and how what you're doing now relates to that.

FIGURE 2.1
PERSPECTIVES ON TEACHER KNOWLEDGE. THE INTERSECTION OF SUBJECT MATTER KNOWLEDGE, PEDAGOGICAL CONTENT KNOWLEDGE, AND CURRICULAR KNOWLEDGE.

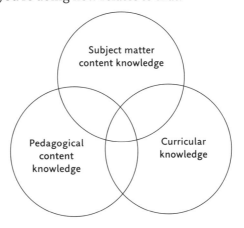

Forms of Knowledge

A second aspect is what Shulman calls forms of teacher knowledge which too is broken down into three forms:

Propositional knowledge

- *Propositional knowledge*: The evidence-informed (Shulman speaks of research-based) propositions relating to good teaching and instruction in terms of
  - *Principles*: theoretical claims derived from empirical research (e.g., instruction before problem solving leads to better learning than discovery),
  - *Maxims*: practical claims (e.g., Never smile until Christmas), and
  - *Norms*: ideological claims or philosophical commitments (e.g., justice, fairness, equity, . . .).

Case knowledge

- *Case knowledge*: Knowledge of specific, well-documented, and richly described events which usually illuminate the theoretical and/or practical in the form of
  - *Prototypes* which exemplify theoretical principles,
  - *Precedents* which capture and convey principles of practice or maxims, and
  - *Parables* which convey norms or values.

Strategic knowledge

- *Strategic knowledge*: Knowing what to do when confronted with a situation or problem where principles "collide and no simple solution is possible" (p. 13). Here one must be metacognitively aware in order to reflect and make professional judgments.

Conclusions

If we look at what teachers needed to know and be able to do at the end of the 19th century and what they needed to know and be able to do at the end of the twentieth, we can see a large discrepancy. This discrepancy is what Lee Shulman called *the missing paradigm*: having knowledge of general pedagogical strategies without the necessary concomitant knowledge of the content area being taught is insufficient for good teaching. His message was that to be a good teacher, one needs both subject matter knowledge and pedagogical content knowledge. Putting this all together, what teachers know should be based upon and teacher training should be organised around the matrix found in Table 2.1.

We'll end this chapter with a final quote from the article (p. 14):

> We reject Mr. Shaw and his calumny. With Aristotle we declare that the ultimate test of understanding rests on the ability to transform one's knowledge into teaching.
>
> Those who can, do. Those who understand, teach.

TABLE 2.1
THE TEACHER KNOWLEDGE MATRIX. THE RELATIONSHIPS BETWEEN THE THREE FORMS OF KNOWLEDGE (PROPOSITIONAL, CASE, STRATEGIC) AND THE THREE PERSPECTIVES ON KNOWLEDGE (SUBJECT MATTER, PEDAGOGICAL CONTENT, CURRICULAR).

		Forms of Knowledge		
		Propositional	**Case**	**Strategic**
Perspectives on Knowledge	**Subject Matter Content**	Principles Maxims Norms	Prototypes Precedents Parables	Reflection Professional judgement
	Pedagogical Content	Principles Maxims Norms	Prototypes Precedents Parables	Reflection Professional judgement
	Curricular	Principles Maxims Norms	Prototypes Precedents Parables	Reflection Professional judgement

Takeaways

- Having knowledge of general pedagogical strategies without the necessary concomitant knowledge of the content area being taught is insufficient for good teaching.
- Any curriculum for teachers should contain a complete mix of three categories of content knowledge and three forms of knowledge.
- Research-based programs of teacher education need to be designed which expand and change to accommodate conceptions of both process and content.
- Teachers cannot be adequately assessed by observing their teaching performance without reference to the content being taught (Shulman, 1987, p. 20).

References

ONG, W. J. (1958). *RAMUS, METHOD AND THE DECAY OF DIALOGUE.* HARVARD UNIVERSITY PRESS.

SHULMAN, L. S. (1986). THOSE WHO UNDERSTAND TEACH: KNOWLEDGE GROWTH IN TEACHING. *EDUCATIONAL RESEARCHER, 15*(2), 4–14.

SHULMAN, L. S. (1987). KNOWLEDGE AND TEACHING: FOUNDATIONS OF THE NEW REFORM. *HARVARD EDUCATIONAL REVIEW, 57*(1), 1–23.

Suggested Readings and Links

SHULMAN, L. S. (1987). KNOWLEDGE AND TEACHING: FOUNDATIONS OF THE NEW REFORM. *HARVARD EDUCATIONAL REVIEW, 57*(1), 1–23.

In this article, which is also highlighted in this book (see Chapter 16), Shulman discusses and answers the four questions: What are the sources of the knowledge base for teaching? In what terms can these sources be conceptualised? What are the processes of pedagogical reasoning and action? and What are the implications for teaching policy and educational reform?

AVAILABLE VIA HTTPS://PEOPLE.UCSC.EDU/~KTELLEZ/SHULMAN.PDF

VIDEOS

A THREE-MINUTE VIDEO ON WHAT MAKES TEACHERS SPECIAL? PEDAGOGICAL CONTENT KNOWLEDGE

What does a teacher need to know? What is the most important thing a new teacher needs to develop? Teachers have a very particular type of knowledge. The old saying that if you can't do, teach, sells short what teachers know. Pedagogical Content Knowledge described the knowledge teachers develop about how to teach particular subjects to particular people. This concept was developed by Lee Shulman in 1986, but is just as relevant for teachers today.

AVAILABLE VIA WWW.YOUTUBE.COM/WATCH?V=PTM9RZC-PQ8

PCK SUMMIT KEYNOTE: DR. LEE SHULMAN

The PCK Summit was held to explore the potential for a common model for how PCK research is understood, conducted, and interpreted.

AVAILABLE VIA WWW.YOUTUBE.COM/WATCH?V=NZJMYVFRYSE

WEBSITES

BLOG: SHULMAN, KNOWLEDGE GROWTH IN TEACHING (1986)

AVAILABLE VIA HTTPS://DLAVERTYDOTCOM.WORDPRESS.COM/2012/01/14/SHULMAN-KNOWLEDGE-GROWTH-IN-TEACHING-1986/

3

TEACHERS ARE MADE, NOT BORN

LINDA DARLING-HAMMOND ON TEACHER TRAINING

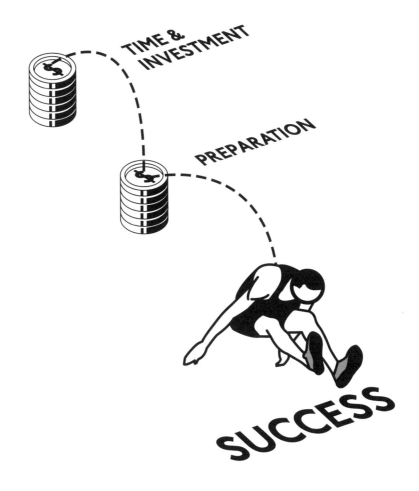

3 TEACHERS ARE MADE, NOT BORN

ARTICLE Teacher quality and student achievement[1]

QUOTE *"Differential teacher effectiveness is a strong determinant of differences in student learning."*[2]

Why You Should Read This Article

In his book *Thinking in Jazz*, Paul F. Berliner (2004) explores the layered complexities of an art form that is all-too-often misunderstood. Unlike Classical musicians who often have bestowed upon them words like "rigour" and "discipline", Jazz is often dealt the back-handed compliment that comes with being a "knack" – in other words, something that you either have a feel for or you don't. As Berliner puts it of Jazz players, "their skills are poorly understood, even downright misunderstood, and their knowledge undervalued by outsiders" (p. 5).

In many ways, teaching might be the Jazz of the professional world. Like Jazz, teaching appears at first glance to be a loosely structured, fluid exercise, heavily dependent on improvisation. Like Jazz, teaching's surface features shroud an underlying structure that is more nuanced and complex by comparison and which can be broken down, understood and improved upon in systematic ways. Like Jazz, teaching is subject to the diminishing characterisation of something one is "born-to-do" – for if becoming good at something is simply a case of having a knack for it, what does that say about the seriousness of the pursuit?

Excellence in teaching, as with all other fields (including Jazz), is actually based on specific things one has learnt and can do to get better. Although there are many excellent teachers who have had no formal

1 DARLING-HAMMOND, L. (2000). TEACHER QUALITY AND STUDENT ACHIEVEMENT: A REVIEW (STATE POLICY EVIDENCE. *EDUCATION POLICY ANALYSIS ARCHIVES, 8*(1), 1–44.
2 IBID., P. 2

training nor ever read any research, it is still fair to suggest that good teaching isn't inborn, it doesn't happen by accident, and seeing it as such fundamentally undervalues its richness, the challenge associated with doing it well, and the effort that good teachers have put into becoming good. Worse still, when teaching is relegated to the status of a "knack" profession in this way, decisions about how to fund the systems that prepare and develop teachers tend to adopt the same lack of seriousness.

In giving teaching its due, researchers and educators alike have strived to better understand which factors contribute to effective teachers and subsequent achievement in students. To address this directly, we might first ask "What makes for a good teacher?" and then, "What conditions help connect teacher preparation, teacher effectiveness, and positive student outcomes?" These were some of the questions Linda Darling-Hammond sought to answer in her influential examination of the relationship between teacher quality and student achievement.

Abstract of the Article

Using data from a 50-state survey of policies, state case study analyses, the 1993–94 Schools and Staffing Surveys (SASS), and the National Assessment of Educational Progress (NAEP), this study examines the ways in which teacher qualifications and other school inputs are related to student achievement across states. The findings of both the qualitative and quantitative analyses suggest that policy investments in the quality of teachers may be related to improvements in student performance. Quantitative analyses indicate that measures of teacher preparation and certification are by far the strongest correlates of student achievement in reading and mathematics, both before and after controlling for student poverty and language status. State policy surveys and case study data are used to evaluate policies that influence the overall level of teacher qualifications within and across states. This analysis suggests that policies adopted by states regarding teacher education, licensing, hiring, and professional development may make an important difference in the qualifications and capacities that teachers bring to their work. The implications for state efforts to enhance quality and equity in public education are discussed.

The Article

Prior to Darling-Hammond's work, little had been done within the US education context to examine the connection between education policy, teacher preparation, and student learning with such a systematic lens.

In order to yoke the big-picture of education policy to the specific conditions necessary for effective teacher preparation, she first set out to define, through reference to the existing literature, those factors most worthy of consideration when understanding the anatomy of an effective teacher. She names them as follows:

- General Intelligence.
- Subject Matter Knowledge.
- Knowledge of Teaching and Learning.
- Teaching Certification Status.

First is the question of whether general intelligence and subject matter knowledge are prerequisites for teaching effectiveness. In the case of the former, most studies reveal a small and statistically insignificant relationship between teachers' intelligence or general academic ability and their teaching performance. In the case of the latter, the extent of the relationship between subject matter knowledge and teacher effectiveness is shown to be "not as strong and consistent as one might suppose" (p. 3). The reason for this is that subject matter alone, without an appreciation and knowledge of teaching and learning, is a necessary but insufficient component of effective teaching.

When compared to subject matter knowledge alone, knowledge of teaching and learning has a stronger and more positive effect on teacher effectiveness, as well as having a regulating relationship with subject specific knowledge. As Darling-Hammond puts it: "It may be that the positive effects of subject matter knowledge are augmented or offset by knowledge of how to teach the subject to various kinds of students. That is, the degree of pedagogical skill may interact with subject matter knowledge to bolster or reduce teacher performance" (p. 5).

In other words, it isn't so much a question of what teachers know *or* what they're able to do but rather what teachers know *and* are able to do with what they know that has the most influence on the success of their practice.

Grounded in this rationale, Darling-Hammond identifies "certification status" as the most reliable predictor of teacher effectiveness, precisely because effective teacher preparation combines aspects of subject matter knowledge with an understanding of teaching and learning that does justice to both. The operative word here is, of course, *effective* and, since not all teacher preparation experiences are created equal, it follows that the variance in standards of preparation counts for a lot when it comes to the teacher-quality-to-student-achievement dynamic. But what precisely accounts for these differences?

Teacher effectiveness

Teacher preparation and certification

IF IT'S NOT IN THE COURSE TEXTBOOKS, IS IT TAUGHT?

POMERANCE ET AL. (2016) looked at the preparation of teachers by examining textbooks used in teacher education programmes in the United States for coverage of six learning/teaching strategies that have been shown to work: that is, proven practices that promote learning for all students, regardless of grade or subject, and that are especially potent with struggling students (Pashler et al., 2007). These strategies were pairing graphics with words, linking abstract concepts with concrete representations, posing probing/epistemic questions, alternating problems with their solutions provided and problems that students must solve, distributed practice, and retrieval practice. What they found was very sparse coverage and discussion of evidence-informed strategies in those textbooks and a logical conclusion is that if the textbooks don't cover the topics, that the teachers also don't. Tim Surma and his colleagues replicated this study for a subset of effective teaching practice (i.e., distributed practice and retrieval practice) in the Netherlands and Flanders, Belgium, and found the same disappointing results (2018).

Where Do Differences in Teacher Preparation and Effectiveness Come From?

In response to this question, much has been written about the implications of various school-based conditions and their effect-size on student achievement. For instance, minimising class sizes and improving pupil-teacher ratios are often seen as an aspirational goal on the road to improved outcomes for students.

Variance in teacher preparation

What makes Darling-Hammond's study so interesting and influential is the way she exposes many of these assumed factors as either insignificant or secondary to the importance of investing in teacher quality. To do this, she examines data on public school teacher qualifications, as well as student characteristics and achievement over time. Her headline findings regarding teacher preparedness go a long way to dispelling (or at the very least repositioning) many of the assumptions we might hold around what gives rise to teacher effectiveness and student achievement. She concludes the following:

Teacher quality characteristics

- Teacher quality characteristics such as certification status and degree in the field to be taught are very significantly and positively correlated with student outcomes. Characteristics such as education level (percentage of teachers with master's degrees) show positive but less strong relationships with education outcomes.

Student characteristics

- Student characteristics such as poverty, non-English language status, and minority status are negatively correlated with student outcomes, and usually significantly so. These student characteristics are also significantly and negatively correlated with the qualifications of teachers; that is, the more socially advantaged the students, the more likely teachers don't hold full certification and a degree in their field and the more likely they are to have entered teaching without certification.
- Other school resources, such as pupil-teacher ratios, class sizes, and the proportion of all school staff who are teachers, show very weak and rarely significant relationships to student achievement when aggregated.

Examining the Impact of Teacher (In)Effectiveness on Student Achievement

To underline the extent of the impact such factors determining the quality of teacher preparation can make, Darling-Hammond turns to Ferguson (1991) whose analysis of over 900 school districts in Texas arrived at a striking conclusion. In the study, Ferguson found that teacher expertise accounted for more of the inter-district variation in students' reading and mathematics achievement (and achievement gains) in grades 1 through 11 than student socioeconomic status. Indeed, Darling-Hammond highlights how the span of teacher expertise is so wide that if you control for socioeconomic status the differences in achievement between black and white students can be attributed more than any other factor to the differences in qualifications and expertise of their teachers.

The Ferguson study is presented in conjunction with others which together offer an increasingly troubling picture, especially with concern to educational equity. Numerous studies found evidence of strong bias when it came to which students were allocated effective and less effective teachers (Jordan et al., 1997), as well as studies showing that African American students are nearly twice as likely to be assigned to the most ineffective teachers and half as likely to be assigned to the most effective teachers (Sanders & Rivers, 1996).

These disparities in teacher preparedness are presented as the result of

Investing in teachers

another disparity: the type and extent of teacher preparation investment from state to state in the US. The size of the gulf between states can be seen in international maths and science assessments, where top-ranking US states are on a par with the highest-scoring countries in the world and lower-ranking states score similarly to the bottom-ranked countries worldwide. This is to say, there are similar degrees of variance in student performance found within the United States alone as there are between countries around the world.

As Darling-Hammond points out, the disparities in teacher investment, as well as the implications this has for student achievement, can be attributed as much to choice as necessity. She illustrates how "a number of high-growth states have enacted and maintained high standards for entry to teaching while many low-growth states have not" and that "policies appear to be at least as important as demographics in determining the qualifications of teachers hired and retained" (p. 11).

A MATTER OF POLICY

TO ILLUSTRATE The choices available to those considering the optimal approach to teacher preparation, Darling-Hammond sets out the policy-based variables that lead to effective teaching practice, or its inverse. Specifically, she shows how differences in teacher investment play out according to the following:

The standards set for acceptance into and graduation from teacher preparation programmes.

High standards for teachers

In a high-standards state (i.e., Minnesota) anyone wishing to teach high school "must complete a bachelor's degree that includes a full major in the subject area to be taught plus coursework covering learning theory, child and adolescent development, subject matter teaching methods, curriculum, effective teaching strategies, uses of technology, classroom management, behavior and motivation, human relations, and the education of students with special needs. In the course of this work, the teacher must complete at least a college semester of student teaching under the supervision of a cooperating teacher who meets minimum standards". In comparison, in a

Low standards for teachers

low-standards state (i.e., Louisiana), "Prospective high school teachers can be licensed without even a minor in the field they will be teaching. The state does not require them to have studied curriculum, teaching strategies, classroom management, uses of technology, or the needs of special education students, and they can receive a license with only six weeks of student teaching" (NASDTEC, 1997; Darling-Hammond, 1997).

(Continued)

(Continued)

Standards enforcement

The extent to which those standards are enforced.

Comparing states that don't allow for the hiring of unqualified teachers with those that consistently accept teachers who have not met their standards she states how, "in Wisconsin and eleven other states, for example, no new elementary or secondary teachers were hired without a license in their field in 1994". while "in Louisiana, 31% of new entrants were unlicensed and another 15% were hired on substandard licenses. At least six other states allowed 20% or more of new public school teachers to be hired without a license in their field (Darling-Hammond, 1997, Appendix A)".

Funding allocation

Funding allocation for pre- and in-service teacher education and the extent to which induction supports for beginning teachers are funded or required.

The extent of funding allocation differentials across states, particularly when it comes to the minimum requirements and mandates, is tied to funding. She found that "Student teaching requirements ranged from five weeks in Massachusetts to 18 weeks in Wisconsin. As of 1994, the proportions of academic high school teachers teaching with both a 12 of 44 license and a major in their field ranged from a low of 52% to a high of 85% across states. The proportions of mathematics teachers teaching with less than a minor in the field ranged from a low of 9% to a high of 56% (Darling-Hammond, 1997, Appendices A and B)".

A Tale of Two States

Priorities in education policy

Darling-Hammond further shows how policy choices play out in real-world contexts, with telling exemplifications of what she calls "geographically proximate, demographically similar states" (p. 21) adopting differing approaches to the preparation and support of teachers over time. She refers to multiple states with varying conditions and fortunes across the span of the paper but two places in particular, North Carolina and Georgia, help to illustrate her point. Examining a period roughly spanning the mid-1980s to late 1990s, a compelling picture is offered of what happens when you prioritise effective teacher preparation, and what happens when you don't.

Starting with North Carolina, Darling-Hammond presents a case of sustained, multi-faceted investment in teachers, showing how the state "coupled major statewide increases in teacher salaries and improvements in teacher salary equity with intensive recruitment efforts and initiatives to improve preservice teacher education, licensing, beginning teacher mentoring, and ongoing professional development" (p. 15). In the aftermath of this many-fronted policy push, Darling-Hammond points out that North Carolina saw the most significant improvement in mathematics and reading of any state in the nation, with an eleven-point gain in NAEP scores from 1992–1996.

During roughly that same period in the 1980s, Georgia launched their own broad-based educational reforms. In their case, efforts were not centred around teacher investment but instead involved big bets on student testing as a driver of change. Extensive testing systems were created, with corresponding rewards and sanctions for students, teachers, and schools.

Even though Georgia mandated tests for teachers, Darling-Hammond points out a critical flaw in the approach when she highlights how "they did not link these assessments to emerging knowledge about teaching or to new learning standards, nor did they invest in improving schools of education or ongoing professional development" (p. 18). This, coupled with the fact that "few districts in [Georgia] required teachers to hold a degree in the field to be taught and full state certification as a condition of hiring" (p. 18), is presented as a significant factor explaining flat-line student achievement in mathematics and declining scores in reading for Georgia during the same period when North Carolina experienced its significant gains.

We have already identified how subject matter knowledge alone offers little without an appreciation of teaching and learning. Here, Darling-Hammond extends that conception to highlight the positive impact thoughtful, robust investment in teachers can have: Investment that acknowledges teachers' emergent knowledge in both subject matter and teaching practice, and which organises its structures of support and accountability in keeping with that conception of teacher excellence and growth.

Conclusions

We started this chapter by saying that teachers are not born but made. In order to better understand what goes into their making, Linda Darling-Hammond offers a roadmap for moving the field from a place where "differential teacher effectiveness is a strong determinant of differences in student learning" (p. 2) towards a professional body of teachers "who are more knowledgeable in their field and are skillful at teaching it to others" (p. 33).

What makes her articulation of that change so compelling is the way she considers not only what we should expect from a good teacher, but also how we might create the conditions necessary for the forging of good teachers. Darling-Hammond:

> Prior to Darling-Hammond's work, little had been done within the US education context to examine the connection between education policy, teacher preparation, and student learning with such a systematic lens. In order to yoke the big-picture of education policy to the specific conditions necessary for effective teacher preparation, she first set out to define, through reference to the existing literature, those factors most worthy of consideration when understanding the anatomy of an effective teacher, namely: General Intelligence, Subject Matter Knowledge, Knowledge of Teaching and Learning, and Teaching Certification Status.

Takeaways

- Two kinds of knowledge are necessary for teachers to succeed: subject matter knowledge and knowledge of teaching and learning.
- These two types of knowledge are interdependent variables: more powerful in concert than when they stand alone.
- Teacher certification, when delivered well, is the best pathway for developing good teachers since it brings together subject matter expertise and knowledge about teaching and learning together to optimal effect.
- Policies and priorities concerning the type and extent of investment in teacher preparation account for much of the difference found in teacher preparedness and, subsequently, differences in student achievement.
- While student demographic characteristics are strongly related to student outcomes, this is because less socially advantaged students are less likely to encounter teachers who are adequately certified and prepared to teach.
- A reconsideration of the standards applied to teacher preparation, the extent to which those standards are enforced, and the degree of investment in teacher preparation are all necessary factors in reforming teacher preparation.
- Investment should aim at improving that point of confluence where teachers' growing knowledge of their subject meets their emerging understanding of teaching and learning.

References

BERLINER, P. F. (2004). *THINKING IN JAZZ: THE INFINITE ART OF IMPROVISATION.* UNIVERSITY OF CHICAGO PRESS.

DARLING-HAMMOND, L. (1997). *DOING WHAT MATTERS MOST: INVESTING IN QUALITY TEACHING.* NATIONAL COMMISSION ON TEACHING AND AMERICA'S FUTURE.

DARLING-HAMMOND, L. (2000). TEACHER QUALITY AND STUDENT ACHIEVEMENT: A REVIEW OF STATE POLICY EVIDENCE. *EDUCATION POLICY ANALYSIS ARCHIVES, 8*(1), 1–44.

FERGUSON, R. F. (1991, SUMMER). PAYING FOR PUBLIC EDUCATION: NEW EVIDENCE ON HOW AND WHY MONEY MATTERS. *HARVARD JOURNAL ON LEGISLATION, 28*(2), 465–498.

JORDAN, H. R., MENDRO, R. L., & WEERSINGHE, D. (1997). *TEACHER EFFECTS ON LONGITUDINAL STUDENT ACHIEVEMENT: A PRELIMINARY REPORT ON RESEARCH ON TEACHER EFFECTIVENESS.* PAPER PRESENTED AT THE NATIONAL EVALUATION INSTITUTE. CREATE, WESTERN MICHIGAN UNIVERSITY, INDIANAPOLIS, IN.

NATIONAL ASSOCIATION OF STATE DIRECTORS OF TEACHER EDUCATION AND CERTIFICATION. (1997). *MANUAL ON CERTIFICATION AND PREPARATION OF EDUCATIONAL PERSONNEL IN THE UNITED STATES AND CANADA.* NASDTEC.

PASHLER, H., BAIN, P. M., BOTTGE, B. A., GRAESSER, A., KOEDINGER, K., MCDANIEL, M., ET AL. (2007). *ORGANIZING INSTRUCTION AND STUDY TO IMPROVE STUDENT LEARNING. IES PRACTICE GUIDE (NCER 2007–2004).* NATIONAL CENTER FOR EDUCATION RESEARCH. AVAILABLE VIA HTTP://IES.ED.GOV/NCEE/WWC/PDF/PRACTICEGUIDES/20072004.PDF

POMERANCE, L., GREENBERG, J., & WALSH, K. (2016, JANUARY). *LEARNING ABOUT LEARNING: WHAT EVERY NEW TEACHER NEEDS TO KNOW.* NATIONAL COUNCIL ON TEACHER QUALITY. AVAILABLE VIA WWW.NCTQ.ORG/DMSVIEW/LEARNING_ABOUT_LEARNING_REPORT.

SANDERS, W. L., & RIVERS, J. C. (1996). *CUMULATIVE AND RESIDUAL EFFECTS OF TEACHERS ON FUTURE STUDENT ACADEMIC ACHIEVEMENT.* UNIVERSITY OF TENNESSEE VALUE-ADDED RESEARCH AND ASSESSMENT CENTER.

SURMA, T., VANHOYWEGHEN, K., CAMP, G., & KIRSCHNER, P. A. (2018). DISTRIBUTED PRACTICE AND RETRIEVAL PRACTICE: THE COVERAGE OF LEARNING STRATEGIES IN FLEMISH AND DUTCH TEACHER EDUCATION TEXTBOOKS. *TEACHING AND TEACHER EDUCATION, 74,* 229–237.

Suggested Readings and Links

POMERANCE, L., GREENBERG, J., & WALSH, K. (2016, JANUARY). *LEARNING ABOUT LEARNING: WHAT EVERY NEW TEACHER NEEDS TO KNOW.* NATIONAL COUNCIL ON TEACHER QUALITY.

AVAILABLE VIA WWW.NCTQ.ORG/DMSVIEW/LEARNING_ABOUT_LEARNING_REPORT

SCOTT, C., & DINHAM, S. (2008). BORN NOT MADE: THE NATIVIST MYTH AND TEACHERS' THINKING, *TEACHER DEVELOPMENT, 12*(2), 115–124.

AVAILABLE VIA WWW.RESEARCHGATE.NET/PUBLICATION/39729741_BORN_NOT_MADE_THE_NATIVIST_MYTH_AND_TEACHERS'_THINKING

VIDEOS

IN THIS VIDEO, LINDA DARLING-HAMMOND, MADELYN GARDNER, AND MARIA E. HYLER FROM THE LEARNING POLICY INSTITUTE REACT TO THE TRUMP ADMINISTRATION'S 2017 PROPOSAL TO ELIMINATE $2.1 BILLION IN FEDERAL FUNDING DESIGNATED FOR TITLE II OF THE EVERY STUDENT SUCCEEDS ACT (ESSA). THEY ASK: DOES INVESTING IN TEACHER PROFESSIONAL DEVELOPMENT MAKE A DIFFERENCE? IF SO, WHAT SEPARATES EFFECTIVE PROFESSIONAL DEVELOPMENT FROM INEFFECTIVE OFFERINGS?

AVAILABLE VIA WWW.YOUTUBE.COM/V/IKSCLXDEPFE&T=535S?START=424&END=1483

IN THIS VIDEO, MARY M. BRABECK, PHD, PROFESSOR OF APPLIED PSYCHOLOGY AND DEAN EMERITA OF THE STEINHARDT SCHOOL OF EDUCATION AT NEW YORK UNIVERSITY, TALKS ABOUT THE CHALLENGES ASSOCIATED WITH DETERMINING THE EFFICACY OF TEACHER PREPARATION PROGRAMS, AND SUGGESTS STRATEGIES FOR ADDRESSING THAT CHALLENGE, INCLUDING THE EFFECTIVE USE OF DATA.

AVAILABLE VIA WWW.YOUTUBE.COM/WATCH?V=2XDBXILF6UK&LIST= PLXF85IZKTYWIRKVD3INQYG2Q7FXLMFUMD

WEBSITES

THE LEARNING POLICY INSTITUTE: EFFECTIVE TEACHER PROFESSIONAL DEVELOPMENT – REPORT AND ACCOMPANYING MATERIALS

AVAILABLE VIA HTTPS://LEARNINGPOLICYINSTITUTE.ORG/PRODUCT/ EFFECTIVE-TEACHER-PROFESSIONAL-DEVELOPMENT-REPORT

DEANS FOR IMPACT: BUILDING BLOCKS OF EFFECTIVE TEACHER PREPARATION.

AVAILABLE VIA HTTPS://DEANSFORIMPACT.ORG/BUILDING-BLOCKS/

4 THE DEATH OF THE TEACHER?

JERE BROPHY AND THOMAS GOOD ON TEACHER BEHAVIOUR

DOI: 10.4324/9781003228165-5

4 THE DEATH OF THE TEACHER?

CHAPTER Teacher behavior and student achievement[1]

QUOTE *"Students achieve more in classes where they spend most of their time being taught or supervised by their teachers rather than working on their own."*[2]

Why You Should Read This Chapter

In 1967, Roland Barthes shook the world of literary and artistic criticism when he published *The Death of the Author*. The central argument of his essay was that our experience of art is determined not by the artist but by the viewer (or reader) who brings art's meaning into being. For Barthes, the creator and their creation are unrelated, for it is the observer who truly creates: hence the erasure of "the author" found in the essay's famous title.

For a generation now, it could be argued that teachers have increasingly been designated a role within the classroom similar to that which Barthes assigned to his idea of the author. That is to say, the advent of an over-literal interpretation of student-centred learning has threatened to render the teacher into a peripheral figure: there to "create the space" in which learning happens at the hands of students, rather than having a direct effect on student learning.

In their exhaustive review of research into teacher behaviour and its effect on student achievement, Jere Brophy and Thomas L. Good articulate the influence a teacher can have in the classroom, how that influence occurs, and the difference all that makes for students. The authors achieve this by establishing a connection between teacher actions and student outcomes, and then by integrating their findings into a series of "research-based conclusions about teacher behaviors

---

1   BROPHY, J. E., & GOOD, T. L. (1986). TEACHER BEHAVIOR AND STUDENT ACHIEVEMENT. IN M. C WITTROCK (ED.), *HANDBOOK OF RESEARCH ON TEACHING* (3RD ED., PP. 328–375). MACMILLAN.

2   IBID., P. 361

that maximise student achievement". In so doing, the authors reposition the teacher's significance in the classroom and define for us a version of teaching practice determined first and foremost by its *effect* on student learning.

Abstract of the Chapter

This paper, prepared as a chapter for the "Handbook of Research on Teaching" (third edition), reviews correlational and experimental research linking teacher behaviour to student achievement. It focuses on research done in K-12 classrooms during 1973–83, highlighting several large-scale, programmatic efforts. Attention is drawn to design, sampling, measurement, and context (grade level, subject matter, student socioeconomic status) factors that must be considered in interpreting this research and comparing the findings of different studies. Topics covered include these: (1) opportunity to learn/content covered, (2) teacher expectations/role definitions/time allocations, (3) classroom management/student engaged time, (4) success level/academic learning time, (5) active instruction by the teacher, (6) group size, (7) presentation of information (structuring, sequencing, clarity, enthusiasm), (8) asking questions (difficulty level, cognitive level, wait-time, selecting respondents, providing feedback), and (9) handling seatwork and homework assignments.

The Chapter

Defining "Teacher Behaviour" and "Student Achievement"

Brophy and Good (1986) begin by laying out their terms of engagement so that everyone is on the same page. They make clear that this will be a review of "teacher effects" as opposed to "teacher effectiveness". In particular, they distinguish "effects" as more specific than broad-based "effectiveness", referring instead to *teacher-effect inputs* (focusing on teacher behaviour rather than other variables such as "student interactions with peers" or "curriculum materials") and *teacher-effect outputs* (focusing on "student achievement gain" rather than other variables such as "personal, social, or moral development") as the basis of the study.

Even though their emphasis on those teacher actions that affect students" "mastery of formal curricula" (p. 328), this is not to say that the role of a teacher shouldn't incorporate broader "effectiveness" traits, such as "socializing students and promoting [students'] affective and personal development" (p. 328). Rather, Brophy and Good are more concerned in this case with how teachers help students acquire to-be-remembered content.

Teacher effects vs. teacher effectiveness

CONTEXT MATTERS

BROPHY AND GOOD offer an important caveat we should bear in mind when reading this (or any) study: "Many findings must be qualified by reference to grade level, student characteristics, or teaching objectives". Instead of offering a list of generic approaches to teaching that can be "copied and pasted" into any setting, they remind us that "effective instruction involves selecting (from a larger repertoire) and orchestrating those teaching behaviors that are appropriate to the context and to the teacher's goals" (p. 360).

Just as this is true for the purposes of Brophy and Good's paper, so should it be true of any evidence-informed approach to teaching: there is no such thing as a hard and fast rule for "what *always* works", but there are teacher behaviours that tend towards more positive outcomes for student learning. To paraphrase our colleague Pedro de Bruyckere: everything works somewhere and nothing works everywhere.

Integrating effective behaviours

The challenge for any teacher should be about how to integrate effective behaviours into an ever-evolving model of what it means to be good at teaching. It is this integration of effect-heavy practices that Brophy and Good hope to facilitate with their review.

The Teacher as Conveyor-of-Information

Having examined a broad swathe of the research, Brophy and Good's synthesise what all this means into a model of teacher effects on student achievement. Their conclusions cover a number of wide-ranging teacher behaviours – but for the purposes of this chapter we're going to focus on a trait that often hides in plain sight but which we consider to be hugely

Conveyor of Information

significant: *teachers as conveyors of information to students.*

Perhaps the archetypal image we have of a teacher, as depicted in popular culture, is that of a figure standing at the front of the classroom communicating items of knowledge to their students. Yet, when it comes to the way teaching has become regarded within the profession, such conceptions of practice have come to been seen by some as antiquated – especially when compared to approaches that promise to "place students at the centre of their own learning".

Don't get us wrong, we believe that students *should* be at the centre of learning – as the primary beneficiaries of it – but this doesn't mean students should be primarily *responsible* for all the learning that needs to happen. In keeping with this, Brophy and Good's work serves as a powerful acknowledgement that a big part of a teacher's job is to convey information to students.

Structuring and sequencing information

Structuring and Sequencing Information

We know that information is more likely to remain in our long-term memories and will be more easily retrieved if it's situated in an organising structure along with associated, relevant knowledge items. Take, for instance, expert chess players who can memorise the configuration of every piece on a board, and across many boards simultaneously, such that they can play multiple games at once. If you were to take those same expert players and ask them to remember the layout of a board that betrayed the rules of chess and had the pieces randomly placed, those chess masters would be just as mediocre at remembering the boards as the rest of us.

Learning as contextually dependent

This is because learning is highly contextually dependent but also because we learn things not in isolated units but as part of interconnected knowledge networks that psychologists refer to as *schemata*. In this example, the schema (or mental model) might accurately be labelled "Possible Positions of Chess Pieces". Within that mental model there are a whole host of interconnected items of knowledge, including how the pieces move and where they are supposed to show up on the board, all of which makes an expert chess player outstanding at one type of remembering and at best average at the other.

For teachers, this idea of how we process, retain, and retrieve information in networks of ideas is really important since effective structuring makes clear the relationship within and between chunks of knowledge, as well as how those chunks hang together.

Brophy and Good remind us that the teacher can play a significant role in determining how information is absorbed by paying attention to how they structure and sequence the presentation of that information. To do this, they reference studies into sequential structuring by Smith and Sanders (1981); explore the work of Gage and colleagues from the 1960s – which was reviewed by Rosenshine in 1968 and came to be known as the Stanford Studies.

From this, Brophy and Good highlight three effective approaches to structuring knowledge that can be integrated into practice:

Overviews and outlines

- *Overviews and outlines of to-be-remembered content*. Any organising structure for information that situates a specific knowledge item within its broader context helps students to integrate parts of knowledge into an overarching, coherent structure.

- In a biology lesson, a teacher might share a diagram that names the parts of a plant and then situate each part according to the role it plays in a given process, like photosynthesis or pollination. In this case, a specific knowledge item (one part of the plant) is being considered in relation to the broader network of knowledge items surrounding it (the other parts and processes of the plant).

Rule-example-rule patterns

- ■ *Rule-example-rule patterns* which invite students to link specific pieces of information to the broader concepts or rules within which they reside.
  - In a history lesson, a teacher might first introduce broad ideological concepts like communism or fascism, then invite students to explore specific leaders and nations in history, before determining the extent to which they might reasonably be defined as communist or fascist. In this case, a rule is established (the ideology), an example is introduced (the leader/nation), and a pattern is then interrogated (the extent to which the leader or nation could be seen as typical of that ideology).

Summaries and sequences

- ■ *Summaries and sequences of learning that revisit and review key concepts and associated rules* which, in Brophy and Good's words, "integrate and reinforce the learning of major points" (p. 362).
  - In a series of elementary Maths lessons, a teacher might move from "Place Value" onto "Addition and Subtraction" but still hold regular low-stakes tests and quizzes on the first of these concepts. In this case, since it's important for students to understand how addition and subtraction fit into the mental model established by their study of place values, the follow-up testing prevents the trace of the original content from fading, and invites students to make sense of new knowledge through reference to prior learning.

Questioning

Conveying Information by Questioning Students

An under-appreciated way of conveying information is the careful articulation of questions that elicit effortful thinking by the learner. The assumption we sometimes make is that the questions we ask students are only there to determine what knowledge has already "stuck" rather than as a means of making it stick. Brophy and Good address this by showing how teachers can convey, situate, and solidify new information through thoughtful questioning (for more on this idea, see Chapter 14 which explores Robert Bjork's work on desirable difficulties).

They begin by exploring studies into effective questioning, including Winne (1979), noting an important distinction about how we tend to interpret the substance of a question: "The cognitive level of a question is conceptually separate from its difficulty level" (p. 363). In other words, just because the subject or content referenced by a question is straightforward, that doesn't mean the cognitive demand required to answer the question is also straightforward, and vice versa. Conflating the complexity of the content found in a question with the cognitive demands of the question can lead to problems. Consider, for instance, questions like, "Why is the sky blue?" or "How does an airplane fly?" The terms of the question might be straightforward and "knowable", even to a child, but the cognitive implications associated with answering the question are much more complex.

Crafting thoughtful questions that build and deepen understanding is therefore trickier than it seems – a truth made all-the-more confounding by the fact that the research remains inconsistent when it comes to when and how to use certain question approaches. Brophy and Good suggest the reason for this inconsistency is, once again, the degree of contextual dependency associated with asking the right question at the right time. They note that the efficacy of a question will always need to "take into account the teacher's goals . . . the quality of the questions (clarity, relevance, etc.) and their timing and appropriateness given the flow of the activity" (p. 363).

At the same time, the authors acknowledge that useful roadmaps for questioning do exist, drawing on previous frameworks such as those developed by Anderson et al. (1982) to articulate those teacher-questioning behaviours that most positively affect student learning. Specifically, they offer two scenarios in which the context of learning would determine the choice of questioning approach:

- **Asking students to suggest a possible application of an idea, and then probing for details about how the suggested application could work** requires more demanding questions followed by less demanding questions.
- **Trying to call students' attention to relevant facts and then stimulate them to integrate the facts and draw an important conclusion** requires less demanding questions followed by more demanding questions (p. 363).

In addition to moderating the complexity of questions to suit the moment, Brophy and Good remind us that teachers can also determine when to ask questions that the students will likely know the answer to, versus when to ask questions that will likely stretch students in productive ways. The authors point out again that the research has yielded mixed results but that there is sufficient agreement on certain approaches that have been shown to correlate with positive student outcomes.

Managing question complexity

Crafting thoughtful questions

They note how "it seems clear that most (perhaps three fourths) of teachers' questions should elicit correct answers, and that most of the rest should elicit overt substantive responses (incorrect or incomplete answers) rather than failures to respond at all" (p. 362). This is in keeping with what has come to be known as "productive struggle", namely that teachers shouldn't only serve up questions that they know students know. Even if that might make the teacher look or feel better, asking questions that are always easily answerable won't lead to deeper, wider learning.

Instead, the challenge is to strike a balance between difficult-to-answer and less-difficult-to-answer questions that will determine when and how students are being stretched. As before, Brophy and Good offer good thinking on when one approach might work over the other, depending on the context:

Drill and practice

- Basic skills instruction requires a great deal of drill and practice, and **thus frequent fast-paced drill-review lessons during which most questions are answered rapidly and correctly** is more contextually appropriate.
- When teaching complex cognitive content, or when trying to stimulate students to generalise from, evaluate, or apply their learning, **teachers will need to raise questions that few students can answer correctly** as well as questions that have no single correct answers at all (p. 363).

Regardless of the qualitative nature of students' responses, the message here seems to be *one way or another, get students to respond*. This calls to mind the old sporting adage in which any in-game decision can be split into three categories: (1) making the right decision, (2) making the wrong decision, and (3) allowing uncertainty to reign and making no decision at all. Most coaches would tell you that they prefer (1), they don't always mind (2), but that (3) is inexcusable. In the same way, Brophy and Good make their point abundantly clear: whether students get a question right or wrong, it's more important that they are made to confront questions and to offer *something* over nothing.

Conclusions

Unsupervised versus supervised learning

One of the standout conclusions made by Brophy and Good is the importance of what they call "active teaching". In defining the concept and articulating its significance, they speak in the plainest possible terms: "Students achieve more in classes where they spend most of their time being taught or supervised by their teachers rather than working on their own" (p. 361).

It would be a little hypocritical, seeing as we have pointed to the dangers of over-interpreting student-centred learning, to invite a similarly absolutist interpretation of active teaching. Therefore, just in case Brophy and Good's headline might lead to the belief that *all* teaching should take the form of instructor-led lecture, we want to make clear that they regard active teaching as "frequent lessons . . . in which the teacher presents information and develops concepts through lecture and demonstration, elaborates this information in the feedback given following responses to recitation or discussion questions" but that they *also* acknowledge active teaching can look like a teacher who "monitors progress in assignments after releasing the students to work independently, and follows up with appropriate feedback and reteaching where necessary" (see Chapters 11 and 12 about direct Instruction and explicit instruction). Moreover, they note that "the teacher carries the content to the students personally rather than depending on the curriculum to do so, but conveys information mostly in brief presentations followed by recitation or application opportunities" (p. 361).

As you can see, committing to active teaching and positioning teachers as conveyors-of-information is *not* synonymous with wall-to-wall lecturing, or a student-stifling, top-down classroom dynamic. What Brophy and Good make clear is that there's an important place for student-led learning but that it is more effective *in light of* teacher-led building of shared understanding. This makes it not so much a question of relative importance or prioritisation but one of *operational order*. For students to learn for themselves, there must be something around which they can huddle and about which they can think. The alternative is tantamount to students pushing around pockets of thin air in what might appear to be industrious activity (i.e., are engaged or busy) but which is materially insubstantial.

In other words, despite recent trends, it's still worth remembering that a teacher's job is first and foremost to *teach*. This is not to rob students of their agency as learners but rather to acknowledge that students' best chances at learning come when relevant information has been conveyed, after which comes the work of what to do with that knowledge. Whether learning happens this way or not is ultimately down to the teacher – a truth Brophy and Good's paper so thoughtfully and convincingly conveys.

Takeaways

- It's possible to articulate teacher behaviours and actions that have the most positive impact on students' mastery of formal curricula.

- One teacher behaviour shown to have positive effects is when the teacher engages in "active teaching" in the guise of a conveyor-of-information.
- Teachers can perform this action through the way they structure and sequence information (paying attention to how knowledge is constructed, retained, and retrieved) as well as in the way they ask questions of students (paying attention to how questions have certain cognitive demands and invite students to think at varying degrees of depth).
- All teaching practice is highly contextually dependent, so rather than adopting and applying these approaches in their entirety, it's useful to integrate them into your evolving model of what good teaching looks like.
- Student-centred learning should not be entirely student-centred, and nor should active teaching be considered as entirely teacher-led. More effective is an approach to teaching in which teachers convey information and then help students wield, manipulate, adapt, and transfer that knowledge.

References

ANDERSON, L., EVERTSON, C., & BROPHY, J. (1982). *PRINCIPLES OF SMALL-GROUP INSTRUCTION IN ELEMENTARY READING* (OCCASIONAL PAPER NO. 58). INSTITUTE FOR RESEARCH ON TEACHING, MICHIGAN STATE UNIVERSITY. AVAILABLE VIA HTTP://FILES.ERIC.ED.GOV/FULLTEXT/ED223981.PDF

BROPHY, J. E., & GOOD, T. L. (1986). TEACHER BEHAVIOR AND STUDENT ACHIEVEMENT. IN M. C. WITTROCK (ED.), *HANDBOOK OF RESEARCH ON TEACHING* (3RD ED., PP. 328–375). MACMILLAN.

ROSENSHINE, B. (1968). TO EXPLAIN: A REVIEW OF RESEARCH. *EDUCATIONAL LEADERSHIP, 26,* 275–280.

SMITH, L., & SANDERS, K. (1981). THE EFFECTS ON STUDENT ACHIEVEMENT AND STUDENT PERCEPTION OF VARYING STRUCTURE IN SOCIAL STUDIES CONTENT. *JOURNAL OF EDUCATIONAL RESEARCH, 74,* 333–336.

WINNE, P. (1979). EXPERIMENTS RELATING TEACHERS' USE OF HIGHER COGNITIVE QUESTIONS TO STUDENT ACHIEVEMENT. *REVIEW OF EDUCATIONAL RESEARCH, 49,* 13–50.

Suggested Readings and Links

BERLINER, D. (1979). TEMPUS EDUCARE. IN P. PETERSON & H. WALBERG (EDS.), *RESEARCH ON TEACHING: CONCEPTS, FINDINGS, AND IMPLICATIONS.* MCCUTCHAN.

BROPHY, J. (1979). TEACHER BEHAVIOR AND ITS EFFECTS. *JOURNAL OF EDUCATIONAL PSYCHOLOGY, 71,* 733–750.

BRADBURY, S., & BERLIN, R. (2021, JUNE 28). BETTER QUESTIONS IN THE CLASSROOM LEAD STUDENTS TO THINK HARDER AND LEARN DEEPER. *EDSURGE.* AVAILABLE VIA WWW.EDSURGE.COM/NEWS/2021-06-28-BETTER-QUESTIONS-IN-THE-CLASSROOM-LEAD-STUDENTS-TO-THINK-HARDER-AND-LEARN-DEEPER

CRUICKSHANK, D. (1976). SYNTHESIS OF SELECTED RECENT RESEARCH C TEACHER EFFECTS. *JOURNAL OF TEACHER EDUCATION, 27(1),* 57–60.

VIDEOS

COLUMBIALEARN: THIS VIDEO FROM THE TEACHERS COLLEGE AT COLUMBIA UNIVERSITY EXPLORES THE CONCEPT OF COGNITIVE LOAD: A KEY REASON WHY TEACHERS SHOULD SEQUENCE INFORMATION WITH STUDENT LEARNING IN MIND.

ACCESSIBLE VIA: WWW.YOUTUBE.COM/WATCH?V=O6WTKEQRJMY

MICHIGAN VIRTUAL: THIS VIDEO EXPLORES DIFFERENT TYPES OF TEACHER QUESTIONING, INCLUDING THE WAYS IN WHICH IT CAN DEEPEN STUDENTS'' PROCESSING OF INFORMATION.

AVAILABLE VIA: WWW.YOUTUBE.COM/WATCH?V=BGBLMDXNTMO

WEBSITES

TEACHING WORKS: A RESOURCE BANK ON THE DESIGNING OF LESSONS AN SEQUENCES OF LESSONS, WITH A FOCUS ON SCIENCE AND SOCIAL STUDIES.

AVAILABLE VIA HTTPS://LIBRARY.TEACHINGWORKS.ORG/ CURRICULUM-RESOURCES/TEACHING-PRACTICES/DESIGNING-LESSONS/

UNIVERSITY OF MICHIGAN: A RESOURCE GUIDE FOR THE QUESTION FORMULATION TECHNIQUE (QFT) WHICH EXTENDS THE IDEA OF EFFECTIVE QUESTION FORMULATION AS A SKILL THAT STUDENTS CAN ALSO UNDERSTAND AND HONE.

AVAILABLE VIA HTTPS://SITES.LSA.UMICH.EDU/INCLUSIVE-TEACHING/ QUESTION-FORMULATION-TECHNIQUE/

5 I THINK, THEREFORE I TEACH

DANIEL MUIJS AND COLLEAGUES ON TEACHER EFFECTIVENESS

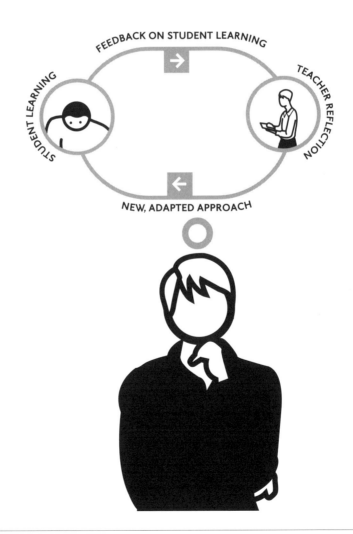

OI: 10.4324/9781003228165-6

5 I THINK, THEREFORE I TEACH

ARTICLE State of the art – teacher effectiveness and professional learning[1]

QUOTE *"If teachers are to become self-regulated learners and take responsibility for their own learning . . . then teachers must set learning goals for themselves as well as their students."*[2]

Why You Should Read This Article

We've all encountered the expression "practice makes perfect": that well-worn phrase is used whenever we hope to refine an aptitude for the better. Utter those words to a top athlete or musician and it will more than likely elicit a grimace of concern, since they know full well that practice alone doesn't make perfect.

Yes, practice is very necessary but platitudes like these only go a fraction of the way to capturing what deliberate, incremental improvement is, particularly when it comes to the complex skills found in activities such as sport, music, and teaching. Even educators who advocate for a fuller appreciation of how teaching capabilities emerge and grow are more likely to ground that in what it means for their students than for themselves. In reality, they would be better placed to focusing on teacher improvement as a necessary prerequisite for student learning.

We've already explored the erroneous belief that teachers are born, not made, and that good teaching doesn't happen by accident. To address these same ideas in service of teacher professional development requires a different approach. It involves exploring effective teaching strategies and their impact on learning but, more than that, calls on careful interrogation of what it takes to get *better* at this immeasurably intricate

---

I   MUIJS, D., KYRIAKIDES, L., VAN DER WERF, G., CREEMERS, B., TIMPERLEY, H., & EARL, L. (2014). STATE OF THE ART – TEACHER EFFECTIVENESS AND PROFESSIONAL LEARNING. *SCHOOL EFFECTIVENESS AND SCHOOL IMPROVEMENT: AN INTERNATIONAL JOURNAL OF RESEARCH, POLICY AND PRACTICE,* 25(2), 231–2! AVAILABLE VIA WWW.TANDFONLINE.COM/DOI/ABS/10.1080/09243453.2014.885451

2   IBID., P. 247.

thing we call teaching. That was the task taken on by Daniel Muijs and his colleagues in their paper: "State of the art – teacher effectiveness and professional learning".

For Muijs and his co-authors, not enough had been done to anticipate how teachers improve in ways that correspond with their context, meaning professional development often falls foul to both a "one-size-fits-all" and a "one-moment-in-time" approach. Instead, they offer a way of thinking about professional learning that brings together the best of what we know about how teachers teach with new ideas about how teachers can learn and improve. Central to Muijs' notion of "better" is the idea that teachers, like their students, are better served by a metacognitive approach that sees improvement itself as subject to intelligent design.

Abstract of the Article

One of the key findings from decades of educational effectiveness research is the importance of the classroom level as a predictor of pupil outcomes. In this review, we therefore look at synthesising our best evidence from research on effective teaching, and its corollary, teacher development. In the 1st section, we will look at key findings from 35 years of research on effective teaching using a process-product research that has led to the identification of a range of behaviours which are positively related to student achievement. A key limitation of this research, however, is its focus on basic skills in English and maths. Therefore, in the 2nd section we review research on "new learning" and teaching for metacognitive and thinking skills. While in these two sections we have discussed key findings from research on teaching, including emerging knowledge on metacognition, it is important to continue to take into account ongoing developments in theories of learning. In the 3rd section of this paper, we develop the argument that a major contributing factor to this situation is that "state-of-the-art" understandings about processes and conditions that promote student learning are typically not used to construct appropriate learning environments for their teachers.

The Article

Change-based
approach to teaching
practice

In his quest to imagine a different approach to teacher development, Muijs begins with the assertion that school improvement efforts have traditionally seen students as a necessary unit of change but not teachers, and even efforts that do focus on teacher effectiveness tend to concentrate on what effective teaching practice looks like, without asking how practice can be *changed*. As Muijs puts it, "If teacher behaviours are key to educational effectiveness, we need to pay attention to ways in which we can change practice as well as looking at what effective practice is" (p. 231). With this as his motivating principle, Muijs sets out to find a new way.

Moving Beyond "Best Practice" to a Dynamic Model of Professional Development

Muijs sets the context for this work by exploring those teacher behaviours that the last 35 years of research have shown to have the most positive and predictable relationship to student achievement. These include opportunity to learn and time on task, effective instruction and interaction, classroom climate, teacher expectations, and differential teacher effectiveness. He also points out how meta-analyses have combined results from different studies to shed new light on teacher effectiveness, particularly regarding the strong impact that reinforcement and feedback have on student outcomes.

While offering a useful picture of "what works", Muijs is quick to note the limitations of the study base, pointing out that it skews heavily towards English and maths instruction at the expense of a broader swathe of instructional contexts. He also suggests the studies represent a comparatively limited approach to codifying teacher effectiveness in entirety, especially when held up against the more robust literature underpinning student learning. In response, Muijs moves us beyond a simple conception of what good teaching looks like towards a multi-dimensional appreciation of what it looks like to get better at teaching.

To do this, he turns to one of the leading lights of theoretical modelling in education – Bert Creemers – whose work in the 1990s and early 2000s developed the idea of education as a complex system, possessing interconnected layers which demand better understanding both in isolation and in concert. This idea of an interconnected system is presented in the form of Creemers' *Comprehensive Model of Educational Effectiveness* (1994) which "strongly stressed the relationship between effectiveness at the different levels, and in particular consistency of effectiveness characteristics between and within levels, cohesion, meaning that all members of staff should show characteristics of effective teaching, and control, meaning that policy and goal attainment in the school should be evaluated" (p. 243).

It's clear that once we conceive of education in this way, attempting to see teaching as a one-dimensional list of best practices fixed in time and place becomes a wholly inadequate approach to professional learning. Tracking the evolution of this idea, Muijs shows how teachers exist as part of the interconnected system, subject like all parts of that system to their own version of incremental improvement. For this, he turns to Creemers and Kyriakides (2006) and their *Dynamic Model of Educational Effectiveness*.

Unlike the usual list of fixed traits, their dynamic model draws two important distinctions. First, it focuses on effective observable instructional behaviour rather than on underlying factors such as teacher beliefs or interpersonal competencies. We might capture this

Education as a complex system

Models of educational effectiveness

Dynamic Model of Educational Effectiveness

in the question, "What do effective teacher actions look like?" Second, it assumes that each factor can be defined and measured in accordance with its application and potential for improvement *in dynamic terms*. We might capture this in the question, "How can I understand and improve the effectiveness of those teacher actions along an imagined continuum of incremental improvement?"

In practical terms, these questions are addressed through those observable elements of teaching practice that have the highest-potential impact on student learning (see Figure 5.1) combined with a metric that states, "each effectiveness factor can be defined and measured using five

Factors		Main elements
1 | Orientation	a	Providing the objectives for which a specific task/lesson/series of lessons take(s) place
	b	Challenging students to identify the reason why an activity is taking place in the lesson
2 | Structuring	a	Beginning with overviews and/or review of objectives
	b	Outlining the content to be covered and signalling transitions between lesson parts
	c	Drawing attention to and reviewing main ideas
3 | Questioning	a	Raising different types of questions (i.e., process and product) at appropriate difficulty level
	b	Giving time to students to respond
	c	Dealing with student responses
4 | Teaching modelling	a	Encouraging students to use problem-solving strategies presented by the teacher or other classmates
	b	Inviting students to develop strategies
	c	Prompting the idea of modelling
5 | Application	a	Using seatwork or small-group tasks in order to provide needed practice and application opportunities
	b	Using application tasks as starting points for the next step of teaching and learning
6 | The classroom as a learning environment	a	Establishing on-task behaviour through the interactions they promote (i.e., teacher-student and student-student interactions)
	b	Dealing with classroom disorder and student competition through establishing rules, persuading students to respect them and using the rules
7 | Management of time	a	Organising the classroom environment
	b	Maximising engagement rates
8 | Assessment	a	Using appropriate techniques to collect data on student knowledge and skills
	b	Analysing data in order to identify student needs and report the results to students and parents
	c	Teachers evaluating their own practices

FIGURE 5.1 MAIN ELEMENTS OF EACH TEACHER FACTOR INCLUDED IN THE DYNAMIC MODEL. (SOURCE: MUIJS ET AL., 2014, P. 244, REPRINTED BY PERMISSION OF THE PUBLISHER, TAYLOR & FRANCIS LTD, WWW.TANDFONLINE.COM).

dimensions: frequency, focus, stage, quality, and differentiation" (p. 245), thus lending a dynamic component to the manner in which each element is enacted and observed.

With the help of Creemers, Muijs begins to offer up a multi-dimensional picture of teacher effectiveness. Rather than seeing effective teacher behaviours as fixed traits, the dynamic model acknowledges them as existing within a complex system and, just like that system, as subject to change along a continuum of increasing (or decreasing) effectiveness over time.

Towards a Unified Model of Professional Development

Having established evolving teacher effectiveness as a dynamic system, Muijs argues that adopting a dynamic model requires shifts in our understanding and perceptions of teacher development, particularly when compared to traditional notions of student growth. He posits that, "'State-of-the-art' understandings about processes and conditions that promote student learning are typically not used to construct appropriate learning environments for their teachers", arguing that there is a dissonance inherent in the more highly evolved understanding we have of student learning and the less-well-developed field of teacher improvement. Indeed, it could be argued that this contributes to the phenomenon of educators who appreciate the value of professional learning as a concept but all-too-often experience it as inadequate in practice.

Just as our understanding of how learning happens becomes more sophisticated, it seems the gap between what we know to be good for students and that which we experience as teachers becomes starker. To address this, Muijs draws on the work of Bransford et al. (2000) to illustrate which conditions of effective learning are common to both students and teachers and arrives at making connections, developing metacognitive awareness, and taking control of one's learning through self-regulation. Muijs stresses the cost of not employing metacognitive strategies with reference to a study by Hammerness et al. (2005) which showed that whenever teachers are not supported in making connections between existing knowledge and new knowledge, "they interpret new ideas within existing frameworks and so make only superficial changes to practice when much deeper changes are required". The phrase used to describe this phenomenon is "over-assimilation".

Muijs further explores these points of connection between teachers and students through reference to yet more meta-analyses and a developing body of international evidence showing that there is more of a relationship between how students learn and how teachers develop than is acknowledged by most school systems.

Common conditions for learning – shared by students and teachers

The conclusions of the professional development studies Muijs pulls together read like a list of learning priorities that any right-minded educator would endorse for the sake of their students, namely that:

- Organising for learning should take account of specificities of context rather than relying on the over-generalised translation of existing approaches.
- Learning should focus on specific and well-defined problems rather than broad-based challenges.
- Definitions of success should be determined by progress towards solving for said problems rather than driven by outcomes.
- Developing a mental model of improvement informed by an understanding of how people learn should guide the way rather than misguided notions of what works.

These, for Muijs, are the activating ingredients for professional learning. If the literature base of the last few decades started to show us what good teaching looks like, and the Creemers' dynamic models of teacher effectiveness showed us what good teaching looks like *and* what it means to get better at it, then metacognitive processes such as these are the key to unlocking the "how" of teacher improvement in action. They do so by lending self-regulated agency to teachers in their development and by giving teachers the tools they need to bridge the gap between an evolving idea of teaching practice and their evolving enactment of it.

The Unified Model

Unified model of professional development

So, what would it mean to bring all of the strands we have explored so far into a single model of professional development? For Muijs, such a model looks like this:

FIGURE 5.2
TEACHER ENQUIRY AND KNOWLEDGE-BUILDING CYCLE TO PROMOTE IMPORTANT OUTCOMES FOR STUDENTS. (SOURCE: MUIJS ET AL., 2014, P. 247, REPRINTED BY PERMISSION OF THE PUBLISHER, TAYLOR & FRANCIS LTD, WWW.TANDFONLINE.COM).

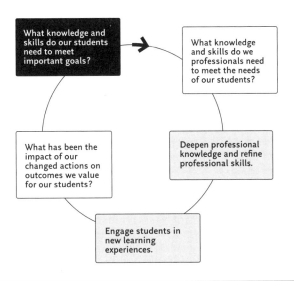

In this unified model lives the most significant pieces of the teacher development journey explored so far:

Student knowledge and skills

- **What knowledge and skills do our students need to meet important goals?** The cycle begins with the aim of understanding "the discrepancy between goals and the current situation" of the students in question. Learning "how to collect the relevant evidence and to develop the necessary understandings" (p. 247) of their students current and prospective states of learning is crucial to this opening step.

Professional knowledge and skills

- **What knowledge and skills do we have as professionals to meet the needs of our students?** Here begins the fractal relationship between student and teacher learning, for "if teachers are to become self-regulated learners and take responsibility for their own learning . . . then teachers must set learning goals for themselves as well as their students". As in the previous step, teachers must establish a sense of what they have versus what they'll need. The risk of teachers who don't know what they don't know can affect this stage, so working alongside someone "with specific expertise in the particular area of inquiry" (p. 247) is important, be that in pedagogical or domain-specific content knowledge.

Deepen professional knowledge

- **Deepen professional knowledge and refine professional skills.** This step is "where traditional approaches to professional development usually begin". The problem of failing to engage with the first two steps is that it normally leads to teachers being given answers to questions they didn't ask, typically with an external source such as a policymaker or researcher offering the unsolicited vision of improvement. Instead, a contextually specific process of inquiry and knowledge-building comes into play. Just as it is true for students, this step acknowledges that learning occurs "by making patterns that connect existing knowledge to new knowledge". As such, improvement resembles an ever-evolving mental model of what it would take to become a better teacher, as opposed to an approach in which teachers "interpret new ideas within existing frameworks and so make only superficial changes to practice when much deeper changes are required" (p. 248).

Engage students / Check impact

- **Engage students in new learning experiences** and then ask: **What has been the impact of our changed actions on outcomes we value for our students?** These steps embody the bounded relationship between teacher and student growth, allowing for "a more iterative process as teachers learn new knowledge and refine existing skills, try things out in practice, work out what is working and not working for students, revisit conceptions and misconceptions, and try again" (p. 248). This is where fixed notions of "best practice" give way to a self-regulated and dynamic approach to professional improvement.

If what teachers learn and are able to do is closely bound to what students end up learning and being able to do, then this phase is about understanding the learning goals of teachers *and the ways in which the realisation of those goals precede and inform subsequent student learning*.

The model's aesthetic suggests a neat cycle but it is important to note that, despite its sequential appearance, it's much more iterative in real life. It involves establishing multiple feedback loops designed to better understand student and teacher learning, and offers multiple opportunities to understand, modify, and refine practice. In other words, a practical model of dynamic professional learning that can be applied to the real-world conditions of teaching.

Conclusions

The model proposed by Muijs and the theories that underpin it remind us to resist fixed notions of "best practice" in teaching. It does so by positioning research and evidence not as a monolithic body of knowledge but rather as the flow of ideas and data that teachers can use and infuse into an ever-evolving mental model for teaching.

Muijs also urges us to resist the fixed notion of a teacher. His work reminds us that teachers are not automata who passively receive and "over-assimilate" inherited ideas and instructions. Rather, he articulates a dynamic model that sees teachers as self-regulating entities and respects their development as complex, iterative, contextually specific, and closely bound to the learning conditions of their students.

For Muijs, teachers can and should think for themselves, and this influential paper is his roadmap for how to do just that.

Takeaways

- Professional development that assumes a "one-size-fits-all" or a "one-moment-in-time" approach does not change teaching practice in meaningful, sustainable ways.
- The "best practice" approach to teaching assumes teaching traits to be fixed and devoid of context.
- A dynamic model of teacher effectiveness acknowledges context and sees practice as subject to iterative improvement relative to that context.
- Professional learning should be grounded in what students need to know and be able to do, leading to a parallel articulation of what teachers need to know and be able to do in meeting student needs.
- Teachers, like students, can benefit from an approach to their learning that employs metacognition, self-regulation, and connecting prior

learning to new information. As such, professional development should follow an organising principle that sees teachers as adaptive learners.

- More should be done to articulate those "state of the art" approaches to teacher learning and development in the same way that understanding of "how learning happens" for students has evolved in recent years.

References

BRANSFORD, J. D., BROWN, A. L., & COCKING, R. R. (2000). *HOW PEOPLE LEARN: BRAIN, MIND, EXPERIENCE, AND SCHOOL: EXPANDED EDITION.* NATIONAL ACADEMY PRESS.

CREEMERS, B. P. M. (1994). *THE EFFECTIVE CLASSROOM.* CASSELL.

CREEMERS, B. P. M., & KYRIAKIDES, L. (2006). CRITICAL ANALYSIS OF THE CURRENT APPROACHES TO MODELLING EDUCATIONAL EFFECTIVENESS: THE IMPORTANCE OF ESTABLISHING A DYNAMIC MODEL. *SCHOOL EFFECTIVENESS AND SCHOOL IMPROVEMENT, 17,* 347–366

HAMMERNESS, K., DARLING-HAMMOND, L., BRANSFORD, J., BERLINER, D., COCHRAN-SMITH, M., MCDONALD, M., & ZEICHNER, K. (2005). HOW TEACHERS LEARN AND DEVELOP. IN L. DARLING-HAMMOND (ED.), *PREPARING TEACHERS FOR A CHANGING WORLD: WHAT TEACHERS SHOULD LEARN AND BE ABLE TO DO* (PP. 358–389). JOHN WILEY & SONS.

MUIJS, D., KYRIAKIDES, L., VAN DER WERF, G., CREEMERS, B., TIMPERLEY, H., & EARL, L. (2014). STATE OF THE ART – TEACHER EFFECTIVENESS AND PROFESSIONAL LEARNING. *SCHOOL EFFECTIVENESS AND SCHOOL IMPROVEMENT: AN INTERNATIONAL JOURNAL OF RESEARCH, POLICY AND PRACTICE, 25*(2), 231–256.

Suggested Readings and Links

HANUSHEK, E. (2008). INCENTIVES FOR EFFICIENCY AND EQUITY IN THE SCHOOL SYSTEM. *PERSPEKTIVEN DER WIRTSCHAFTSPOLITIK, 9*(SUPPL. 1), 5–27.

MUIJS, D., & REYNOLDS, D. (2000). SCHOOL EFFECTIVENESS AND TEACHER EFFECTIVENESS IN MATHEMATICS: SOME PRELIMINARY FINDINGS FROM THE EVALUATION OF THE MATHEMATICS ENHANCEMENT PROGRAM (PRIMARY). *SCHOOL EFFECTIVENESS AND SCHOOL IMPROVEMENT, 11,* 273–303.

TEDDLIE, C., CREEMERS, B. P. M., KYRIAKIDES, L., MUIJS, D., & FEN, Y. (2006). THE INTERNATIONAL SYSTEM FOR TEACHER OBSERVATION AND FEEDBACK: EVOLUTION OF AN INTERNATIONAL STUDY OF TEACHER EFFECTIVENESS CONSTRUCTS. *EDUCATIONAL RESEARCH AND EVALUATION, 12,* 561–582.

VIDEO

IN THIS VIDEO, DYLAN WILIAM ASKS OF TEACHER QUALITY: WHAT IS IT, WHY IT MATTERS, AND HOW TO GET MORE OF IT?

AVAILABLE VIA WWW.YOUTUBE.COM/WATCH?V=BACHTPRH-QQ

WEBSITES

SCIENCE DIRECT: A COLLECTION OF ARTICLES, BOOKS, BOOK CHAPTERS AND STUDIES ON THE TOPIC OF TEACHER EFFECTIVENESS.

AVAILABLE VIA WWW.SCIENCEDIRECT.COM/TOPICS/SOCIAL-SCIENCES/TEACHER-EFFECTIVENESS

TNTP: A SERIES OF PUBLICATIONS EXPLORING TEACHER EFFECTIVENESS, SET ALONGSIDE THE BROADER CHALLENGE OF RECRUITING, SUPPORTING AND RETAINING HIGH-QUALITY TEACHERS.

AVAILABLE VIA HTTPS://TNTP.ORG/PUBLICATIONS/SCROLL/TEACHER-TRAINING-AND-CLASSROOM-PRACTICE

6 WHEN THINKING AND ACTING BECOME ONE

DONALD SCHÖN ON REFLECTIVE PRACTICE

ONCE YOU START PAYING ATTENTION TO THE REFLECTIVE BACK-AND-FORTH WITH THE PHENOMENA OF DAILY LIFE IN THIS WAY...

...IT CAN BEGIN TO FEEL LIKE A DANCE

DOI: 10.4324/9781003228165-7

6 WHEN THINKING AND ACTING BECOME ONE

BOOK The reflective practitioner[1]

QUOTE *"Our knowing is in our action."*[2]

Why You Should Read This Book

There was once a village situated on the banks of a river. One day, as the villagers worked in a nearby field, they saw an alarming sight: a baby floating towards them down stream. They rushed to the baby's aid, pulling it to safety, but that was far from the end of their worries. A few minutes later, *another* baby was seen drifting down the river, followed moments later by another. Over the coming days and weeks, a steady stream of babies kept coming and it soon became clear that something had to be done.

In desperate response, the village set up watchtowers to stop babies from drifting past unnoticed; they established a dedicated day care to look after the youngsters; and community meetings turned to questions of the long-term welfare of the children, who would need loving homes and a good education. Meanwhile, one villager who had just retrieved yet another baby from the river, had a revelation. He ran straight to a community meeting that was already in session, flung open the doors and posed a question nobody had yet thought of, let alone voiced because they were too wrapped up in action than thought: "When is someone going to head upstream and find out how those babies ended up in the river in the first place?!"

The parable of the river (McKinlay, 1975) has often been used to examine root causes but it's also a study in the power of thoughtful in-the-moment reflection. In this case, set against the reactionary

---

1   SCHÖN, D. (1983) *THE REFLECTIVE PRACTITIONER.* BASIC BOOKS. REPUBLISHED WITH PERMISSION O
HACHETTE BOOKS GROUP, PERMISSION CONVEYED THROUGH COPYRIGHT CLEARANCE CENTEI
INC.
2   IBID., P. 49

behaviours of the community at large, it takes one villager to catch themselves, reframe the situation, and identify what was laying beneath the surface all along: a potentially solvable problem that can only be attended to if it is first articulated as such.

Thinking through and reacting to one's engagement in a task *while engaged in it* is a difficult but not impossible skill. It requires one to reflect-in-action and consider the possibilities that exist outside our initial field of view. Indeed, it turns out professionals engage in this kind of reflection all the time, and one of the most influential books ever written about such practices is the focus of this chapter: *The Reflective Practitioner* by Donald A. Schön.

Abstract of the Book

A leading M.I.T. social scientist and consultant examines five professions, engineering, architecture, management, psychotherapy, and town planning to show how professionals really go about solving problems. The best professionals, Donald Schön maintains, know more than they can put into words. To meet the challenges of their work, they rely less on formulas learned in graduate school than on the kind of improvisation learned in practice. This unarticulated, largely unexamined process is the subject of Schön's provocatively original book, an effort to show precisely how reflection-in-action works and how this vital creativity might be fostered in future professionals.

The Book

The Illusion of Order

Schön begins his book by asserting that much of what we *think* we know about professional knowledge and practice is based on a misguided understanding of how professions are structured to begin with – a phenomenon he refers to as *Technical Rationality*.

Technical Rationality

The basic premise of technical rationality rests on what we might call "the illusion of order". That is to say, the erroneous belief that there exists a straight line between the knowledge underpinning a given practice and its successful enactment. To show us what he means, Schön turns to Edgar Schein (1973) who described three components to professional knowledge:

1. An *underlying discipline* or *basic science* component upon which the practice rests or from which it is developed.
2. An *applied science* or *"engineering"* component from which many of the day-to-day diagnostic procedures and problem-solutions are derived.

3. A *skills* and *attitudinal* component that concerns the actual performance of services to the client, using the underlying basic and applied knowledge.

Hierarchies of understanding

For Schön, organising any professional domain in this way represents the illusion of order because it relies on an unrealistically neat and predictable relationship between one part of the professional structure and the next. According to such a construction, anyone preparing to enter a profession must *first* learn the underlying principles governing it, *then* consider their application, before *finally* graduating to the point of enacting that understanding.

This has been true of our approach to teaching for the longest time, where we so often assume that teachers must first "know their stuff" in a theoretical sense before arriving at a level of understanding that means they're "ready" for clinical experience. This is akin to making a five-year-old complete sixth months' worth of worksheets on how to ride a bike before deeming them "ready" to operate one for the first time.

Technical rationality also assumes that the progression of professional knowledge flows neatly in the opposite direction. As such, when someone becomes part of a profession and faces a problem to be solved, all they need to do is retrace their steps back through the bread-crumbed path of applied understanding and foundational principles governing the problem and, "Hey presto!" the solution will present itself. Again, this would look something like the five-year-old falling off the bike at the first attempt and returning to their worksheets to diagnose what went wrong.

The assumption is that everything we need to solve the problem can be found in the long-established foundations of knowledge that preceded us: reminiscent of the villagers from the parable of the river, who know how to set up watchtowers and day cares and school systems but have fallen into the convenience of relying *only* on such prior knowledge as the presumptive answer to the problem of floating babies.

Managing complexity

Schön argues that this conception of how knowledge passes neatly back and forth through practice fails to appreciate a fundamental truth: the world is *much* more complex than that. To illustrate his point, he offers a case from the world of medicine (p. 41):

> A physician who recognizes a case of measles can map it onto a system of techniques for diagnosis, treatment and prognosis. But a unique case falls outside the categories of applied theory; an unstable situation slips out from under them. A physician cannot apply standard techniques to a case that is not in the books.

In this example (which we hope you will see as imminently transferable to the world of teaching) Schön reveals the reality behind the curtain of technical rationality. For starters, the case doesn't end with the physician giving up on the patient altogether. In the *real* world the physician would never say, "Ah well, the answer isn't in one of my textbooks so . . . good luck kid!" and neither would a teacher in an analogous situation. In the real world, a professional would try to find the means of diagnosing the problem, not because of technical rationality but despite it. To shine a light on what technical rationality has missed, Schön therefore turns to the nature of problem solving itself.

From Problem Solving to Problem Setting

From Problem Solving to Problem Setting

For Schön, the main limitation of technical rationality is that it has very little to say about how real people solve real problems. He draws this distinction by arguing that, "From the perspective of Technical Rationality, professional practice is a process of problem *solving*" for which "problems of choice or decision are solved through the selection, from available means, of the one best suited to established ends" (p. 39).

Problem solving vs problem setting

Since we've already seen in the parable of the river that problems don't always present us with "established ends", problem *solving* falls short as a description for how to deal with such challenges. In language borrowed from John Dewey (1938) Schön states that "The situations of practice are not problems to be solved but problematic situations characterized by uncertainty, disorder and indeterminacy" (p. 16), and since real-world problems "do not present themselves to the practitioner as givens" they must be "constructed from the materials of problematic situations, which are puzzling, troubling and uncertain" (p. 40). In other words, when faced with uncertainty and complexity, simply turning to "what is known" in order to engage in problem *solving* will often prove inadequate. Instead, Schön offers a more realistic definition of what professionals actually do, namely *problem setting*.

Naming and setting problems

To illustrate the difference, Schön offers the example of engineers setting about the task of building a road. Rather than simply "building a road" engineers "deal usually with a complex and ill-defined situation in which geographic, topological, financial, economic and political issues are all mixed up together". For Schön, these overlapping concerns cannot technically be defined as "a problem", in much the same way that "what to do with babies floating down a river" is not yet "a problem" in the fullest sense of the term. Rather, these are problematic *situations* that first need to be *set* (or problematised) in terms that can be managed and to which one can reasonably respond. Schön therefore defines problem *setting* as the process by which "we *name* the things to which we will attend and *frame* the context in which we will attend to them" (p. 40).

So how might people, be they physicians, engineers, or teachers, move from problem *solving* to problem *setting* in their own practice? To answer this question, Schön introduces us to two fundamentally important ideas: *knowledge-in-action* and *reflection-in-action*.

Knowing and Reflecting in Action

Knowing and acting at once

Schön's argument about the nature of problems and how we meet them is closely linked to his ideas about knowledge and action. As we've already explored, technical rationality would have us believe that knowledge *precedes* action, serving as the logical precursor for the challenges we face. For Schön, this is misguided because, "Our knowing is ordinarily tacit, implicit in our patterns of action and in our feel for the stuff with which we are dealing". Indeed, he goes on to suggest that knowing and doing likely happen all at once: "It seems right to say that our knowing is *in* our action" (p. 49).

Acting and reflecting at once

Schön then suggests a logical extension to the idea of knowledge-in-action which he introduces in deceptively simple terms. He plainly states that, "we sometimes think about what we are doing" (p. 54) and that this is why we have found so many ways to describe "thinking on your feet" or "keeping your wits about you". This is the language we turn to when knowledge-in-action becomes reflection-in-action.

Schön offers a variety of reflection-in-action examples, such as the tight-rope walker (who knows how to make tiny but life-saving adjustments in balance from moment-to-moment); the baseball pitcher (who begins to get a "feel" for the ball and how to manipulate it within a series of pitches); or the jazz musician (who can take the fundamental structure of a tune but improvise their way to ever-more creative variations in real time). All such examples show people who are displaying both knowledge-in-action *and* reflection-in-action: an ability to think and act (then reflect and adjust and act again) seemingly in complete concert, with apparent fluidity, and often in ways that escape easy definition – even by those doing the task.

Actualising Reflection-in-Action

If knowledge- and reflection-in-action are identifiable in the ways described, it follows that there must be specific traits that one might hope to emulate. To this end, Schön breaks down features of a reflection-in-action approach to professional practice. We'll explore some of them here, with reference to what each might look like in the context of teaching.

Understanding the Nature of Your Own "Problem Setting"

When considering what it means to "set" a problem, Schön reminds us of important questions that effective practitioners tend to ask themselves along the way (p. 133):

- Can I solve the problem I have set?
- Do I like what I get when I solve this problem?
- Have I made the situation coherent?
- Have I made it congruent with my fundamental values and theories?
- Have I kept inquiry moving?

New problem, new context

The idea of "keeping inquiry moving" in the last of these questions essentially means that once a complex situation has been reframed into a problem to be solved, that then becomes a new context all its own, thus demanding fresh inquiry. A school leader might identify that the school's perception of a dip in reading scores is based on an inaccurate premise, only to replace that theory with yet another misguided one. The questions Schön offers are a way of checking that the new world you've created for yourself by setting the problem is in fact the one you want and need to be occupying.

Past experiences

Bringing Past Experiences to Bear on New Situations

It might seem contradictory, especially given what we have had to say about technical rationality up till now, to champion the impact of prior knowledge on new problems. Of course, applying received wisdom carelessly rarely meets the needs of a novel challenge. What Schön argues instead is that (p. 139):

- Prior experience provides a practitioner with, "a repertoire of examples, images, understandings, and actions".
- When a practitioner makes sense of a new situation, they "see the unfamiliar situation as both similar to and different from the familiar one".
- The familiar "functions as a precedent or a metaphor . . . for the unfamiliar" which means we can "see unfamiliar situations as familiar ones".

Building mental models

Every experience we have contributes to an ever-growing mental model, filled with examples and non-examples which can be "held up alongside" new situations to render them more familiar. A highly experienced teacher can walk into a classroom that is not their own and immediately gain a sense of what's happening. This is because they have the accumulated wisdom of *every* classroom they've *ever* entered to help them make sense of this one.

Running on-the-Spot Experiments

If technical rationality defines "experimentation" in the classical sense, reflection-in-action adopts a more pragmatic approach in which the uncertainty of the real world can't always be controlled as though in laboratory conditions. Instead, Schön defines three forms of real-time experimentation for reflective practice:

Exploratory experiments

- *Exploratory Experiments* is described as "the probing, playful activity by which we get a feel for things". It happens "when action is undertaken only to see what follows, without accompanying predictions or expectations". A teacher spends the early weeks of the new year getting to know their students and finds ways for them to get to know each other. The stakes are low and the main intent is to build relationships but there's much to reflect on from these early interactions.

Move-testing experiments

- *Move-Testing Experiments* happen when we introduce something new into a new situation to see what happens. For Schön, "Any deliberate action with an end in mind is, in this sense, an experiment". Based on what they've come to know about their students and the working dynamic of the classroom in the opening weeks, the same teacher tries out a new seating plan before reflecting on the impact it has on classroom dynamics.

Hypothesis-testing experiments

- *Hypothesis-Testing Experiments* involve making predictions about what we think will happen in a given circumstance before confirming or denying the hypothesis in question based on observable evidence. The same teacher who started the new year getting to know students and then made a move to put them in a new seating plan is now making bets about what approaches to instruction will work best for *these* students in *this* context given *those* prior choices.

Running experiments of which you are a part

Unlike classical hypothesis experimentation (in which the subject of the experiment is not to be interfered with for fear of biasing the results) reflection-in-action inevitably leads to direct involvement because the practitioner is necessarily a part of what's being observed. Indeed, reflection-in-action is perhaps best captured when the practitioner displays, and finds themselves a part of, all three forms of experimentation at once.

It's seen in the teacher who is simultaneously observing classroom dynamics in light of what was learned early in the year; determining the effectiveness of the seating plan in supporting the students as they go about a given task; adjusting instructional practice in real time to meet the needs of each new instructional situation; setting and solving problems almost as quickly as they can be defined. In other words, what we call *teaching*.

Conclusions

Schön's ideas have proved hugely influential because of the way he invites us to rethink our very relationship with the world around us, the knowledge we bring to bear on it, and the thoughts and actions we engage in – all at once. Once you start paying attention to this reflective back-and-forth with the phenomena of daily life it can begin to feel like a dance, or, as Schön puts it, "a practitioner's reflective conversation with a situation".

In order to conduct such conversations, Schön reminds us that we must stay attentive: to ourselves, to the choices we make as practitioners, and to the "back-talk" of those situations with which we converse. Schön talks of reflection-in-action as requiring a kind of "double vision" in which we "must act in accordance with the view [we have] adopted" but remain open to the reality that we "can always break it open later, indeed, *must* break it open later in order to make sense of [our] transaction with the situation" as we set and frame and change it through our evolving practice.

Every time we bring something to bear on a situation, the situation becomes new again and so does our relationship with it, thus making it ripe for fresh inquiry. This is what makes complex, rich practices like teaching so very rewarding; it's also why any teacher who tells you that they have it licked is either deluded or a liar. Indeed, in a world defined by reflective practice, it can truly be said that "the end of all our exploring/Will be to arrive where we started/And know the place for the first time" (Eliot, 1942).

Takeaways

- We have come to see professional practice through a lens of *technical rationality* in which rational problem solving, grounded in underlying principles is the way to go.
- This conception is misguided because real-world problems are complex and messy.
- To meet this complexity, we must move from a problem-*solving* stance (in which it is assumed we know all we need to know to meet what we think is up) to a problem-*setting* stance (in which we first name and frame the terms of the thing we are hoping to address).
- In order to make this shift, Schön offers us *reflection-in-action*: the ability to think about, reflect upon, and make changes to our practice in ways that are directly connected to and sometimes indistinguishable from that practice.
- In practical terms, any practitioner can do this by understanding the nature of the problems we face and the way we "set" them, bringing

past experiences to bear on new situations, and running on-the-spot experiments to determine whether our hypotheses and actions are contributing to our desired aims.

References

DEWEY, J. (1938). *LOGIC: THE THEORY OF INQUIRY.* HOLT.

ELIOT, T. S. (1942). *LITTLE GIDDING.* FABER AND FABER.

MCKINLAY, J. B. (1975). A CASE FOR REFOCUSING UPSTREAM: THE POLITICAL ECONOMY OF SICKNESS. IN J. D. ENELOW & J. B. HENDERSON (EDS.), *APPLYING BEHAVIORAL SCIENCE TO CARDIOVASCULAR RISK* (PP. 9–25). AMERICAN HEART ASSOCIATION.

SCHEIN, E. (1973). *PROFESSIONAL EDUCATION.* MCGRAW-HILL.

SCHÖN, D. (1983). *THE REFLECTIVE PRACTITIONER.* BASIC BOOKS.

Suggested Readings and Links

ARGYRIS, C., & SCHÖN, D. (1974). *THEORY IN PRACTICE: INCREASING PROFESSIONAL EFFECTIVENESS.* JOSSEY-BASS PUBLISHERS.

GIBBS, G. (1988). *LEARNING BY DOING: A GUIDE TO TEACHING AND LEARNING METHODS.* FURTHER EDUCATION UNIT.

RYLE, G. (1949). *THE CONCEPT OF MIND.* HUTCHINSON'S UNIVERSITY LIBRARY.

SHULMAN, L. S. (2004). *THE WISDOM OF PRACTICE: VOL. 1: ESSAYS ON TEACHING, LEARNING, AND LEARNING TO TEACH.* JOSSEY-BASS INC.

SIMON, H. A., & LAIRD, J. (2019). *THE SCIENCES OF THE ARTIFICIAL.* MIT.

VIDEOS

IN THIS VIDEO, DONALD SCHÖN DESCRIBES IN HIS OWN WORDS THE ORIGINS OF TECHNICAL RATIONALITY AND THE FUNDAMENTAL PRINCIPLES BEHIND REFLECTION-IN-ACTION.

AVAILABLE VIA WWW.YOUTUBE.COM/WATCH?V=LD9QJCMINMO

THIS VIDEO SHOWS HOW REFLECTING-IN-ACTION AND REFLECTING-ON-ACTION CAN BE USEFUL TOOLS FOR TEACHERS

AVAILABLE VIA WWW.YOUTUBE.COM/WATCH?V=X2MFNE91JLK

WEBSITES

GETTING STARTED WITH REFLECTIVE PRACTICE: THIS RESOURCE OFFERS FRAMEWORKS FOR THE EFFECTIVE IMPLEMENTATION OF REFLECTIVE PRACTICE IN TEACHING.

AVAILABLE VIA HTTPS://TINYURL.COM/BHHD7R3N

REFLECTIVE PRACTICE: THIS WEBSITE OFFERS A USEFUL DISTILLATION OF TEACHER-FOCUSED REFLECTIVE PRACTICES, INCLUDING A BANK OF REFLECTION-IN-ACTION QUESTIONS.

AVAILABLE VIA HTTPS://TINYURL.COM/3E35ZTR2

SECTION 2

CURRICULUM DEVELOPMENT/ INSTRUCTIONAL DESIGN

In *Alice's Adventures in Wonderland*,[1] written by Lewis Carroll and first published in 1865, 7-year-old Alice is walking around Wonderland aimlessly trying to figure out how to get home when she comes across the Cheshire Cat. The following conversation ensues:

ALICE: *"Would you tell me, please, which way I ought to go from here?"*
THE CHESHIRE CAT: *"That depends a good deal on where you want to get to".*
ALICE: *"I don't much care where".*
THE CHESHIRE CAT: *"Then it doesn't much matter which way you go".*
ALICE: *". . . so long as I get SOMEWHERE".*
THE CHESHIRE CAT: *"Oh, you're sure to do that, if only you walk long enough".*

The Cheshire Cat's sardonic response to Alice at the end of this exchange offers a telling insight into the nature of our intentions, our actions, and the results that arise whenever we set out on a journey of discovery. In this moment, the Cat suggests to Alice that even her *lack* of direction will result in her getting somewhere; it's just difficult to say for certain where that "somewhere" will be.

This relationship between intentions and outcomes is perhaps best summed up by a phrase often attributed to W. Edwards Deming: "Every system is perfectly designed to get the results it gets". If this is true, the question then becomes whether the system in question *intended* to arrive at its results or, like Alice, it ended up "somewhere" by happenstance more than design.

That is a question that has challenged educators for the longest time. Answering it can come in forms as simple as developing a set of goals for the end of the semester or the year, like getting a good grade or evaluation, or it can be as complicated as articulating how best to teach or learn something rich and complex in a meaningful way.

---

[1] WWW.ADOBE.COM/BE_EN/ACTIVE-USE/PDF/ALICE_IN_WONDERLAND.PDF

DOI: 10.4324/9781003228165-8

In the real world, we have different kinds of maps that help us get to where we want to go; in education we have curricula to guide us – and it is through the designing and enacting of curricula that the intentions of education become realised. As such, whatever the aim of learning, a crucial factor is the manner in which those intentions are articulated, understood, and enacted – such that what is intended to be taught and what is eventually learned are closely related.

In this section, we consider these challenges by asking these questions: How do we align our teaching so that what we want students to learn, how we teach them, and how we evaluate their learning form a consistent whole? How can we then best develop our instruction to achieve what we set out to achieve? And, How do we formulate objectives so that we can teach effectively, efficiently, and enjoyably?

7 IT'S ALL ABOUT ALIGNMENT

JOHN BIGGS ON CONSTRUCTIVE ALIGNMENT

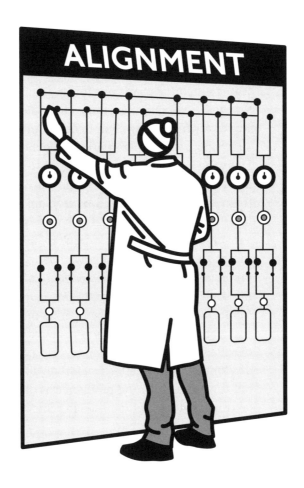

7 IT'S ALL ABOUT ALIGNMENT

ARTICLE Enhancing teaching through constructive alignment[2]

QUOTE *"When curriculum and assessment methods are aligned, the results of instruction are massively improved."*[3]

Why You Should Read This Article

Paul once held a learning and research chair as professor of computer-supported collaborative learning (learning together with other in teams supported by various forms of information and communication technologies; computers linked together via the Internet), and this was a very frustrating chair to hold. Collaborative learning and its sister approach cooperative learning didn't suffer from lack of interest. Everyone jumped on the bandwagon to use this approach to learning and instruction, dividing their classes into groups/teams and giving them tasks to carry out and/or problems to solve. But while the approach had many users and advocates, both with and without computers, a major problem was that it didn't really work well. One reason was that most teachers didn't know or hadn't learnt how to design tasks or problems that were complex enough to warrant collaboration, and thus the students didn't collaborate. An expensive way to say this is that the *transactive costs*[4] of working together on the task (i.e., communication about and coordination of group activities) were greater than the *benefits* of collaborating on the task (i.e., being able to do something you couldn't do alone or to do it better/faster than doing it alone). But this wasn't the only problem. A second problem was that while the goals of collaborative learning and the method used to achieve those goals were well-suited to

Transactive costs: Cost-benefit analysis made by students

---

2   BIGGS, J. (1996). ENHANCING TEACHING THROUGH CONSTRUCTIVE ALIGNMENT. *HIGHER EDUCATION, 32*, 347–364.
3   IBID., P. 350.
4   KIRSCHNER, P.A., SWELLER, J., KIRSCHNER, F., & ZAMBRANO, J. (2018). FROM COGNITIVE LOAD THEORY TO COLLABORATIVE COGNITIVE LOAD THEORY. *INTERNATIONAL JOURNAL OF COMPUTER-SUPPORTED COLLABORATIVE LEARNING, 13*, 213–233.

each other – they were well-aligned – most if not all teachers ultimately assessed learners individually. There were many reasons for this: it's unfair to give everyone the same grade if some worked harder than others, we need to know if everyone learnt what they were supposed to learn, we have to hinder social loafing and free-riding by some of the students, the school's examination rules don't allow for giving individual grades on a group project, and so forth. In other words, though the goals and pedagogy were aimed at working together, the assessment was individual and competitive; the assessment wasn't properly aligned with the learning objectives and the instructional method. In 1996, John Biggs introduced the term "constructive alignment" to describe the situation where objectives, methods, and assessment are properly aligned.

Abstract of the Article

Two lines of thinking are becoming increasingly important in higher educational practice. The first derives from constructivist learning theory, and the second from the instructional design literature. Constructivism comprises a family of theories but all have in common the centrality of the learner's activities in creating meaning. These and related ideas have important implications for teaching and assessment. Instructional designers for their part have emphasised alignment between the objectives of a course or unit and the targets for assessing student performance. "Constructive alignment" represents a marriage of the two thrusts, constructivism being used as a framework to guide decision-making at all stages in instructional design: in deriving curriculum objectives in terms of performances that represent a suitably high cognitive level, in deciding teaching/learning activities judged to elicit those performances, and to assess and summatively report student performance. The "performances of understanding" nominated in the objectives are thus used to systematically align the teaching methods and the assessment. The process is illustrated with reference to a professional development unit in educational psychology for teachers, but the model may be generalised to most units or programs in higher education.

The Article

Systems-based approach to teaching

Constructive alignment is basically a three-step, systems-based approach to teaching and learning where (1) the intended or desired learning outcomes that students are meant to achieve are defined before teaching takes place, (2) the chosen instructional approaches are well-suited for achieving the intended or desired outcomes, and (3) the assessment methods used are designed to reliably assess whether the intended or desired learning outcomes have been achieved. Figure 7.1 illustrates the

Constructive alignment concept of constructive alignment. This isn't about "teaching to the test", it's about ensuring that student learning goals, teaching, and learning activities, and assessments are aligned in relation to what students are expected to know and be able to do.

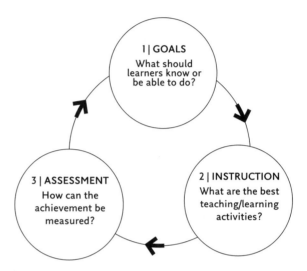

FIGURE 7.1
CONSTRUCTIVE ALIGNMENT BETWEEN GOALS, INSTRUCTION, AND ASSESSMENT.

Biggs situated his article as an attempt to translate what he considered to be important features of constructivism on teaching and assessment. This is important because, as we discussed in *How Learning Happens*, constructivism is a theory of knowledge and knowing and not a theory of instruction. He distinguishes between what he calls the *objectivist* tradition based on a dualism between knower and known where teachers transmit knowledge and *constructivism* and *phenomenography* where learners construct meaning. He notes that teachers have a real problem in moving from focussing on the learner and their world and organising instructional experiences to do this. He calls this "the familiar hiatus between espoused theory and theory-in-use" (p. 349). In other words, how do you actualise the principles of constructivism in a nonprescriptive instructional way?

Phenomenography

Instruction as an Internally Aligned System

Biggs saw teaching as a complex system. In the classroom it involves teachers, students, teaching contexts, student learning activities, and outcomes. Characteristic of systems is that its components interact with each other with the goal of achieving what Von Bertalanffy (1968) calls a stable equilibrium. Stepping away from the goals and the instruction,

Tail wagging the dog

he illustrated this as what can be called *the tail wagging the dog*. He wrote "if the set assessment tasks address lower cognitive level activities than those nominated in the curriculum objectives, equilibrium will be achieved at a lower level; the system will be driven by backwash from testing, not by the curriculum. Attempts to enhance teaching need to address the system as a whole, not simply add "good" components, such as a new curriculum or methods" (p. 350). Put simply, if you test for factual knowledge, kids will learn facts no matter what the goals were and/or how hard you try to teach them to apply the facts or principles etc.

Instructional alignment

He then borrowed from (one could also say stole) Cohen's idea of *Instructional alignment*. Cohen (1987) wrote, "Instructional alignment describes the extent to which stimulus conditions match among three instructional components: intended outcomes, instructional processes, and instructional assessment" (p. 19) and that when "critical features of instructional stimuli match those of assessment, effect sizes routinely reach 1.2 to 3 sigma" (Bloom's 2-sigma effect is discussed in *HLH*, Chapter 13). The problem here is that Cohen discussed this in a mastery learning framework which Biggs, as a constructivist, considered to be too objectivist and narrow. He wrote: "While mastery learning produces positive results when dealing with narrow, quantitatively defined performances, there is no evidence that mastery learning is of value to those interested in achieving broader outcomes" (p. 350). Crucial here, and possibly the reason why he changed instructional alignment to constructive alignment, is that the benefits of alignment can also be found when the system is aligned to achieving high cognitive level goals where learners need to construct their own meaning.

From Aims to Objectives

As can be seen in Figure 7.1 there's a strong relationship between the goals, the instruction, and the assessment. You can do all you want with the first two, but if the student knows the way they will be assessed and on what, then the only thing that they're interested in is the assessment. In this way, the assessment which follows the goals and instruction in time (i.e., is the tail end of the alignment) drives the learning and thus, the wags the dog. Based on this backwash-/tail-wagging-the-dog-effect,

Five levels of task performance

Biggs saw learning objectives in terms of five levels of task performance, namely:

1. Prestructural: The task is carried out wrong; the student hasn't under-stood the point.
2. Unistructural: One or a few aspects of the task are picked up (nominal understanding).

3. Multistructural: Some task aspects are learned but aren't integrated (knowing about).
4. Relational: All aspects are integrated into a coherent whole (application, appreciating relationships).
5. Extended abstract: Reconceptualised at a higher abstraction level (reflect, generalise, and far transfer involving metacognition).

SOLO: Structure of the Observed Learning Outcome

He, along with Kevin Collis, originally proposed this in 1982 and called it the SOLO taxonomy (Structure of the Observed Learning Outcome; discussed further in Chapter 27). At that time, he saw it as way to classify learning outcomes in terms of their complexity. This taxonomy allowed teachers to assess students' work in terms of its quality not in terms of how many pieces of information they got right. Having a performative notion of understanding would, in his view, enable teachers to specify those things that students need to do to demonstrate particular levels of understanding.

Teaching/Learning Activities

Teaching/learning activity (TLA)

The next step is to choose the proper teaching/learning activities. The methods chosen must engage students in activities that are most likely to necessitate their performing in the way designated in the objectives. Another way of approaching this is determining what activities which teaching methods are most likely to produce; that is, selecting teaching/learning activities (TLAs) that specifically address one or more desired levels of performance. Take, for example, a teacher who wants their students to be able to apply a principle in different specific situations. They shouldn't have the students simply recite the principle on a test or ask them to apply it in the situation in which it was taught. Better would be to ask them which principles would work in what situations (and why) and then present them with different situations in which they needed to apply it.

Biggs emphasises that the teacher doesn't have sole responsibility for setting up the TLAs as individual and social activities also, in his words, lead to "construction of knowledge". In the first place, the *teacher* has primary control over formal teaching activities such as lectures, tutorials labs as well as setting up formal cooperative activities involving peers, such as discussion groups and brainstorming. In addition there are *peer-controlled activities* which can range from formal activities initiated by the teacher (e.g., groupwork) to informal and/or spontaneous collaboration inside and outside the classroom. Finally, there are *self-controlled activities* which include "anything that goes under the heading of independent

Teacher control

Peer control

Self control

learning and study, including specific strategies for extracting meaning from text such as summarizing and note-taking, general study skills, and metacognitive strategy use" (p. 354–355).

Assessment and Grading

Assessment

Assessment is about judging the whole performance of the student against predetermined and public criteria. In deciding the assessment tasks, it is necessary to judge the extent to which they embody the target performances of understanding, and how well they lend themselves to evaluating individual student performances. Again, another way of approaching this is asking what levels of understanding assessment tasks are likely to elicit.

Biggs then walks the reader through what he calls "typical" assessment tasks (remember, he is looking at all of this through a constructivist lens) and comments on each. Here he conflates what students study during assessment and what the assessment meant to measure. He begins with a discussion of research by Tang (1991) in which he asked students how they prepared for an essay exam. The answers were rote learning, question spotting, going through past papers, underlining, organising study time and materials, memorising . . . He concludes that few of the activities employed address high level curriculum objectives and [remarkably] that

> The practice of marking examinations "analytically" (by aggre-gating marks as points are made), which is common in large classes with multiple markers, means that higher level under-standing performances tend not to be in focus . . . One student . . . answered a "compare-and-contrast" [history] question . . . simply by listing the life histories of each. She didn't answer the ques-tion, but made many points, thereby obtaining the highest mark in the class. (p. 356)

Biggs judges the assessment based upon the answers!

He continues this for "objective/multiple choice-tests" (p. 357) on the one hand stating that they can assess high-level thinking and then excoriating them because teachers implement them improperly. He calls this the "insurmountable problem with quantitative approaches to assessment" concluding that "All the above modes of assessment, then, are inadequate for much tertiary teaching".

BIGGS' NON SEQUITUR: AN ANALOGY

WHEN PAUL gives a presentation, he often asks the audience if they feel that people should follow a healthy diet and they almost unanimously answer yes. Then he asks them to list the foods that they prefer to eat. [BTW: He does this to show them that what they prefer is not always what's best for them: learning styles]. The results are always the same, namely the foods are either fatty, salty, or sweet or a combination thereof. Does this mean that the people in the audience don't want to eat in a healthy way? Does he conclude that their own health isn't in focus? And should he conclude that everything that people eat is inadequate for good nutrition? No! The only conclusion is that while the goal is to live healthily (by analogy taking an essay exam) what the audience does doesn't always achieve this (by analogy deep understanding).

Guidelines for choosing the proper assessment technique

Biggs gives three general guidelines for choosing the proper assessment technique which, in our opinion, are valid for all assessments, from memorisation to far transfer namely, determine (1) th qualities you're looking for, (2) if the assessment should be taken out of its practical context or should be presented in a practical or subject-rich situation, and (3) who should set the criteria, provide evidence, and assess the evidence.

He concludes with a model of instruction that he considers to be simple and intuitive where:

- Teachers are clear about what they want students to learn, and how they should show this.
- Performance objectives are arranged in a hierarchy from most to least acceptable (*a propos* his levels), which become the grading system (A, B, C, D, and F).
- Students are being put in situations which are likely to provoke required learnings.
- Students provide evidence that their learning matched the objectives

Conclusions

Effective learning is a matter of alignment. The goals, methods, and assessment need to be aligned. It's extremely important to note here tha while Biggs based part of his constructive alignment in constructivism (renaming it constructive as opposed to instructional), the concept of alignment is universal. If your goal is to learn something by rote, then you need to choose an approach to teaching that's aimed at effective, efficient, and enjoyable rote learning (yes, all three are possible even for rote learning), and you need to assess the rote learning with a proper assessment of rote learning. The same is true for applying, evaluating, or any other goal that you can choose for your teaching.

What this means is that you as the teacher need to step back from the one-size-fits-all mentality presented by modern-day educational gurus, that one specific pedagogy works and should be applied. Yes, learning in teams has its place in the teachers' toolkit, but not for everything. The same is true for drill-and-practice, story-telling, working on problems or projects, or whatever. This doesn't mean that all approaches are good (i.e., are effective, efficient, enjoyable/successful). Some just don't like learning to solve problems by solving problems or doing things by discovery learning because discovery is so motivating and engaging. What it does mean is that after acquiring the knowledge needed to solve a problem, the next step is to have students practice solving problems if your goal is to have them be able to do this.

Takeaways

- Alignment means that there's a match among the intended outcomes, the instructional/teaching processes, and the assessment.
- Teachers must be clear about what they want students to learn, and how they would show this.
- A performative notion of understanding enables you to specify what students need to do to demonstrate particular levels of understanding.
- Students need to be put in situations where they are likely they can exhibit the required learning/performance.
- Good teaching/instruction means good alignment.

References

BIGGS, J. B. (1996). ENHANCING TEACHING THROUGH CONSTRUCTIVE ALIGNMENT. *HIGHER EDUCATION, 32,* 1–18.
AVAILABLE VIA HTTPS://TINYURL.COM/4U57PZS6
BIGGS, J. B., & COLLIS, K. F. (1982). *EVALUATING THE QUALITY OF LEARNING: THE SOLO TAXONOMY (STRUCTURE OF THE OBSERVED LEARNING OUTCOME).* ACADEMIC PRESS.
COHEN, S. A. (1987). INSTRUCTIONAL ALIGNMENT: SEARCHING FOR A MAGIC BULLET. *EDUCATIONAL RESEARCHER, 16*(8), 16–20.
TANG, K. C. C. (1991). *EFFECTS OF DIFFERENT ASSESSMENT METHODS ON TERTIARY STUDENTS" APPROACHES TO STUDYING.* UNPUBLISHED PHD DISSERTATION, UNIVERSITY OF HONG KONG.
VON BERTALANFFY, L. (1968). *GENERAL SYSTEMS THEORY.* BRAZILLER.

Suggested Readings and Links

BIGGS, J. B. (2014). CONSTRUCTIVE ALIGNMENT IN UNIVERSITY TEACHING. *HERDSA REVIEW OF HIGHER. EDUCATION, 1* (5), 5–22.

AVAILABLE VIA WWW.HERDSA.ORG.AU/SYSTEM/FILES/ HERDSARHE2014V01P05_0.PDF

BIGGS. J. B. (2003). ALIGNING TEACHING FOR CONSTRUCTING LEARNING. *THE HIGHER EDUCATION ACADEMY, 1* (4).

AVAILABLE VIA HTTPS://TINYURL.COM/7H3DZPA8

VIDEOS

WHY SHOULD ASSESSMENTS, LEARNING OBJECTIVES, AND INSTRUCTIONAL STRATEGIES BE ALIGNED?

Assessments should reveal how well students have learned what we want them to learn while instruction ensures that they learn it. For this to occur, assessments learning objectives, and instructional strategies need to be closely aligned so that they reinforce one another.

AVAILABLE VIA WWW.CMU.EDU/TEACHING/ASSESSMENT/BASICS/ ALIGNMENT.HTML

JOHN BIGGS, CONSTRUCTIVE ALIGNMENT AND S.O.L.O. – COURSERA.

AVAILABLE VIA HTTPS://TINYURL.COM/BA5833S5

WEBSITES

WEBSITE OF JOHN BIGGS

AVAILABLE VIA WWW.JOHNBIGGS.COM.AU/ACADEMIC/ CONSTRUCTIVE-ALIGNMENT/

8

PEBBLE IN THE POND

M. DAVID MERRILL AND JEROEN VAN MERRIËNBOER ON
INSTRUCTIONAL DESIGN

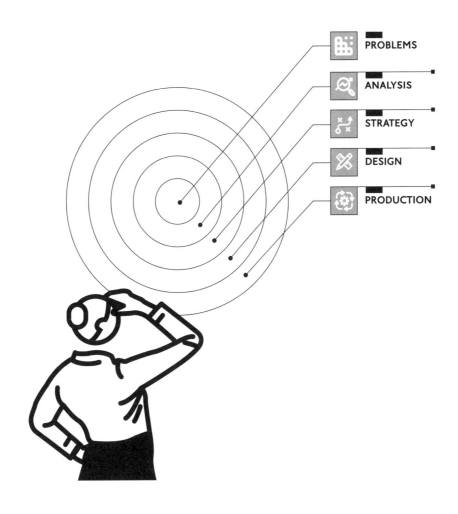

PROBLEMS

ANALYSIS

STRATEGY

DESIGN

PRODUCTION

DOI: 10.4324/9781003228165-10

8 PEBBLE IN THE POND

ARTICLES   Training complex cognitive skills: A four-component instructional design model for technical training[1]

A pebble-in-the-pond model for instructional design[2]

QUOTE   *"Merely following a series of steps, when there is insufficient guidance as to quality, is likely to result in an inferior product."*[3]

Why You Should Read These Articles

The famous Dutch philosopher (and football player, or is it the other way around?) Johan Cruijff once said, "Something has to happen before something happens". Cruijff's "words of wisdom" are often, at first glance, waved off by many as nonsensical or trite but behind the seemingly trite phrase there lies hidden wisdoms about the elusive nature of expertise. Take the moment in 1995 in the Champions League final between Ajax Amsterdam and AC Milan when Louis van Gaal, the Ajax coach, got really mad about what an opposing player from AC Milan did – it's called dangerous play when you raise your leg so high that it can injure an opposing player – which the ref didn't penalise. To make his point, he jumped and gave a demonstrative "karate-kick" in the air. It could have gotten him a red card (it didn't), but what it did do according to the players was shake the team up and Ajax won the match on a late goal by Patrick Kluivert and were the European champions. Van Gaal needed to shake things up; something needed to happen to get something to happen.

When you throw a pebble into a pond, you get a series of ripples starting from where the pebble hit the water and emanating out from

---

1   VAN MERRIENBOER, J. J. G. (1997). *TRAINING COMPLEX COGNITIVE SKILLS: A FOUR-COMPONEN INSTRUCTIONAL DESIGN MODEL FOR TECHNICAL TRAINING.* EDUCATIONAL TECHNOLOG PUBLICATIONS.

2   MERRILL, M. D. (2002). A PEBBLE-IN-THE-POND MODEL FOR INSTRUCTIONAL DESIGN. *PERFORMANC IMPROVEMENT, 41* (7), 39–44.

3   MERRILL, M. D. (2002). A PEBBLE-IN-THE-POND MODEL FOR INSTRUCTIONAL DESIGN. *PERFORMANC IMPROVEMENT, 41* (7), 39–44.

that point. This one thing happening causes other things to happen. David Merrill came up with his Pebble-in-the-Pond design model in 2002 which consists of a series of expanding activities initiated by first casting in a pebble, that is, a whole task or problem of the type that learners will be taught to accomplish by the instruction: the content to be learned. This is followed by a series of design activities which he notes is a version of the 4C/ID model proposed in 1992 and expanded in 1997 by Jeroen van Merriënboer.

Abstracts of the Articles

Training Complex Cognitive Skills

Our society is characterised by fast technological changes. More and more routine tasks are taken over by machines. As a result, complex cognitive tasks that must be performed by humans because they require flexible problem-solving behaviour are becoming increasingly important. . . . While there is an increasing need for instructional guidelines that may help to design efficient training programs for complex cognitive skills, and to make those training programs more effective in terms of learning outcomes, only a few of those guidelines have been discussed in the literature. . . . The main purpose of this book is to fill this gap by giving a comprehensive description of the **Four-Component Instructional Design** model (**4C/ID**-model) . . . . This model presents diverse guidelines and heuristics for the development of training programs for complex cognitive skills . . . [through] the integration of theoretical developments and empirical results . . .

A Pebble-in-the-Pond Model for Instructional Design

Instructional systems development (ISD) has recently come under attack to suggestions that it may not be an appropriate methodology for developing effective instruction (Gordon & Zemke, 2000). ISD is accused of being too slow and clumsy, of claiming to be a technology when it is not, of producing bad instruction, and of being out of touch with today's training needs. The aphorism that a bad craftsman blames his tools is helpful here. It should be obvious to the thoughtful observer that the problem may be the implementation of ISD, not a systematic approach itself.

The Articles

4C/ID: Four Component Instructional Design

Let's begin with Jeroen van Merriënboer's, 1997 ground-breaking book *Training complex cognitive skills: A four-component instructional design model for technical training*. His 4C/ID model has become a go-to model for designing instruction for teaching, training, and curricula that can be applied to real world problems. According to van Merriënboer and colleagues (2002), it "addresses at least three deficits in previous instructional design models". First, [it] focuses on

> the integration and the coordinated performance of task-specific constituent skills rather than on knowledge types, context or presentation-delivery media. Second, [it] makes a critical distinction between supportive information[4] and required just-in-time information. . . . And third, traditional models use either part-task or whole-task practice; the 4C/ID model recommends a mixture where part-task practice supports very complex, "whole-task" learning. (p. 39)

4C/ID is a holistic design approach based upon authentic whole learning task. This is the opposite of atomistic design where complex contents and tasks are usually reduced to their simplest or smallest elements. Such a holistic design approach deals with complexity without losing sight of the separate elements and the interconnections between them. In this holistic approach, each learning task confronts the learner with all or almost all of the constituent skills needed to perform the task, including the knowledge and attitudes associated with them. This approach solves three common educational problems, namely, compartmentalisation (i.e., separation of a whole into distinct parts or categories), fragmentation (i.e., breaking something down into small, incomplete, or isolated parts which cannot magically be integrated when needed), and the transfer paradox (i.e., where methods that work best for reaching isolated, specific objectives are not best for reaching integrated objectives and transfer of learning.

PROBLEMS WITH TRADITIONAL EDUCATION/ INSTRUCTIONAL DESIGN

Compartmentalisation, Fragmentation, Transfer paradox

Compartmentalisation: The tendency in traditional education to teach knowledge, skills, and attitudes separately. This approach hinders complex learning and competence development.

(Continued)

---

4 INFORMATION RELEVANT FOR LEARNING THE NON-RECURRENT (I.E., PROBLEM SOLVING REASONING AND DECISION-MAKING) ASPECTS OF LEARNING TASKS THROUGH ELABORATION AND UNDERSTANDING.

(Continued)

Fragmentation: The tendency in traditional education to analyse a complex learning domain in small pieces which often correspond with specific learning objectives, and then teach the domain piece-by-piece without paying attention to the relationships between pieces. This hinders complex learning and competence development.

Transfer paradox: The tendency in traditional education to use instructional methods that are highly efficient for achieving specific learning objectives (e.g., blocked practice), but that are not efficient for reaching a transfer of learning. This hinders complex learning and competence development.

Four components: Learning tasks, Supportive information, Procedural information, Part-task practice

A basic assumption of the 4C/ID model is that educational programs designed for acquiring complex cognitive skills can be described in terms of four basic components, namely (a) learning tasks, (b) supportive information, (c) procedural information, and (d) part-task practice (see Figure 8.1). Learning tasks provide the backbone of the educational program; they provide learning from varied experiences and explicitly aim at the transfer of learning. The three other components are connected to this backbone.

Van Merriënboer teamed up with Paul A. Kirschner and expanded the 4C/ID model into a design process of *Ten steps to complex learning* (2018). The steps are organised into the four basic components (see Figure 8.2 and Table 8.1).

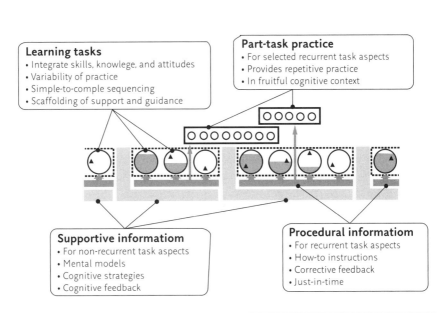

FIGURE 8.1
A GRAPHICAL VIEW OF THE FOUR COMPONENTS OF THE 4C/ID MODEL. LEARNING TASKS, SUPPORTIVE INFORMATION, PROCEDURAL INFORMATION, AND PART-TASK PRACTICE. (*SOURCE:* VAN MERRIËNBOER & KIRSCHNER, 2018).

Learning tasks
- Integrate skills, knowlege, and attitudes
- Variability of practice
- Simple-to-comple sequencing
- Scaffolding of support and guidance

Part-task practice
- For selected recurrent task aspects
- Provides repetitive practice
- In fruitful cognitive context

Supportive informatiom
- For non-recurrent task aspects
- Mental models
- Cognitive strategies
- Cognitive feedback

Procedural informatiom
- For recurrent task aspects
- How-to instructions
- Corrective feedback
- Just-in-time

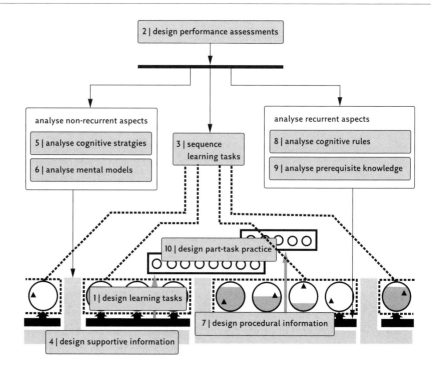

FIGURE 8.2
THE TEN STEPS
TO COMPLEX
LEARNING
(*SOURCE:* VAN
MERRIËNBOER &
KIRSCHNER, 2018).

TABLE 8.1
THE TEN STEPS

Learning Tasks	Supportive Information	Procedural Information	Part-Task Practice
1. Design learning tasks 2. Sequence task classes 3. Set performance objectives	4. Design supportive information 5. Analyse cognitive strategies 6. Analyse mental models	7. Design procedural information 8. Analyse cognitive rules 9. Analyse prerequisite knowledge	10. Design part-task practice
Authentic, whole-task experiences based on real tasks that integrate the necessary skills, knowledge, and attitudes organised in stages, with each stage having diminished learner support. A series of increasingly complex learning tasks serves as the backbone of an educational program.	Helps learners perform non-routine aspects (problem solving, reasoning, decision making) of learning tasks. It is presented to them before they start working on learning tasks and/or made available to them while they are working on these tasks.	Tells learners how to perform routine aspects of learning tasks (how-to instructions). It's best presented to them just-in-time, precisely when they need it during their work on learning tasks.	Here students perform/practice routine activities to develop a high level of automaticity Part-task practice requires huge amounts of repetition and should only start after the routine has been introduced within a whole, meaningful learning task.

First principles of
instruction

Activate prior
experience,
Demonstrate skills,
Apply skills. Integrate
skills

Strongly related to this is David Merrill's *Pebble in the Pond model for instructional design* which (2002b), in turn, is based upon his *First Principles of Instruction* (2002a). In his view, effective learning is problem-centred[5] where learners are involved in a cycle of learning with four distinct phases: (1) activating prior experience, (2) demonstrating skills, (3) applying skills, and (4) integrating these skills into real-world activities. Note here that it's necessary to have adequate prior knowledge and experiences, otherwise weak problem-solving (means-ends analysis; *HLH*, Chapter 1). He then comes with five basic principles, namely:

1. Present instruction in the context of real-world problems.
2. Ensure that the instruction activates relevant prior knowledge or experience.
3. Have instruction demonstrate what is to be learned rather than merely giving information about what is to be learned.
4. Give learners an opportunity to practice and apply their newly acquired knowledge or skill.
5. Have instruction provide techniques that encourage learners to integrate (transfer) the new knowledge or skill into their everyday life.

Having defined his first principles, he uses a pebble in a pond as an analogy (see Figure 8.3) for a series of expanding activities initiated by

> first casting in a pebble, a whole task or problem of the type that learners will be taught to accomplish by the instruction. Having identified an initial problem the second ripple in the design pond is to identify a progression of such problems of increasing difficulty or complexity, such that if learners are able to do all of the whole tasks thus identified, they would have mastered the knowledge and skill to be taught. The third ripple in the design pond is to identify the component knowledge and skill required to complete each task or solve each problem in the progression. The fourth ripple is to determine the instructional strategy that will be used to engage learners in the problems and help them acquire the component knowledge and skill required to complete the tasks or solve the problems. The fifth ripple is interface design. It is at this point in the design process that the content to be learned and the strategy used to engage learners is adapted to the delivery system and instructional architecture of

---

5 NOTE: PROBLEM- OR TASK-CENTRED DESIGN IS NOT THE SAME AS PROBLEM-BASED LEARNING. PROBLEM-CENTRED DESIGN CONTEXTUALISES WHAT IS TO BE LEARNT WHILE PROBLEM-BASED LEARNING IS A SPECIFIC TEACHING- OR LEARNING STRATEGY AIMED AT SOLVING A PROBLEM WITH LEARNING AS RESIDUAL OF THE SOLUTION PROCESS.

the learning situation or product. The ripples have now expanded sufficiently to engage in the production of the instructional materials or situation. (p. 40–41)

Sound familiar? It should as Merrill wrote in his article on First Principles (2002a, p. 53) "Van Merriënboer provided perhaps the most comprehensive recent model of instructional design that is problem-centered and involves all of the phases of instruction identified in this paper. His model integrated more directive approaches to instruction with problem-based approaches all in the context of what is known about cognitive processing". He even went as far as to say that his model was a version of Van Merriënboer's 4C/ID model.

Merrill noted that traditional instruction usually begins with the specification of a mass of atomistic instructional objectives which are "abstract representations of the knowledge to be taught rather than the knowledge itself" (p. 41): in other words, in a fragmented and compartmentalised way. Pebble-in-the-Pond (see Figure 8.3) avoids this by starting (first ripple) with what the learner should be able to do after instruction (i.e., the whole tasks to be completed or the problems to be solved) rather than abstract representations of this (i.e., the list of learning objectives). In other words, it begins with an instructional goal and not detailed objectives. After this, it specifies a progression of problems (ripple 2) that begin simple and that gradually increase in complexity, difficulty or the amount of component knowledge or number of component skills required to carry out the task/solve the problem. To solve each problem in the progression from simple to complex, learners need to use all of the necessary knowledge and skill required by the instructional goals. The third ripple comprises the analysis and identification of what knowledge and skills are needed to complete each task in the progression. This component knowledge "consists of the information, parts, kinds, how-to and what-happens knowledge and skill required to solve each problem" (p. 42). Ripple 4 is determining the instructional strategy to be used. An instructional strategy combines four modes of instructional interaction with the components of the to-be-learned knowledge: tell, ask, show, and do. The fifth and final ripple is what Merrill calls production is where "the content to be learned and the strategy used to engage learners i adapted to the delivery system and instructional architecture of the learning situation or product" (p. 42).

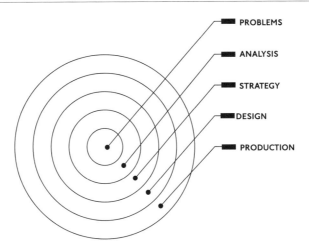

FIGURE 8.3
ADAPTED FROM
PEBBLE-IN-THE-
POND. (SOURCE:
MERRILL, 2002B).

What characterises Merrill's Pebble-in the-Pond model and his First Principles is that they are very general and can be implemented in many ways. They are fundamental foundational principles of instruction. If these first principles of instruction are implemented they should result "in instruction that is more effective, efficient and appealing" (Merrill, 2002a).

Conclusions

The major conclusion that we can draw from the work of both Jeroen van Merriënboer and David Merrill is that our approach to curriculum design and teaching should radically shift away from our traditional atomistic, fragmented, and compartmentalised definition of learning objectives followed by developing instruction for each of those separate objectives hoping at the end that the sum will be greater than the individual parts. Rather, our teaching should embrace a holistic, coherent, and unified determination of what the ultimate goals that you, as teacher and instructional design (yes, we consider teachers to be the ultimate instructional designers), want your students to be able to reach. What tasks should they be able to carry out or what problems should they be able to solve when they've finished your course? This is the pebble that's thrown into the learning pond that causes the first ripple. The next step/ripple is to analyse what component knowledge and skills your students need to successfully carry out the tasks or solve the problems. Then determine the most effective, efficient, and enjoyable (Merrill uses the word "appealing") way to engage your students in the tasks/problems and help them acquire the component knowledge and skills required to complete the tasks or solve the problems (i.e., determine the proper teaching and learning strategy). Finally, you need to design and then develop (i.e., produce) the teaching or instructional environment to reach the goal or goals.

Takeaways

- Teachers are the ultimate instructional designers.
- Designing a curriculum based on a mass of learning objectives that students need to learn and then teaching to those objectives leads to learning that is fragmented and compartmentalised and where transfer is minimal.
- Designing a curriculum based on what tasks a student should be able to carry out or what problems they should be able to solve and then teaching to those goals leads to learning that is coherent and unified where transfer is maximised.
- Take a note from Reigeluth's *elaboration theory* (see Chapter 16 in *HLH*) and work in classes of authentic whole tasks. Begin with simple versions of those tasks and add complexity (i.e., more components) to new tasks as students advance.
- Good instruction should present what is to be learned in the context of real-world problems, activate relevant prior knowledge and experience, demonstrate what is to be learned rather than just telling it, allow students to apply their newly learned knowledge and skills, and finally integrate or transfer the knowledge and skills in authentic situations.

References

CORE KNOWLEDGE. (2021, SEPTEMBER 16). *GROUPING ANIMALS* [SAMPLE LESSON PLAN]. AVAILABLE VIA FROM WWW.COREKNOWLEDGE.ORG.UK/RESOURCES/SCIENCE%20RESOURCE%20PACK-%20YEAR%201-%20ANIMALS.PDF

GORDON, J., & ZEMKE, R. (2000). THE ATTACK ON ISD. *TRAINING, 37*(4), 42–45.

MERRILL, M. D. (2002A). FIRST PRINCIPLES OF INSTRUCTION. *EDUCATIONAL TECHNOLOGY RESEARCH & DEVELOPMENT, 50*(3), 43–59.

MERRILL, M. D. (2002B). A PEBBLE-IN-THE-POND MODEL FOR INSTRUCTIONAL DESIGN. *PERFORMANCE IMPROVEMENT, 41*(7), 39–44.

VAN MERRIËNBOER, J. J. G. (1997). *TRAINING COMPLEX COGNITIVE SKILLS*. EDUCATIONAL TECHNOLOGY PUBLICATIONS.

VAN MERRIËNBOER, J. J. G., CLARK, R. E., & DE CROOCK, M. B. M. (2002). BLUEPRINTS FOR COMPLEX LEARNING: THE 4C/ID-MODEL. *EDUCATIONAL TECHNOLOGY, RESEARCH AND DEVELOPMEN 50*(2), 39–64.

VAN MERRIËNBOER, J. J. G.V., & KIRSCHNER, P.A. (2018). *TEN STEPS TO COMPLEX LEARNING: A SYSTEMATIC APPROACH TO FOUR-COMPONENT INSTRUCTIONAL DESIGN* (3RD ED.). ROUTLEDGE.

Suggested Readings and Links

MERRILL, M. D. (2002A). FIRST PRINCIPLES OF INSTRUCTION. *EDUCATIONAL TECHNOLOGY RESEARCH & DEVELOPMENT, 50*(3), 43–59.

AVAILABLE VIA HTTPS://DOI.ORG/10.1007/BF02505024

MERRILL, M. D. (2002B). A PEBBLE-IN-THE-POND MODEL FOR INSTRUCTIONAL DESIGN. *PERFORMANCE IMPROVEMENT, 41*(7), 39–44.

AVAILABLE VIA HTTPS://DOI.ORG/10.1002/PFI.4140410709

SWELLER, J., VAN MERRIËNBOER, J., & PAAS, F. (1998). COGNITIVE ARCHITECTURE AND INSTRUCTIONAL DESIGN. *EDUCATIONAL PSYCHOLOGY REVIEW, 10*, 251–296.

AVAILABLE VIA HTTPS://DOI.ORG/10.1023/A:1022193728205

KIRSCHNER, P. A., & VAN MERRIËNBOER, J. J. G. (2009). TEN STEPS TO COMPLEX LEARNING: A NEW APPROACH TO INSTRUCTION AND INSTRUCTIONAL DESIGN. IN T. L. GOOD (ED.), *21ST CENTURY EDUCATION: A REFERENCE HANDBOOK* (PP. 244–253). SAGE.

AVAILABLE VIA HTTPS://CORE.AC.UK/DOWNLOAD/PDF/55535269.PDF

VAN MERRIËNBOER, J. J. G. (2019). *THE FOUR-COMPONENT INSTRUCTIONAL DESIGN MODEL: AN OVERVIEW OF ITS MAIN DESIGN PRINCIPLES.* MAASTRICHT UNIVERSITY.

This report gives a concise description of the main characteristics of the 4C/ID model, describing the four components from which competence-based education is built and briefly explains how an integrated curriculum based on the four components helps to reach transfer of learning.

AVAILABLE VIA WWW.4CID.ORG/WP-CONTENT/UPLOADS/2021/04/VANMERRIENBOER-4CID-OVERVIEW-OF-MAIN-DESIGN-PRINCIPLES-2021.PDF

VIDEOS

WHOLE TASK LEARNING 4C ID MODEL AS PRESENTED BY JEROEN VAN MERRIËNBOER

AVAILABLE VIA WWW.YOUTUBE.COM/WATCH?V=IRK5UHE6QOI

THIS IS A WEB LECTURE BY JEROEN VAN MERRIËNBOER THAT YOU CAN DOWNLOAD AND LISTEN TO. IT IS AN INTERACTIVE POWERPOINT PRESENTATION WITH BASIC INFORMATION ABOUT THE 4C/ID MODEL. THE VIDEOS ARE ONLINE AND WILL OPEN IN YOUR BROWSER.

WWW.4CID.ORG/WP-CONTENT/UPLOADS/2021/04/WEBLECTURE4CID-MET_VIDEOLINKS.PPSX

THIS IS A BRIEF INTRODUCTION TO DAVID MERRILL'S THOUGHTS ABOUT INSTRUCTIONAL DESIGN.

AVAILABLE VIA WWW.YOUTUBE.COM/WATCH?V=I_TKAO2-JXA

THIS IS THE SECOND OF TWO BRIEF VIDEOS ON FIRST PRINCIPLES OF INSTRUCTION. THIS VIDEO INTRODUCES THE PEBBLE-IN-THE-POND MODEL OF INSTRUCTIONAL DESIGN.

AVAILABLE VIA WWW.YOUTUBE.COM/WATCH?V=SUG2U_V56L0

WEBSITES

THE OFFICIAL 4C/ID WEBSITE

AVAILABLE VIA WWW.4CID.ORG/

FIRST PRINCIPLES OF INSTRUCTION EDUTECH WIKI

AVAILABLE VIA HTTP://EDUTECHWIKI.UNIGE.CH/EN/FIRST_PRINCIPLES_OF_INSTRUCTION

9 HOW TO TELL THE STORY OF AN IDEA

JEROME BRUNER ON REPRESENTING KNOWLEDGE

DOI: 10.4324/9781003228165-11

9 HOW TO TELL THE STORY OF AN IDEA

BOOK   Toward a theory of instruction[1]

QUOTE   *"Any idea or problem or body of knowledge can be presented in a form simple enough so that any particular learner can understand it in a recognizable form."*[2]

Why You Should Read This Book

Whenever a movie deals with cognitively complex subject matter, filmmakers find themselves in a difficult bind. They want to do justice to the source material but whenever the main aim is to engage and entertain they can't saturate the viewer with overly dense content. For instance, how would you capture the sophistication of John Nash's ideas on game theory in the movie *A Beautiful Mind* without losing the attention of an audience who on the whole are unlikely to understand advanced mathematics?

Filmmakers address this as a question of representation, employing a host of visual and storytelling techniques to convey (or at least suggest) that complexity. In *A Beautiful Mind*, Nash's ideas are variously presented through analogy – such as the famous scene when Nash and his two friends use an aspect of game theory to decide which of three girls each should ask out in a bar – as well as through the visual expression of mathematical symbols in those scenes where Nash is seen writing out equations on the windows of his study.

It can be easy to sneer at Hollywood depictions of such content as either dumbing down or misrepresenting the original ideas entirely. After all, that bar scene has been criticised by mathematicians for its theoretical inaccuracies, and seeing Russell Crowe write equations on a

---

[1]   TOWARD A THEORY OF INSTRUCTION BY JEROME S. BRUNER, CAMBRIDGE, MASS.: THE BELKNA PRESS OF HARVARD UNIVERSITY PRESS, COPYRIGHT © 1966 BY THE PRESIDENT AND FELLOWS C HARVARD COLLEGE. USED BY PERMISSION. ALL RIGHTS RESERVED.

[2]   IBID., P. 44.

window doesn't actually tell us anything about Nash's theories unless we understand those theories to begin with. Nevertheless, there are aspects to the challenge of representation in storytelling that hold true with what we know about teaching.

Whenever we plan to teach, the question of how to represent an idea or set of ideas should be central to our thinking. This is because knowledge can't be conveyed in its fullest and rawest form at first blush, especially if learners are to stand a chance of understanding, retaining, retrieving, and using it effectively. Because of this, teachers can and should represent ideas in ways conducive with durable learning, while accurately conveying the necessary features of the content to be learned.

Unlike many Hollywood movies, teachers cannot use poetic license to gloss over the important details of knowledge. However, like any gifted storyteller, it turns out there are ways for teachers to present information that will make it memorable *and* maintain its essential qualities. Addressing this question of how best to render information with learning in mind is a central concern of Jerome S. Bruner's seminal work, *Towards a Theory of Instruction* (1966).

Abstract of the Book

Jerome Bruner presents a distillation of half a decade's research and reflection. His theme is dual: how children learn, and how they can best be helped to learn – how they can be brought to the fullest realisation of their capacities.

At the conceptual core of the book is an illuminating examination of how mental growth proceeds, and of the ways in which teaching can profitably adapt itself to that progression and can also help it along. Closely related to this is Mr. Bruner's "evolutionary instrumentalism", his conception of instruction as the means of transmitting the tools and skills of a culture, the acquired characteristics that express and amplify man's [*sic*] powers – especially the crucial symbolic tools of language, number, and logic. Revealing insights are given into the manner in which language functions as an instrument of thought.

The Book

Teaching as Telling the Story of an Idea

Bruner's theories on instruction evoke natural comparisons to storytelling because both are concerned with representational structure. For Bruner, "Any idea or problem or body of knowledge can be presented in a form simple enough so that any particular learner can understand it in a recognizable form" (p. 44). This is a refreshing way to take on

Representational structure

complexity in that it doesn't rely on surface notions of what students are "ready for" or "capable of" learning. The onus, rightly so, is on whether information is organised in such a way that it is ready to be learned – and that's the job of the teacher.

In exploring how ideas can be made ready for learning, Bruner lays out three structural characteristics of knowledge, each of which can affect the ability of any learner to master it: Mode of Representation, Economy, and Power.

Mode of
Representation

Mode of Representation

For Bruner, the form an idea takes is the first significant factor to bear in mind when considering how to present it for learning. In much the same way we might break down the formal means of delivering a good story, he posits that any item of knowledge can be represented by a set of:

1. Actions appropriate for achieving a set result (*enactive representation*).
2. Summary images or graphics that stand for a concept without defining it fully (*iconic representation*).
3. Symbolic or logical propositions drawn from a symbolic system governed by rules for forming and transforming propositions (*symbolic representation*).

To illustrate each, Bruner provides the analogy of a playground seesaw. He talks us through how even a young child sitting on one side

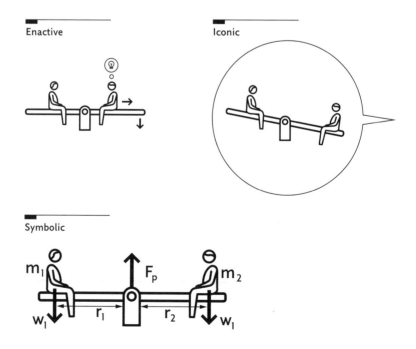

FIGURE 9.1
BRUNER'S THREE
FORMS OF
REPRESENTATION.

of a see-saw can intuitively ascertain that moving further out from the centre will increase the chances of that side going down (*enactive representation*); an older child would be able to represent this same phenomenon by drawing what that looks like or describing it in words (*iconic representation*); and, finally, that the nuanced specificity of a see-saw's movement "can be even better described mathematically through reference to Newton's Law of Moments in inertial physics" (p. 45) (*symbolic representation*).

As you can see from Bruner's example, the essential content being presented in each case is the same (placing weight further to the edge of a fulcrum increases the likelihood of that side going down) but the *mode of representation* in which that essential point is conveyed differs across the three. Understanding why each is important and applying that to a model for teaching is something we will return to later.

Economy

In an early nod to what we now refer to as cognitive load theory, Bruner defines "economy" when representing any domain of knowledge as "the amount of information that must be held in mind and processed to achieve comprehension" (p. 45). In much the same way as the storyteller who hopes to keep their audience informed but not overwhelmed, teachers must also find the "Goldilocks Zone" between too much information to cope and not enough to matter. In addressing this tension, Bruner helps us see that "too much vs. not enough" might in fact be a false choice in the first place. Instead, applying a lens of economy to our representation of knowledge means we can translate knowledge into ever-more compact and palatable forms. Once again, Bruner offers elegant examples to convey what he means (thus illustrating his point).

His first representation comes from mathematics when he argues that, "It is more economical to summarise the characteristics of free-falling bodies by the formula $S=1/2\ gt^2$ than to put a series of numbers into tabular form summarizing a vast set of observations made on different bodies dropped different distances in different gravitational fields" (p. 46). The second, drawn from literacy, posits that even though the sentence, "This is the squirrel that the dog that the girl that the man loved fed chased" holds exactly the same meaning as, "This is the man that loved the girl that fed the dog that chased the squirrel" it is the *economy* of meaning found in the latter sentence that allows it to be more efficiently and effectively processed by the reader. Bruner refers to the first type of representation as "requiring carriage of much information" whereas the second is reliant on "a pay-as-you-go type of information processing" (p. 46).

[margin notes]
Economy of representation

Goldilocks Zone

Too much information v. not enough

Economical representations of knowledge

You may already be starting to notice that Bruner's theories on how to present knowledge don't stand alone. For instance, the above equation on falling bodies relies on *symbolic representation* to make it more economical. There's a telling and somewhat ironic lesson for teachers here: even though the modes of representation begin with more simplistic renderings of ideas and move to seemingly more complex ones, the closer you can get learners to understanding and utilising those more advanced modes, the *easier* it will in fact become for them to represent and make sense of new information themselves.

This relationship between representation and economy offers a hugely generative challenge that can be laid down to learners and inform their approach to complexity: the more you know, the more elegantly you'll be able to represent what you know. This has been expressed in more ways than we can count by thinkers down the years but perhaps Goethe said it best with, "Beschränkung zeigt sich erst der Meister" or "Only in limitation does the master show himself" (Esterhammer, 2002).

Power

Bruner's definition of "power" as a characteristic of knowledge is perhaps the most abstract of the three and is tied up in ideas similar to those espoused by Goethe above. Bruner presents "power" in the representation of an idea is "its capacity, in the hands of the learner, to connect matters that, on the surface, seem quite separate" (p. 48). This is similar to what Chi et al. (1981) were talking about with respect to novices and experts which we discussed in Chapter 1 of *HLH*.

Power of representation

In short, Bruner suggests that power equates to straightforward usefulness. That is to say, knowledge that is in some way useful to the learner (because aspects of it can be transferred and applied to other contexts), and knowledge that is useful to the process of learning itself (because the learner comes to know more about how knowledge is constructed and how learning happens).

As before, Bruner points out the interconnectedness between power and economy, even though the two are theoretically independent. He offers that, "It is clear that a structure may be economical but powerless. But it is rare for a powerful structuring technique in any field to be uneconomical". For Bruner, there exists a version of knowledge that is powerful precisely *because* it is economical, even elegant. He suggests that this could explain, "the faith shared by many scientists that nature is simple" and that "perhaps it is only when nature can be made reasonably simple that it can be understood" (p. 48).

This is a profound realisation with significant implications for our approach as teachers to the representation of knowledge. All-too-often in teaching, simplicity is seen as a necessary evil. Just like the Hollywood movie that dumbs down the source material in exchange for keeping the audience entertained, the price we feel we must pay whenever we teach something is to strip it of the things that make it rich, just so it can be understood. Bruner reminds us that the richness and simplicity of knowledge can co-exist and, moreover, that the richness of knowledge is best expressed *as simplicity itself*. That beauty in simplicity, for Bruner, is where the power of knowledge lies; and conveying the beauty and simplicity of elegant ideas is something to which all teachers should rightly aspire.

The power of simplicity in teaching

From Structure to Sequence – Building the Foundations of Knowledge

From structure to sequence

One caveat we might put on the above articulation of how knowledge ought to be structured relates to its sequencing. Even though there's an elegance to understanding something well enough to render it in beautiful simplicity, that doesn't mean one can necessarily head straight to that end point without stopping at any stations along the way. Indeed, we've already seen how simplicity is often a marker of mastery so we cannot assume that such elegant representations of knowledge are ready for most learners to pick up straight away.

Bruner himself states that, "If it is true that the usual course of intellectual development moves from enactive through iconic to symbolic representation of the world, it is likely that an optimum sequence will progress in the same direction" and even when he does acknowledge that, "when the learner has a well-developed symbolic system, it may be possible to by-pass the first two stages" (p. 49) he adds that the learner would likely do so at their own risk.

Order matters when sharing knowledge

So, why does the sequence in which we present information matter just as much as the mode it takes, or the economy and power bound up within it? To answer this question, we can return to Bruner's ideas on modes of representation, to three important ideas observed in the difference between the modes, and to the significant implications all that has for teaching:

1. Appreciating the difference between representational modes allows us as teachers to structure the presentation of content in ways that mean learners will be more likely to understand it well. This is why an elementary mathematics textbook would rely on the diagram of a see-saw whereas a graduate-level mathematics textbook would more likely opt for algebraic representations of Newton's Law.

2. Since each mode offers a more sophisticated picture of a given idea than the previous representation, we as teachers can acknowledge that the more a learner comes to know, the more they can *do* with what they know. This is why an advanced mathematician would be able to tell us more about the nuances of how a see-saw operates than a four-year-old child – and why they would use the language of mathematics to do so.

3. Presenting this continuum of sophistication and an idea of how learners move along it, Bruner demonstrates something wonderful through his observations of learners coming to terms with new ideas. He shows us how, even when learners move from concrete simplicity to more abstract and nuanced symbolic representations of knowledge – they *still* return to and rely on those original, simpler representations whenever they encounter that knowledge in new and different forms. In other words, even when a mathematician encounters and understands a symbolic, purely mathematical representation of how a see-saw works, they almost certainly still rely on some iconic (the image of a see-saw) or enactive (the experience of being on a see-saw) mode of representation to help them as they make sense of it in those abstract, algebraic terms.

Conclusions

This last point offered here by Bruner is particularly profound since it shows teachers that the structuring and sequencing of knowledge isn't just about simple scaffolding, or offering information to learners in ways that meet their immediate needs. It can also serve as a representation of how knowledge itself gets built and, as such, how even the seemingly simple foundations of that knowledge come to be relied upon whenever we recall and apply it to a new situation. As Bruner puts it, "While, once abstraction is achieved, the learner becomes free in a certain measure of things, he nonetheless continues to rely upon the stock of imagery that permits him to work . . . [through] means of exploring problems and relating them to problems already mastered" (p. 68).

In this sense, Bruner's work addresses a long-held misunderstanding about the nature and role of constructivism in education – namely that it is a pedagogical theory stating learners learn best when they actively engage in building their own knowledge and understanding. An understanding of Bruner instead positions constructivism as much closer to a theory of the mind, explaining how we build knowledge through the construction of ever-more nuanced representational model (Kirschner et al., 2006). Knowing this becomes useful for teachers and their practice, not because it urges us towards "discovery learning" but because it instead tells us how the structure of knowledge, and the forms in which we represent it, have hugely significant implications for how it is learned.

Takeaways

- Any idea or problem or body of knowledge can be presented in a form simple enough so that any particular learner can understand it in a recognisable form.
- Knowledge can be rendered more or less recognisable and understandable by teachers when they consider its mode of representation, its economy and its power.
- Within "modes of representation", there are ways to structure and sequence knowledge for student learning, namely moving from enactive, to iconic, and then symbolic representations of ideas.
- Even when learners become more advanced and begin to see knowledge in ever-more abstracted and symbolic ways – they still tend to ground this complexity in the foundational understanding they acquired from the earlier, enactive stage.
- Based on the above, ask not whether the learner is ready to understand a piece of knowledge; ask whether a piece of knowledge is ready to be understood by the learner.

References

BRUNER, J. (1966). *TOWARD A THEORY OF INSTRUCTION.* HARVARD UNIVERSITY PRESS.

CHI, M., FELTOVICH, P. J., & GLASER, R. (1981). CATEGORIZATION AND REPRESENTATION OF PHYSICS PROBLEMS BY EXPERTS AND NOVICES. *COGNITIVE SCIENCE, 5,* 121–152.

ESTERHAMMER, A. (2002). *ROMANTIC POETRY.* JOHN BENJAMINS PUBL. CO.

KIRSCHNER, P. A., SWELLER, J., & CLARK, R. E. (2006). WHY MINIMAL GUIDANCE DURING INSTRUCTION DOES NOT WORK: AN ANALYSIS OF THE FAILURE OF CONSTRUCTIVIST, DISCOVERY, PROBLEM-BASED, EXPERIENTIAL, AND INQUIRY-BASED TEACHING. *EDUCATIONAL PSYCHOLOGIST, 41*(2), 75–86.

Suggested Readings and Links

BRUNER, J. S. (1977). *THE PROCESS OF EDUCATION.* HARVARD UNIVERSITY PRESS.

BRUNER, J. S., GOODNOW, J. J., & AUSTIN, G. A. (1956). *A STUDY OF THINKING.* WILEY.

AVAILABLE VIA HTTPS://TINYURL.COM/R5SACUD4

BRUNER, J. S. (1964). THE COURSE OF COGNITIVE GROWTH. *AMERICAN PSYCHOLOGIST, 19,* 1, 1–15.

AVAILABLE VIA WWW.UKY.EDU/~GMSWAN3/544/BRUNER_1964_COCG.PDF

VIDEOS

IN THIS VIDEO, JEROME BRUNER TALKS ABOUT HOW TEACHING INFLUENCES LEARNING AND WHAT IT MEANS TO GO BEYOND THE INFORMATION GIVEN.

AVAILABLE VIA WWW.YOUTUBE.COM/WATCH?V=ALJVAUXQHDS

WEBSITES

TEACHING WORKS: A COLLECTION OF RESOURCES AND VIDEOS THE HIGH-LEVERAGE PRACTICE "EXPLAINING AND MODELLING CONTENT", WITH AN EMPHASIS ON REPRESENTATIONAL MODELS.

AVAILABLE VIA HTTPS://TINYURL.COM/HMB8ETBK

10 IF YOU DON'T KNOW WHERE YOU'RE GOING, YOU MIGHT WIND UP SOMEPLACE ELSE[1]

ROBERT MAGER ON LESSON OBJECTIVES

1 YOGI BERRA: WWW.NOTABLE-QUOTES.COM/B/BERRA_YOGI.HTML

10

IF YOU DON'T KNOW WHERE YOU'RE GOING, YOU MIGHT WIND UP SOMEPLACE ELSE

BOOK Preparing Instructional Objectives[2]

QUOTE *"Instruction is successful, or effective, to the degree that it accomplishes what it sets out to accomplish."*[3]

Why You Should Read This Book

Imagine you're setting out with five friends on a day-long trek across unfamiliar terrain. You're the more seasoned trekker of the group so you volunteer to take the lead on navigation. You print out detailed maps of the journey ahead, complete with staging posts and estimated timings for each leg, hand them out to the members of your party, and set out in high spirits.

Fast forward eight hours and the mood has changed for the worse: you and your fellow trekkers are tired, frustrated, and very, very lost. The day has been filled with argument and contradiction, and at every point along the way your friends have either been confused by your choice of direction or downright adamant that you're heading the wrong way.

With the sun quickly setting, you decide to call it a day and set up camp – at which point you realise what had been going wrong all along: when first handing out the maps at the start of the day, you had somehow managed to mix up the copies to such an extent that everyone on the team was operating from an ever-so-slightly-different version to one another. The journey was destined for failure because everyone in the

2   MAGER, R. F. (1962). *PREPARING INSTRUCTIONAL OBJECTIVES.* FEARON.
3   IBID., P. 1

group had subtle but significant differences in their sense of where they were going and how you intended to get there.

Now imagine if this same phenomenon were to play out in a classroom – with the teacher as "trek leader" and the various competing maps standing in for the varying perceptions of the learning that was about to take place. How would you know that your directions for that learning were the same as the ones the learner had in their head? What would be the implications for learning if there existed competing depictions of the journey to come?

As you can see, beginning an instructional journey *without* drawing an accurate picture of the stuff of instruction can land learners and teachers in all kinds of trouble. Exploring the importance of instructional objectives so that learning doesn't get lost before it has been found is the purpose of Robert F. Mager's seminal work: *Preparing Instructional Objectives*.

Abstract of the Book

Instructional objectives are the cornerstone of successful instruction. When written well, they enable you to identify appropriate content for your instruction, organise your instruction in the best way possible, and create tools to accurately determine if instruction is achieving your goals. *Preparing Instructional Objectives* is a systematic guide to identifying, selecting, and writing objectives that create the foundation for instructional success.

The Book

Why Instructional Objectives Matter

Mager begins his book by stating the case for instructional objectives in the clearest possible terms: "Instruction is successful, or effective, to the degree that it accomplishes what it sets out to accomplish" (p. 1). This might sound disarmingly straightforward but there's a fair amount going on here that can easily get overlooked if we don't attend to it.

For Mager, instruction is successful whenever it is "Changing students . . . in desired directions . . . and not in undesired directions" (p. 1). Therefore, in order to ensure that enacted learning doesn't stray from its original intent, it's imperative that we name precisely what is to be learned and done. The alternative, in Mager's eyes, is akin to buying a bus ticket without knowing where you're going, building a factory without knowing what you're intending to manufacture, or throwing a pie without knowing whom you intend to hit (p. 13).

Well-defined instructional objectives	More concrete and useful for our understanding, Mager then lays out the utility of well-defined instructional objectives as follows (pp. 14–19):
Right tools	■ *It helps you pick the right tools for the job* – A surgeon wouldn't select their instruments before they knew the aim of the surgery. Mager puts it like this: "If you don't know where you're going, how will you know which road to take to get there?"
Variation in approach	■ *It helps you play with variations around your main approach to the learning* – Jazz musicians get to improvise not because of an absence of musical structure but because there exists a tune around which they can riff. Mager puts it like this: "The existence of the objectives can free instructors to be creative and flexible".
Consistent results	■ *It helps you achieve consistent results* – If you're teaching a group of students to perform the triple jump, it's clear that some will jump further than others. but if you clarify from the start that everyone will at least be able to hop, skip, and jump by the end of the session, you would have set clear and achievable expectations. This resonates with the idea that formative assessment can clarify the objectives of learning – which we discuss in Chapter 26 of this book on Bloom et al. Mager puts it like this: "Some will learn more or reach a higher performance level than the objectives require, of course, but everyone can be expected to at least accomplish each objective".
Measure learning	■ *It helps you measure the results of learning* – The *only* way to demonstrate the instructional objective "Be able to ride a bike" is to have that person attempt to ride a bike. If the objective was instead, "Understand bike riding" then the means of demonstration would become unclear. Mager puts it like this: "Without clear objectives, it simply isn't possible to decide which measuring instrument will tell you what you want to know".
Learner organisation	■ *It helps learners organise for learning* – Setting out on a days-long hike without knowing what the weather has in store would mean having to make shot-in-the-dark choices about clothing and equipment – all of which could either weigh you down unnecessarily or leave you dangerously unprepared. Mager puts it like this: "When the instructional intent has been clarified – and revealed to the students – it is no longer necessary for them to guess what an instructor might have in mind for them to accomplish.
Streamline instruction	■ *It helps you streamline and direct your instruction* – If you spent a series of lessons teaching car mechanics how to spot the signs of a faulty gear box and then set them the task of fixing one – you shouldn't be surprised if they failed in their task. This is because you will have taught them how to spot symptoms, not how to solve problems. By noticing such distinctions, you can do away with redundancy. Mager puts it like this: "When good objectives have been derived,

existing instruction can be drastically shortened . . . [or] sometimes be eliminated altogether".

A WORD ON THE APPLICATIONS AND LIMITATIONS OF INSTRUCTIONAL OBJECTIVES

SOME ASPECTS OF MAGER'S work on instructional objectives have been subject to "toxic mutations" in recent years. In particular, the reasoning behind the triple-jump example above is reminiscent of an approach to objective setting which many saw as contributing to the workload crisis affecting the profession. Specifically, an over-interpretation of Mager's approaches by some schools saw teachers spending countless hours articulating continuums of expectation ("some will do this, most will do this, all will do this") that could be mapped onto the perceived ability levels of their students. This, I'm sure we'd all agree, is a misapplication of the approach and a misuse of teachers' time.

In addition to the rise in paperwork that came from taking Mager too far, there's also cause for concern about the form that instructional objectives take. Since language is often too ambiguous and slippery to faithfully articulate exactly what a teacher wants their students to know and be able to do, we run the risk of things getting lost in translation. Mager would likely argue that this is precisely why we need to concentrate on language we use in the first place — but Michael Polanyi's work on Tacit Knowledge and Donald Schon's assertion that our knowing is in our action (Chapter 6 of this book) underline the problems that can arise when we attempt to articulate the ineffable aspects of learning. More recently, we've seen how modelling in the form of worked examples (Zhu & Simon, 1987) and the comparison of examples and non-examples (Richland et al., 2007) help convey gradations of expected quality in ways that are less reliant on the ambiguities of language — both of which are vital contributions to this conversation and one of which (worked examples) we cover in Chapter 15 of this book.

The Qualities of Useful Objectives

Clarity in communicating instructional objectives

As with the trekking mishap described at the beginning of this chapter, one of the key challenges of setting instructional objectives relates to clarity in communication. Ambiguity can affect both the teacher and the learner, for even when we think we've described an instructional objective in unequivocal terms, the extent to which it remains open to interpretation can even surprise its author. This is why, as Mager puts it, "the best statement is the one that excludes the greatest number of possible meanings *other than* your intent".

To help build instructional objectives that say exactly what we mean them to say, Mager sets out three important characteristics: *Performance*, *Conditions* and *Criterion*.

Performance

Mager defines "performance" as, "What the learner is expected to be able to do" (p. 51) before breaking that down into two performance types: *overt* and *covert*.

Overt demonstrations of performance are the more straightforward of the two and have already been captured in our "be able to ride a bike" example. But there are the less-clear-cut demonstrations of performance that risk muddying the waters. Which is where one of Mager's many useful aphorisms comes into play: "*If a statement does not include a visible performance, it isn't yet an objective*" (p. 52). He illustrates what he means with the following two examples (p. 55):

1.   Be able to write a news article.
2.   Be able to develop an appreciation of music.

Since we can tell when someone is successfully writing a news article, that satisfies the definition of a "visible performance"; since we can't tell when (or whether) someone is developing an appreciation of music, that doesn't. The key here is to concentrate on those verbs that indicate demonstrable action, not their opposite. So, "stating, writing, drawing, listing" are preferable to "developing, valuing, appreciating, and internalizing" (p. 63). The latter describes a process of knowing, while the former describes something a person will be able to *show* once they *know*.

So far, so overt. But what happens when the overt becomes covert? Mager points out that "not all performances are visible to the naked eye" so an extra step is required. This is where we get to enjoy another of Mager's missives: "*Whenever the performance stated in an objective is cover add a performance indicator*" (p. 77).

To illustrate, Mager explains how an objective like, "Recognise tactless statements" isn't a visible performance since a person could do it without anyone being able to tell. So, what happens if we change it to, "Be able to recognise tactless statements by ringing a bell every time you hear one"? *Then* this becomes performance that can be *seen in action*. Mager's reminder that we need to "see" learning-in-performance is critical

Performance — margin note

Overt performance — margin note

Covert performance — margin note

because it makes explicit those aspects of learning that would otherwise remain shrouded from view.

THE VARIOUS USES OF "PERFORMANCE"

THE TERM "PERFORMANCE" has come to mean slightly different things, depending on which educational theorist you ask.

Mager's use of the term "predominantly" means to carry out or accomplish something. This is why he often speaks in the language of what a learner should "be able to do" as a result of what they've learnt.

Elizabeth and Robert Bjork (2011) see performance more as being able to do something immediately after having studied it. For them, it is that which we can observe or measure during instruction and is the means by which we infer the nature of the learning taking place.

You can see traces of both interpretations in the conditions of overt and covert performance described in the above section.

Conditions

Mager defines this component as, "The conditions under which the performance is expected to occur" (p. 51). To illustrate what can be lost when the conditions of an instructional objective are *not* stated, Mager offers the difference between, "Be able to run the hundred-yard dash" and "Be able to run the hundred-yard dash barefoot up a slippery slope" (p. 85).

Performance conditions

To help guard against the critical absence of "conditions" Mager offers a three-point guide as follows (p. 87):

1. What will the learner be expected to use when performing (e.g., tools, forms, etc.)?
2. What will the learner not be allowed to use while performing (e.g., checklists or other aids)?
3. What will be the real-world conditions under which the performance will be expected to occur (e.g., on top of a flagpole, under water, in front of a large audience, in a cockpit, etc.)?

We could add to this list the possibility that *no* context would be required for certain objectives, such that "Be able to ride a bicycle . . ." would likely *not* need to be concluded with the phrase, ". . . on a bicycle" but might well need to be concluded with "on a mountain path" if that's the setting in which it will take place.

Criterion

Criteria of
competency

Mager defines "criterion" as, "How well someone would have to perform to be considered competent" (p. 51). He argues that whenever we add information describing "the yardstick by which accomplishment of the objective will be measured" it can have significant and enhancing effects, including these (p. 110):

1. You will have a standard against which to test the success of the instruction.
2. Students will know how to tell when they have met or exceeded the performance expectations.
3. You will have the basis for proving that your students can, in fact, do what you set out to teach them.

On the last of these points, Mager pushes back on the argument that certain aspects of certain subjects are "intangible" and therefore "resist simple definition in the form of criteria". He argues that teachers already have a sense of what it means to achieve expertise in their domain (since they have done so) and that they "already make decisions about whether or not students can or cannot perform to your satisfaction". The only thing missing in such cases is the *naming* of the basis for that satisfaction – otherwise known as success criteria.

Speed

How long someone has to do something will have a qualitative impact on how they go about doing it. Consider giving someone thirty seconds to draw a self-portrait. Or three hours? What about three weeks? Each of those time frames confer something about how one might go about the work. Of course, it would still be important to state other terms (its *Performance* and *Conditions* aspects) but time would play its own part in communicating expectation.

Speed, sequence,
and rate of task

To help us make sense of the role speed and timing play, Mager offers three considerations to bear in mind, all of which affect the terms of the task at hand (p. 119):

1. Consider how fast something has to be done (e.g., within five seconds).
2. Consider what has to be done before another event begins (e.g., before the red light comes on).
3. Consider how often something must be done per unit of time (e.g., must fire at least three rounds within two seconds).

Accuracy

Accuracy

Doing something and doing something accurately are two very different things. The prompt, "Kick a football" is a far cry from, "Kick a football over a wall of defenders into the top-right hand corner of the goal avoiding the outstretched arm of the goalkeeper". That said, prompts for greater accuracy don't necessarily make a task more difficult, as shown by Mager's examples, which should all feel familiar (p. 123):

. . . and solutions must be accurate to the nearest whole number.
. . . with materials weighed accurately to the nearest gram.
. . . correct to at least three significant figures.

In this regard, details stating expectations of accuracy can have a similar effect to the establishment of *Conditions* within the objective. Sometimes the specificity with which the task is bound can have a clarifying and simplifying effect, and knowing exactly what's needed in one aspect can free up students' attention to concentrate on other components of their performance.

Freeing up student attention

Quality

If someone was judging a cooking competition, it's unlikely they'd pay much mind to the speed with which contestants prepared the dish (unless that was a stated factor as in *The Great British Bake-Off*) or the accuracy with which they followed the cooking instructions (unless that affected the final product). More important, and an ever-present criterion for success, would be the quality of the dish they cooked.

Even though quality can be difficult to determine, it's possible. Mager defines how *Quality* criteria work by mismatching an example with an *Accuracy* criterion in the following objective: "Be able to compose a sonata with 90 percent accuracy". Such an objective strikes us as inherently bizarre because determining what it would take to compose a sonata is so obviously reliant on quality rather than accuracy. The challenge therefore becomes this: How would you articulate the necessary qualities of a sonata, such that someone preparing to compose one would understand what "good" looked like for the purposes of the exercise? In this case, defining such qualitative criteria would be more useful for the student-composer than any expectations of accuracy or speed.

Quality

Conclusions

One of the most popular advertisements coming out of the UK in the early 1990s was for a wood stain called Ronseal. The tagline of the commercial quickly became a household phrase for anything that delivered on its promise without fuss: "*Ronseal quick-drying wood stain. It does exactly what it says on the tin*". This refreshingly honest piece of marketing works so well because doesn't say anything other than what Ronseal *actually does*. It stains wood and dries quickly – no more, no less. If we are to take anything from this chapter, it's that the same can be said for the power of an effective instructional objective.

As mentioned earlier, there have been no shortage of reactions to Mager's work in recent years – after all, what seminal work *hasn't* been wrestled with, subject to (un)successful refutation, or applied in troubling ways at one time or another. We *don't* think Mager's work should mutate into teachers filling out lengthy Learning Objective forms, and we agree with recent thinking that there is a powerful utility to *showing* as well as *telling* students what excellence looks like. Nevertheless, we believe that there is still much to learn from Mager when it comes to the thoughtful articulation of objectives – particularly the belief that an effective objective is one that passes the Ronseal Test by "doing exactly what it says on the tin".

Takeaways

- Instruction is successful when it accomplishes what it sets out to accomplish.
- Stating what you expect learners to know and be able to do as a result of your instruction provides an important roadmap for the instruction to come, and helps learners organise for learning.
- High-quality instructional objectives pay close attention to *Performance* (What the learner is expected to be able to do); *Conditions* (The conditions under which the performance is expected to occur); and *Criteria* (How well someone would have to perform to be considered competent).
- Any instructional objective worth its salt should *do exactly what it says on the tin*.

References

BJORK, E., & BJORK, R. (2011). MAKING THINGS HARD ON YOURSELF, BUT IN A GOOD WAY: CREATING DESIRABLE DIFFICULTIES TO ENHANCE LEARNING. *PSYCHOLOGY AND THE REAL WORLD: ESSAYS ILLUSTRATING FUNDAMENTAL CONTRIBUTIONS TO SOCIETY*, 56–64.

MAGER, R. F. (1962). *PREPARING INSTRUCTIONAL OBJECTIVES*. FEARON.

RICHLAND, L. E., ZUR, O., & HOLYOAK, K. J. (2007). COGNITIVE SUPPORTS FOR ANALOGIES THE MATHEMATICS CLASSROOM. *SCIENCE, 316*(5828), 1128–1129.

ZHU, X., AND SIMON, H. (1987). LEARNING MATHEMATICS FROM EXAMPLES AND BY DOING. *COGNITIVE INSTRUCTION*, 4, 137–166.

Suggested Readings and Links

BLOOM, B. S. (1965). *TAXONOMY OF EDUCATION OBJECTIVES: THE CLASSIFICATION OF EDUCATIONAL GOALS.* DAVID MCKAY.

GRONLUND, N. E. (1970). *STATING BEHAVIORAL OBJECTIVES FOR CLASSROOM INSTRUCTION.* MACMILLAN.

VIDEOS

THIS VIDEO OFFERS A CONCISE OVERVIEW OF THE STRUCTURE OF INSTRUCTIONAL OBJECTIVES AND BUILDS OUT EXAMPLES/NON-EXAMPLES IN REAL TIME.

AVAILABLE VIA WWW.YOUTUBE.COM/WATCH?V=OLOSOL0YPL4

THIS VIDEO EXPLORES WHAT MAKES AN OBJECTIVE MEASURABLE, WITH REFERENCE TO BLOOM'S TAXONOMY.

AVAILABLE VIA WWW.YOUTUBE.COM/WATCH?V=TDXDHT9BQ58

WEBSITES

A PRACTICAL RESOURCE COVERING THE FEATURES OF INSTRUCTIONAL OBJECTIVES, WITH GUIDED STEPS FOR CREATING YOUR OWN.

AVAILABLE VIA WWW.WKU.EDU/STE/OBJECTIVES/INDEX.PHP

A GUIDE FOR CRAFTING INSTRUCTIONAL OBJECTIVES, SET WITHIN THE WIDER CONTEXT OF DESIGNING A COURSE OF STUDY.

AVAILABLE VIA WWW.CMU.EDU/TEACHING/DESIGNTEACH/DESIGN/LEARNINGOBJECTIVES.HTML

SECTION 3

TEACHING TECHNIQUES

We know from Kierkegaard that even though life is lived forwards, it must be understood backwards. This distinction between our experience of life and how we make sense of it after the fact is particularly striking when it comes to learning something for the first time.

One definition of learning is the bringing together of previously disorganised information into a coherent, recognisable, and retrievable form. Organising knowledge in this way can often lead us to mis-characterise the act of learning itself as something that was similarly ordered and straightforward when this is far from the case.

For instance, any memory you have of learning to ride a bike or speak a new language might *feel* like it was a natural, consistent trajectory of progression but that's almost certainly a case of revisionist history. In reality, learning is a messy and counterintuitive process that must be broken down in order for it to be fully understood.

Just as this is true of learning, so is it true of teaching. Indeed, one of the problems we often encounter with teaching is the assumption that it, too, is intuitive, predictable, and forever adhering to a natural order that "just happens" rather than requiring a well-thought-out design and thoughtful enactment. All of which can lead to the meme on the next page.

The reason this meme makes us chuckle is due to the assumptions we sometimes make about the linear inevitability of teaching. It is as though teaching is prone to a brand of magical thinking that leaves out or skips over the very components that make it work in the first place. Thankfully, there are plenty of ways to think about how teaching and teaching techniques actually work which we will explore in this chapter.

To get at these ideas, we ask among other things: What is Direct Instruction and how does it differ from di? What is explicit instruction and how does it differ from chalk-and-talk? And we know that learning isn't and shouldn't be passive, but how do we make it generative?

DI: 10.4324/9781003228165-13

How to draw an Owl.

"A fun and creative guide for beginners"

Fig 1. Draw two circles   Fig 2. Draw the rest of the damn Owl

THERE'S NO SUCH THING AS A CHILD WHO CAN'T BE TAUGHT

SIEGFRIED ENGELMANN ON DIRECT INSTRUCTION

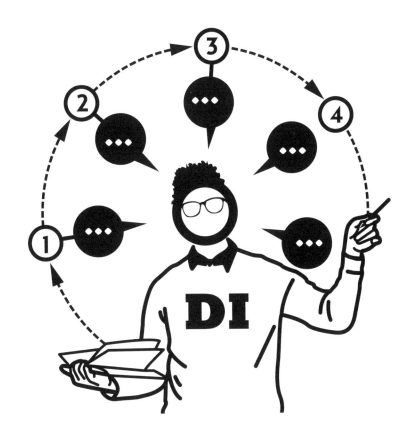

OI: 10.4324/9781003228165-14

11 THERE'S NO SUCH THING AS A CHILD WHO CAN'T BE TAUGHT

BOOK: Direct Instruction[1]

QUOTE *"The students [would] increase their self-esteem and self-confidence through their academic achievement, providing motivation for subsequent tasks."*[2]

Why You Should Read This Book

We perhaps can conjure an idea of what we think a scientist at NASA does to get a rocket into space, or the things an archaeologist does when excavating an ancient settlement – but do we really know? Could we speak to the details? I think we would all agree that the answer to that is "No" – so why is it the case that people think that they have an intuitive sense of what "goes into" teaching? Even within the teaching profession, there exists another misconception from afar: that people think they know what goes into something like Direct Instruction. In the absence of the facts, people fill in the blanks about a drill and kill, chalk and talk approach where the teacher is there to talk and students are there to listen etc.

Siegfried Engelmann's Direct Instruction (DI) is both a theory of and a design model for instruction based on two premises or assumptions, namely "that learners perceive qualities, and that they generalize upon the basis of *sameness* of qualities" (Engelmann & Carnine, 1991, preface). The point of examining his work here is (1) to set the record straight about what DI is (and isn't) and (2) to learn from the wisdom of his work.

---

[1] ENGELMANN, S. (1980). *DIRECT INSTRUCTION*. EDUCATIONAL TECHNOLOGY PUBLICATION REPUBLISHED WITH PERMISSION OF EDUCATIONAL TECHNOLOGY PUBLICATIONS, INC.

[2] MAGLIARO, S. G., LOCKEE, B. B., & BURTON, J. K. (2005) DIRECT INSTRUCTION REVISITED: A KEY MOD FOR INSTRUCTIONAL TECHNOLOGY. *EDUCATIONAL TECHNOLOGY RESEARCH & DEVELOPMENT, 53(* 41–55.

Abstract of the Book

The Direct Instruction approach begins with the question, "What is the most efficient way to teach each skill?" not with the question, "How do children typically learn each skill?"

The learner is assumed to act in a perfectly reasonable way, which means that the learner will always derive an interpretation that is consistent with the presentation the learner receives. If the presentation of examples is consistent with more than one interpretation, the learner will derive one of these interpretations – not necessarily the one the teacher wishes. Conversely, the presentation that is consistent with only one interpretation will work with virtually all learners who have necessary preskills.

Complex routines for solving problems are constructed so the same routine works for all problems of a given type. The steps that lead to the outcome are made functional and overt. The teacher now has the opportunity to provide precise feedback.

The Book

One thing we need to realise here is that DI isn't a theory of learning, but rather a theory of instruction. A *theory of learning* deals with how people learn, regardless of the instruction used[3] (e.g., Sweller's Cognitive Load Theory, Reigeluth's Elaboration Theory, Paivio's Dual Coding Theory . . . all discussed in *HLH*). A *theory of instruction*, on the other hand, deals with the form of the instruction itself, implying or even advocating there's a "best way" to provide effective and efficient instruction (e.g., Biggs' Constructive Alignment Theory (Chapter 7) or Merrill's First Principles of Instruction/Van Merriënboer's Four Component Instructional Design Theory (Chapter 8 of this book).

Theory of learning

Theory of instruction

> **Direct Instruction (DI),** referred to as "capital or uppercase DI", is an explicit, carefully sequenced, and scripted model of instruction as prescribed by Engelmann. It's a collection of formal, highly scripted, and formatted curricula in the form of lessons, textbooks, and sequencing.
>
> *(Continued)*

---

3 THIS DOESN'T MEAN THAT THERE ISN'T AN INTERPLAY BETWEEN THEM OR THAT A LEARNING THEORY DOESN'T SUGGEST A CERTAIN INSTRUCTIONAL DESIGN, BUT RATHER THAT A THEORY OF LEARNING IS JUST ABOUT HOW WE LEARN.

(Continued)

direct instruction (di), also referred to as "small or lowercase di", is a term that Barak Rosenshine, based upon his own teacher effectiveness studies (see Chapters 4 and 5 about teacher effectiveness) gave to a set of variables found to be significantly related to student achievement. It is an instruction strategy, not a curriculum. In his original work, he referred to it as "explicit instruction" (see Chapter 12).

Siegfried Engelmann is the scientist and educator known for "inventing" (DI), a technique and a theory he described as an efficient and effective way to teach *any skill*. It's important to note here that when speaking of Engelmann's theory or model, we use capital letters.

DI versus di

While the first DI programs were about teaching basic reading, writing, and mathematics skills, "Direct Instruction applies to nearly al instructional problems, from the teaching of very unfamiliar behaviors to a [child with a learning disability][4] to turning on older students who are not easy to motivate. It applies to the teaching of college level skills and to the teaching of subjects not taught well through traditional approaches – reading, spelling, arithmetic, and the sciences (Engelmann, 1980, p. 3).

Philosophy underlying DI

The philosophy underlying DI is a very positive one. He believed that:

- There's no such thing as a child who can't be taught.
- Taught properly, every child can learn well and attain a positive self-image.
- With suitable training and instructional materials, all teachers can succeed.
- Low performers/disadvantaged learners need to be taught at a faster pace than what's normally the case as only then can they catch up to their peers.

For mastery, new instruction reinforces what has already been learnt

- Instruction must be carefully planned and controlled to avoid learners misinterpreting what's being taught and to benefit from the "reinforcing effect of instruction".

Unambiguous communication

Central to DI is unambiguous communication with students and that the basis for a theory of instruction is "making the communication faultless and then observing the performance of the learner".

---

4   ENGELMAAN, IN 1980, ACTUALLY USED THE TERM "HANDICAPPED YOUNGSTER".

(Engelmann & Carnine, 1991, p. 3). To this end, he arrived at seven communication conventions for instruction, namely:

1. Instructional presentations must be clearly and concisely scripted to assure that the same wording is used for similar tasks. This is required, as he and we already stated, for "learners [to] perceive qualities, and . . . generalize upon the basis of *sameness* of qualities".
2. The pace of instruction should be rapid for better student attention and higher student performance.
3. The teacher should present many tasks to the group, with the children responding together at the same time (in unison).
4. The teacher should use clear and unequivocal signals to let the group know exactly when they should respond to make sure that it's not only a few students who initiate the response and others who simply copy it.
5. After group tasks, the teacher should give individual turns so as to gather information about each individual student.
6. Learning isn't errorless. Each instructional programme should anticipate and specify the precise steps that need to be made in correcting the more common errors.
7. Learners will enjoy the material and work on it better and more diligently if they're reinforced for good performance and hard work via "praise and challenges, exhortations, and expressed amazement over the performance of the student" (p. 13).

Engelmann's first DI model came in collaboration with Carl Bereiter (Bereiter & Engelmann, 1966) which in itself is rather strange. Carl Bereiter had made his mark as strong proponent of *knowledge building*, a constructivist approach to learning, which he developed with Marlene Scardamalia (Computer Supported Intentional Learning Environment [CSILE] which begat Knowledge Forum®). Engelmann's approach to instruction, in contrast, is firmly rooted in behaviourism. Their 1966 model involves a 3-stage process with continuous assessment playing a role in each stage. Stage 1 introduces the new, to be learnt, content based on previously mastered knowledge and skills: that is, refreshing what has previously been learnt. Stage 2 is the presentation of the lesson; that is what is to be learnt. This is a fast-paced, scripted explanation or demonstration designed to elicit only one interpretation of the concept which is "reinforced with appropriate examples and nonexamples" (Magliaro et al., 2005, p. 46). Stage 3 is lots of practice with immediate feedback. The practice begins as a completely teacher-directed activity requiring the whole class to respond in unison to rapid-fire scripted questioning by the teacher. These group-based interactions allow the teacher to determine how well the students are grasping the targeted content and to correct any misconceptions that may arise. When the teacher is confident that the newly learnt facts, concepts, and skills have been mastered, the teacher-controlled practice is replaced by independent practice with the teacher closely monitoring so as to determine that the acquired facts, concepts, and skills are properly applied. This has remained the basis of all of Engelmann's iterations of DI that have followed.

For Engelmann (1980), DI requires "a careful analysis of the skill to be taught, a careful analysis of the learner, and very careful execution of the presentation that is designed to 'teach' or to establish the new behavior" (p. 4) and as such requires a lot of work. In that book he notes that, in the DI model, the lessons and tasks were (almost) completely scripted for two reasons. The first was to control "every controllable variable that, affects the learner's performance" (p. 4). The second was, as Magliaro et al. (2005) write, to free the teacher to focus on the following:

- Presenting information and communicating with students.
- Determining the prerequisite skills and capabilities students need to carry out the targeted task.
- Identifying potential problems students might have (via task analysis).
- Understanding how students learn by identifying examples of learner success and the strategies they use when successful.
- Learning how to construct well-designed tasks.

Task analysis

Noteworthy here is that key to Engelmann's DI was his conviction that students "would increase their self-esteem and self-confidence through their academic achievement, providing motivation for subsequent tasks" (Magliaro et al., 2005, p. 45).

Oliver Caviglioli summarises nine key features of DI in Figure 11.1.

Does DI Work?

We could go on and on about DI, but the question is actually "does it work?". For this we refer the reader to *Project Follow Through*, initiated in the U.S. in 1967 and which lasted ten years. It was set up to determine the best way of teaching at-risk children from kindergarten through grade 3 (i.e., children at or around the 20th percentile), often in the poorest areas. Originally intended to reach 200,000 children in 178 communities, comparing 22 different models of instruction clustered in three types of approaches. The first cluster – *Basic-Skills Models* – included, amongst others, Engelmann's DI. The approaches focused on the acquisition of basic knowledge and skills in language and numeracy and assumed that higher-order thinking, problem-solving skills, and self-esteem would arise from mastery of component skills. It was basically a bottom-up approach to learning. The second cluster – *Cognitive-Conceptual Models* – emphasised developing higher-order cognitive skills. This was more a

Project Follow Through

Basic-skills models

Cognitive-conceptual models

THE EVIDENCE–BASED CLASSROOM SERIES

BEN GORDON

ASSISTANT PRINCIPAL (MATHS TEACHING & LEARNING), MATHS SLE, BLACKPOOL

4: ENGELMANN'S DIRECT INSTRUCTION

One of the forms of direct instruction that Barak Rosenshine identified in his research behind effective teachers was Siegfried Engelmann's Direct Instruction. Have you ever wondered what are its key features?

(1) BELIEFS AND VALUES

Engelmann believed that all children can learn and develop a positive self-image. He saw failure to learn as faulty curriculum and instructional design, not faulty children.

(2) MINIMAL NEW CONTENT EACH LESSON

Only 15% of content in each lesson is new. 85% is prior content through review, practice, application, and testing, often the opposite of most traditional lessons.

15% NEW   85% OLD

(3) STRAND CURRICULUM

Each lesson is organized around multiple skills or topics rather than around a single skill or topic. Skills are then intelligently distributed into future lessons through review, practice, application, and testing.

(4) MASTERY STAIRWAY

Students begin with basic concepts that develop in complexity of application over time. Students do not move up the stairs if they are not ready to do so and are re-grouped if necessary.

(5) SEQUENCING

A great deal of thought goes into the sequencing of examples, task chaining, and series of lessons. Principles include separating confusing concepts in time and teaching consistent instances of a strategy before exceptions.

(6) HOMOGENOUS GROUPINGS

Ensuring that students are placed in the correct grouping depending on their level of mastery, not pre-conceived ability, in the unit is vital.

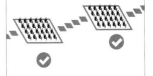

(7) FAULTLESS COMMUNICATION

Engelmann has extremely specific requirements for what constitutes faultless communication so that students do not form "misrules". The use of scripts is prevalent to integrate consistency.

(8) HIGHLY INTERACTIVE

Teaching new content may occur for 6–12 minutes of a lesson. The rest of the lesson is application with high frequency questioning and feedback, often using choral response.

(9) GENERALISATION

The goal of a DI programme is to teach the concepts and strategies that can be applied to the greatest possible range of contexts. First, specific instances of a concept are taught followed by a sequence of generalizable instances.

Oliver Caviglioli | @olicav | teach SECONDARY | teachwire.net

FIGURE 11.1 KEY FEATURES OF ENGELMANN'S DIRECT INSTRUCTION MODEL. (SOURCE: OLIVER CAVIGLIOLI, WWW.OLICAV.COM/S/4-DIRECT-INSTRUCTION-V2.PDF).

top-down approach targeting thinking and problem-solving skills, assuming that lower-order basic skills and self-esteem would be acquired automatically while mastering complex problems. This is comparable to many present day 21st-century-skills approaches

Affective models

to learning. The third cluster – *Affective Models* – focused on promoting positive self-esteem to improve learning and development and assumed that experiences that raised the children's self-esteem would provide a motivational catalyst to learning and achievement. This is similar to what we see today in the Growth Mindset and Grit approaches to learning. For a description of all of the individual approaches, see Watkins (1997).

Widely used and validated tests

The measures used to determine the efficacy of the different programmes included widely used and validated tests of problem-solving ability, self-esteem, responsibility for success or failure, along with a small battery of standardised language and mathematics achievement tests. When all of the results were in, it was clear that children who received lessons falling into the Basic Skills models cluster, and especially DI, not only had significantly higher academic achievement scores than those in any of the other programmes but also higher self-esteem and self-confidence scores. Specifically, in a study by Watkins (1997) which looked at the original national evaluation of Follow Through, as well as three major reanalyses of the Follow Through data showed that:

- Models emphasising basic skills succeeded better than other models in helping children gain these skills.
- Where models put their primary emphasis elsewhere than on basic skills, the children scored lower on tests of these skills than they would have done without Follow Through. That is, those models had a negative effect.
- No type of model was notably more successful than the others in raising scores on cognitive conceptual skills.
- Models that emphasised basic skills produced better results on tests of self-concept than the other models. In other words, the basic-skills programmes also had better affective outcomes than the programmes specifically designed to do this!

To end on an unhappy note, although all evaluations of *Project Follow Through* clearly showed that DI works, the results of the original evaluation were suppressed by the U.S. Office of Education and the results of follow-up evaluations showing the same have been either ignored or demonised. In a letter,[5] the then Commissioner of Education, Ernest Boyer (Watkins, 1997), wrote that "Since only one of the sponsors (Direct Instruction) was found to produce positive results more consistently than any of the others, it would be inappropriate and irresponsible to disseminate information on all of the models". Yes, you read that right. As only one approach proved to work, it would be "inappropriate or irresponsible" to let the public know what didn't work! And why is this? The theory and methods of Direct Instruction

---

5 THE LETTER CAN BE FOUND HERE: WWW.NIFDI.ORG/WHAT-IS-DI/PROJECT-FOLLOW-THROUGH

were inconsistent with the dominant constructivist thinking of American educators at that time and are still. They were not prepared for the findings that only one program would excel in basic skills and cognitive skills, in reading, spelling, and math and would also have children develop the strongest self-image. Boyer admitted that the results didn't match how experts predicted and thus he suppressed the results. This type of instruction is still painted into a corner by many policymakers and so-called educational innovators as being child-unfriendly and if any good at all, only good for cognitive results while the results prove the opposite. Opinion, philosophy, and dogma triumphed over data.

Conclusions

Direct Instruction works. On the one hand it's a highly scripted and teacher-led form of education while on the other hand it's a dynamic and proven effective way to teach. It requires much forethought and planning. It requires investing a lot of time on planning and preparation but yields results not only on cognitive but also on affective learning and development.

And why, then is DI so maligned? The answer is both simple and sad. The theory underlying DI and its methods conflict with more progressive and romantic philosophies of teaching and learning which are developmental, constructivist, and child-driven and which assume that education should allow children to determine what and how they learn, that how a child learns depends on their developmental stage, that children can and should be let free to construct or derive understanding, and/or that we all learn best when our own unique learning style or preference is respected and used.

There is also the fact that for many teachers, autonomy about what is taught in their classroom and how it is taught is a central part of their identity.

Chapter 12 will continue in this vein, discussing Barak Rosenshine's direct instruction (di), or as he called it: explicit instruction.

Takeaways

- DI is a stimulating and varied approach to instruction based on prior knowledge, scripted lessons, and much practice with extensive feedback in all three.
- DI involves:
  1. Communicating learning goals
  2. Examining whether students have prerequisite knowledge and skills to understand the new lesson
  3. Presenting key principles of the new lesson through clear instruction

4. Checking student mastery and understanding by posing questions, providing examples, and correcting misconceptions
5. Providing opportunities for guided practice
6. Assessing performance and providing feedback on the guided practice
7. Providing opportunities for independent practice through group or individual work in class or as homework

- DI is mastery-based and systematic.
- DI not only leads to better academic achievement in children, but also to higher self-esteem and a better self-concept.
- Dismissing teaching strategies that work in favour of fashionable fads or unproven methods and/or methods that been shown not to work hurts the very students who are most at risk.

References

BEREITER, C., & ENGELMANN, S. (1966). *TEACHING DISADVANTAGED CHILDREN IN THE PRESCHOOL.* PRENTICE HALL.

COOMBS, M. K. (1998, MARCH 24). HONEST FOLLOW-THROUGH NEEDED ON THIS PROJECT. *THE WASHINGTON TIMES.* AVAILABLE VIA WWW.MATHEMATICALLYCORRECT.COM/HONESTFT.HTM

ENGELMANN, S. (1980). *DIRECT INSTRUCTION.* EDUCATIONAL TECHNOLOGY PUBLICATIONS.

ENGELMANN, S., & CARNINE, D. (1991). *THEORY OF INSTRUCTION: PRINCIPLES AND APPLICATIONS.* ADI PRESS.

MAGLIARO, S. G., LOCKEE, B. B., & BURTON, J. K. (2005). DIRECT INSTRUCTION REVISITED: A KEY MODEL FOR INSTRUCTIONAL TECHNOLOGY. *EDUCATIONAL TECHNOLOGY RESEARCH & DEVELOPMENT, 53*(4), 41–55.

WATKINS, C. L. (1997). *PROJECT FOLLOW THROUGH: A CASE STUDY OF THE CONTINGENCIES INFLUENCING INSTRUCTIONAL PRACTICES OF THE EDUCATIONAL ESTABLISHMENT.* (MONOGRAPH). CAMBRIDGE CENTER FOR BEHAVIORAL STUDIES. AVAILABLE VIA WWW.BEHAVIOR.ORG/RESOURCES/901.PDF

Suggested Readings and Links

 CARNINE, D. (2000). *WHY EDUCATION EXPERTS RESIST EFFECTIVE PRACTICES (AND WHAT IT WOULD TAKE TO MAKE EDUCATION MORE LIKE MEDICINE).* THOMA FORDHAM FOUNDATION.

AVAILABLE VIA WWW.WRIGHTSLAW.COM/INFO/TEACH.PROFESSION.CARNINE.PDF

 STOCKARD, J., WOOD, T. W., COUGHLIN, C., & KHOURY, C. R. (2018). THE EFFECTIVENESS OF DIRECT INSTRUCTION CURRICULA: A META-ANALYSIS OF A HALF CENTURY OF RESEARCH. *REVIEW OF EDUCATIONAL RESEARCH, 88,* 479–507.

AVAILABLE VIA HTTPS://TINYURL.COM/2MKHXXNM

VIDEOS

 PRESCHOOL STUDENTS DEMONSTRATE EXCEPTIONAL MATH SKILLS

AVAILABLE VIA HTTPS://YOUTU.BE/GKYVMBJJIGC

NIFDI VIDEO LIBRARY

AVAILABLE VIA WWW.NIFDI.ORG/VIDEOS.HTML

INTRO TO DI VIDEO SERIES

THIS NINE-PART INTRODUCTION IS FREE AND COVERS A RANGE OF TOPICS ADDRESSING THE FUNDAMENTALS OF DIRECT INSTRUCTION. DESIGNED TO PROVIDE INFORMATION RELEVANT TO INDIVIDUALS NEW TO DI.

AVAILABLE VIA WWW.NIFDI.ORG/VIDEOS/INTRO-TO-DI

WEBSITES/BLOGS

PSYCHOLOGY LEARNING RESOURCES: SIEGFRIED ENGELMANN AND DIRECT INSTRUCTION

This interactive tutorial is for use by Psychology students at Athabasca University. It was written by Dr. Joseph A. Parsons and Dr. David Polson of the University of Victoria.

AVAILABLE VIA HTTPS://PSYCH.ATHABASCAU.CA/OPEN/ENGELMANN/INDEX.PHP

NATIONAL INSTITUTE FOR DIRECT INSTRUCTION

THE NATIONAL INSTITUTE FOR DIRECT INSTRUCTION IS THE WORLD'S FOREMOST DIRECT INSTRUCTION (DI) SUPPORT PROVIDER. IT PROVIDES INFORMATION AND RESOURCES FOR ADMINISTRATORS, TEACHERS, AND PARENTS TO HELP THEM MAXIMISE STUDENT ACHIEVEMENT THROUGH DI. IT ALSO CONTAINS INFORMATION ON DI'S EXTENSIVE AND BROAD RESEARCH BASE, INCLUDING A SEARCHABLE DATABASE OF MORE THAN TWO HUNDRED ARTICLE SUMMARIES.

AVAILABLE VIA WWW.NIFDI.ORG/

DIRECT INSTRUCTION GETS NO RESPECT (BUT IT WORKS)

AVAILABLE VIA HTTPS://3STARLEARNINGEXPERIENCES.WORDPRESS.COM/2018/05/01/DIRECT-INSTRUCTION-GETS-NO-RESPECT-BUT-IT-WORKS/

DIRECT INSTRUCTION: THE RODNEY DANGERFIELD OF CURRICULUM

AVAILABLE VIA HTTPS://TINYURL.COM/2W8UTKYJ

OLIVER CAVIGLIOLI'S DIRECT INSTRUCTION SUMMARY

AVAILABLE VIA WWW.OLICAV.COM/BLOG/2018/5/15/DIRECT-INSTRUCTION

12

BURNING THE STRAWMAN

BARAK ROSENSHINE ON EXPLICIT INSTRUCTION

DOI: 10.4324/9781003228165-15

12 BURNING THE STRAWMAN

ARTICLE Synthesis of Research on Explicit Teaching[1]

QUOTE *"A decade of research on teaching has firmly established the effectiveness of systematic, step-by-step instruction."*[2]

Why You Should Read This Article

We're often told that explicit instruction is boring, demotivating, and if we believe the late Ken Robinson even that it kills learning. And we hear that this is especially the case for younger learners. We should let them, among other things, play freely, discover new knowledge, and self-direct their own learning. But is that so?

Paul often brought his granddaughter Elsa to day care on his bike, she in a bike-seat on the handlebars in front of him. On the way they talked about everything from unicorns to Paw Patrol, and in those discussions the meaning of red and green lights in traffic was naturally also part of the mix (Grandpa, why do we have to wait here?). When she was a little older they were walking in the city, the following conversation ensued:

- Paul: Elsa, can we cross the street? [The light was red.]
- Elsa: No Grandpa, the light's red; you know that. [She'd previously learnt while biking to the day care that you had to stop for a red light.]
- Paul: And now? [The light had changed to green.]
- Elsa: Yeah, let's go!
- Paul: No, wait a second.
- Elsa: Why Grandpa?
- Paul: Because we first have to look left[3] to see if a car is coming [exaggerated looking left]; Elsa, which way is left? [I wait for an answer

---

[1] ROSENSHINE, B. V. (1986). SYNTHESIS OF RESEARCH ON EXPLICIT TEACHING. *EDUCATIONAL LEADERSHIP, 43*, 60–69.
[2] IBID., P. 464.
[3] FOR SOME READERS IT MIGHT BE THE OTHER WAY AROUND.

and acknowledge that she knows this.] Then right [exaggerated looking right], and then left [ditto left].

- Elsa: Why Grandpa? They have a red light and we have green!
- Paul: Because maybe some naughty person doesn't stop for their red light and hits us.
- Elsa: Oh, but why do we have to look left a second time?
- Paul: Because maybe while looking right, a car or bike turns the corner and could hit us. [Looking at the light which has turned green.] It's green; can we now cross? First let's look left and right and left.
- [We both look left and right and left and Paul saying,] No naughty people coming from either direction. Can we go?
- Elsa: Yes Grandpa. [She makes a move to walk.]
- Paul: OK, but hold my hand.
- Paul [at the next intersection]: OK Elsa, it's your turn now.

This is an example of explicit instruction. It's not boring or demotivating. It's lively and playful, and also effective and efficient! It includes explicit explaining (instruction), checking prior knowledge before and whether something has been learnt after (assessing), allowing independent but guided action, etc. Actually, it's fun for both of us and gives Elsa a feeling of accomplishment (and Paul too that she grasped it). We really don't want to think about what would have happened if Paul had let her playfully and self-directedly discover how to safely cross the busy street! As is clear, explicit instruction is much different from the talk-and-chalk strawman that some people paint it to be. This chapter is about one of Barak Rosenshine's articles on what explicit instruction really is.

Abstract of the Article

The research on effective teaching conducted since 1974 has yielded a pattern of instruction that is particularly useful for teaching a body of content or well-defined skills. This pattern is a systematic method for presenting material in small steps, pausing to check for student understanding, and eliciting active and successful participation from all students. Although this method was derived primarily from reading and mathematics research conducted in elementary and junior high schools, the results are applicable to any "well-structured" discipline where the objective is to teach performance skills or mastery of a body of knowledge. Specifically, these results are most applicable to the teaching of mathematical procedures and computations, reading decoding, explicit reading procedures such as distinguishing fact from opinion, science facts and concepts, social studies facts and concepts, map skills, grammatical concepts and rules, and foreign language vocabulary and grammar.

The Article

Direct instruction

In the previous chapter, Siegried Engelmann's *Direct Instruction* was discussed with an uppercase "DI" and a very strict approach to how it is carried out. In 1976 and 1979, Barak Rosenshine developed his own, though similar, approach (direct instruction; lowercase "di') where instructors (1) emphasise academic goals, (2) ensure that learners are involved in learning, (3) select learning objectives and monitor learner progress, (4) structure learning activities and give immediate, academically focused, feedback, and (5) create a task-oriented yet "relaxed" learning environment. In 1986, he took it a step further and

Explicit instruction

dubbed it *explicit instruction* as, in his words, "researchers have found that when effective teachers teach concepts and skills explicitly" (p. 464), students learn better.

Rosenshine begins his 1986 article with what those researchers found to be effective for stimulating concept and skills learning, namely:

Goals
- Beginning lessons by concisely stating the lesson's goals (explicitly letting students know what's expected of them).

Prior knowledge
- Beginning lessons by reviewing previous and/or prerequisite learning (in *HLH* we discussed David Ausubel's premise that the most important factor in learning is what the learner already knows).

Small steps
- Presenting new material in small steps (minimising intrinsic cognitive load) and having students practice after each step (ensuring storage in long-term memory).

Clear instructions
- Ensuring that instructions and explanations are detailed and clear (minimising extraneous cognitive load).

Active practice
- Providing/requiring active practice (requires cognitive effort to process information for better learning and retention).

Checking understanding
- Asking questions, checking student understanding, and obtaining responses from all students (lets teacher and learner know if something's been learnt, but this retrieval practice is also a "desirable difficulty" – Chapter 14 – which benefits learning).

Guidance
- Guiding students during their initial practice (guidance minimises extraneous cognitive load and can be faded as learning occurs).

Systematic feedback
- Providing systematic feedback and corrections (corrective, directive, and/or epistemic feedback as either feed-forward, feed-through, or feedback, both in Chapter 19 in *HLH*).

Lots of practice
- Continuing to practice until students are independent and confident (learning and overlearning helps automatise what has been learnt, making it instantaneously usable (i.e., retrievable from long-term memory) in new situations).

MISINTERPRETATION PROBLEM

THE AFOREMENTIONED has led to problems because, seeing these techniques, teachers (and teacher trainers) first tended to see this as a checklist or algorithm (i.e., a process or set of rules to be followed that bring us to a desired end-state: learning) and, second, that each and every action should be carried out in each and every class (it's not). Teachers also assumed that it's something that can and should be used for all students. Rosenshine himself says that "[I]t would be a mistake to say that this small-step approach applies to all students or all situations. It is most important for young learners, slow learners, and for all learners when the material is new, difficult, or hierarchical . . . when teaching older, brighter students, or when teaching in the middle of a unit, the steps are larger; that is, the presentations are longer, less time is spent in checking for understanding or in guided practice, and more independent practice can be done . . . because the students do not need as much help and supervision. But even for these situations, it is more efficient to return to small-step instruction when the material becomes difficult" (p. 465).

Rosenshine drew these techniques from research on human information processing such as how our working memory is very limited (too much new information overloads it), how practice helps move information from our working memory to our long-term memory (e.g., using things now called generative learning activities or desirable difficulties such as elaboration, review, rehearsal, summarisation, or enhancement), and how continuing until fluency allows what has been learnt to be effortlessly (i.e., automatically) recalled from long-term memory when needed.

Generative learning activities

Rosenshine also looked at research on what good teachers do (teaching effectiveness studies). In summarising those studies, he divided what he found into what he called "six teaching functions (see Table 12.1): review, presentation of new material, guided practice, feedback and corrections, independent practice, and weekly and monthly reviews" (p. 466).

Teaching effectiveness studies

TABLE 12.1
TEACHING
FUNCTIONS
(ADAPTED FROM
AND EXPANDED
ON ROSENSHINE,
1986)

Seductive details

Activity (What)	Implementations (How)
Review	Review homework from the previous day with the class Review relevant previous learning (from yesterday, last week, last month) either by presenting it or via forms of retrieval practice like quizzes or flashcards Review prerequisite knowledge and skills explaining how it's related to what's coming
Presentation	Make the lesson goals explicit and/or provide an outline that remains visible Segment what you're going to teach in small steps Model procedures; demonstrate a procedure including not on what you're doing but also why you're doing something (or not doing something else) Provide specific and tangible positive and negative examples Use clear language; avoid jargon but also explain and use technical terms Check constantly for student understanding by asking questions and cold-calling or requiring that everyone puts their answer on an individual whiteboard Don't digress or resort to using other seductive details
Guided practice	Allow students to practice alone, but with proper guidance from you. Continue during practice to ask questions frequently to keep students thinking Don't let them raise they hands, but require all students respond (group answers, cold-calling, whiteboards) Make sure that you obtain a high success rate (i.e., mastery) before going further Continue practicing until the students have automatised the learning
Corrections and feedback	Give not only product feedback (i.e., correct or incorrect followed by what it should have been) but also process-oriented feedback, especially if a student gives the correct answer but is hesitant Reteaching when necessary but try a different approach
Independent practice	Once you're fairly certain that the student has achieved (near) mastery, let the students do new tasks or solve new problems themselves! Provide assistance only when necessary
Weekly and monthly reviews	At the beginning of each week, review the previous week's lesson At the end of the month review what students learnt the last four weeks. Don't allow students to forget past lessons once they've moved on or passed an exam

In the article, Rosenshine elaborates on all of the aforementioned functions with references to both the research and how to implement them in the classroom. Especially interesting, for example, is what he says on guided practice and active participation. In his opinion, the purpose of guided practice is to "supervise students initial practice on a skill and provide the active practice, enhancement, and elaboration necessary to move new learning from working memory into long-term memory" (p. 469).

Active participation

Active Participation

Rosenshine propagates active participation during explicit instruction, but how can you do this in a class? He presents a few ways to increase active participation, for example by asking all students to:

- Tell their answer to a peer.
- Make a short summary (one or two sentences) and share this orally with a peer or with the class.
- Write the answer on a whiteboard and then hold it up so that the teacher can see who understood it and who didn't.
- Give a thumbs-up when they think they have the answer so that the teacher can check the whole class and then cold-call one or two.
- Raise different coloured cards when the answer is a, b, or c.

Suitable for different learners

Rosenshine also gave some tips on how explicit instruction can be modified to suit different learners. He noted that when students have learning problems, are less knowledgeable, or are younger or when the material is complex or difficult, more review is necessary and the steps should be smaller and less is presented (i.e., fewer new things are presented). There's also a great need for well-guided practice and independent practice in the classroom setting where the teacher is always available as these students need lots of help and supervision. On the other hand,

> when students are faster or older, or when the material is less difficult, less review is necessary and more time can be spent on presenting new material There is also less need for guided practice and independent practice in class, and more of the independent practice can be done as homework because the students do not need as much help and supervision. (p. 474)

He followed up this article with a widely read article written explicitly for teachers published in *The American Educator* (Rosenshine, 2012), the journal of the American Federation of Teachers. There, he presents ten instructional principles that he distilled from research on (1) how our brains acquire and use new information (i.e., cognitive psychological research), (2) classroom practices of successful teachers whose students show the highest learning gains (i.e., teacher effectivity studies), and (3) findings from studies that taught learning strategies to students (i.e., empirical intervention studies). See Figure 12.1.

01 | Begin a lesson with a short review of previous learning: Daily review can strengthen previous learning and can lead to fluent recall.	**02** | Present new material in small steps with student practice after each step: Only present small amounts of new material at any time, and then assist students as they practice this material.
03 | Ask a large number of questions and check the responses of all students: Questions help students practice new information and connect new material to their prior learning. 	**04** | Provide models: Providing students with models and worked examples can help them learn to solve problems faster.
05 | Guide student practice: Successful teachers spend more time guiding students' practice of new material. 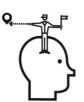	**06** | Check for student understanding: Checking for student understanding at each point can help students learn the material with fewer errors. 
07 | Obtain a high success rate: It is important for students to achieve a high success rate during classroom instruction.	**08** | Provide scaffolds for difficult tasks: The teacher provides students with temporary supports and scaffolds to assist them when they learn difficult tasks. 
09 | Require and monitor independent practice: Students need extensive, successful, independent practice in order for skills and knowledge to become automatic.	**10** | Engage students in weekly and monthly review: Students need to be involved in extensive practice in order to develop well-connected and automatic knowledge. 

FIGURE 12.1
ROSENSHINE'S
TEN PRINCIPLES
(OLIVER
CAVIGLIOLI).

In that article (as well as in a pamphlet that he wrote for UNESCO in 2010), Rosenshine discusses each of the ten techniques beginning with a short discussion of the *research findings* underlying the techniques (the why) followed by a section on *In the classroom* (the how). For example, when discussing the first principle – beginning lessons with a short review of previous learning – he first discusses research on how daily review strengthens previous learning and leads to fluent recall and then proceeds to present a number of practical ways to do this in the classroom. He writes: "In addition, teachers might consider doing the following during their daily review:

■ Correct homework.
■ Review the concepts and skills that were practiced as part of the homework.
■ Ask students about points where they had difficulties or made errors
■ Review material where errors were made.
■ Review material that needs overlearning (i.e., newly acquired skills should be practiced well beyond the point of initial mastery, leading to automaticity)".

For Rosenshine, in order to learn effectively, students first must acquire new knowledge, rehearse it, and connect it to what they already know. Though many of the activities carried out may be hands-on, they're always carried out after learning/acquiring the foundation and not before. Further, it's imperative for teachers to spend significant amounts of time in guided practice, to ask loads of questions, and then to check for understanding and correct errors.

Conclusions

Barak Rosenshine was a very special researcher. On the one hand he did quite a lot of research on teacher effectiveness, a field of research that looks at the instructional procedures that are used by the most successful teachers. On the other hand, he was deeply into empirical research which looks at how the mind acquires and uses information as well as the procedures invented by researchers to help students learn. This convergence of these fields makes his writing all the more important and relevant for both theory and practice. Rosenshine best sums up the conclusions and implications we should draw from his work in his UNESCO pamphlet (p. 6), writing:

> Each of these three sources [cognitive science theory, classroom observation, cognitive research on instruction] has suggestions for classroom practice that are included in this pamphlet. An interesting

finding is that there is *no conflict at all* [italics are ours] between the instructional suggestions that come from each of these three sources. In other words, these three sources supplement and complement each other. And the fact that the instructional ideas from three different sources supplement and complement each other gives us faith in the validity of these findings.

Takeaways

Let's just use Barak Rosenshine's own takeaways filled in with one of our own (the first):

- Explicit instruction isn't lecturing, boring, or demotivating. Burn the strawman!
- Start lessons by correcting the previous night's homework and/or reviewing what was recently been taught.
- Alert students to the goals of the lesson and then present new information a little at a time.
- Model procedures, give clear examples, and check often to make sure students understand.
- Allow substantial practice with the new information under your direction.
- Ask lots of questions to allow students to correctly repeat or explain a procedure or concept.
- Give lots of feedback during guided practice. See *How Learning Happens*, Chapter 20 for more on the what and how.
- Let students practice on their own and intervene only when necessary.
- Let students help each other.
- At the beginning of each week, review the previous week's lesson and at the end of the month review what students have learned during the last four weeks.

References

ROSENSHINE, B.V. (1976). CLASSROOM INSTRUCTION. IN N. GAGE (ED.), *THE PSYCHOLOGY OF TEACHING METHODS, 75TH YEARBOOK OF THE NATIONAL SOCIETY FOR THE STUDY OF EDUCATION.* UNIVERSITY OF CHICAGO PRESS.

ROSENSHINE, B.V. (1979). CONTENT, TIME, AND DIRECT INSTRUCTION. IN P. L. PETERSON & H. J. WALBERG (EDS.), *RESEARCH ON TEACHING: CONCEPTS. FINDINGS AND IMPLICATIONS* (PP. 28–56). MCCUTCHAN PUBLISHING.

ROSENSHINE, B.V. (1986). SYNTHESIS OF RESEARCH ON EXPLICIT TEACHING. *EDUCATIONAL LEADERSHIP, 43,* 60–69.

AVAILABLE VIA HTTPS://TINYURL.COM/YA9DD9T9

ROSENSHINE, B.V. (2010). *PRINCIPLES OF INSTRUCTION; EDUCATIONAL PRACTICES SERIES* (VOL. 21). THE INTERNATIONAL ACADEMY OF EDUCATION.

AVAILABLE VIA HTTPS://TINYURL.COM/UDCC7K5C

ROSENSHINE, B.V. (2012). PRINCIPLES OF INSTRUCTION: RESEARCH-BASED STRATEGIES THAT ALL TEACHERS SHOULD KNOW. *AMERICAN EDUCATOR, 36*(1), 12–39.

AVAILABLE VIA HTTPS://FILES.ERIC.ED.GOV/FULLTEXT/EJ971753.PDF

Suggested Readings and Links

BOXER, A. (2019). *THE RESEARCHED GUIDE TO EXPLICIT & DIRECT INSTRUCTION: AN EVIDENCE-INFORMED GUIDE FOR TEACHERS.* JOHN CATT.
In this book, Adam Boxer examines direct instruction, editing contributions from a broad swath of writers with theoretical and practical knowledge of direct instruction.

AVAILABLE VIA WWW.JOHNCATTBOOKSHOP.COM/ THE-RESEARCHED-GUIDE-TO-DIRECT-INSTRUCTION

VIDEOS

WHY EXPLICIT INSTRUCTION?

Explicit instruction expert, Dr Anita Archer, provides the rationale and overview of explicit instruction and its benefit to students.

DESCRIPTION – PREFERABLY APA6

AVAILABLE VIA WWW.YOUTUBE.COM/WATCH?V=I-QNPFTCYNI

NATIONAL CENTER ON INTENSIVE INTERVENTION: EXPLICIT INSTRUCTION MODULE 5

Module 5 begins a series of modules on the topic of explicit instruction. Explicit instruction is about modelling and practicing to help students reach academic goals.

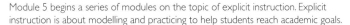

AVAILABLE VIA WWW.YOUTUBE.COM/WATCH?V=OWFGF0RDEC0

THIS VIDEO OF BARAK ROSENSHINE TALKING ABOUT EXPLICIT INSTRUCTION AND "HIGHER ORDER THINKING SKILLS" IS ONE OF THE SINGLE MOST IMPORTANT THINGS FOR TEACHERS TO KNOW ABOUT LEARNING.

AVAILABLE VIA WWW.YOUTUBE.COM/WATCH?V=N3KNHHRFTLA

WEBSITES

EXPLICIT INSTRUCTION: WHAT YOU NEED TO KNOW

Kim Greene discusses how explicit instruction is a way to teach skills or concepts to students using direct, structured instruction. It helps make lessons clear by modelling for students how to start and succeed on a task and giving them ample time to practice.

AVAILABLE VIA HTTPS://TINYURL.COM/3JF3BRW7

WHAT IS EXPLICIT INSTRUCTION?

AVAILABLE VIA HTTPS://MY.VANDERBILT.EDU/SPEDTEACHERRESOURCES/ WHAT-IS-EXPLICIT-INSTRUCTION/

WHAT DOES EXPLICIT INSTRUCTION IN SCIENCE LOOK LIKE?

ADAM BOXER, A BRILLIANT CHEMISTRY TEACHER AT A SCHOOL IN NORTH LONDON, EXPLAINS DIRECT INSTRUCTION AND SHOWS HOW TO IMPLEMENT IT IS CHEMISTRY LESSONS.

AVAILABLE VIA HTTPS://TINYURL.COM/4RP7JYCS

13 MAKE SOMETHING OF WHAT YOU'VE LEARNT

LOGAN FIORELLA & RICHARD MAYER ON WAYS TO GENERATE LEARNING

DOI: 10.4324/9781003228165-16

13 MAKE SOMETHING OF WHAT YOU'VE LEARNT

ARTICLE Eight ways to promote generative learning[1]

QUOTE *"The mind . . . is not a passive consumer of information", rather, "i* *actively constructs its own interpretations of information and draw: inferences on them."*[2]

Why You Should Read This Article

We have many tools at our disposal as teachers or learners. Take Microsoft Excel® as an example. One way to use this programme is to simply fill in the cells following a recipe that you've learnt or have been given for setting up and filling in the spreadsheet. As such, it can be a great production tool to help you keep track of your administration in th classroom (expenditures, time spent, students and their progress, and sc further). Excel is a tool that you can use in a very limited capacity but it can also be used in myriad useful ways if you know how to employ it to i fullest potential.

This same tool can also be used to get learners to think about (and generate) relationships between the different variables in the spreadsheet, to understand why when one parameter changes within the spreadsheet other parameters change too, to see the spreadsheet as a dynamic system. If you employ Excel in this way, the simple production tool becomes a mindtool; a tool for thinking and generating learning.

In the same way, there are teaching and learning tools (i.e., pedagogie strategies) that can be used in highly evolved ways, such that they become mindtools. This idea of using learning tools to generate new thoughts, ideas, and knowledge is similar to what Logan Fiorella and

---

1   FIORELLA, L., & MAYER, R. E. (2016). EIGHT WAYS TO PROMOTE GENERATIVE LEARNING. *EDUCATION PSYCHOLOGY REVIEW, 28,* 717–741. HTTPS://LINK.SPRINGER.COM/ARTICLE/10.1007/S10648-015-934: REPRINTED BY PERMISSION FROM SPRINGER NATURE.
2   WITTROCK, M. C. (1989). GENERATIVE PROCESSES OF COMPREHENSION. *EDUCATIONAL PSYCHOLOG 24,* 345–376. (P. 348)

Richard Mayer proposed when they introduced the term "generative learning."

Abstract of the Article

Generative learning involves actively making sense of to-be-learned information by mentally reorganising and integrating it with one's prior knowledge, thereby enabling learners to apply what they have learned to new situations. In this article, we present eight learning strategies intended to promote generative learning: summarising, mapping, drawing, imagining, self-testing, self-explaining, teaching, and enacting. First, we provide an overview of generative learning theory, grounded in Wittrock's (1974) generative model of comprehension and reflected in more recent frameworks of active learning, such as Mayer's (2014) select-organise-integrate (SOI) framework. Next, for each of the eight generative learning strategies, we provide a description, review exemplary research studies, discuss potential boundary conditions, and provide practical recommendations for implementation. Finally, we discuss the implications of generative learning for the science of learning, and we suggest directions for further research.

Select-Organise-Integrate (SOI) Framework

The Article

Generative learning activities/strategies

In 2015, Richard Mayer and Logan Fiorella published their book *Learning as a Generative Activity* describing eight generative learning activities or strategies. They're called generative (and sometimes also productive) because they allow or coerce learners to remould the information that they are presented and based on that, create their own output, such as a summary or a drawing. In other words, learners generate/produce something themselves based on and that goes further than what they've learned.

Learning as construction

Fiorella and Mayer trace the roots of generative learning back to Frederic Bartlett, the man who in 1932 first referred to knowledge structures in our heads as schemas, who regarded learning as an act of schema construction. Fast forward to Merlin Wittrock's (1974) generative model of learning based on the idea that learners "generate perceptions and meanings that are consistent with their prior knowledge" (p. 88) and that "learning with understanding involves the process of generating and transferring meaning for stimuli and events from one's background, attitudes, abilities, and experiences" (p. 93).

Select, Organise, and Integrate (SOI) memory model

In their article, they present eight learning strategies intended to promote generative learning, namely summarising, mapping, drawing, imagining, self-testing, self-explaining, teaching, and enacting. Each strategy prompts learners to apply Mayer's Select, Organise, and Integrate (SOI) memory model (1996). This model stipulates that there are three cognitive processes involved in meaningful learning, namely *selecting* relevant information from what is presented, *organising* selected information into coherent representations, and *integrating* presented information with existing knowledge (see Figure 13.1).

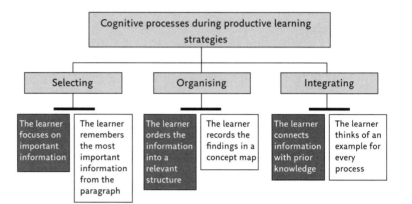

FIGURE 13.1
MAYER'S
SELECTION,
ORGANISING,
AND
INTEGRATING
(SOI) MEMORY
MODEL (BASED
ON *FIORELLA &
MAYER, 2016*).

These strategies ensure that learners engage with what they're learning in a cognitively active way. It makes them seek out and connect pieces of information in whatever the form of instruction, verbally or visually generate and show the relationships between the different pieces, and, thus, construct their own idiosyncratic ways of thinking about it. The astute reader who possibly also read *HLH* will remember Section 1 on how the brain works where we presented what our cognitive architecture looks. This SOI model fits that perfectly (see Figure 13.2).

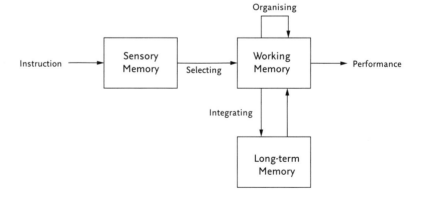

FIGURE 13.2
THE SOI MODEL
IN RELATION
TO COGNITIVE
ARCHITECTURE
(ADAPTED FROM
*FIORELLA & MAYER,
2016*).

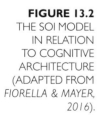

Generative learning:
Transforming
information into
knowledge

In short, generative learning is the process of transforming incoming information (e.g., words and pictures) into usable knowledge (e.g., mental models, schemas). As such, generative learning depends not only on how information is presented to learners (i.e., instructional methods) but on how learners try to make sense of it (i.e., learning strategies). Although much research focuses on instructional methods – that is, what the instructor can do to promote learning.

The Eight Techniques

As stated, the authors propose eight techniques or study strategies to promote generative learning, namely summarising, mapping, drawing, imagining, self-testing, self-explaining, teaching, and enacting. Let's discuss each of them.

Summarising Summarising: When you make a summary you must succinctly give the main ideas of what you heard or read in your own words. To be generative, the summary must be more than verbatim transcription of a lesson or writing down the exact words or phrases from what you've read. It requires selecting the key ideas from a lesson, organising them, and integrating it in what you already know (prior knowledge). Often, it will also include your own interpretation of those ideas based on your prior knowledge.

Mapping Mapping: Mapping isn't one specific thing, but rather a group of techniques to convert printed or spoken text into a spatial arrangement of words and links connecting them. Three examples are concept maps, knowledge maps, and graphic organisers.

Concept map

THREE EXAMPLES OF MAPPING

A *concept map* is a visual representation of information depicting the main concepts and ideas of a lesson, often as boxes or circles, and the relationships among them, often as lines or arrows with linking phrases specifying the relation.

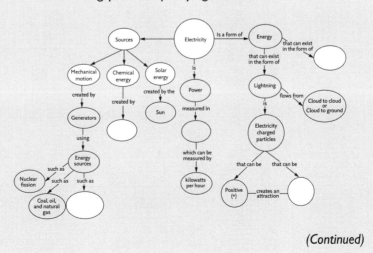

(Continued)

(Continued)

Knowledge map

A *knowledge map* "is a particular kind of concept map in which the links are restricted to a set of basic predefined relations such as part of, type of, leads to, and characteristic of" (p. 722).

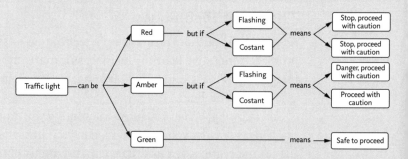

Graphic organiser

A *graphic organiser* is itself a collection of graphical displays, but where the key ideas are arranged within a predefined structure, such as a matrix, flow chart, or hierarchy which, respectively, can be used for comparing-and-contrasting, cause-and-effect, and a classification hierarchy.

Comparison Matrix					
Nutrients	Broccoli	Steak	Bread	Pizza	Apple
Proteins					
Fats					
Carbohydtrates					
Sugar Carbs					
Salt					
Other					

Comparison Matrix					
Nutrients	Broccoli	Steak	Bread	Pizza	Apple
Proteins					
Fats					
Carbohydtrates					
Sugar Carbs					
Salt					
Other					

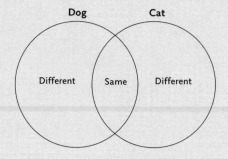

Drawing

Drawing: When drawing, you create a drawing depicting the lesson content. You can do this either by hand (paper and pen/pencil) or electronically with a computer or tablet. When you draw, you have to translate a text (written or audio) to a pictorial representation. This requires selecting the key ideas from a lesson, organising them spatially, and using your prior knowledge to clarify the meaning of the text and its relation to the drawing.

Imagining

Imagining: When imagining, you form mental images of the content of a lesson while reading or listening.

Self-testing

Self-Testing: Self-testing is a form of retrieval practice (testing effect) which usually involves multiple testing or quizzing over a period of time where you have to recall the material from memory, helping to make the material "stick". This was discussed in Chapter 19 of *HLH* as assessment for learning.

Self-explaining

Self-Explaining: When self-explaining you explain the lesson content to yourself while studying. John Dunlosky and colleagues (2013; also Chapter 21 of *HLH*) define it as "Explaining [to yourself] how new information is related to known information, or explaining steps taken during problem solving". In a way, it's similar to what teachers do when the use elaborative interrogation. For example, if you're reading a text on how car brakes work, you could try to explain to yourself how disc-brakes differ from drum-brakes, focusing on any conclusions or inferences relating to them and their use (why one works better or worse than the other and in what situations), determining what you need to clarify or have clarified about the brakes, and/or thinking of situations where one or the other would be better.

Teaching

Teaching: Learning by teaching (peer-teaching) is similar to learning by self-explaining but here you have to explain the to-be-learned material to someone else with the goal of helping them understand and learn. Thus, you need to place yourself in the shoes of a peer who possibly knows less than you. You need to think up examples that will help them, analogies that will make the content clearer to them, and so further. Ideally, you should also test whether they understand what you've taught them which would involve a form of self-testing.

Enacting

Enacting: Enacting involves carrying out task-relevant movements during learning, such as when you manipulate objects or make gestures in coordination with the lesson content. An example might be to place dolls in a formation similar to how the three witches, Hecate, and Macbeth were in the famous cauldron scene. Why enacting works is usually explained in terms of embodied theories of cognition and instruction which holds that our cognitive processes are grounded in our physical interactions with our surroundings.

Conclusions

Along with presenting scientific evidence about how and when the strategies work or don't work, Fiorella and Mayer also give practical recommendations on how to implement the strategies and what the obstacles/problems of using them are. Of course, it's best to read them yourself, but we'll present a few here.

Strategies must be taught and practised

Summarising: Summarising isn't something that comes naturally without instruction and practise. It's only effective when learners have *learnt, practised*, and *mastered* the "art" of summarising. Students – particularly younger ones – need extensive training in how to summarise (i.e., selecting main ideas and stating them in their own words). Nota bene, this is true for all of the techniques!

Mapping: Fiorella and Mayer note two major obstacles for mapping, namely that students here too may need extensive training in how to create useful maps and that they may lose interest in constructing maps it's too tedious and time-consuming.

Drawing: You must be careful in how to implement drawing. Students need very specific directions on what to draw (i.e., what should or shouldn't be included. The authors also recommend that you minimise "the mechanics of drawing", for example by giving students a "predrawn background and simple elements in the margins that can be easily copied" (p. 723).

Pre-drawn background and simple elements

Imagining: As a teacher, you need to understand potential difficulties involved in generating useful mental images. First, students need sufficient prior knowledge to effectively imagine especially when the material is complex for the learner. Second, it's helpful to provide very specific prompts on what to imagine going as far as explicitly telling them what to include.

Self-Testing: Unlike the preceding techniques, self-testing doesn't require extensive training. If you use self-testing, remember that practice testing should be (1) combined with immediate feedback (see *How Learning Happens*, Chapters 19 and 20) to correct errors or misconceptions and (2) carried out frequently and repeatedly.

Self-Explaining: Self-explaining can't be used for everything. It works extremely well for understanding and learning complex conceptual material, but not for simple facts. This is because it's intended to help students reflect on their own understanding of the material, recognize misconceptions, and repair faulty mental models" (p. 728). It can also be very useful when the learning involves complex diagrams or examples.

Reflect on understanding

Teaching: Teaching isn't just telling (as you know better than anyone! It involves preparing, explaining, and interacting. Students need to understand the stages and go through them. Also, studying something, knowing that you'll have to teach it to a peer (i.e., preparing) may help develop better quality explanations when actually peer-teaching. Answering a peer's questions may also lead to deeper cognitive processing as you're forced to reflect on your own understanding and elaborate it beyond the material itself.

Enacting: To use enacting effectively, students need "explicit guidance in how to perform specific actions intended to promote learning – that is, guidance in how to map specific gestures to problem-solving strategies . . . or how to map other body movements or specific object manipulations to underlying events described in a story" (p. 731).

Takeaways

- Generative learning involves *selecting* relevant information, *organising* it into coherent representations, and *integrating* it with existing (prior) knowledge.
- Generative learning ensures that learners engage with what they're learning in a cognitively active way, making them seek out and connect pieces of information in whatever the form of instruction.
- Generative learning techniques are skills that need to be acquired. Many, if not all, need to be learnt and extensively practised by students before they can work.
- Students don't carry out the activities by themselves. Left to their own devices, research shows that they'll revert to rereading or highlighting, both of which have been shown to be ineffective. This means that they must be told to do the activities. Hopefully they'll experience that these *desirable difficulties* (see Chapter 14) lead to better learning and eventually use them without external direction.
- Nothing works everywhere and everything works somewhere so be careful to choose the proper strategy for your goals and the content.

References

DUNLOSKY, J., RAWSON, K. A., MARSH, E. J., NATHAN, M. J., & WILLINGHAM, D. T. (2013). IMPROVING STUDENTS' LEARNING WITH EFFECTIVE LEARNING TECHNIQUES: PROMISING DIRECTIONS FROM COGNITIVE AND EDUCATIONAL PSYCHOLOGY. *PSYCHOLOGICAL SCIENCE IN THE PUBLIC INTEREST, 14*, 4–58.

FIORELLA, L., & MAYER, R. E. (2016). EIGHT WAYS TO PROMOTE GENERATIVE LEARNING. *EDUCATIONAL PSYCHOLOGY REVIEW, 28*, 717–741.

MAYER, R. E. (1996). LEARNING STRATEGIES FOR MAKING SENSE OUT OF EXPOSITORY TEXT: THE SOI MODEL FOR GUIDING THREE COGNITIVE PROCESSES IN KNOWLEDGE CONSTRUCTION. *EDUCATIONAL PSYCHOLOGY REVIEW, 8*, 357–371.

MAYER, R. E. (2014). COGNITIVE THEORY OF MULTIMEDIA LEARNING. IN R. E. MAYER (ED.), *THE CAMBRIDGE HANDBOOK OF MULTIMEDIA LEARNING* (SECOND EDITION, PP. 43–71). CAMBRIDGE UNIVERSITY PRESS.

WITTROCK, M. C. (1974). LEARNING AS A GENERATIVE PROCESS. *EDUCATIONAL PSYCHOLOGIST, 11*(2), 87–95.

WITTROCK, M. C. (1989). GENERATIVE PROCESSES OF COMPREHENSION. *EDUCATIONAL PSYCHOLOGIST, 24,* 345–376.

Suggested Readings and Links

BROD, G. (2021). GENERATIVE LEARNING: WHICH STRATEGIES FOR WHAT AGE? *EDUCATIONAL PSYCHOLOGY REVIEW, 33,* 1295–1318.
AVAILABLE VIA HTTPS://LINK.SPRINGER.COM/ARTICLE/10.1007/S10648-020-09571-9

ENSER, Z., & ENSER, M. (2020). *FIORELLA & MAYER'S GENERATIVE LEARNING IN ACTION.* JOHN CATT EDUCATION LTD.

Generative Learning in Action helps to answer the question: which activities can students carry out to create meaningful learning? It does this by considering how we, as teachers, can implement the eight strategies for generative learning set out in the work of Fiorella and Mayer in their seminal 2015 work *Learning as a Generative Activity: Eight Learning Strategies that Promote Learning.*

VIDEOS

AN INTRODUCTION TO GENERATIVE LEARNING BY ZOE AND MARK ENSER. IN THIS VIDEO, THEY EXPLAIN THE PRINCIPLES BEHIND THE THEORY AND EXPLORE HOW IT COULD BE PUT INTO ACTION.

AVAILABLE VIA WWW.YOUTUBE.COM/WATCH?V=SUC0MG3BEOM

WEBSITES

LET'S GET TO WORK WITH PRODUCTIVE LEARNING STRATEGIES: SUMMARISING: THE FIRST IN A SERIES OF EIGHT BLOGS, ORIGINALLY WRITTEN BY TINE HOOF, TIM SURMA & PAUL A. KIRSCHNER ON FIORELLA AND MAYER'S GENERATIVE LEARNING STRATEGIES. FOLLOW THIS FOR THE OTHER SEVEN.

AVAILABLE VIA HTTPS://TINYURL.COM/2J9P36D6

VISUAL TOOLS CAN NOT ONLY LEAD TO STUDENTS SIGNIFICANTLY IMPROVING CONTENT AND CONCEPTUAL LEARNING BUT ENGENDER SELF REFLECTION AND EMPATHIC UNDERSTANDING. IN ADVANCE OF HIS COURSE FOR TEACHINGTIMES, DAVID HYERLE, PROVIDES AN INSIGHT IN THEIR POWER AND PROMISE

AVAILABLE VIA WWW.TEACHINGTIMES.COM/VISUAL-TOOLS-FOR-THINKING-AND-LEARNING/

A LIST OF TYPES OF GRAPHIC ORGANIZERS ACCOMPANIED BY A TEMPLATE FOR USING THEM

AVAILABLE VIA HTTPS://CREATELY.COM/BLOG/DIAGRAMS/TYPES-OF-GRAPHIC-ORGANIZERS/

14 LEARNING: NO PAIN, NO GAIN

ROBERT BJORK ON DESIRABLE DIFFICULTIES

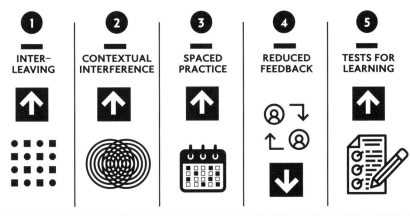

1	2	3	4	5
INTER-LEAVING	CONTEXTUAL INTERFERENCE	SPACED PRACTICE	REDUCED FEEDBACK	TESTS FOR LEARNING

DESIRABLE DIFFICULTIES

DOI: 10.4324/9781003228165-17

14 LEARNING: NO PAIN, NO GAIN

CHAPTER Memory and metamemory considerations in the training of human beings[1]

QUOTE *"Conditions that yield a high rate of correct responses during training can fail to support performance in the posttraining environment; conversely, conditions that appear to slow or impede performance during training can enhance the subsequent real-world performance."*[2]

Why You Should Read This Chapter

Imagine you're training to play a sport like football (soccer for our American friends) – and the coach trains you in all of the aspects of the game but without an opponent. Or that you're practicing free kicks but with a row of dummy defenders and without a goalkeeper. While you may perfect some specific aspects of the different situations, you'll probably be near worthless in a match. Why? Because you haven't practiced dribbling while a defender has tried to steal the ball or when two or more defenders converge on you or . . . for the free kick, you've learned to kick the ball, but there were no defenders jumping and/or rushing you, no teammates ready to change the ball's trajectory and no goalkeeper who tried to break your concentration or who dove to block your shot. These are some of the things, among many, that you encounter in a real life match. A good trainer will add these to the training. They'll make all of the things more difficult to carry out, but these difficulties are desirable because only with them will you learn and acquire the skills needed to play your position in a match situation. The trainer has

---

1 BJORK, R. A. (1994B). MEMORY AND METAMEMORY CONSIDERATIONS IN THE TRAINING OF HUMA BEINGS. IN J. METCALFE & A. SHIMAMURA (EDS.), *METACOGNITION: KNOWING ABOUT KNOWIN* (PP. 185–205). MIT PRESS.
2 BJORK, R. A. (1994A). INSTITUTIONAL IMPEDIMENTS TO EFFECTIVE TRAINING. IN D. DRUCKMAN & R BJORK (EDS.), *LEARNING, REMEMBERING, BELIEVING: ENHANCING INDIVIDUAL AND TEAM PERFORMAN* (PP. 295–306). NATIONAL ACADEMY PRESS.

employed "desirable difficulties"; strategically chosen and implemented impediments that have helped you learn and ultimately function better when you really need to.

Robert Bjork is the man who coined the phrase desirable difficulties with respect to learning and training. This chapter discusses what desirable difficulties are, how and why they work, and what a number of desirable difficulties for learning are.

Abstract of the Chapter

In recent papers, Christina and Bjork (1991) and Schmidt and Bjork (1992) have argued that training programs are often much less effective than they could be. A central part of the argument is that individuals responsible for training are often misled as to what are, and are not, effective conditions of practice. Conditions that enhance performance during training are assumed, implicitly or explicitly, to be the conditions of choice with respect to enhancing the goal of training: namely, long-term posttraining performance. That assumption, however, is frequently questionable and sometimes dramatically wrong. Manipulations that speed the rate of acquisition during training can fail to support long-term posttraining performance, while other manipulations that appear to introduce difficulties for the learner during training can enhance posttraining performance.

The Chapter

Remember and recall
The goal of education or teaching is, or at least should be, that learners can remember and recall what they've learnt long after it's been taught and that they can transfer what they've learnt to new/other situations both inside and outside the school environment. In other words the learning should be durable, not only until the exam or the end of the term but much later in the next class, school level, and the rest of their lives even after not using it for a while.

Cognitive schema
A second goal of education is to help learners form a representation (we call this a mental or cognitive schema) that they can quickly and easily access the knowledge or skill when it's needed. That learners can draw upon that schema in situations that differ from the learning situation and generalise it to those situations. In Bjork's words, "Stated in terms of human memory, then, we would like a training program not only to produce a stored representation of the targeted knowledge in long-term memory, but also to yield a representation that remains accessible (recallable) as time passes and contextual cues change" (p. 186–187).

Human memory is peculiar in that we don't store information in our long-term memories as literal recordings that we can play back when needed, but rather that we store it in a semantic way in terms of what it means to us and how it's associated to other things in our memory.

SEMANTIC VS. EPISODIC MEMORY

Semantic and episodic memory

Semantic memory is the knowledge that we have accumulated in our long-term memories about what we know of the world around us. It consists of facts, ideas, and concepts and is entwined in our experiences and is dependent on our culture. Examples of what we can have in our semantic memory include the number of lines in a sonnet and the possible rhyme schemes used, what the northern lights (aurora borealis) are, how to bake cookies, and knowing what animals are mammals and what the characteristics of mammals are.

Episodic memory, on the other hand, is a type of long-term memory that involves the recollection of specific events, situations, and experiences that we have encountered (i.e., episodes in our lives). Examples of what we can have in our episodic memory are what you remember about how you felt when you first read a Shakespeare sonnet, how your grandmother's cookies tasted and smelled, what the northern lights looked like in Finland when you camped there with your partner, and how amazed you were when you saw a tree shrew and a blue whale at a museum exhibition and learned that they were both mammals.

Encoding and Retrieval

The more often and the more ways we store (encode) it, the better. A second peculiarity of our memory is that retrieving information itself is a powerful learning event. The information that we recall isn't left in the same state it was prior to our retrieving it. Retrieving the information actually makes that information more recallable in the future. Bjork calls the act of retrieval a *memory modifier*. The more often and the more ways we retrieve information the better and easier future recall is. He posits that "as a learning event . . . a successful retrieval can be considerably more potent than an additional study opportunity, particularly in terms of facilitating long-term recall" (p. 188). In other words, durable and flexible learning is partly determined by how that information is encoded/stored (i.e., whether and how it is understood) and partly by practicing the retrieval process.

The Need to Introduce Difficulties for the Learner

Bjork at this point asks the question: "What specific manipulations of training, then, are best able to foster the long-term goals of training, whether stated in terms of measures of posttraining performance or in terms of underlying memory representations?" (p. 189). While being cognisant of the fact that the exact blend of techniques is debatable, one general characteristic of that mixture is that it would introduce difficulties and challenges for the learner. At this point he introduces five – in his words – manipulations that we today call desirable difficulties.

The first manipulation (desirable difficulty) is *varying the conditions of practice*. Similar to what Van Merriënboer posits in his 4 *Component Instruction Design model* (4C/ID; see Chapter 8) Bjork states that "introducing variation and/or unpredictability in the training environment causes difficulty for the learner but enhances long-term performance – particularly the ability to transfer training to novel but related task environments" (p. 189). We now call this *interleaving*. Yes, practicing the same thing over and over in the same situation will lead to speed and accuracy at that moment (for example practicing calculating the area of a right-angle triangle for ten such triangles and a day later doing the same for an obtuse triangle, and so on), but when confronted with all different types of triangles where you need to calculate the area, it would have been better to have mixed all the different types of triangles during learning and practice. Practicing tasks in random fashion, rather than blocking by task type, might impair performance during learning but enhances long-term performance.

Interleaving

The second desirable difficulty is *providing contextual interference*. Very similar to the first, here you make the task environment – not the task – more variable or unpredictable "in a way that creates, at least temporarily, interference for the learner" (p. 190). Here, things are practiced under conditions in which certain contextual factors prohibit quick and smooth mastery like varying the difficulty or the redundancy of information (sometimes certain information is present and sometimes it isn't). Consider troubleshooting and then remedying a process like distilling whisky. In one task the process is disrupted by one factor (the heat of the stoking fire) and in the other the amount of sugar in the malted barley. Anyone learning to distil whisky would have to contend with this kind of contextual interference, yet an approach such as this has been shown to lead to better retention and transfer performance than practice under non-interfering conditions.

Contextual interference

The third difficulty is *distributing practice on a given task*. We as teachers and students as learners tend to mass practice or study sessions

Distributed practice or Spaced practice

into one long whole (e.g., cramming for an exam the night before) which produces better short-term performance or recall on the exam, while distributing practice or study sessions on a given task over time (e.g., studying for the exam over a few shorter study sessions spread over time) is markedly superior for long-term performance or recall.

Reducing feedback

Difficulty number four is *reducing feedback to the learner*. Bjork notes that while it's commonly held that giving feedback aids in skill acquisition, and the more immediate, frequent, and/or accurate it is, the better it is for learning and performance. In contrast, he states that based upon research by Richard Schmidt and colleagues (e.g., Schmidt, 1991; Winstein & Schmidt, 1990), reducing feedback frequency makes life more difficult for the learner *during* training, but can enhance post-training performance. The reason for this is that frequent feedback can guide learners toward expected performance and even create a dependency where they rely on the feedback to guide their behaviour. When this happens, "the learning needed to produce proficient posttraining performance in retention or transfer either does not occur or occurs only at a weak level" (Christina & Bjork, 1991, p. 47), putting the learner at a disadvantage when there is little or no feedback.

Retrieval practice

The fifth and final desirable difficulty is *using tests as learning events*, what we now call retrieval practice. In this respect, retrieving what has been learnt is considerably better for long-term retention than restudying what you've learnt in facilitating future recall. Also, prior testing increases the learning on subsequent study trials (that is, reading, testing and then rereading). As is the case with the other desirable difficulties, using tests rather than restudy or increasing the difficulty of such tests, may seem counterproductive *during* learning as measured by a test at the end of the study session, but leads to better recall after a delay. This success is increased when the testing events are spaced over time (see difficulty 3).

The Million Dollar Question

The question is then, if we know all of this then why "are massed practice, excessive feedback, fixed conditions of training, and limited opportunities for retrieval practice – among other nonproductive manipulations – such common features of real-world training programs?" (p. 193). Bjork chalks this up to three things: misperceptions of the trainer, metamemory considerations, and misperceptions of the learner.

Teacher misperceptions

"Misperceptions of the teacher" is an umbrella term for a number of phenomena. First, teachers are overexposed to the daily performance and evaluative reactions of their students. Teachers are vulnerable to, in Bjork's words, "a type of operant conditioning, where the reinforcing events are improvements in the performance and/or happiness" (p. 193) of students. Second, teachers are often evaluated in terms of their students" performance and satisfaction. Short-term performance and ease of study determine the evaluation score more than long-term learning and transfer. Third, teachers don't see the long-term results. Students go off to other grades with other teachers or even other schools so later success or failure isn't seen.

Performance vs.
Learning

PERFORMANCE VS. LEARNING

When we speak of "learning" we're talking about relatively long-lasting/permanent changes in our long-term memory (Kirschner et al., 2006) or behaviour. On the other hand, when we speak of "performance" we're talking about temporary changes or variations in our knowledge or behaviour that is usually determined during or directly after the learning experience. In other words, performance is a short-term change while learning is long-term change. One is observable while the other is largely invisible.

Metacognition

Metamemory, or what we nowadays call metacognition, is the extent to which learners can validly and reliably judge their own learning or competence. Bjork states, "Individuals who have illusions of comprehension or competence pose a greater hazard to themselves and others than do individuals who correctly assess that they lack some requisite information or skill" (p. 194). Judging one's own learning isn't something that children or adolescents (and very often also adults) are very good at. Rereading gives the illusion of having learnt something because when you reread something you think "Yeah, I recognise that", but recognising that you've read something before is quite different from being able to recall it later. Also, rapid progress which one experiences when doing the same calculation of triangle area ten times in a row is comforting to the learner, though little learning may be happening. Struggling and making errors, on the other hand, are distressing, even though real learning may be happening. This misreading of progress can lead students to prefer less effective study strategies above effective ones.

Learner
misperceptions

Finally, *misperceptions of the learner* where one index is used to predict another can inhibit using successful strategies. Learners, for example, may be fooled by their own successes during learning. They observe their own performance during learning and then assume that their success in the learning situation (i.e., the ability to calculate a right-angle triangle's area after the fourth or fifth of ten massed tasks) predicts future success and that instances of failure inherent to desirable difficulties (i.e., varying practice conditions or contextual interference) predict future failure. In effect, they rely on an "unreliable index – the current ease of access to a correct answer or procedure – as a measure of the extent to which learning in a broader sense has been achieved" (p. 196). A second unreliable index is familiarity or fluency. When something looks familiar to you, as just mentioned with respect to rereading, you use that familiarity, wrongly, as an index for learning.

An implication of these misperceptions is that both the learner and the teacher don't receive meaningful objective information on the teaching/learning process, but rather misleading subjective experiences. In this way we risk denying both the feedback essential for valid assessment of their current state of knowledge.

SEEING TEACHING AS AN INNATE GIFT IS TOXIC

TEACHING IS A COMPLEX skill requiring strong initial learning, but also effective life-long formal, informal, and nonformal learning. Both school management and teachers often see teaching not as something learnt, but, rather, as a gift bestowed on certain people. If you view teaching ability as an innate talent, criticism of your teaching — however constructive and specific it is — will often be seen as a personal attack on you and will subsequently be rejected and/or lead to bad feelings towards the critic. On the other hand, the well-meant criticism might be accepted, but then as evidence of your limited potential as a teacher which could make you less inclined to seek advice and feedback in the future, as well as limit your exploring alternative techniques and methods.

This "innate ability" notion is remarkably widespread. At lunch and elsewhere, we talk to each other about family, politics, sports, the weather, the stock market . . . "but rarely, if ever, about teaching strategies and techniques. It is as though talking about such matters is off limits — possibly because one is at risk of implying that a colleague has failings as a teacher or that one has an elevated opinion of one's own 'gifts' as a teacher" (Bjork, 1994a).

Conclusions

The best way to ensure that learners (1) remember and recall what they've learnt long after it's been taught and that (2) they can transfer what they've learnt to new/other situations both inside and outside the school environment involves making the learner's life a little more difficult in the short term. A way to do this is to introduce study and teaching strategies like varying the training conditions, inducing contextual interference, distributing practice in time and space, reducing feedback frequency, and using tests to learn. This requires a number of dramatic changes in all those in the education system.

At the teacher level, Robert Bjork's work means that teachers must gather information on student learning, not only from the tests and exams they give, but from longer term assessment experiences. It also means that they need to throw off the yoke of judging their own teaching in terms of student satisfaction and fluency of the teaching. That students like it, find it to be fun, think that they've understood and learnt, and/or can go through the lesson quickly doesn't mean that they actually learnt something and can recall and apply it in the long-term and in different situations.

Parallel to this, two other changes are needed. First, teachers must prove to (not just show) students that having things go a little slower and be a little harder are not bad things; that is, that the saying "No pain, no gain" is true for learning. Second, schools and other organisations must stop evaluating teachers and their teaching in terms of student performance, satisfaction, and/or self-reported judgements of learning during the lessons or at the end of the semester. They need to carry out comprehensive objective analyses of real, long-term learning looking at later successes and failures in settings far removed from both the original learning and the teacher.

Takeaways

- Intuition and standard practice are poor guides to teaching.
- Learning and performance are not the same thing.
- Introducing one or more desirable difficulties leads to better, long-term learning and transfer; no pain, no gain.
- Practicing tasks in random fashion, rather than blocking by task type, might impair performance during learning but enhances long-term performance.
- Providing contextual interference leads to better retention and transfer performance than practice under non-interfering conditions.
- Distributing practice on a given task instead of massing it is markedly superior is for long-term performance or recall.
- Though reducing feedback frequency makes life more difficult for the learner *during* training, it can enhance post-training performance.
- Using tests as learning events and not only as assessment moments is better for long-term retention than restudying what you've learnt in facilitating future recall.

- Using desirable difficulties is hindered by teacher misperceptions, student metacognition, and teacher misperceptions.
- Employing desirable difficulties requires a change in how the teacher assesses their own teaching and their students' learning as well in how schools and organisations evaluate teachers.

References

BJORK, R. A. (1994A). INSTITUTIONAL IMPEDIMENTS TO EFFECTIVE TRAINING. IN D. DRUCKMAN & R. A. BJORK (EDS.), *LEARNING, REMEMBERING, BELIEVING: ENHANCING INDIVIDUAL AND TEAM PERFORMANCE* (PP. 295–306). NATIONAL ACADEMY PRESS.

BJORK, R. A. (1994B). MEMORY AND METAMEMORY CONSIDERATIONS IN THE TRAINING OF HUMAN BEINGS. IN J. METCALFE & A. SHIMAMURA (EDS.), *METACOGNITION: KNOWING ABOUT KNOWING* (PP. 185–205). MIT PRESS.

CHRISTINA, R. W., & BJORK, R. A. (1991). OPTIMIZING LONG-TERM RETENTION AND TRANSFER. IN D. DRUCKMAN & R. A. BJORK (EDS.), *IN THE MIND'S EYE: ENHANCING HUMAN PERFORMANCE* (PP. 23–56). NATIONAL ACADEMY PRESS.

KIRSCHNER, P. A., SWELLER, J., & CLARK, R. E. (2006). WHY MINIMAL GUIDANCE DURING INSTRUCTION DOES NOT WORK: AN ANALYSIS OF THE FAILURE OF CONSTRUCTIVIST, DISCOVERY, PROBLEM-BASED, EXPERIENTIAL, AND INQUIRY-BASED TEACHING. *EDUCATIONAL PSYCHOLOGIST*, 46(2), 75–86.

SCHMIDT, R. A. (1991). FREQUENT AUGMENTED FEEDBACK CAN DEGRADE LEARNING: EVIDENCE AND INTERPRETATIONS. IN G. E. STELMACH & J. REQUIN (EDS.), *TUTORIALS IN MOTOR NEUROSCIENCE* (PP. 59–75). KLUWER ACADEMIC PUBLISHERS.

SCHMIDT, R. A., & BJORK, R. A. (1992). NEW CONCEPTUALIZATIONS OF PRACTICE: COMMON PRINCIPLES IN THREE PARADIGMS SUGGEST NEW CONCEPTS FOR TRAINING. *PSYCHOLOGICAL SCIENCE*, 3, 207–217.

WINSTEIN, C. J., & SCHMIDT, R. A. (1990). REDUCED FREQUENCY OF KNOWLEDGE OF RESULTS ENHANCES MOTOR SKILL LEARNING. *JOURNAL OF EXPERIMENTAL PSYCHOLOGY: LEARNING, MEMORY, AND COGNITION*, 16, 677–691.

Suggested Readings and Links

BJORK, E. L., & BJORK, R. A. (2011). MAKING THINGS HARD ON YOURSELF, BUT IN A GOOD WAY: CREATING DESIRABLE DIFFICULTIES TO ENHANCE LEARNING. IN M. A. GERNSBACHER, R. W. PEW, L. M. HOUGH, J. R. POMERANTZ, & FABBS FOUNDATION (EDS.), *PSYCHOLOGY AND THE REAL WORLD: ESSAYS ILLUSTRATING FUNDAMENTAL CONTRIBUTIONS TO SOCIETY* (PP. 56–64). WORTH PUBLISHERS.

AVAILABLE VIA HTTPS://BJORKLAB.PSYCH.UCLA.EDU/WP-CONTENT/ UPLOADS/SITES/13/2016/04/EBJORK_RBJORK_2011.PDF

AN INTERVIEW WITH ELIZABETH AND ROBERT BJORK

AVAILABLE VIA HTTPS://BJORKLAB.PSYCH.UCLA.EDU/WP-CONTENT/ UPLOADS/SITES/13/2016/04/EBJORK_RBJORK_2011.PDF

VIDEOS

ROBERT BJORK AND ELIZABETH BJORK: MAKING THINGS HARD ON YOURSELF, BUT IN A GOOD WAY

Address given upon receiving the James McKeen Catteell Fellow Award May 201 in Chicago at the 28th Annual Convention of the Association for Psychological Science.

AVAILABLE VIA WWW.YOUTUBE.COM/WATCH?V=HSZDN8WMUZ4

HOW TO STUDY TO MAXIMISE PERFORMANCE: ELIZABETH BJORK & ROBERT BJORK:
In their informative, research-based TEDx talk, Elizabeth and Robert Bjork offer invaluable study skills for everyone who wants to maximise performance when it really counts.

AVAILABLE VIA WWW.YOUTUBE.COM/WATCH?V=0NIXM74NWXS

A presentation by plus a Q&A with Blake Harvard on Bjork and Bjork's desirable difficulties. He discusses four conditions that promote desirable difficulties for learning, how he creates these conditions in his classroom, and how teachers can work to make their learners desire these difficulties.

AVAILABLE VIA HTTPS://THEEFFORTFULEDUCATOR.COM/2020/07/23/DESIRABLE-DIFFICULTIES-PRESENTATION/

WEBSITES

THE BJORK LEARNING AND FORGETTING LAB

AVAILABLE VIA HTTPS://BJORKLAB.PSYCH.UCLA.EDU/

15

STEP FOR STEP

ROBERT ATKINSON AND COLLEAGUES ON EXAMPLES

15 STEP FOR STEP

ARTICLE Learning from examples: Instructional principles from the worked examples research[1]

QUOTE *"The worked examples literature is particularly relevant to programs of instruction that seek to promote skills acquisition, a goal of many workplace training environments as well as instructional programs in domains such as music, chess, athletics, programming, and (arguably) basic mathematics."*[2]

Why You Should Read This Article

You're just starting work on an essay for your CPD course about "Learning Styles: Myth or Reality?" so you have to collect the literature you'll need. What we often see is that people (both students and adults) type "learning styles" into Google (that is, if they know that quotes bring back sources that contain these exact words in this exact order), see what comes up (8,180,000 Google results with and 1,180,000,000 without quotes at the time of writing), choose some sources (from the more than eight million that Google returned!), and then begin reading and writing.

A better way would be to first select proper databases to search. Google returns everything including the kitchen sink, ranging from scientific literature to book reviews to blogs and opinion pieces written by Eduquacks[3] to paid content by companies propagating their own learning styles products for profit. Maybe it would be better to use a

---

[1] ATKINSON, R. K., DERRY, S. J., RENKL, A., & WORTHAM, D. (2000). LEARNING FROM EXAMPL INSTRUCTIONAL PRINCIPLES FROM THE WORKED EXAMPLES RESEARCH. *REVIEW OF EDUCATION RESEARCH, 70*(2), 181–214.

[2] IBID., P. 185.

[3] AN EDUQUACK (NEOLOGISM MADE UP BY PAUL YEARS AGO; PORTMANTEAU WORD COMBININ *EDUCATION + QUACKERY*) IS THE EDUCATIONAL VARIANT OF WHAT IS COMMONLY KNOWN AS QUACKADEMIC: AN ACADEMIC WITH LITTLE OR NO REAL KNOWLEDGE OF WHAT THEY'RE TALKIN ABOUT BUT WHO HAS NO PROBLEM VENTING THAT IGNORANCE. THE URBAN DICTIONA CALLS THEM FRAUDULENT OR IGNORANT PRETENDERS; A QUACKISH OR PSEUDOSCIENTIF ACADEMIC.

more specific database like EBSCO or ERIC and to choose a time period. Next, instead of just using the term "learning styles" you might want to set up a proper search query. To do this you'll need to choose proper search terms and operators to limit or expand your search (so-called Boolean operators such as "and", "or", not", an asterisk (*) as a wildcard, and so forth). The next step would be to do the search which involves operating the chosen search programme (not all databases work the same) including determining which search-fields (e.g., author, title, abstract, book/article, patent) need to be chosen or not. Finally, you'll need to select – out of all of the studies found – the ones most relevant to your question, download them from different online libraries or order them from physical ones, store them in a reference system like EndNote® or Mendeley® on your own computer, root out duplicates, and then finally read them. We've now explained how to carry out a proper literature search, but we wouldn't be the least bit surprised if you, as novice "documentalist", were now a bit dizzy and weren't able to do this on your own.

What would have been a lot better was to give you, for one or more similar search problems, examples of a proper search with the steps delineated with the results of each step and then let you take a stab at doing it yourself. In other words, if we had used worked examples (also called worked-out examples). In this chapter we'll discuss an article by Robert Atkinson, Sharon Derry, Alexander Renkl, and Donald Wortham which reviewed research on worked examples and then synthesised it to present both principles and a framework for using worked examples in instruction.

Abstract of the Article

Worked examples are instructional devices that provide an expert's problem solution for a learner to study. Worked-examples research is a cognitive-experimental program that has relevance to classroom instruction and the broader educational research community. A framework for organising the findings of this research is proposed, leading to instructional design principles. For instance, one instructional design principle suggests that effective examples have highly integrated components. They employ multiple modalities in presentation and emphasise conceptual structure by labelling or segmenting. At the lesson level, effective instruction employs multiple examples for each conceptual problem type, varies example formats within problem type, and employs surface features to signal deep structure. Also, examples should be presented in close proximity to matched practice problems. Moreover, learners can be encouraged through direct training or by the structure of the worked example to actively self-explain examples. Worked examples are associated with early stages of skill development . . .

The Article

Examples, though a staple in most teaching, were first studied by cognitive and educational psychologists starting in the 1950s. Worked examples, as such, were probably first studied by Micki Chi and her colleagues in 1989 (see Chapter 2 in *HLH*). In her research, she looked at the effect of the quality of the self-explanations that learners gave while solving problems after first receiving worked examples. Simply stated, *worked examples* are composed of three elements namely a problem statement with the *givens* of a problem (the what), a procedure for solving the problem set out in the steps – the *solution steps* – that need to be carried out to arrive at a solution (the how), and the final *solution* itself. Optimally, a worked example could also contain an explanation of why certain steps are carried out or certain information is used (the why), but this isn't a requirement. "In a sense, they provide an expert's problem-solving model for the learner to study and emulate" (pp. 181–182).

Worked examples

EXAMPLE OF A SIMPLE WORKED EXAMPLE

GIVEN: You're given a canvas bag containing four black and three white balls. You're asked to put your hand in the bag and randomly pull out two balls, one at a time, without returning the ball you first chose to the bag. What's the probability that you'll first pull out a black ball and then a white ball?

SOLUTION STEPS:

STEP 1:
  Total number of balls: 7
  Number of black balls: 4
  Probability that you pick a black ball first: 4/7

STEP 2:
  Total number of balls after your first draw: 6
  Number of white balls after the first draw: 3
  Probability that you pick a white ball second: 3/6

STEP 3:
  Probability that you pick a black ball first and a white ball second:
  $4/7 * 3/6 = 12/42 = 2/7$

SOLUTION: The probability that you first pick a black ball and a white ball second is 2/7.

The first wave of empirical studies on worked examples dealt primarily with how selecting and ordering examples to illustrate a principle or pattern affected learning. The next wave focussed on complex forms of knowledge and learning and more specifically on how experts and novices differ. This research showed that "experts typically focus on deeper structural aspects of problems, whereas novices are often misled by surface features" (p. 183). The third wave looked at how students acquire schemas or patterns that help them solve problems, focussing on how to increase novices' awareness of problem structure through practice.

WORKED EXAMPLES VS. PROCESS WORKSHEETS

While worked examples are often, but not exclusively, usable in more exact domains (math, natural sciences, economics) where many of the tasks to be carried out or problems that need to be solved are algorithmic, there's a sister approach that's very usable for domains with more *heuristic* tasks or problems like writing or art; the process worksheet (Van Merriënboer & Kirschner, 2018). A *process worksheet* presents learners not with the exact steps, but rather with the phases for carrying out a task and guides them through the process. In other words it gives learners what's known as a *systematic approach to a problem-solving* (SAP) and *rules-of-thumb* for carrying out the learning task.

A process worksheet may be as simple as a sheet of paper indicating the problem-solving phases (and, if relevant, sub phases) that the learner uses to guide their work. Within the phases, rules-of-thumb that could help the learner to successfully finish the phase are provided, for example as statements (e.g., when preparing a presentation, consider the audience's prior knowledge and take it into account) or as guiding questions (e.g., what aspect[s] of your audience should you take into account when preparing a presentation and why?).

Process worksheet

Worked Examples and Acquiring Cognitive Skills

ACT-R: Adaptive Control of Thought-Rational

Worked examples are particularly useful for skills acquisition, and are most important in the early stages of acquisition. Atkinson and his colleagues frame this in Anderson et al. (1997) four-stage ACT-R model. In Stage 1, learners solve problems via analogies, referring to known examples and then relating them to the problem at hand. Stage 2 finds learners developing "abstract declarative rules, verbal knowledge that guides their problem solving" (p. 185). After much practice, they move to Stage 3 where their skill performance becomes fluent. Here, learners no longer "follow their learned verbal rules, which is a slow process, but can deal with familiar problems or aspect of problems quickly and automatically, without using many attention resources" (p. 185). In Stage 4, learners have practiced so many different types of problems that they can retrieve a solution quickly and directly from memory. "From the viewpoint of skills acquisition, then, the importance of studying examples relative to pure problem solving practice is very high when a student is in the first stage (analogy) or is beginning to enter the second stage (abstract rules of learning)" (p. 186).

Instructional Principles for Teaching by Worked Examples

When using worked examples, it's important to consider specific factor that can moderate their effectiveness. The authors divide these factors into three categories, namely: *intra-example features* (i.e., how they are designed), *inter-example features* (i.e., the relationships between multiple examples and practice problems), and *individual differences in example processing* by students, especially how they self-explain the examples.

Intra-Example Features

Intra-example features

The design or structure of worked examples to a large part determines their effectiveness. To this end, the authors suggest three intra-example features which influence how they function.

Integrating text and diagrams

Split-attention effect

The first is *integrating text and diagrams* in the worked example. Here the authors directly reference what is known as the split-attention effect first posited by John Sweller where "requiring a student to split attention among multiple sources of information might impose a heavy cognitive load" (p. 186) which interferes "with the student's acquisition of schema representing the basic domain concepts and principles that students should learn from examples" (p. 187). In other words, a worked example that requires the student to attend to a number of different sources of information (e.g., text and accompanying diagrams) which subsequently have to be mentally integrated with each other (e.g., a diagram with the descriptive or clarifying text in a legend or in a paragraph apart from the diagram) increases the cognitive demand on the student and interferes with, rather than facilitate, learning.

Integrating aural and visual information

The second is *integrating aural and visual information* in the worked example. Here the authors discuss the benefits of integrating aural (i.e., spoken) and visual presentation of material boost to problem-solving performance and facilitate problem solving. This is often referred to as the *modality effect* which holds that we learn best from visuals and spoken words than from visuals and printed words as long as the two are not redundant (i.e., exactly the same).

Integrating steps and subgoals

The final intra-example aspect is *integrating steps and subgoals* in the worked example. Based on research by Richard Catrambone, Atkinson et al. discuss how "formatting an example's solution to accentuate its subgoals, by either affixing a label to them or simply visually isolating them, can assist a learner in actively inducing the example's underlying goal structure, which can guide a learner to discovering useful generalizations" and that "these structural cues enhance learning by encouraging learners to determine first the goal or function of the subgoals and then to explain to themselves why a series of steps are grouped together [helping to] promote induction of deeper structure representing domain principles, or schemas" (p. 190).

Inter-example features

Inter-Example Features

The sequencing and arrangement of worked examples in a lesson also plays a role in their effectiveness. To this end, the authors suggest four inter-example features which influence how they function.

Using multiple examples

The first inter-example feature is the *use of multiple examples*. According to Atkinson and colleagues, research on worked examples ranging from Rand Spiro and colleagues (cognitive flexibility) to John Sweller (cognitive load) has found that multiple examples or analogues are needed if your goal is to have students learn complex concepts or skills during instruction. Also, students who receive a combination of simple and complex examples learn better than those who receive either a single example or even those who received an example along with procedures for solving the problem.

Varying problem types

The second deals with *how and whether problem types should be varied* within a lesson. While this now sounds trivial as know that variability of practice or *interleaving* as it is known has a positive effect on learning (see Chapter 14 and Chapter 21 in this book on desirable difficulties), in 2000 this was a relatively open question. Citing research by Van Merriënboer and Paas, "increasing the variability [in problem type] within a lesson makes sense, if acquisition of robust problem-solving schemas depends upon understanding the range of conditions under which solution procedures may be effectively applied. On the other hand, increased variability in example design may increase cognitive demand, which interferes with learning" (p. 192). What they found was that variability in the types of problems to be solved did in fact lead to better transfer, but only when the rest of the instruction was designed to minimise cognitive load using worked examples.

Varying surface stories   The third feature is how themes or *"surface stories"* might be varied. Often, if not always, you want your students to learn how to discriminate between two or more types of problems and solve each correctly.[4] We know that sometimes things that look or sound the same or similar on the surface differ in their deeper structure.

SURFACE AND DEEP FEATURES

Baking bread at sea level or on a mountain top looks the same at the surface but at a deeper conceptual level the effect of atmospheric pressure on the process of rising and baking is different. On the other hand, things that look different on the surface can have the same deeper structure. For example, cooking spaghetti or boiling an egg on a mountain look different but at a deeper conceptual level, the effect of atmospheric pressure on water's boiling point and a food's cooking time is the same.

The problem you want to broach is the tendency of novices (i.e., your students) to base their choice of problem-solving strategy on the surface level attributes (see *HLH*, Chapter 1). You, thus, need to wean students "away from their reliance on superficial similarities until they are able to categorize the problems by structural aspects only" (p. 193). This means that you need to emphasise how, independent of the surface level features, underlying concepts can differ. This requires using what the authors call "structure-emphasising techniques" to demonstrate that a reliance on surface features doesn't work.

---

4   HERE WE HAVE TO GO BACK TO CHI'S WORK ON HOW EXPERTS AND NOVICES LOOK AT AN INTERPRET PROBLEMS (HLH, CHAPTER 1) AND CRAIK AND LOCKHART'S WORK ON DEPTH PROCESSING (HLH, CHAPTER 3).

The final feature is the *intermingling of practice and worked examples*. Simply stated, there are two approaches namely intermingling worked examples and practice problems throughout the lesson or blocking the examples followed by blocking the practice. It should by this time not be at all surprising to learn that intermingling works better both in terms of learning time and learning result.

Explanation Effects

This final factor doesn't relate directly to the worked example, but rather to how the worked example is used and understood by the learner. More specifically, it's about the learners' practice of explaining the examples to themselves or others (see Chapter 13 on generative strategies). Going back to Chi and her colleagues, we know that students who explained to themselves what they were doing while studying examples learned more effectively (i.e., were more successful solving subsequent problems) than those who didn't. She called this the *self-explanation effect*. But what to do with those learners (possibly most of them) who don't do this spontaneously? Atkinson and colleagues present three approaches to remedy this.

The first is *fostering self-explanations through structural manipulations*. They report, for example, how Catrambone assumed that that labelling subgoals would lead learners to group steps together and then to try to self-explain why those steps go together. What he found was that this labelling actually improved self-explanation and subsequent learning and transfer. Another approach reported was Robin Stark's work on omitting text and inserting blanks into worked examples. "[C]ompared to studying complete examples, incomplete examples fostered explanations and reduced ineffective self-explanations, such as rereading or paraphrasing. As a consequence, incomplete examples enhanced the transfer of learned solution methods" (p. 198).

The second is *training self-explanations*. Here, there are unequivocal results reported that explicitly training students to self-explain led to a fostering of self-explanations and concomitant better learning outcomes

Finally, Atkinson et al. speak of the *use of social incentives* such as assigning a student to the role of explainer in cooperative/peer learning settings. The results here were less promising. In particular, students with little or no prior tutoring experience and who are also novices within the domain seem to experience stress and overload when asked to provide instructional explanations.

Atkinson and colleagues summed up the causal relationships among the three categories of factors influencing learning from worked examples in Figure 15.1.

Intermingling practice and worked examples

Self-explanation effect

Fostering self-explanations

Training self-explanations

FIGURE 15.1
FRAMEWORK
OF FACTORS
INFLUENCING
LEARNING
FROM WORKED
EXAMPLES (FROM
ATKINSON
ET AL., LEARNING
FROM EXAMPLES:
INSTRUCTIONAL
PRINCIPLES FROM
THE WORKED
EXAMPLES
RESEARCH,
70:20, P. 203,
©2000, BY SAGE
PUBLICATIONS.
REPRINTED BY
PERMISSION
OF SAGE
PUBLICATIONS).

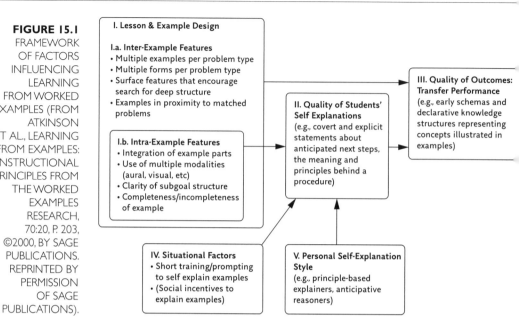

I. Lesson & Example Design

I.a. Inter-Example Features
• Multiple examples per problem type
• Multiple forms per problem type
• Surface features that encourage search for deep structure
• Examples in proximity to matched problems

I.b. Intra-Example Features
• Integration of example parts
• Use of multiple modalities (aural, visual, etc)
• Clarity of subgoal structure
• Completeness/incompleteness of example

II. Quality of Students' Self Explanations
(e.g., covert and explicit statements about anticipated next steps, the meaning and principles behind a procedure)

III. Quality of Outcomes: Transfer Performance
(e.g., early schemas and declarative knowledge structures representing concepts illustrated in examples)

IV. Situational Factors
• Short training/prompting to self explain examples
• (Social incentives to explain examples)

V. Personal Self-Explanation Style
(e.g., principle-based explainers, anticipative reasoners)

Conclusions

It's clear that worked examples are very useful for making learning and instruction more effective, more efficient, and more enjoyable. First, it challenges the teacher to think through all of the steps that the learner needs to carry out a task or solve a problem. In this way they can partially alleviate the curse of expertise that teachers can experience (i.e., they don't remember what it was to be a novice) as well as allow the teacher to double check if all of the required knowledge and skills have already been covered by them. Also, when designed and implemented properly, worked examples can facilitate both the learning of the procedures and skills needed to solve particular problems as well as the transfer of what has been learnt to novel problems and new situations. Well-designed modelling examples or process-oriented worked examples provide maximum guidance because they confront learners with how they should carry out the task, explaining why the task is being performed the way it i and how to do it. What's especially interesting is that worked examples ca be used in all types of instructional settings ranging from the "traditional classroom" through so-called authentic learning environments.

Takeaways

- Worked examples, when used properly, really work for both learning and transfer of skills.
- Structure worked examples to include cues that highlight meaningfu chunks of information which emphasise a problem's underlying conceptual meaning.

- Transfer is enhanced when there are at least two examples presented for each type of problem taught.
- Have students "experience a variety of different problem cases and example solutions for each to-be-learned concept" (p. 206).
- Represent the different to-be-solved problems by worked examples with a limited set of cover stories that are used across the various problem types.
- Pair worked examples with practice problems in close proximity to each other rather than using a blocked series of practice problems.
- Prompting students to self-explain improves transfer of learning.
- Social incentives to explain don't foster self-explanation.

References

ANDERSON, J. R., FINCHAM, J. M., & DOUGLASS, S. (1997). THE ROLE OF EXAMPLES AND RULES IN THE ACQUISITION OF A COGNITIVE SKILL. *JOURNAL OF EXPERIMENTAL PSYCHOLOGY: LEARNING, MEMORY, AND COGNITION, 23,* 932–945.

ATKINSON, R. K., DERRY, S. J., RENKL, A., & WORTHAM, D. (2000). LEARNING FROM EXAMPLES: INSTRUCTIONAL PRINCIPLES FROM THE WORKED EXAMPLES RESEARCH. *REVIEW OF EDUCATIONAL RESEARCH, 70*(2), 181–214.

CHI, M. T. H., BASSOK, M., LEWIS, M. W., REIMANN, P., & GLASER, R. (1989). SELF-EXPLANATIONS: HOW STUDENTS STUDY AND USE EXAMPLES IN LEARNING TO SOLVE PROBLEMS. *COGNITIVE SCIENCE, 13,* 145–182.

VAN MERRIËNBOER, J. J. G., & KIRSCHNER, P. A. (2018). *TEN STEPS TO COMPLEX LEARNING: A SYSTEMATIC APPROACH TO FOUR-COMPONENT INSTRUCTIONAL DESIGN.* ROUTLEDGE.

Suggested Readings and Links

RENKL, A. (1997). LEARNING FROM WORKED-OUT EXAMPLES: A STUDY ON INDIVIDUAL DIFFERENCES. *COGNITIVE SCIENCE, 21,* 1–29.

RENKL, A., STARK, R., GRUBER, H., & MANDL, H. (1998). LEARNING FROM WORKED-OUT EXAMPLES: THE EFFECTS OF EXAMPLE VARIABILITY AND ELICITED SELF-EXPLANATIONS. *CONTEMPORARY EDUCATIONAL PSYCHOLOGY, 23,* 90–108.

SWELLER, J., & COOPER, G. A. (1985). THE USE OF WORKED EXAMPLES AS A SUBSTITUTE FOR PROBLEM SOLVING IN LEARNING ALGEBRA. *COGNITION AND INSTRUCTION, 2,* 59–89.

WEBSITES

ONLINE CPD: MAKING THE MOST OF WORKED EXAMPLES

Craig Barton presents here an online course on worked examples. He teaches about four significant mistakes he used to make with his worked examples and goes through how he uses worked examples, incorporating the principles of Example-Problem Pairs, Silent Teacher, Show Call and more.

AVAILABLE VIA HTTPS://TINYURL.COM/ED94AK7P

THREE BLOGS BY MIRJAM NEELEN AND PAUL A. KIRSCHNER

Designing Winning Worked Examples 1 – Intra Example Features

AVAILABLE VIA HTTPS://TINYURL.COM/2WNBBPA6

DESIGNING WINNING WORKED EXAMPLES 2 – INTER EXAMPLE FEATURES

AVAILABLE VIA HTTPS://TINYURL.COM/UDKZPJYZ

DESIGNING WINNING WORKED EXAMPLES 3 – EXPLANATION EFFECTS

AVAILABLE VIA HTTPS://TINYURL.COM/DRMYKMTC

SECTION 4

PEDAGOGICAL CONTENT KNOWLEDGE

A piece of personal history. Before Paul studied psychology and then majored in educational psychology, he was an electrical engineering major. After a year at Syracuse University, a semi-Ivy league university where his fellow students were more interested in fast expensive cars and drinking at fraternities than societal problems and the war in Vietnam, he transferred to SUNY at Stony Brook; a more down-to-earth, state university to continue his studies. In his first semester there, he took a required engineering course in calculus from a professor at the university who was a Nobel prize winner in physics (he shall remain nameless). The man was a theoretical physicist who specialised in statistical mechanics, integrable systems, gauge theory, and both particle physics and condensed matter physics. As such, you can probably assume that he also had a comprehensive knowledge of calculus. While acing his courses at Syracuse including the math courses and having never received less than an A at the Bronx High School of Science, Paul was at a loss in that calculus course. It didn't matter what he did, how hard he worked, how many questions he asked in the class, the course was a lost cause for him. Long story short, this experience caused him to change majors and the rest is history.

What went wrong? One plausible explanation could be that while this Nobel prize winner was a great scientist and probably also a great mathematician, he wasn't a great teacher. The National Association for Research on Science Teaching (NARST) would say that he missed the type of knowledge that differentiates science teachers from scientists. "Teachers differ from scientists, not necessarily in the quality or quantity of their subject matter knowledge, but in how that knowledge is organized and used".[1] Specifically, teachers' knowledge is organised with teaching in mind and has the aim of developing students' understanding, while scientists' knowledge is organised with the domain itself in mind and has the aim of developing new knowledge in that domain. In other

---

[1] HTTPS://NARST.ORG/RESEARCH-MATTERS/PEDAGOGICAL-CONTENT-KNOWLEDGE

DI: 10.4324/9781003228165-19

words, that professor lacked pedagogical content knowledge (PCK); the combination of what they know about teaching and what they know about what they teach. He didn't understand where his students (or at least where Paul) were coming from or what they needed when it came to the subject he was teaching.

Thanks to this professor's lack of PCK, the world might have lost a great engineer or even physicist, but it gained a dedicated, enthusiastic, and sometimes grumpy educational psychologist. You decide whether you should blame or thank that professor!

This section is about PCK. It looks at what PCK is, what PCK looks like in different domains such as math, science, and language. Finally it takes on a new branch on the PCK tree, namely Technological Pedagogical Content Knowledge (TPACK).

If you want to learn about PCK before reading the chapters, here's a nice video of Lee Shulman, the godfather of PCK about the missing paradigm – PCK – as the "essence of great teaching". Likening the art of teaching to a seemingly ordinary game of golf, Shulman explains the importance of a "pedagogical swing" that must change to fit current needs and conditions.

 WWW.YOUTUBE.COM/WATCH?V=TOKLQND5BSI

16 WHY YOU CAN'T TEACH WHAT YOU DON'T KNOW

LEE SCHULMAN ON TEACHER KNOWLEDGE

16 WHY YOU CAN'T TEACH WHAT YOU DON'T KNOW

ARTICLE Knowledge and teaching: Foundations of the new reform[1]

QUOTE *"Perhaps the most enduring and powerful scholarly influences on teachers are those that enrich their images of the possible."*[2]

Why You Should Read This Article

In his 1958 magnum opus *Personal Knowledge*, Michael Polanyi defines "tacit knowledge" as anything we know how to do but cannot explicitly explain how we do it, such as the complex set of skills needed to ride a bike or the instinctive ability to stay afloat in water. It is the ephemeral, elusive form of knowledge that resists classification or codification and that can only be gleaned through immersion in the experience itself. In most cases it's not even something that can be expressed through language. As he so beautifully puts it, "we can know more than we can tell".[3]

Explicit versus tacit knowledge

For Polanyi, explicit knowledge is hugely important in becoming proficient at anything but without the tacit dimension of knowing how to use and *apply* that knowledge, one can only arrive at an abstract and approximate appreciation of it:

> Textbooks of diagnostics teach the medical student the several symptoms of different diseases, but this knowledge is useless, unless the student has learnt to apply it at the bedside. The identification of the species to which an animal or plant belongs, resembles the task of diagnosing a disease; it too can be learnt only by practicing it under a teacher's guidance.[4]

---

1   SHULMAN, L., (1987) KNOWLEDGE AND TEACHING: FOUNDATIONS OF THE NEW REFORM. *HARVARD EDUCATIONAL REVIEW, 57*(1), 1–23. REPUBLISHED WITH PERMISSION OF HARVARD EDUCATION REVIEW; PERMISSION CONVEYED THROUGH COPYRIGHT CLEARANCE CENTER, INC.

2   IBID., P. 10.

3   POLANYI, M. (1966) *THE TACIT DIMENSION* (P. 4). DOUBLEDAY & CO (REPRINTED PETER SMITH GLOUCESTER, MA, 1983).

4   POLANYI, M. (1962). *PERSONAL KNOWLEDGE: TOWARDS A POST-CRITICAL PHILOSOPHY* (P. 602). UNIVERSITY OF CHICAGO PRESS.

The really difficult thing about teaching is that a lot of it is invisible and so there is always an ongoing debate about standards to be used to not only monitor but also to observe teacher effectiveness. In this article, Lee Schulman argues for a more cohesive knowledge base for the teaching profession in terms of curricular knowledge and pedagogical content while also acknowledging the elusive nature of the kinds of knowledge that need to be systematised. He calls for a particular kind of scrutiny of teaching which he terms "wisdom-of-practice" studies where the complexities and subtleties of effective teacher knowledge are closely observed and recorded: "Practitioners simply know a great deal that they have never even tried to articulate" (p. 12). However he is clear that for effective learning to happen, clear instruction is vital: "teaching requires a special kind of expertise or artistry, for which explaining and showing are the central features" (p. 12). Essentially, Schulman argues for a systematic and cohesive knowledge base for teaching that should replace the "currently incomplete and trivial definitions of teaching" (p. 20) held by the wider community.

Abstract of the Article

Lee S. Shulman builds his foundation for teaching reform on an idea of teaching that emphasises comprehension and reasoning, transformation, and reflection. "This emphasis is justified", he writes, "by the resoluteness with which research and policy have so blatantly ignored those aspects of teaching in the past". To articulate and justify this conception, Shulman responds to four questions: what are the sources of the knowledge base for teaching? In what terms can these sources be conceptualised? What are the processes of pedagogical reasoning and action? and What are the implications for teaching policy and educational reform? The answers – informed by philosophy, psychology, and a growing body of case-work based on young and experienced practitioners – go far beyond current reform assumptions and initiatives. The outcome for educational practitioners, scholars, and policymakers is a major redirection in how teaching is to be understood and teachers are to be trained and evaluated.

The Article

There are two central questions in this article; firstly what should teachers know and secondly what should they know how to do? There have been calls for many years for the training and development of teachers to follow other professions where there is a systematic base of knowledge, extended internship and training periods, and a more cohesive model of national certification of standard however an ongoing issue in the teaching profession is that "richly developed portrayals of expertise" (p. 1) are rare.

To that end, Shulman sketches an example of teaching expertise in the form of Nancy, a veteran English teacher teaching a unit on *Moby Dick* in which she is likened to a "symphony conductor, posing questions, probing for alternative views, drawing out the shy while tempering the boisterous" (p. 2). A key aspect of Nancy's expertise is a "mental index" for books she had taught many times before and which she was able to deftly combine with pedagogical knowledge with great effect. However, her teaching style is not prescriptive or static in any sense but highly flexible and adaptable to meet the needs of her students to such an extent that she's able to get the students to work independently. He notes that she can "not only conduct her orchestra from the podium, she can sit back and watch it play with virtuosity by itself" (p. 3).

He then asks the questions "What does Nancy believe, understand, and know how to do that permits her to teach as she does?" and "Can other teachers be prepared to teach with such skill?" (p. 3). He makes the interesting point that while there are plenty of descriptions of the management of pupils in the classroom there's precious little of the management of *ideas* in the classroom.

Expert versus novice teachers

In attempting to address these questions, he borrows from Piaget's model of observing how the very young collate and organise knowledge and observes "neophyte" teachers in their journey from complete novices towards experts with all the attendant mistakes along the way. Indeed, what he describes as "error, success, and refinement" (p. 4) are seen as an integral part of a teacher gaining expertise. These observations were then compared with veteran teachers like Nancy who display expertise regularly while novice teachers display this "haltingly although occasionally masterfully also. The key question Shulman asks is, again, what do teachers know (or not know) that allows them to teach in such a way?

Running concurrently with this, Shulman notes that he's also working to systematise this knowledge at a policy level seeking to establish a set teacher standards which

> must be closely tied to the findings of scholarship in the academic disciplines that form the curriculum (such as English, physics, and history) as well as those that serve as foundations for the process of education (such as psychology, sociology, or philosophy); they must possess intuitive credibility (or "face validity") in the opinion of the professional community in whose interests they have been

designed; and they must relate to the appropriate normative conceptions of teaching and teacher education. (p. 5)

Subject specific expertise matters

Shulman notes that most teacher training comprises a general aptitude test, some evidence of competency in a subject domain followed by classroom observations to establish expertise and worthiness. This represents a trivialisation of teaching for him claiming that "Teachers themselves have difficulty in articulating what they know and how they know it" (p. 6). In addition, he also warns against genericism where the subject matter to be taught and the context of the classroom are over ignored. This mistake is then compounded according to him where observers who are observing teachers have no subject expertise in the lesson being observed. We might pause to ask the question, should a Biology teacher be observing and evaluating a History teacher or vice versa? For Schulman, the observer can only really comment on generic pedagogical elements of the lesson, a mistake which he claims "an acceptable strategy for research became an unacceptable policy for teacher evaluation" (p. 7).

Categories of the Knowledge Base

Schulman then attempts to list the categories of knowledge that underlie the teacher understanding as they might be in the headings of a book on effective teaching: content knowledge, general pedagogical knowledge, curriculum knowledge, pedagogical content knowledge ("that special amalgam of content and pedagogy that is uniquely the province of teachers, their own special form of professional understanding" [p. 8]), knowledge of learners and their characteristics, knowledge of educational contexts, knowledge of educational ends, purposes, and values, and their philosophical and historical grounds.

Knowledge allows for more creative flexibility

    In the classroom, subject knowledge is integral to effective teaching as it frees teachers to improvise like a jazz musician, however pedagogical content knowledge is also an important category because it's the one "most likely to distinguish the understanding of the content specialist from that of the pedagogue" (p. 8). In terms of what research or as he calls it, "formal education scholarship" teachers should know, Schulman poetically notes that possibly the most powerful influences on teachers are those that "enrich their images of the possible: their visions of what constitutes good education, or what a well-educated youngster might look like if provided with appropriate opportunities and stimulation" (p. 10).

    A very interesting point made is that research on teaching is more applicable to some subjects than others: "Rosenshine (1986) has observed that effective teaching research has much less to offer to the teaching of understanding, especially of complex written material; thus, the research applies more to teaching a skill like multiplication than to teaching critical interpretations of, say, the Federalist Papers" (p. 10). Certainly the rendering of Nancy's virtuosic performance as an English teacher would bear this out. Another issue highlighted about the teaching profession is its "extensive individual and collective amnesia" (p. 11), meaning there's no enduring representation of great achievements in the way that other professions do such as architecture, law, or medicine. He writes "teaching is conducted without an audience of peers. It is devoid of a history of practice" (p. 10). In addition, he warns against turning research into a prescription noting that to codify general principles runs the risk of simplifying the "otherwise outrageously complex activity of teaching" (p. 11). Despite this, he does categorise what he refers to as "aspects of pedagogical reasoning" [see Table 16.1].

TABLE 16.1
A MODEL OF PEDAGOGICAL REASONING AND ACTION (*SHULMAN, L., 1987,* REPUBLISHED WITH PERMISSION OF HARVARD EDUCATIONAL REVIEW; PERMISSION CONVEYED THROUGH COPYRIGHT CLEARANCE CENTER, INC.).

A Model of Pedagogical Reasoning and Action

Comprehension
Of purposes, subject matter structures, ideas within and outside the discipline

Transformation
Preparation: critical interpretation and analysis of texts, structuring, and segmenting, development of a curricular repertoire, and clarification of purposes
Representation: use of a representational repertoire which includes analogies, metaphors, examples, demonstrations, explanations, and so forth
Selection: choice from among an instructional repertoire which includes modes of teaching, organising, managing, and arranging
Adaptation and Tailoring to Student Characteristics: consideration of conceptions, preconceptions, misconceptions, and difficulties, language, culture, and motivations, social class, gender, age, ability, aptitude, Interests, self concepts, and attention

Instruction
Management, presentations, Interactions, group work, discipline, humour, questioning, and other aspects of active teaching, discovery or Inquiry Instruction, and the observable forms of classroom teaching

Evaluation
Checking for student understanding during Interactive teaching
Testing student understanding at the end of lessons or units
Evaluating one's own performance, and adjusting for experiences

Reflection
Reviewing, reconstructing, re-enacting and critically analysing one's own and the class's performance, and grounding explanations in evidence

New Comprehensions
Of purposes, subject matter, students, teaching, and self
Consolidation of new understandings, and learnings from experience

"ADMIRAL FARRAGUT" TEACHING

CAN A GOOD TEACHER TEACH *ANY* SUBJECT? No not really. Schulman goes to great lengths to illustrate the fact that without a solid understanding of what's to be taught, a teacher can't harness the improvisational techniques that are so characteristic of experts in any given domain. A useful analogy here is the jazz musician whose playing appears to be completely random in nature but who's only able to do so because of a solid understanding of the standard on which they're playing. He gives an excellent example of this from his research which describes a teacher (Colleen) who when teaching English literature and the close reading of poetry is highly confident, able to draw students in, and harness her considerable knowledge to flexibly improvise and respond to any student misunderstanding. However, when teaching a unit on grammar she's far less at home because she's trained in literature not language and as a result, the lesson suffers:

"Colleen looked like a different teacher during that lesson. Her interactive style evaporated. In its place was a highly didactic, teacher-directed, swiftly paced combination of lecture and tightly controlled recitation: Socrates replaced by DISTAR. I sometimes refer to such teaching as the Admiral Farragut style, 'Damn the questions, full speed ahead'. Students were not given opportunities to raise questions or offer alternative views".

Content and pedagogy are intertwined

The article ends by warning against the dangers of prescription and that we should aim to "achieve standards without standardization" (p. 20). Moreover, teachers can't be adequately assessed by observing their teaching performance without reference to the content being taught. For Schulman, evaluation and reflection are retrospective in nature as opposed to the prospective nature of preparing and "knowing" material to be taught. Really successful teachers are reflective practitioners engage in a process where the teacher "reconstructs, reenacts, and/or recaptures the events, the emotions, and the accomplishments" (p. 20) of what has transpired in the teaching and learning process. As a result of this, teachers arrive at a form of "new comprehension" of what is to be taught, its broader purposes and of the students themselves.

Conclusions

Teaching a group of children over an extended period of time is one of those highly specialised acts where tacit knowledge is perhaps more of a prerequisite than others. It involves a million subtle nuances that are often invisible to the untrained eye, and as Schulman reminds us, are often invisible to teachers themselves. Knowing what will work last period on a Friday, knowing how one particular student will respond to a particular kind of feedback, knowing how to phrase that question just right to a particular kind of class who is struggling, knowing when students need to read in silence or have an animated discussion, knowing how to pitch a tricky concept at just the right point in the term or knowing how to deal with a 12-year-old who has recently been bereaved and still get them through the year are all forms of tacit knowledge that are difficult to truly understand unless experienced first-hand. On top of that, knowing how to assimilate all those elements *and* navigate the demands of an ever-changing curriculum, parental engagement, marking and assessment and the undulating rhythms of the school year are all forms of tacit knowledge that are difficult to even define by its very best practitioners, never mind codify and teach to someone else.

Knowing content in "several ways"

A key claim in this article is that being a really effective teacher means being knowledgeable about what they're teaching. They don't just need to understand it but they should understand it in "several ways". This knowledge gives a teacher the confidence to explain the content in a clear and cohesive fashion, address any student misconceptions or questions as they arise, be able to draw links and analogies with other knowledge that might illuminate student understanding or as Schulman puts it "understand how a given idea relates to other ideas within the same subject area and to ideas in other subjects as well" (p. 16). In addition, teachers need to be aware of the broader purposes of what they're doing to attend to the "equality of opportunity and equity among students of different backgrounds and cultures" (p. 15). Ultimately, Schulman argues that knowledge of subject is not enough and that effective teaching lies "the intersection of content and pedagogy" (p. 15).

Takeaways

- A sound knowledge of what you are teaching is essential to becoming an expert teacher.
- It's not enough to know what you are teaching. You need to know it in "several ways".
- "Explaining and showing" are an essential part of the artistry of teaching.

- A "representational repertoire" of examples, analogies and connections to other knowledge is vital.
- Being a good teacher in one subject doesn't mean you're a good teacher in another.

References

POLANYI, M. (1962). *PERSONAL KNOWLEDGE: TOWARDS A POST-CRITICAL PHILOSOPHY.* UNIVERSITY OF CHICAGO PRESS.

POLANYI, M. (1966). *THE TACIT DIMENSION.* GLOUCESTER, DOUBLEDAY & CO. (REPRINTED PETER SMITH, GLOUCESTER, MA, 1983).

ROSENSHINE, B. (1986, APRIL). *UNSOLVED ISSUES IN TEACHING CONTENT: A CRITIQUE OF A LESSON ON FEDERALIST PAPER NO. 10.* PAPER PRESENTED AT THE MEETING OF THE AMERICAN EDUCATIONAL RESEARCH ASSOCIATION, SAN FRANCISCO, CA.

SHULMAN, L. (1987). KNOWLEDGE AND TEACHING: FOUNDATIONS OF THE NEW REFORM. *HARVARD EDUCATIONAL REVIEW, 57*(1), 1–23. AVAILABLE VIA HTTP://HEPGJOURNALS.ORG/DOI/PDF/10.17763/HAER.57.1.J463W79R56455411

Suggested Readings and Links

LOUGHRAN, J., BERRY, A., & MULHALL, P. (2012). PEDAGOGICAL CONTENT KNOWLEDGE. IN J. LOUGHRAN, A. BERRY, & P. MULHALL (EDS.), *UNDERSTANDING AND DEVELOPING SCIENCE TEACHERS' PEDAGOGICAL CONTENT KNOWLEDGE. PROFESSIONAL LEARNING* (VOL. 12). SENSE PUBLISHERS. HTTPS://DOI.ORG/10.1007/978-94-6091-821-6_2

SCHULMAN, L. (1986). THOSE WHO UNDERSTAND: KNOWLEDGE GROWTH IN TEACHING. *EDUCATIONAL RESEARCHER, 15*(2), 4–14.

AVAILABLE VIA HTTPS://JOURNALS.SAGEPUB.COM/DOI/10.3102/0013189X015002004

VIDEOS

PCK SUMMIT KEYNOTE: DR. LEE SHULMAN

AVAILABLE VIA WWW.YOUTUBE.COM/WATCH?V=NZJMYVFRYSE

WHY CONTENT KNOWLEDGE MATTERS IN TEACHING AND THE IMPLICATIONS FOR TEACHER EDUCATION

AVAILABLE VIA HTTPS://YOUTU.BE/ZRTW4A1ITO4

17 MATHEMATICAL KNOWLEDGE FOR TEACHING

HEATHER HILL, DEBORAH HALL AND COLLEAGUES ON
MATHEMATICS PCK

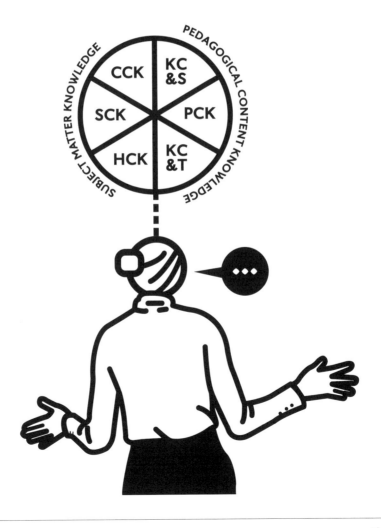

OI: 10.4324/9781003228165-21

17 MATHEMATICAL KNOWLEDGE FOR TEACHING

ARTICLES Unpacking pedagogical content knowledge: Conceptualizing and measuring teacher's topic-specific knowledge of students[1]

Content knowledge for teaching: What makes it special?[2]

QUOTE *"By 'mathematical knowledge for teaching', we mean the mathematical knowledge used to carry out the work of teaching mathematics."*[3]

Why You Should Read These Articles

Ever hear of something called *faux amis* (false friends)? It's a French term to describe words which are the same, or very alike, in two languages, but whose meanings are different. For example, the French word *histoire* means story and not history and *libraire* means bookseller and not library. In Dutch *paragraaf* means section of an article or chapter and not paragraph, for which the Dutch use the word *alinea*. False friends can also be found within one language but across cultures. Let's take the word *biscuit*. If a British person asks for a biscuit in the United States, they would most probably receive something approximating a *scone* while what they really wanted is what Americans call a *cookie*. Paul, born in the United States, saw on his first trip to England a sign in a pub with the words *refuse tip*. In his mind, that meant that the servers were not to accept gratuities, but it actually meant what he knew as a *garbage dump*. This can get even more difficult when it comes to cultures

1 HILL, H. C., BALL, D. L., & SCHILLING, S. C. G. (2008). UNPACKING PEDAGOGICAL CONTENT KNOWLEDGE: CONCEPTUALIZING AND MEASURING TEACHERS' TOPIC-SPECIFIC KNOWLEDGE OF STUDENTS. *JOURNAL FOR RESEARCH IN MATHEMATICS EDUCATION, 39*, 372–400.
2 BALL, D. L., THAMES, M. H., & PHELPS, G. (2008). CONTENT KNOWLEDGE FOR TEACHING: WHAT MAKES IT SPECIAL? *JOURNAL OF TEACHER EDUCATION, 59*, 389–407.
3 HILL ET AL. (2008, P. 373).

What an American says that they know and understand football is quite different from what the rest of the world knows and understands to be football (soccer to Americans), and what a Dutch person sees as hockey (field hockey) is quite different from what a Canadian sees as hockey (ice hockey).

This is also the case with mathematics. Mathematical knowledge for most of what we need and do to function in our jobs and in society is quite different from the mathematical knowledge that a math teacher needs to know to be a good teacher. Maybe we can add a little to Shulman's thesis (see Chapter 2) that *those who can, do, those who understand, teach and those who teach a subject do and understand their subject area*. This chapter discusses the different types of knowledge that a math teacher needs to know: mathematical knowledge for teaching or as it also is sometimes called, content knowledge for teaching mathematics.

Abstracts of the Articles

Unpacking pedagogical content knowledge: Conceptualising and measuring teachers' topic-specific knowledge of students

There is widespread agreement that effective teachers have unique knowledge of students' mathematical ideas and thinking. However, few scholars have focused on conceptualising this domain, and even fewer have focused on measuring this knowledge. In this article, we describe an effort to conceptualise and develop measures of teachers' combined knowledge of content and students by writing, piloting, and analysing results from multiple-choice items. Our results suggest partial success in measuring this domain among practicing teachers but also identify key areas around which the field must achieve conceptual and empirical clarity. Although this is ongoing work, we believe that the lessons learned from our efforts shed light on teachers' knowledge in this domain and can inform future attempts to develop measures.

Content knowledge for teaching: What makes it special?

This article reports the authors' efforts to develop a practice-based theory of content knowledge for teaching built on Shulman's (1986) notion of pedagogical content knowledge. As the concept of pedagogical content knowledge caught on, it was in need of theoretical development, analytic clarification, and empirical testing. The purpose of the study was to investigate the nature of professionally oriented subject matter knowledge in mathematics by studying actual mathematics teaching and identifying mathematical knowledge *for* teaching based on analyses of the mathematical problems that arise in teaching. In conjunction, measures of mathematical knowledge for teaching were developed. These lines of research indicate at least two empirically discernible subdomains within pedagogical content knowledge (*knowledge of content and students* and *knowledge of content and teaching*) and an important subdomain of "pure" content knowledge unique to the work of teaching, *specialised content knowledge*, which is distinct from the *common content knowledge* needed by teachers and nonteachers alike. The article concludes with a discussion of the next steps needed to develop a useful theory of content knowledge for teaching.

The Articles

This was a tough one! There are so many different articles that can be called seminal when it comes to teaching mathematics while at the same time each of them is simply a part of the puzzle as to what it is and what it entails. Here we've made a choice for an article by Heather Hill, Brian Rowan, and Deborah Loewenberg Ball and an article by Deborah Ball, Mark Thames, and Geoffrey Phelps, but at the end we give a list of references that we just as easily could have chosen.

In their chapter on research in teaching mathematics in the 4th edition of the *Handbook of research on teaching* (2001), Deborah Ball, Sarah Lubienski, and Denise Mewborn ask: "Why does it work to add a zero on the right when multiplying by 10 . . . ? Why, when the number includes a decimal, do we move the decimal point over instead of adding zeros? What does it mean to divide *by one-half*? . . . . Is a square a rectangle?" (p. 433). Most people can't answer these questions. Many mathematicians can answer them, but aren't really able to explain their answers to others or to teach them about it. What is that special thing that makes it possible to teach mathematics well?

Pedagogical content knowledge

Until the beginning of the 21st century pedagogical content knowledge (PCK), a concept introduced by Lee Shulman in 1986 (see Chapter 2), was considered specific enough to help us think about how teachers taught their subjects. Shulman lamented that teachers' readiness was evaluated based on what they knew about classroom practice and classroom management skills along with the different strategies and behaviours that could lead to improved student performance. There was, however, no real connection between those things that teachers had learnt and the specific content that they were teaching. There was, essentially, a generic view of teaching. Shulman called this omission of subject content the *missing paradigm*; that is "a blind spot with respect to content programs of teacher evaluation and teacher certification, . . . questions about the content of the lessons taught, the questions asked, and the explanations offered" (pp. 7–8). In this blind spot were subject matter content knowledge, pedagogical content knowledge (that which "distinguishes the understanding of the content specialist from that of the pedagogue"), and curricular knowledge. Clearly, this generic PCK wasn't enough.

Mathematical Knowledge for Teaching (MKT) or Content Knowledge for Teaching Mathematics (CKTM)

In a superb review of how PCK "pervaded mathematical research", Fien Depaepe et al. (2013) present criticisms of PCK and how, via a series of iterations, it has been broadened, culminating in the interchangeable terms *mathematical knowledge for teaching* (MKT) or *content knowledge for teaching mathematics* (CKTM). Math teachers not only have to be able to "do the math", but also have to be able to represent mathematical concepts and procedures to their students via pictures, graphs, or diagrams, give their students explanations for how and why rules and procedures work, and analyse their students' solutions and explanations. MKT is, thus, the mathematical knowledge that teachers use to carry out their work of teaching math. Examples of this "include explaining terms and concepts to students, interpreting students' statements and solutions, judging and correcting textbook treatments of particular topics, using representations accurately in the classroom, and providing students with examples of mathematical concepts, algorithms, or proofs" (Hill et al., 2005, p. 373).

Knowledge of content and students

Hill and her colleagues first dissect teachers' knowledge of content and students (KCS) which they define as "content knowledge intertwined with knowledge of how students think about, know, or learn this particular content. KCS is used in tasks of teaching that involve attending to both the specific content and something particular about learners" (p. 375). This is a primary element in Shulman's (1986) PCK, namely "an understanding of what makes the learning of specific topics easy or difficult: the conceptions and preconceptions that students of different ages and backgrounds bring with them to the learning of those most frequently taught topics and lessons" (p. 9).

As can be seen in Figure 17.1, on the left-hand side we have subject-matter knowledge or mathematical knowledge for teaching which encompasses

Common content knowledge

- *Common Content Knowledge*: Mathematical knowledge that is required, but not unique to teaching. In other words knowledge used both in teaching and in settings other than teaching (e.g., engineering, accounting), including things like recognising errors, making correct calculations, and pronouncing terms correctly. It's the math that they themselves have learnt and what they need to carry out the tasks and solve the problems that they give their students.

Specialised content knowledge

- *Specialised Content Knowledge*: Mathematical knowledge that goes further than the required procedural knowledge of math that a math-using professional would use; the mathematical knowledge and skill unique to teaching and according to Ball et al. (2008) it's "mathematical knowledge not typically needed for purposes other than teaching" (p. 400). You could compare this to football or almost any sport, in that a good coach needn't have been a star player. Here it's about a deeper understanding and ability to communicate that understanding to students such as "how to accurately represent mathematical ideas, provide mathematical explanations rules and procedures, and examine and understand unusual solution methods to problems" (p. 377–378) or the ability to recognise the nature of student errors and student interpretations.

Knowledge at the mathematical horizon

- *Knowledge at the Mathematical Horizon*: This knowledge is an "orientation to and familiarity with the discipline(s) that contribute to the teaching of the school subject at hand, providing teachers with a sense for how the content being taught is situated in and connected to the broader disciplinary territory" (Jakobsen et al., 2012, p. 4642). This includes being aware of how different mathematical topics are related to each other, of core disciplinary orientations and values, and of major structures of the discipline.

On the right-hand side we have what can be called traditional PCK, namely:

Knowledge of content and students

- *Knowledge of Content and Students*: This type of knowledge is a combination of knowing about mathematics and knowing about students. It's knowledge of how students think mathematically, including their mathematical conceptions and misconceptions. It allows them to "anticipate what students are likely to think and what they will find confusing" (Ball et al., 2008, p. 401). It also includes interpreting student understanding as it evolves and though student language.

Knowledge of content and teaching

- *Knowledge of Content and Teaching*: This knowledge is a combination of knowledge of mathematics with knowledge of teaching. This type of knowledge deals with instructional decisions that you make, including things like ordering and designing instruction, determining the advantages and disadvantages of different representations, and so forth. In other words, it's about knowing how to design mathematical instruction such that the chosen instructional approach/pedagogy interacts with mathematical understanding.

Knowledge of content and curriculum

- *Knowledge of Content and Curriculum*: Knowing how the mathematical content relates to the curriculum in two ways, narrow and broad. In a narrow sense it's about how one subject topic that you're teaching in your year relates to other math topics in that year but also to topics in other subject areas that year (e.g., for math that might be economics or the natural sciences). In the broad sense it's about how one subject topic that you're teaching in your year relates to what your students have learned in previous years of what they'll need to learn in future years. This knowledge also relates to how to use instructional materials to organise your study programme.

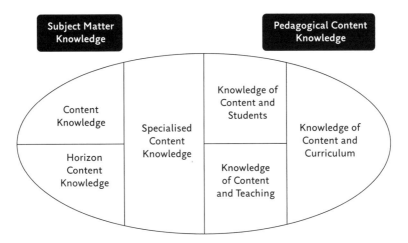

FIGURE 17.1
MATHEMATICAL
KNOWLEDGE
FOR TEACHING
(ADAPTED FROM
HILL ET AL. [2008]
AND BALL ET AL.
[2008]).

WHAT'S WHAT?

Let's take the following list of actions relating to decimals:

- Ordering a list of decimals.
- Generating a list of decimals that would reveal key mathematical issues.
- How decimals are used and represented in different ways.
- Recognising which decimals are hardest for students to understand and why.
- Deciding what to do about the student problems.
- How decimals relate to powers of a number (both positive and negative) or types of fractions and repeating decimals.

Each action uses a different kind of knowledge.

- Ordering a list of decimals can be considered to be "simple" common content knowledge. If you know math, you should be able to do this.
- Generating a list of decimals to reveal key math issues is an example of specialised content knowledge. You need to be able to recognise the nature of student errors and student interpretations to do this.

(Continued)

(Continued)

- Using and representing the relationships between decimals in different forms like fractions or ratios or understanding how, why, and when to use a leading decimal is an example of horizon content knowledge as you're aware of how different mathematical topics are related to each other.
- Recognising that this is difficult for students and why requires knowledge of content and students because you must know and understand how students think mathematically, including their mathematical conceptions and misconceptions.
- Deciding what to do requires knowledge of content and teaching as it relates to the instructional decisions that you make.
- Teaching how and when to teach these relationships requires knowledge of content and curriculum. Fractions usually come before decimals, understanding that .333 is a repeating decimal that approximates 1/3 but isn't the same is often done in the same year, but powers of ten, especially negative powers ($10^{-1} = .1$ or $1/10$), are often handled in later years.

Conclusions

The concept of mathematical knowledge for teaching as an advancement of Shulman's pedagogical content knowledge is important for a number of reasons. First, mathematical knowledge for teaching, in contrast to what Shulman proposed in 1986, was the result of "empirical research on the knowledge teachers need for and apply in mathematics teaching, and as such provides an empirical grounding to pedagogical content knowledge" (Depaepe et al., 2013, p. 14). Second, the research carried out by Heather Hill and her colleagues through the years has allowed for the operationalisation of the concept and has yielded a valid measure of teachers' mathematical knowledge for teaching (Hill et al., 2004, 2005). Finally, the concept of mathematical knowledge for teaching has provided "empirical evidence for a positive relation between teachers' PCK and student learning outcomes" (Depaepe et al., 2013, p. 14).

Takeaways

- Math teachers need not only know the same math that any other educated members of our society know, but also more. They need an "understanding of the insides of ideas, their roots and connections, their reasons and ways of being represented" (Ball, 2003, p. 7).

- Knowledge for teaching mathematics differs from the mathematical knowledge used for other mathematically intensive occupations and professions.
- Math teachers must be able to anticipate and interpret student errors, represent mathematical ideas in multiple forms, develop alternative explanations, etc.
- "The mathematical knowledge needed for teaching, even at the elementary level, is not a watered-down version of 'real' mathematics. Teaching mathematics is a serious and demanding arena of mathematical work" (Ball, 2003, p. 8).

References

BALL, D. L. (2003). *WHAT MATHEMATICAL KNOWLEDGE IS NEEDED FOR TEACHING MATHEMATICS.* PRESENTATION FOR THE SECRETARY'S SUMMIT ON MATHEMATICS, U.S. DEPARTMENT OF EDUCATION, FEBRUARY 6, WASHINGTON, DC.

BALL, D. L., LUBIENSKI, S., & MEWBORN, D. (2001). RESEARCH ON TEACHING MATHEMATICS: THE UNSOLVED PROBLEM OF TEACHERS' MATHEMATICAL KNOWLEDGE. IN V. RICHARDSON (ED.), *HANDBOOK OF RESEARCH ON TEACHING* (4TH ED., PP. 433–456). MACMILLAN.

BALL, D., THAMES, M., & PHELPS, G. (2008). CONTENT KNOWLEDGE FOR TEACHING: WHAT MAKES IT SPECIAL? *JOURNAL OF TEACHER EDUCATION, 59*(5), 389–407.

DEPAEPE, F., VERSCHAFFEL, L., & KELCHTERMANS, G. (2013). PEDAGOGICAL CONTENT KNOWLEDGE: A SYSTEMATIC REVIEW OF THE WAY IN WHICH THE CONCEPT HAS PERVADED MATHEMATICS EDUCATIONAL RESEARCH. *TEACHING AND TEACHER EDUCATION, 34*, 12–25.

ENGAGE NY. (2021, SEPTEMBER 17). *GRADE 2 MATHEMATICS, MODULE 1, TOPIC A, LESSON 2,* [SAMPLE LESSON PLAN]. AVAILABLE VIA WWW.ENGAGENY.ORG/RESOURCE/GRADE-2-MATHEMATICS-MODULE-1-TOPIC-LESSON-2.

HILL, H. C., BALL, D. L., & SCHILLING, S. C. G. (2008). UNPACKING PEDAGOGICAL CONTENT KNOWLEDGE: CONCEPTUALIZING AND MEASURING TEACHERS'' TOPIC-SPECIFIC KNOWLEDGE OF STUDENTS. *JOURNAL FOR RESEARCH IN MATHEMATICS EDUCATION, 39*, 372–400.

HILL, H. C., ROWAN, R., & BALL, D. L. (2005). EFFECTS OF TEACHERS'' MATHEMATICAL KNOWLEDGE FOR TEACHING ON STUDENT ACHIEVEMENT. *AMERICAN EDUCATIONAL RESEARCH JOURNAL, 41*, 371–406.

HILL, H., SCHILLING, S., & BALL, D. L. (2004). DEVELOPING MEASURES OF TEACHERS' MATHEMATICS KNOWLEDGE FOR TEACHING. *THE ELEMENTARY SCHOOL JOURNAL, 105*, 11–30.

JAKOBSEN, A., THAMES, M. H., RIBEIRO, C. M., & DELANEY, S. (2012). USING PRACTICE TO DEFINE AND DISTINGUISH HORIZON CONTENT KNOWLEDGE. IN *PRE-PROCEEDINGS OF THE 12TH INTERNATIONAL CONGRESS IN MATHEMATICS EDUCATION* (PP. 4635–4644). INTERNATIONAL CONGRESS IN MATHEMATICS EDUCATION.

SHULMAN, L. S. (1986). THOSE WHO UNDERSTAND TEACH: KNOWLEDGE GROWTH IN TEACHING. *EDUCATIONAL RESEARCHER, 15*(2), 4–14.

Suggested Readings and Links

THIS IS A SAMPLE OF THE ITEMS DEVELOPED BY BALL ET AL. TO MEASURE TEACHERS' MATHEMATICAL KNOWLEDGE FOR TEACHING.

AVAILABLE VIA WWW.UMICH.EDU/~LMTWEB/FILES/LMT_SAMPLE_ITEMS.PDF

VIDEOS

MATHEMATICAL KNOWLEDGE FOR TEACHING WITH DR DEBORAH LOEWENBERG BALL

DR LOEWENBERG BALL SHARES TEACHING STRATEGIES FOR GETTING STUDENTS AND TEACHERS EXCITED ABOUT MATHEMATICS.

AVAILABLE VIA WWW.YOUTUBE.COM/WATCH?V=-UOXUQ2JUL4

DR BALL GIVES AN INTERACTIVE LECTURE ON MATHEMATICAL KNOWLEDGE FOR TEACHING INCLUDING MANY EXAMPLES OF WHAT IT IS AND HOW TO MEASURE IT.

AVAILABLE VIA WWW.YOUTUBE.COM/WATCH?V=LEASL_KK8XM

HEATHER C. HILL, PROFESSOR AT THE HARVARD GRADUATE SCHOOL OF EDUCATION, WORKS ON DEVELOPING NEW MEASURES OF MATHEMATICS TEACHING QUALITY, AND USING THESE MEASURES TO INFORM CURRENT POLICIES AND INSTRUCTIONAL IMPROVEMENT EFFORTS. PROFESSOR HILL SPOKE TO EMILY FREITAG ABOUT HER RESEARCH ON EFFECTIVE PROFESSIONAL DEVELOPMENT PROGRAMS.

AVAILABLE VIA WWW.YOUTUBE.COM/WATCH?V=Z72JL6PTM2W

HEATHER HILL AT THE PCK SUMMIT ON MATHEMATICS PCK

AVAILABLE VIA HTTPS://TINYURL.COM/8NBF38NC

WEBSITES/BLOGS

A BLOG EXPLAINING THE BALL, THAMES, AND PHELPS ARTICLE CONTENT KNOWLEDGE FOR TEACHING: WHAT MAKES IT SPECIAL?

AVAILABLE VIA HTTPS://TINYURL.COM/53U8SAWF

18

THE SCIENCE OF SCIENCE TEACHING

JAN VAN DRIEL AND COLLEAGUES ON SCIENCE PCK

18 THE SCIENCE OF SCIENCE TEACHING

ARTICLE Developing science teachers' pedagogical content knowledge[1]

QUOTE *"As a consequence of this emphasis on general aspects of PCK, the explicit attention for science teachers' knowledge and beliefs with respect to the teaching of specific topics is still marginal."*[2]

Why You Should Read This Article

If we were to pick a physical object that typifies how science is and has been taught it would probably be a pendulum. Of all school subjects, science possibly has the longest and most transitional history of approaches, swinging from lab apprenticeship to rote memorisation to a combination of labs and classroom work (and the fight between lab-classroom vs. classroom-lab) to discovery learning back to didactic instruction and then to constructivist enquiry. . . . Along with reading and mathematics, science forms the top-three of hotly debated school subjects in relation to its pedagogy. While it didn't begin then, a key moment in our thinking about how to teach science occurred in 1957 when the Soviet Union launched Sputnik 1, the world's first artificial satellite. The Americans, to put it mildly, completely flipped out. There was now a "space gap" and the U.S. determined that this needed to be rectified as quickly as possible.[3] To do this, they needed lots of new scientists and engineers and it was the job of schools to deliver them as quickly as possible. The knee-jerk reaction, which by the way sounded plausible at the time, was to look at how scientists do science and use thi as template for how to teach and train new scientists. The reasoning was that the essence of the natural sciences is doing, experimenting, and

---

1   VAN DRIEL, J. H., VERLOOP, N., & DE VOS, W. (1998). DEVELOPING SCIENCE TEACHERS'' PEDAGOGIC, CONTENT KNOWLEDGE. *JOURNAL OF RESEARCH IN SCIENCE TEACHING, 35,* 673–695.
2   IBID., P. 680.
3   FUN FACT: THIS ALSO LED TO THE ESTABLISHMENT OF ADVANCED RESEARCH PROJECTS AGENC (ARPA, LATER DARPA) IN FEBRUARY 1958. ONE OF THE PROJECTS WAS DARPANET, THE FORERUNN OF THE INTERNET!

inquiring. In those domains, scientists gain new knowledge by experimenting (both via physical- and thought experiments) and, thus, discovering new phenomena. This expert-approach quickly became the blueprint for teaching science. The problem here is that while scientists are doing science, learners are learning science and that learners should be aided in this learning through the application of an effective pedagogy and good instructional design. This means we should not use the epistemology of the scientist as pedagogy for the learner. Two ways of saying this are as follows: The science of learning and the learning of science are radically different but need to also work together and to become an expert scientist, don't do what expert scientists do.

We had a hard time here choosing between Jan van Driel, Nico Verloop, and Wobbe de Vos' article on *Developing Science Teachers' Pedagogical Content Knowledge* (1998) and Richard White and Richard Tisher's (1986) chapter *Research on Natural Sciences* in the *Handbook of Research on Teaching 3rd edition* (1986). While van Driel et al. specifically discuss the concept of PCK within the context of science teaching, White and Tisher didn't specifically discuss how to teach science but rather what research said about what's needed to teach science well. After much soul-searching we chose the former, but definitely recommend everyone read the latter!

Abstract of the Article

This article discusses the concept of pedagogical content knowledge (PCK) within the context of science teaching. First, an attempt is made to define this concept within the tradition of research on teachers' craft knowledge and to identify possible purposes of research on PCK. From this point of view, recent research on science teaching is investigated. This investigation identifies teaching experience as the major source of PCK, whereas adequate subject-matter knowledge appears to be a prerequisite. Finally, an empirical study is presented which focuses on PCK with respect to a specific topic – that is, chemical equilibrium. The effects on teachers' PCK of participation in an in-service workshop and conducting an experimental course in classroom practice are reported. This leads to the identification of elements of PCK teachers can use to promote student understanding. It is concluded that research on topic-related PCK may complement research on student learning of specific topics.

The Article

Van Driel, Verloop, and de Vos' article revolves around the question of to what extent PCK can been seen as "a valuable concept within the field of research on science teaching" (p. 673). They begin with a discussion

Teachers' craft knowledge

of what they call *teachers' craft knowledge* which they see as "integrated knowledge which represents teachers' accumulated wisdom with respect to their teaching practice. As this knowledge guides the teachers actions in practice, it encompasses teachers' knowledge and beliefs with respect to various aspects such as pedagogy, students, subject matter, and the curriculum" (p. 674). It's neither about idiosyncratic examples of individual behaviour or a prescriptive knowledge base of teaching behaviour but rather to look at common patterns in craft knowledge to ultimately develop what Grimmett and MacKinnon (1992, in this article) call a "framework for helping prospective and experienced teachers develop their repertoire of responses, understandings, and magical tricks" (p. 674).

Transformation of subject matter knowledge

Van Driel and colleagues see PCK as a specific type of teachers' craft knowledge where subject matter knowledge is transformed "so that it can be used effectively and flexibly in the communication process between teachers and learners during classroom practice" (p. 675). This could come from teachers' own teaching practice from analysing problems they've had in their teaching and from in-service courses on student conceptions. This can be knowledge of (1) strategies and representations for teaching particular topics, (2) students' understanding, conceptions, and misconceptions of these topics (see also Chapters 2 and 16; Lee Shulman), (3) the purposes for teaching particular topics, and (4) curriculum materials available for teaching. As such when teaching, their actions are determined primaril by their PCK.

> **NOTE HERE** that they exclude pre-service instruction, and explicitly state that "PCK is developed through an integrative process rooted in classroom practice, implying that prospective or beginning teachers usually have little or no PCK at their disposal. This supports our view that PCK is indeed a specific type of teachers' craft knowledge" (p. 677).

They then discuss science teacher's craft knowledge as being determined by teachers' conceptions of the

Nature of science

- *Nature of science* – Science is dynamic and constantly in flux. What may have been "true" yesterday may be questioned today and be eith· amended or discarded tomorrow. This, unfortunately, isn't always reflected in school or university curricula where it's often taught as a series of truths and rules. Possibly as a result of this, science teachers appear to "possess limited knowledge of the history and philosophy of science' and, thus, "hold inadequate or naive conceptions of the nature of science" along with "positivist views, believing that the substantive content of science is fixed and unchangeable rather than tentative" (p. 678).

Teaching and learning of science

- *Teaching and learning of science* – When the article was written (1998), in-service and pre-service teacher training programmes focussed teachers' conceptions of teaching and learning in science, firmly rooted in a constructivist epistemology emphasising conceptual change which proved to be problematic as teachers' positivist belief structures or their commitment to the existing curriculum appeared to hinder implementation.

- *Relations between the two* – Here we see a large difference between experienced and beginning teachers. Experienced teachers have a conceptual framework where their knowledge and beliefs about science, subject matter, teaching and learning, and students are coherently interrelated and are consistent with their teaching behaviour. Beginning teachers, on the other hand, don't have this framework. They experience conflicts between their personal views of science and science teaching and their own actual classroom practice.

Problems of less-experienced teachers

The article then transitions from a discussion of teachers' craft knowledge to their PCK in science. They note that when teaching unfamiliar topics, less-experienced teachers (1) are unaware of potential problems that students may incur and of their specific preconceptions (or to say this another way: not only don't they know what they don't know, but they also don't know what their students don't know!), (2) have problems choosing appropriate representations of subject matter to explain or illustrate concepts, (3) themselves tend to have more misconceptions about the topic in question, and (4) talk longer and more often limit themselves to posing questions of low cognitive level. Experienced teachers, on the other hand, "when teaching a topic out of their area of certification, seem to be sustained by their wealth of general pedagogical knowledge, while their PCK is limited" and "quickly learn the new content as well as adequate content-specific instructional strategies, while relying on their knowledge of general pedagogy" (p. 679). In other words, citing Sanders et al. (1993, p. 733) their general "pedagogical knowledge provides them with a framework for teaching that is filled in by content knowledge and pedagogical content knowledge . . . when teachers taught within and outside their science area".

Experienced
teachers vs. Expert
teachers

EXPERIENCED TEACHERS VS. EXPERT TEACHERS

JOHN HATTIE (2003), in discussing the difference between experienced and expert teachers, noted that expert teachers:

- have deep conceptual representations of the learning content, the teaching of that content, and how learners learn. As a result of this, their knowledge is better organised, they're better at seeing and explaining connections between (new) content and learners' prior knowledge, are able to connect learning content to other topics in the curriculum, and so forth;
- set challenging goals for learners and give them difficult tasks; and
- are better at monitoring problems from learners and give the learners more relevant and useful feedback.

The second and third characteristics of expert teachers are very close to what can be considered to be PCK: setting goals, designing tasks, monitoring the learning process, and giving feedback. These things are only possible if the first characteristic is the case.

PCK comes
after domain
knowledge and
general pedagogic
knowledge

Sobering, as far as what can and/or has been achieved in teacher training institutions (i.e., in pre-service teacher training) is their conclusion that knowledge of instructional strategies to teach their subject comes from the beginning teachers' experiences as learners themselves and as teacher or teaching assistants, and not from their training. According to them, it's not really realistic to expect them to have readily accessible subject-matter knowledge that's translatable into classroom practice until they've gained adequate teaching experience and have mastered basic (i.e., generic) classroom skills. The changes in both teachers' pedagogical knowledge and the subject-matter domain which are necessary to become good science teachers take place as a result of teaching experiences and, consequentially, preservice teachers don't (or possibly can't) integrate these domains. Van Driel et al. conclude that "with the benefit of experience and continual use of one's subject matter structure for purposes of teaching, the division between pedagogical knowledge and subject matter knowledge may become blurred. Thus, the development of PCK may be postponed until teachers reach this stage" (p. 681). Or to say it another way, PCK is best developed when the teacher has a sufficient basis in both the subject matter itself and the general theories of teaching. Good coaching in the first years of teaching could help bridge this gap.

The authors conclude with a description of their own empirical study on teachers' PCK of a specific topic (i.e., chemical equilibrium) in the context of an "educational innovation" *[our quotes]* to promote conceptual change among students. They designed an experimental course for upper-secondary/high school students on chemical equilibrium for realising student conceptual change and implemented an in-service workshop for chemistry teachers to help them teach it. The results showed that, though the teachers were experienced, they

> lacked theoretical arguments to promote student understand-
> ing . . . [admitting] that their usual arguments are weak and not
> very convincing . . . [and that] the best they felt they could do was to
> demonstrate the dynamic equilibrium conception with the help of
> metaphors or analogies. In their eyes, the status quo isn't adequate.
> (p. 686)

Teachers' need to supplement their subject-matter knowledge "by studying the structure and evolution of students' ideas about particular topics" and that "teacher training programs should provide opportunities to use PCK in teaching situations and to reflect on these practical experiences" (p. 690). They go so far as to suggest teacher-training programmes include

> a course on topic-related PCK [that] includes activities which invite
> teachers to (a) critically review schoolbooks, (b) perform scientific
> experiments, and (c) study authentic student responses. Through
> specific assignments and discussions, participants may be stimulated
> to integrate these activities and to reflect on both academic subject
> matter and on classroom practice. In this way, participants' PCK may
> be improved. (p. 691)

Conclusions

Teachers' *craft knowledge* comprises a framework which integrates the teachers' knowledge and beliefs about teaching and learning science, the nature of science, the subject matter, and students. Their conceptions about what teaching and learning science is are rather stable (i.e., positivist, constant) and are often formed in the time that they themselves were students. This exerts a major influence on their teaching practice.

Studies on science teachers' PCK indicate that a thorough coherent understanding of subject matter acting together with teaching experience are necessary but not sufficient for PCK development.

Even experienced teachers need in-service training around specific topics to develop PCK. This explains why future or beginning science teachers who may have the necessary subject-matter knowledge but who miss experience teaching that topic exhibit little to no PCK. Unfortunately, teacher training programs – at least when the article was published – seemed primarily to concentrate on general pedagogical knowledge and/or subject-matter knowledge and, thus, usually don't exert a major influence on the development of science teachers' PCK (see also Chapter 30 of this book).

Takeaways

- The science of learning and the learning of science are radically different but need to also work together.
- PCK doesn't come easy or quickly.
- General pedagogical knowledge functions as a supporting framework for the development of PCK.
- Familiarity with specific topics in combination with teaching experience therein positively contributes to PCK.
- Experienced science teachers' PCK may differ considerably, even when their subject-matter knowledge is similar and when they teach the same curriculum.
- Preservice teacher training isn't effective for helping prospective teachers gain the PCK they need to teach their subject properly.
- PCK is best developed when the teacher has a sufficient basis in both the subject matter itself and the general theories of teaching.

References

GRIMMETT, P., & MACKINNON, A. (1992). CRAFT KNOWLEDGE AND THE EDUCATION OF TEACHERS. IN G. GRANT (ED.), *REVIEW OF RESEARCH IN EDUCATION* (VOL. 18, PP. 385–456). AMERICA EDUCATIONAL RESEARCH ASSOCIATION.

HATTIE, J. A. C. (2003, OCTOBER). *TEACHERS MAKE A DIFFERENCE: WHAT IS THE RESEARCH EVIDEN* PAPER PRESENTED AT THE BUILDING TEACHER QUALITY: WHAT DOES THE RESEARCH TELL US ACER RESEARCH CONFERENCE, MELBOURNE, AUSTRALIA. AVAILABLE VIA HTTP://RESEARCH.ACEF EDU.AU/RESEARCH_CONFERENCE_2003/4.

SANDERS, L. R., BORKO, H., & LOCKARD, J. D. (1993). SECONDARY SCIENCE TEACHERS' KNOWLEDGE BASE WHEN TEACHING SCIENCE COURSES IN AND OUT OF THEIR AREA OF CERTIFICATION. *JOURNAL OF RESEARCH IN SCIENCE TEACHING, 3,* 723–736.

VAN DRIEL, J. H., VERLOOP, N., & DE VOS, W. (1998). DEVELOPING SCIENCE TEACHERS' PEDAGOGICAL CONTENT KNOWLEDGE. *JOURNAL OF RESEARCH IN SCIENCE TEACHING, 35,* 673–69

Suggested Readings and Links

KIND, V. (2009). PEDAGOGICAL CONTENT KNOWLEDGE IN SCIENCE EDUCATION: POTENTIAL AND PERSPECTIVES FOR PROGRESS. *STUDIES IN SCIENCE EDUCATION*, *45*(2), 169–204.

WHITE, R. T., & TISHER, R. P. (1986). RESEARCH ON NATURAL SCIENCES. IN M. C. WITTROCK (ED.), *HANDBOOK OF RESEARCH ON TEACHING* (3RD ED., PP. 874–905). MACMILLAN.

VIDEOS

PRESENTATION BY JAN VAN DRIEL AT THE PCK SUMMIT

AVAILABLE VIA WWW.YOUTUBE.COM/USER/BSCSVIDEOS

WEBSITES

PEDAGOGICAL CONTENT KNOWLEDGE IN SCIENCE TEACHING FROM *THE SOURCEBOOK FOR TEACHING SCIENCE*.

INCLUDES A BIBLIOGRAPHY ON PCK, A BIBLIOGRAPHY ON PCK IN SCIENCE, AND FRAMEWORKS FOR REPRESENTING SCIENCE TEACHERS' PCK

AVAILABLE VIA WWW.CSUN.EDU/SCIENCE/REF/PEDAGOGY/PCK/

19 THREE CHORDS AND THE TRUTH

PAMELA GROSSMAN AND LEE SHULMAN ON PCK AND ENGLISH

DOI: 10.4324/9781003228165-23

19 THREE CHORDS AND THE TRUTH

CHAPTER   Knowing, believing, and the teaching of English[1]

QUOTE   *"The question of what teachers should understand if they wish to teach a domain responsibly is no simple challenge. In the field of English teaching, where canons are under question and 'consensus' is more frequently misspelled than accomplished, th problem of teacher knowledge is daunting."*[2]

Why You Should Read This Chapter

In the 1950s, Harlan Howard who had written hit songs for huge names in the music industry like Patsy Cline, Ray Charles, and Johnny Cash was asked about song writing, specifically country music. According to Howard, all you need to write a good country song is "three chords and the truth".[3] Many years later, Lou Reed would claim that "One chord is fine. Two chords is pushing it. Three chords and you're into jazz". Now of course there's nothing wrong with complex music featuring more than three chords but there's a certain nobility to early gospel, blues, and country which all rock music is based on. Unfortunately, a lot of research in the field of English education is less "three chords and the truth" and more like Spinal Tap's free form and radically experimental progressive rock piece *Jazz Odyssey*. Very often, the mechanics of English teaching has been reified into highly complex jargon that has its roots in political ideology or postmodern philosophy without attending to curricular concerns or the cognitive architecture of how we learn. What's refreshin about Shulman's work on pedagogical content knowledge is that he's

"Three chords and the truth"

---

1   GROSSMAN, P. L., & SHULMAN, L. S. (1994). KNOWING, BELIEVING, AND THE TEACHING OF ENGLI IN T. SHANAHAN (ED.), *TEACHERS THINKING, TEACHERS KNOWING: REFLECTIONS ON LITERACY A LANGUAGE EDUCATION* (PP. 3–22). NATIONAL COUNCIL OF TEACHERS OF ENGLISH

2   IBID., P. 3.

3   DANSBY, A. (2002, MARCH 5). COUNTRY SCRIBE HARLAN HOWARD DIES. *ROLLING STC MAGAZINE* (ONLINE EDITION). AVAILABLE VIA WWW.ROLLINGSTONE.COM/MUSIC/MUSIC-NEV COUNTRY-SCRIBE-HARLAN-HOWARD-DIES-197596/

essentially steering the conversation back to "three chords and the truth" and explicitly asking, "what do English teachers need to know and do?'

In fairness, English teaching is not like other subjects. Using pedagogical content knowledge for teaching English gets into problems when we deal with things other than the language aspect of the discipline of English (or possibly any first-language teaching such as Dutch in the Netherlands and Flanders or even art or music). So for the authors here, a central problem with English as a subject is its ongoing identity crisis. There's broad agreement in other subjects like Maths, Science, Economics, Geography et cetera in terms of curriculum and definitions of success however the same cannot be said of English or other arts. Indeed, as one commentator puts it, English is "the least subject-like of subjects, the least susceptible to definition" (Rosen, 1981, p. 5).

Abstract of the Chapter

What do good teachers know and how do they construct their insights about literacy, interpretation, and craft? Pamela Grossman and Lee Shulman reflect on the scope of English education, and consider the nature of knowledge in English. They then carefully explore the development of teacher knowledge in English language arts instruction. On the basis of their analysis, they propose a professional education focused on the interpretation of "cases of teaching". . . . How can we think about teacher knowledge in English? What are the grounds on which competing claims for needed teacher knowledge can be supported or dismissed? What are the implications of such positions for views of teacher preparation that include the liberal arts component of undergraduate education, as well as coursework in pedagogy? What kinds of research in learning, teaching, and teacher development can be fruitfully pursued in conjunction with these questions?

The Chapter

The Diffuse Nature of English as a Subject Area

In many ways, trying to parse out what English[4] as a subject is can be considered an attempt to define the indefinable. For a start when we talk about "English" as a subject, we are really talking about two subjects: English language (i.e., the discipline) and English literature (i.e., the art) of which there are two key components, reading and writing. In their chapter, Grossman and Shulman begin by trying to define what we mean

---

[4] THOUGH THIS CHAPTER IS ABOUT ENGLISH, ONE COULD CONSIDER WHAT BOTH GROSSMAN AND SHULMAN AND WE WRITE VALID FOR ANY LANGUAGE TAUGHT AS A FIRST LANGUAGE OR EVEN ANY OTHER SUBJECT THAT CAN BE ALSO CONSIDERED TO BE AN "ART".

by English teaching, invoking Applebee's (1974) assertion that whether we are talking about the three basic disciplines of language, literature, or composition the fact remains that inevitably, "the edges of the subject have blurred and wavered, creating for the teacher of English a perpetual crisis of identity" (p. 245–246).

This identity crisis is not so present in other subjects. While there's often broad agreement in other subjects in terms of curriculum and definitions of success, the same cannot be said of English. As a result of this ambiguity, research in this area has proved difficult with researchers focusing on reading, writing, or oracy. "The areas of language, literature, and writing are not as detachable in practice as we sometimes represent them to be in research. So the multifaceted and diffuse nature of English as a subject area poses dilemmas for research on teacher knowledge" (p. 4).

Reading, writing, oracy

Furthermore, individual teacher autonomy is perhaps more present in English teaching than any other subject. Although there may be poetry or prose or drama prescribed by a curriculum at a particular time, many English teachers are free to choose the novels or poems they wish to cover: "The inherent complexity of the subject, with its separate domain and subcomponents, may also offer teachers greater autonomy in developing curriculum" (Grossman, 1993, p. 7). This makes research into English teaching extremely difficult as quite often the variation within this one subject is greater than the variation between many others.

Teacher autonomy

The Nature of Knowledge in English

As a result of this diffusion, the next big question is this: What do we mean by knowledge in English? There has been much research into teacher knowledge in Science and Maths where practitioner knowledge is compared with experts in the field however, knowledge in English teaching is still largely characterised by what Bruner (1986) terms "paradigmatic ways of knowing". In other words, English teachers tend to understand their subject in a *narrative* way as opposed to a classificatory way where for example, if two teachers are teaching Romantic poetry, they may consider the topic in a thematic way with a focus on context and broader concepts such as The Enlightenment and Burke's notion of the Sublime but then choose very choose different poems and poets. So two English teachers might have very different knowledge bases even on the same topic. As the authors state, "if English represents a set of competing schools of thought regarding the very nature of reading and writing, what does it mean to know English well enough to teach it?" (p. 5). In answering this, the authors claim that teachers themselves must be "fully literate" (p. 5) in which they invoke Wells' (1990, p. 374) definition of the term:

> This, then, is the empowerment that comes from engaging with texts epistemically: as a reader or writer (and particularly as a writer), by conducting the transaction between the representation on the page and the representation in the head, one can make advances in one's intellectual, moral, or affective understanding to an extent that would otherwise be difficult or impossible to achieve. To be fully literate, therefore, is to have both the ability and the disposition to engage with texts epistemically when the occasion demands.

A key aspect of English literature, indeed one that is deemed an integral part of it, is the notion that two different interpretations can be true at the same time. In fact multiple interpretations of the same text are what characterise the kind of theoretical literary analysis English are trained in at university level. This capacity to engage with texts on an epistemic level may be the "legacy of a liberal education" (p. 6) as the authors put it where there is a tacit acknowledgement that all sources of knowledge are rooted in certain times and places and the fact that "some texts manage to transcend the particularities of their times and places, that 'King Lear', for example, can be read by contemporary Japanese readers, is testimony to a certain greatness in the text" (p. 6).

English literature is about multiple interpretations

Knowing what students don't know

KNOWING WHAT STUDENTS DON'T KNOW

But it's not just about knowing the narrative, language and context of a play like *King Lear*, teachers also need to have explicit knowledge about their own theoretical stances, or their "predominant orientations toward literature, in order to help others see the assumptions guiding a particular reading of a text" (p. 6). If English teachers want to be able to teach students multiple ways of reading a text, then they need to know what those multiple readings are. This leads to a familiar refrain from the research on PCK which is reiterated here, namely that it's not enough to know what students understand, teachers need to know what students *misunderstand*. Having a strong conceptualisation of where student misunderstandings and misconceptions come from means having a strong grasp of subject knowledge and the theoretical assumptions underpinning it.

Procedural and declarative knowledge

Take the area of writing for example where there's a hugely important distinction between procedural and declarative knowledge. Teachers can teach declarative knowledge about writing quite easily but teachers also

The curse of knowledge

have procedural knowledge about their own writing which is often at an expert level compared to their students, which can lead to an inability to understand why students can't grasp certain basic aspects of writing (or what seem to them at least basic), a phenomenon known as the curse of knowledge. An important question then is, what is the relationship between "knowing about writing and knowing how to write?" (p. 6).

For many English teachers, much of what they have learned is tacit knowledge which is not easily codifiable: "For teachers who grew up speaking standard or mainstream English, the process of internalizing the rules was not a self-conscious one; in detecting and remediating errors, they may rely on what "sounds right" (p. 6). So how should teachers then respond to students who have radically different knowledge and experiences with language and dialect? In other words, the experienced English teacher who has read 600 novels will have a fairly complex mental model of what sophisticated fiction looks like, and while you can break that down into component parts to a certain extent with a focus on sentence structure, more complex vocabulary, accurate spelling and so on, trying to teach a novice to write sophisticated fiction is like telling a stand-up comedian to be funnier.

Knowledge Growth in Teaching Research

In an earlier work on PCK, *Knowledge and Teaching*, Shulman (1987; see also Chapter 16) set forth a model in which teaching is seen as an "alternating and simultaneous interaction of teacher understanding, transformation, action, evaluation and reflection, and progressive development of new understandings" (p. 7). What follows in this section is a closer examination of evidence collected by the researchers on the relationship disciplinary and pedagogical knowledge.

The purpose of the *Knowledge Growth in Teaching* studies was to track the growth and use of subject-matter knowledge among preservice teachers during their year of preparation and their first year of teaching Of particular interest was how English teachers used the knowledge they had learned during their undergraduate training and how they constructed new understandings based on how they learned to teach. Due to some of the difficulties outlined above, more robust research methodologies gave way to self-report, interviews, and teachers responding to literature or a piece of writing. In response to the question "what is the meaning of this poem?" two English teachers gave the following answers:

> Because you can't capture in prose what poetry does. I mean it's always this illusion that the poem meant, is saying, this thing and

that . . . you could just say it. But you can't just say it. And so it pro-
motes this kind of bad way of thinking about poetry, which isn't a
good idea, I think. (Lance)

I don't like these [questions] as well, because they're too specific. . . .
I like to give my kids questions that they can't copy and that they can
each have their own answer to and support them, and that way they'll
have to and they will get more excited about what they're doing if
they have to support what they're doing. This kind of stuff is good to
help them start understanding a poem. (Vanessa, p. 8)

What's notable here is that Lance's response is an objection on
disciplinary grounds, while the Vanessa's is an objection on pedagogical
grounds. In other words, one is taking issue with the *appreciation* of
poetry while the other is disputing the *teaching* of it. The confusion
between these two conceptions lies at the heart of many debates about
English teaching.

The appreciation of literature versus the teaching of it

Implications for Professional Education

The authors note that there's a significant evidence base[5] emphasising
the importance of subject specific training in English teaching and
the dangers of generic pedagogy. Teaching is highly variable and one
of the most difficult aspects of the profession is the ability to "draw
upon and integrate multiple knowledge domains under conditions
of uncertainty and novelty" (p. 10). In this sense, the authors call for
a series of cases to be put to new teachers (see the case of Nancy the
veteran English teacher in Chapter 16) in order to allow them to build a
flexible mental model of expert English teaching which can respond to
novel situations:

A mental model of success through multiple cases

Cases of teaching, as opposed to prescriptive proclamations of best
practice, can attempt to represent the messy world of actual practice, in which often neither the problem nor the solution is clear.
To prepare prospective teachers for the widely diverse settings in
which they will teach, proponents of case methods argue that it is
better to engage them in discussions of ten cases of the teaching of
Hamlet in a host of different contexts than to offer them the one
best way. (p. 10)

---

5   (COMEAUX & GOMEZ, 1990, 1991; FLORIO-RUANE ET AL., 1990; GROSSMAN, 1990; GROSSMAN &
RICHERT, 1988; RITCHIE & WILSON, 1993).

In the domain of English teaching, the signal to noise ratio between research on how to teach, the messiness of pedagogical content knowledge, and the actuality of the classroom means that teachers nee to build up a specific kind of flexible knowledge which is "composed largely of a repertoire of cases, of what happened in particular classes with specific kids" (p. 11). English teaching is highly complex but if we bring it back to "three chords and the truth" then the expert teacher is able to achieve the counter-intuitive notion of complexity through simplicity by drawing on sophisticated models of success to automate their practice. In other words, the teacher who has a rich yet flexible understanding of Shakespeare, how to teach it and an internal bank of how to *vary* that practice according to age, ability or time of day/ year will be operating at a very high level. Once these key components are automated, then the teacher's bandwidth is freed up to focus on behaviour issues, questions from students, addressing misconceptions and attending to the students who need help.

Conclusions

The importance of subject knowledge

Firstly, the authors state quite plainly that "subject-matter knowledge matters" (p. 8). The knowledge teachers had about the subject and wha their beliefs as a result of this knowledge affected "how they planned for instruction, how they selected texts and organized curricula, and how they interacted with students in the classroom" (p. 8). However, subject knowledge alone is not enough. Knowing Shakespeare is not th same as knowing how to teach Shakespeare to a "diverse set of learners in particular contexts" (p. 8). Without an understanding of how to teach subject knowledge, or make it come alive, beginning teachers in particular can struggle as this account indicates. Lance spoke of his lac of success in teaching *Romeo and Juliet* to ninth graders:

> It was really hard for me to adjust my expectations in the sense tha I was always interested in pushing ideas to the extreme, like provin the most obscure theses and showing little nuances in the languag that no one had even seen and why that works. And these kids, of course I know that now, wanted nothing to do with that. That was j totally irrelevant to them. (Grossman, 1990, p. 107)

This also highlights the necessity for other forms of knowledge to interact with subject and pedagogical content knowledge. For example Lance would later learn that in order for him to have that envisioned classroom where his students are exchanging a range of different interpretations in a collegiate and constructive manner, he needed to learn how to manage the group dynamics in other to create the conditions where student thinking can flourish. As the authors note, the "different domains of teacher knowledge are inevitably interactive and interdependent" (p. 9).

Takeaways

- English as a first language, as is the case of any first language or other subjects that could be considered to be an "art", has two components namely English as a discipline (i.e., the language) and English as an art (i.e., literature).
- English teachers need to be "fully literate" with a strong subject knowledge of what they're teaching.
- English teaching is largely about giving students the ability to become "critical consumers" of a text and be able to construct multiple meanings.
- English teachers must also have "explicit knowledge about their own theoretical stances" toward literature.
- It's not enough to know what a student understands, teachers need to know what they *don't understand* or *misunderstand*.
- However, "knowing English is not the same as knowing how to teach English to a diverse set of learners in particular contexts" (p. 8).

References

APPLEBEE, A. N. (1974). *TRADITION AND REFORM IN THE TEACHING OF ENGLISH: A HISTORY.* NATIONAL COUNCIL OF TEACHERS OF ENGLISH.

BRUNER, J. S. (1986). *ACTUAL MINDS, POSSIBLE WORLDS.* HARVARD UNIVERSITY PRESS.

COMEAUX, M. A., & GOMEZ, M. L. (1990). *WHY SARAH DOESN'T TEACH LIKE SANDRA: EXPLORING THE DEVELOPMENT OF PROSPECTIVE TEACHERS' KNOWLEDGE, BELIEFS, AND DISPOSITIONS ABOUT TEACHING WRITING.* PAPER PRESENTED AT THE ANNUAL MEETING OF THE AMERICAN EDUCATIONAL RESEARCH ASSOCIATION, APRIL, BOSTON.

DANSBY, A. (2002, MARCH 5). COUNTRY SCRIBE HARLAN HOWARD DIES. *ROLLING STONE MAGAZINE* (ONLINE EDITION). AVAILABLE VIA WWW.ROLLINGSTONE.COM/MUSIC/MUSIC-NEWS/COUNTRY-SCRIBE-HARLAN-HOWARD-DIES-197596/

FLORIO-RUANE, S., MOSENTHAL, J., DENYER, J., HARRIS, D., & KIRSCHER, B. (1990). *CONSTRUCTING KNOWLEDGE IN CLASSROOM INTERACTION: A PROBLEM IN LEARNING TO TEACH ABOUT TEXT.* PAPER PRESENTED AT THE ANNUAL MEETING OF THE AMERICAN EDUCATIONAL RESEARCH ASSOCIATION, APRIL, BOSTON.

GROSSMAN, P. L. (1990). *THE MAKING OF A TEACHER: TEACHER KNOWLEDGE AND TEACHER EDUCATION.* TEACHERS COLLEGE PRESS.

GROSSMAN, P. L. (1993). *ENGLISH AS CONTEXT: ENGLISH IN CONTEXT. TECHNICAL REPORT S93-2.* CENTER FOR RESEARCH ON THE CONTEXT OF SECONDARY SCHOOL TEACHING.

GROSSMAN, P. L., & RICHERT, A. E. (1988). UNACKNOWLEDGED KNOWLEDGE GROWTH: A RE-EXAMINATION OF THE EFFECTS OF TEACHER EDUCATION. *TEACHING AND TEACHER EDUCATION,* 4(1), 53–62.

GROSSMAN, P. L., & SHULMAN, L. S. (1994). KNOWING, BELIEVING, AND THE TEACHING OF ENGLISH. IN T. SHANAHAN (ED.), *TEACHERS THINKING, TEACHERS KNOWING: REFLECTIONS ON LITERACY AND LANGUAGE EDUCATION* (PP. 3–22). NATIONAL COUNCIL OF TEACHERS OF ENGLISH.

REED, L. (2021, OCTOBER 26). AVAILABLE VIA WWW.ROLLINGSTONE.COM/MUSIC/MUSIC-NEWS/ LOU-REED-VELVET-UNDERGROUND-LEADER-AND-ROCK-PIONEER-DEAD-AT-71-100874.

RITCHIE, J. S., & WILSON, D. E. (1993, MAY). DUAL APPRENTICESHIPS: SUBVERTING AND SUPPORTING CRITICAL TEACHING. *ENGLISH EDUCATION, 25*(2), 67–83.

ROSEN, H. (1981). *NEITHER BLEAK HOUSE NOR LIBERTY HALL.* UNIVERSITY OF LONDON INSTITUTE OF EDUCATION. CITED IN PROTHEROUGH 1989.

SHULMAN, L. (1987). KNOWLEDGE AND TEACHING: FOUNDATIONS OF THE NEW REFORM. *HARVARD EDUCATIONAL REVIEW, 57*(1), 1–23.

WELLS, G. (1990). TALK ABOUT TEXT: WHERE LITERACY IS LEARNED AND TAUGHT. *CURRICULUM INQUIRY, 20,* 369–405.

Suggested Readings and Links

PAPER IN WHICH PAM GROSSMAN INVESTIGATED THE INFLUENCE OF SUBJECT-SPECIFIC COURSE- WORK IN THE DEVELOPMENT OF PEDAGOGICAL CONTENT KNOWLEDGE IN ENGLISH THROUGH CONTRASTING CASE STUDIES OF SIX BEGINNING ENGLISH TEACHERS, ONLY THREE OF WHOM GRADUATED FROM TEACHER EDUCATION.

HOWEY, K. R., & GROSSMAN, P. L. (1989). A STUDY IN CONTRAST: SOURCES OF PEDAGOGICAL CONTENT KNOWLEDGE FOR SECONDARY ENGLISH. *JOURNAL OF TEACHER EDUCATION, 40*(5), 24–31. DOI:10.1177/002248718904000504

VIDEOS

DESCRIPTION – PAM GROSSMAN GIVING THE DEMARZANO LECTURE ON TEACHING EXCELLENCE BASED ON HER OWN RESEARCH ON ENGLISH TEACHING.

AVAILABLE VIA HTTPS://YOUTU.BE/FXFOQX5FPHU

20 HOW SHOULD WE TEACH READING?

ANNE CASTLES AND COLLEAGUES ON THE SCIENCE OF READING

DOI: 10.4324/9781003228165-24

20 HOW SHOULD WE TEACH READING?

ARTICLE Ending the Reading Wars: Reading Acquisition From Novice to Expert[1]

QUOTE *"Learning to read transforms lives."*[2]

Why You Should Read This Article

A philosophy is not a pedagogy

Imagine you are learning to drive a car. You meet your instructor who shows your all the pedals, the gearstick, the safety features and all the buttons and dials on the dashboard. He then shows your how to turn the key in the ignition to switch the engine on and then turns to you with a knowing smile and says "ok, away you go". Not only is this a bad way to learn how to drive but it would also be very dangerous. Yet similar approaches are often used with young children when they're faced with learning possibly the most important thing they'll ever learn in their lives: how to read. This also illustrates a dominant theme in this book, namely that the relationship between teaching and learning is often a confusing one where you often have to do the *opposite* of what seems necessary in the early stages and where the biggest error is to confuse th outcome with the method: a pedagogical philosophy or desired outcome is not always a good basis for designing instruction for that outcome. In other words, the aim of learning to drive a car is to be able to drive on your own with no support but as a means of *teaching* someone to drive, that approach would be disastrous. In the early stages of learning to driv a car you need clear and explicit instruction, careful scaffolding and close monitoring of progress. Sadly, similar approaches have been used to teach young children to read despite strong evidence to the contrary resulting in decades of fierce debate on how to teach reading.

---

1   CASTLES, A., RASTLE, K., & NATION, K. (2018). ENDING THE READING WARS: READING ACQUISITIC FROM NOVICE TO EXPERT. *PSYCHOLOGICAL SCIENCE IN THE PUBLIC INTEREST, 19*(1), 5–51. REPRINTE BY PERMISSION OF SAGE PUBLICATIONS.

2   IBID., P. 5.

Broadly speaking the "reading wars" are a long running series of skirmishes between two schools of thought: those who favour a "whole-language" approach in the teaching of early reading where children discover meaning through an immersion in reading and being read *to* with a focus on whole words as opposed to the more mechanistic approach of phonics-based instruction where children are explicitly taught the relationships between letters and sounds. This article by Anne Castles et al. seeks to end those wars by presenting the overwhelming body of evidence which favours the latter.

Abstract of the Article

There is intense public interest in questions surrounding how children learn to read and how they can best be taught. Research in psychological science has provided answers to many of these questions but, somewhat surprisingly, this research has been slow to make inroads into educational policy and practice. Instead, the field has been plagued by decades of "reading wars". Even now, there remains a wide gap between the state of research knowledge about learning to read and the state of public understanding. The aim of this article is to fill this gap. We present a comprehensive tutorial review of the science of learning to read, spanning from children's earliest alphabetic skills through to the fluent word recognition and skilled text comprehension characteristic of expert readers. We explain why phonics instruction is so central to learning in a writing system such as English. But we also move beyond phonics, reviewing research on what else children need to learn to become expert readers and considering how this might be translated into effective classroom practice. We call for an end to the reading wars and recommend an agenda for instruction and research in reading acquisition that is balanced, developmentally informed, and based on a deep understanding of how language and writing systems work.

The Article

The reading wars have a long and chequered history. They go back more than 200 years when Horace Mann (Secretary of the Massachusetts Board of Education) took great issue with the teaching of letter-sound correspondences referring to letters as "skeleton-shaped, bloodless, ghostly apparitions" and claiming "It is no wonder that the children look and feel so death-like, when compelled to face them" (Adams, 1990, p. 22). Not much has changed since then but this article seeks to synthesise the most reliable research available in the hope of providing clarity.

Despite the years of confusion, over many years the tide has slowly turned towards approaches favouring a phonics approach, in which the

Whole language vs phonics

sounds that letters make are taught explicitly, over a whole-language approach, which "emphasizes the child's discovery of meaning through experiences in a literacy-rich environment" (p. 5). Despite this, there still exist many misconceptions in early reading instruction due to gaps in teacher knowledge and patchy teacher training.

As we illustrated in our first book in Chapter 2 (evolutionary psychology), most children learn to understand spoken language and speak it themselves with relative ease. Indeed, as Pinker (2009) puts it, "there is almost no way to prevent it from happening, short of raising a child in a barrel" (p. 29). However, learning to read and write is a different story. Most children have a relatively complex understanding of the meanings of many words at a relatively early age but the challenge of reading is to "learn to associate arbitrary visual symbols – patterns of lines, curves, and dots – with those meanings" (p. 8).

Literacy is more than decoding letters and words

Although there have been many reviews showing the strength of phonics instruction, there have been little in showing *why* it works. To that end the authors claim that once we understand how and *why* the reading and writing system works, it becomes obvious that phonics should be used in the early stages of instruction. Secondly, there has not been a discussion in the public domain which examines the fact that even if children can decode letters and words, their domain specific knowledge can limit their understanding and internal construction of meaning which is the ultimate point of literacy. Literacy isn't simply the recognition of letter/sound relationships. In order to be confident successful readers, "children need to learn to recognize words and compute their meanings rapidly without having to engage in translation back to sounds" (p. 6).

The aforementioned "wars" are often characterised by discussions around pedagogical philosophy, over how children can best learn to link the written word to oral language. However, a crucial point is that "the most appropriate way to learn this mapping is governed not by pedagogical philosophy but by the nature of the writing system the child needs to learn" (p. 9). In other words, when we learn what reading *actually is* through the alphabetic systems that are used, we are in a better place to consider what approaches work best.

WHAT IS READING?

The authors define the goal of reading quite simply as "to understand what has been read" (p. 7). To illustrate this, consider the following two sentences:

"Denise was stuck in a jam. She was worried what her boss would say".

(Continued)

(Continued)

Firstly, the student needs to comprehend the individual words. This means they need to distinguish the word *jam* from similar words such as *ham* or *jar*. Then they need to find a way of understanding unfamiliar words such as *Denise* or words in an unusual form such as *worried*. But comprehension does not mean merely decoding words. They need to understand the underlying meaning of these words. So the word *jam* here needs to be understood in the context of traffic as opposed to the context of a fruit preserve and that *she* and *her* need to be understood as relating to Denise in the first sentence.

The importance of background knowledge

Furthermore, these two sentences demonstrate the fundamental requirement of *background knowledge*. Integrating this new information with existing knowledge places a strain on working memory especially if there's no existing knowledge with which to integrate it. Knowing what to focus on and what to *ignore* is a largely automatic process for the expert reader but for the novice reader it can quickly result in a feeling of being overwhelmed.

Learning to Read

Alphabetic systems function primarily through the phonemes of the language (sounds) being represented by letters or groups of letters (graphemes; e.g., b → /b/, ph → /f/). The decoding of this relationship determines the child's ability to make meaning of what they're reading. In the English alphabetic system this is complicated by the relative *orthographic depth* of the system, in other words the extent to which the letters are consistent in their meaning. For example, the letter-pairing *gh* in the word *ghost* makes one sound whereas *gh* in the word *rough* makes a completely different sound. Another example is the fact that vowel sound in *wash* appears unusual compared with *cash, stash*, and *dash*.

Why is it so important to crack the alphabetic code? Wouldn't it be better for children to learn whole words instead? Castle et al. cite several studies on preliterate children with exactly this aim. The results were clear:

> Children who knew no letter names were taught to read aloud pairs of written words, such as *fat* and *bat*. Subsequently, they were challenged with a transfer task in which they were shown, for instance, the written word fun and then asked whether the word was "fun" or "bun". The results were clear: Across more than 80 preschool children who participated in the various experiments, virtually none

succeeded on the transfer task. When left to their own devices, the children showed no evidence of inducing the alphabetic principle.

(p. 10)

A follow up study was done and which showed that reliable success on the transfer task was achieved "only when children were trained such that they could (a) segment phonemes in spoken words and identify their initial phonemes and (b) recognize the graphic symbols that corresponded to the key sounds in the transfer task" (p. 10). The authors show that these findings are corroborated with a wide body of research. What this clearly shows is that learning the relationship between letters and sounds and thus being able to make meaning of the written word is a skill which doesn't come naturally to children and must be taught explicitly. As the authors demonstrate, the evidence for the effectiveness of phonics instruction is "extensive and has been surveyed comprehensively elsewhere" (p. 12) but despite this there's a widespread misunderstanding in the wider public domain. Some of these myths can be seen in Table 20.1.

TABLE 20.1
SOME MYTHS ABOUT PHONICS INSTRUCTION (CASTLES ET AL. P. 15, REPRINTED BY PERMISSION OF SAGE PUBLICATIONS)

Box 2. Some Myths About Phonics Instruction

Myth	Evidence	References
1. Phonics teaches children to read nonwords	The aim of phonics instruction is to equip children with the skills to sound out words independently. Nonwords are primarily used not for teaching but for assessment, to index children's phonic skills independently of their word knowledge. An analogy would be measuring heart rate to assess cardiovascular fitness: we don't train the heart to beat more slowly, but we assess this function to measure how effective a fitness training programme has been.	Castles et al. (2009)
2. Phonics interferes with reading comprehension	At a basic level, phonics supports comprehension by allowing the child to align an unfamiliar printed word with a familiar word in oral vocabulary. Phonics also supports the development of fluent word reading ability, which in turn frees up the child's mental resources to focus on the meaning of a text. Ehri et al.'s (2001) meta-analysis found that children taught by a systematic phonics method made gains in text comprehension as well as in word reading and spelling.	Perfetti & Hart (2002) Ehri et al. (2001)

2. Phonics interferes with reading comprehension	It is true that the English writing system is complex, and many words violate typical letter-sound mappings. However, learning phonics will still take a child a long way. More than 80% of monosyllabic words are completely regular and, for those that are not, a "partial decoding" will often bring a child close to the correct pronunciation, which can then be refined using oral vocabulary knowledge.	Share (1995)
4. Phonics is boring for children and turns them off reading	Phonics instruction is often portrayed as robotic and mechanical, but this is at odds with the array of engaging and enjoyable structured phonics programs currently available. And, through its positive effects on reading attainment, phonics instruction is associated with greater motivation to read, more extensive reading for pleasure, and higher academic self-esteem.	Kirsch et al. (2002) Anderson et al. (1988) McArthur & Castles (2017)

The importance of cracking the alphabetic code

Once children can crack the alphabetic code, they gain expertise and become fluent in word reading skills where they're able to decipher a wide range of words by sight alone, a process the authors term *orthographic learning*. From here, they're able to leverage their knowledge to not only become independent readers but to even *self-teach*. Essentially, they improve and refine their knowledge of spelling through every encounter with words. For example, we all have words that we're unsure about or frequently get wrong, but repeated exposure to that word can affect a kind of self-correcting mechanism where the expert reader sees the word in its correct form as distinct from their incorrect version of it.

Developing readers will also use a combination of reading words on sight blended with slowing down and using alphabetic decoding with new or unfamiliar words. This is experienced even by adults when encountering novel printed words for example, *biotope*, *macabre*, or *unapologetic*. An important part of becoming a skilled reader is *lexical quality* where the reader has store of mental representation of words which is flexible and accurate which in turn, frees up precious cognitive bandwidth for comprehension. This means the reader can focus on the deeper meaning and underlying structure of what they're reading.

The authors also claim that there's a need for explicit *morphological instruction* (the shape and form of words including prefixes and suffixes) because of the importance of relating word forms to their meanings however there's a gap in teachers' knowledge in this area. One reason which may account for this is that a significant number of English teachers have a degree in English literature not language.

THE MATTHEW EFFECT AND MOTIVATION

ANDERSON ET AL. (1988) studying out of school reading found that "those at the 10th percentile of time spent reading were estimated to be exposed to approximately 60,000 words per year; those at the 50th percentile, 900,000 words; and those at the 90th percentile, more than 4 million words" (p. 27). This is an example of the *Matthew Effect*; rich get richer and the poor get poorer. This comes from the parable of the talents in the bible:

> *"For to everyone who has, more will be given, and he will have abundance; but from him who does not have, even what he has will be taken away".*[3]

This is particularly evident in education and very prominently in levels of literacy where a large gap can appear between children in a relatively short space of time.

On top of this problem is motivation. This is a multifaceted problem, but possibly most important and easiest to solve is the intrinsic link between the desire to read and *reading ability itself*. If you're good at something then you're more likely to engage in that activity than if the activity is a slog with little reward. In that sense, the authors stress that the question of how to *motivate* children to read should be closely aligned with *how* to teach them to read.

Matthew effect

The simple view of reading

Citing Gough and his colleagues (Gough & Tunmer, 1986), Castles et al. note that the "Simple View of Reading" claims that reading comprehension is the product of two sets of interlinked skills: decoding and linguistic comprehension. In other words, being able to understand letters and words is useless if you don't know what they *mean*. For example, give any well-read adult the front page of a newspaper and they'll be able to read it in the sense that they can decode the printed words and assimilate what they read into their own general knowledge about a range of topics. But give them a textbook on quantum physics and they might be able to *read* it but probably not understand it. Decoding is a key limitation of the novice reader who is learning words

---

3 *NEW KING JAMES BIBLE*, MATTHEW 25:29.

like *cat* and *hat* but as children become expert readers their ability to comprehend texts becomes constrained by their broader background knowledge of the topic they are reading about: "Even if a word is known by a child, it might be known less well or in a way that is less connected to other words, relative to the connections that other children might form" (p. 30).

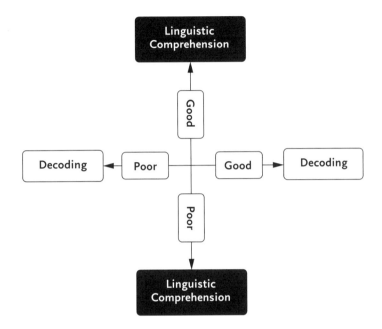

FIGURE 20.2
THE SIMPLE VIEW
OF READING
(CASTLES ET AL.
P. 27, REPRINTED
BY PERMISSION
OF SAGE
PUBLICATIONS).

When people construct meaning from reading a text, they don't store what they have read verbatim but rather form a *situation model* which grows dynamically as they read and make mental connections to things not explicitly stated in what has been written. Where there are holes in knowledge of a particular topic, misunderstanding and misconception can occur. As Perfetti (1994) states, "there is room for lots of things to go wrong when comprehension fails" (p. 885).

Furthermore, rich vocabulary knowledge is not enough to understand a text. For example, the meanings of many idioms such as "kick the bucket" or "break the ice" are not understood merely by knowledge of the individual words but depend on relevant background knowledge: "As with vocabulary, the availability of background knowledge in long-term memory allows relevant knowledge to be activated as the situation model builds during reading" (p. 30). Here, while the authors stress that written language differs from spoken language with individual complexities and subtleties in both forms, the importance of oral language is highlighted as "in skilled readers, the correlation between listening comprehension and reading comprehension is almost perfect" (p. 34).

relevant background knowledge

The core claim made in this article is that *the writing system matters* (p. 7). Once that's understood it then becomes clear what the more effective way is to help children become independent readers and thus be introduced to the wondrous worlds that the printed word can offer them. The focus on a whole language approach is not supported by the wider body of evidence surveyed here. As the authors illustrate:

> If instruction instead focused on teaching children to associate printed words with their meanings directly, then learning to read would require memorization of tens of thousands of individual printed words. Thus, systematic phonics instruction should be viewed as a natural and logical consequence of the manner in which alphabetic writing systems represent spoken language. (p. 12)

Conclusions

A central point made in this article is that on the balance of evidence, the reading wars should be over by now. Those who don't accept the importance of phonics instruction don't understand *why* phonics works for alphabetic systems. Secondly there are many myths about phonics such as the notion that it's the *only* game in town which of course it's not.

The authors further note that while explicit vocabulary instruction works when children are tested on passages containing the taught words but appears not to transfer to standardised assessments of reading comprehension. This points to the importance of teaching "content-relevant vocabulary before children are expected to use that vocabulary to learn from text" (p. 36). This is illustrated by the number of words that are highly context dependent. Take the word *mean* which can well, *mean* several different things depending on the situation. For example the word *set* can be used in over 400 different senses! Also teaching a particular *kind* vocabulary is important such as Tier 2 words, described by Beck et al. (2013) which crop up more often than others such as *important, fascinate,* or *explore.*

Tier 2 words are less complex but more common

So helping children to establish flexible and durable situation models in their long term memory through explicit instruction and oral discussion appears to have a strong evidence base but what about the training of working memory? The answer is no. As the authors point out "Simons et al. (2016) provided an extensive review of cognitive training programs in this journal and found little evidence that such training affects everyday cognitive performance, including reading" (p. 37).

Additionally, the importance of oral language cannot be overstated. A rich dialogic environment where children are exposed to new and novel talk and given opportunity to voice their own ideas is crucial: "Eve before children can read, interventions that target oral language lead to improvements in reading comprehension" (p. 38).

Castles, Rastle, and Nation stress in their article that there have been many misconceptions about phonics which miscast it as merely the teaching of sounds (and often nonsense sounds) but the authors show that a more holistic approach is the key to success stressing the importance of oral language skills alongside the explicit instruction of letter-sound relationships. Lastly the importance of background knowledge is stressed, after all there is little point in learning to decode letters and words if you don't know what they mean.

Takeaways

- Just because we learn to talk naturally, doesn't mean we learn to read naturally.
- The writing system matters.
- The explicit teaching of letter-sound correspondences is a powerful way of creating readers.
- Whole word approaches are not supported by the wider body of evidence.
- Explicit vocabulary instruction does not always lead to comprehension
- Oral language instruction is an important part of comprehension.

References

ADAMS, M. J. (1990). *BEGINNING TO READ: THINKING AND LEARNING ABOUT PRINT.* MIT PRESS.

ANDERSON, R. C., WILSON, P. T., & FIELDING, L. G. (1988). GROWTH IN READING AND HOW CHILDREN SPEND THEIR TIME OUTSIDE OF SCHOOL. *READING RESEARCH QUARTERLY, 23,* 285–303.

BECK, I. L., MCKEOWN, M. G., & KUCAN, L. (2013). *BRINGING WORDS TO LIFE: ROBUST VOCABULARY INSTRUCTION.* NEW YORK, NY: THE GUILFORD PRESS.

CASTLES, A., COLTHEART, M., WILSON, K., VALPIED, J., & WEDGWOOD, J. (2009). THE GENESIS OF READING ABILITY: WHAT HELPS CHILDREN LEARN LETTER–SOUND CORRESPONDENCES? *JOURNAL OF EXPERIMENTAL CHILD PSYCHOLOGY, 104,* 68–88

CASTLES, A., RASTLE, K., & NATION, K. (2018). ENDING THE READING WARS: READING ACQUISITION FROM NOVICE TO EXPERT. *PSYCHOLOGICAL SCIENCE IN THE PUBLIC INTEREST, 19(1),* 551. AVAILABLE VIA HTTPS://DOI.ORG/10.1177/1529100618772271

EHRI, L. C., NUNES, S. R., WILLOWS, D. M., SCHUSTER, B. V., YAGHOUB-ZADEH, Z., & SHANAHAN, T. (2001). SYSTEMATIC PHONICS INSTRUCTION HELPS STUDENTS LEARN TO READ: EVIDENCE FROM THE NATIONAL READING PANEL'S META-ANALYSIS. *READING, 36,* 250–287.

GOUGH, P., & TUNMER, W. (1986). DECODING, READING, AND READING DISABILITY. *REMEDIAL AND SPECIAL EDUCATION, 7,* 6–10.

KIRSCH, I., DE JONG, J., LAFONTAINE, D., MCQUEEN, J., MENDELOVITS, J., & MONSEUR, C. (2002). *READING FOR CHANGE PERFORMANCE AND ENGAGEMENT ACROSS COUNTRIES. RESULTS FROM PISA 2000.* ORGANISATION FOR ECONOMIC CO-OPERATION AND DEVELOPMENT. AVAILABLE VIA HTTPS://WWW.OECD.ORG/EDU/SCHOOL/PROGRAMMEFORINTERNATIONALSTUDENTASSESSMENTPISA/33690904.PDF.

MCARTHUR, G., & CASTLES, A. (2017). HELPING CHILDREN WITH READING DIFFICULTIES: SOME THINGS WE HAVE LEARNED SO FAR. *NPJ SCIENCE OF LEARNING, 2(1),* ARTICLE 7.

PERFETTI, C. A. (1994). PSYCHOLINGUISTICS AND READING ABILITY. IN M. A. GERNSBACHER (ED.), *HANDBOOK OF PSYCHOLINGUISTICS* (PP. 849–894). ACADEMIC PRESS.

PERFETTI, C. A., & HART, L. (2002). THE LEXICAL QUALITY HYPOTHESIS. IN L. VERHOEVEN, C. ELBR, & P. REITSMA (EDS.), *PRECURSORS OF FUNCTIONAL LITERACY* (PP. 189–212). JOHN BENJAMINS.

PINKER, S. (2009). *LANGUAGE LEARNABILITY AND LANGUAGE DEVELOPMENT.* HARVARD UNIVERSITY PRESS.

SHARE, D. L. (1995). PHONOLOGICAL RECODING AND SELF-TEACHING: SINE QUA NON OF READING ACQUISITION. *COGNITION, 55,* 151–218.

SIMONS, D. J., BOOT, W. R., CHARNESS, N., GATHERCOLE, S. E., CHABRIS, C. F., HAMBRICK, D. Z., STINE-MORROW, E. A. L. (2016). DO "BRAIN TRAINING" PROGRAMS WORK? *PSYCHOLOGICAL SCIENCE IN THE PUBLIC INTEREST, 17,* 103–186.

Suggested Readings and Links

CLARKE, P. J., TRUELOVE, E., HULME, C., & SNOWLING, M. J. (2013). DEVELOPING READING COMPREHENSION. WEST SUSSEX, ENGLAND: WILEY.

DEHAENE, S. (2009). READING IN THE BRAIN. NEW YORK, NY: PENGUIN VIKING.

MOATS, L. C. (2010). SPEECH TO PRINT: LANGUAGE ESSENTIALS FOR TEACHERS. BALTIMORE, MD:

SEIDENBERG, M. (2017). LANGUAGE AT THE SPEED OF SIGHT: HOW WE READ, WHY SO MANY CAN'T, AND WHAT CAN BE DONE ABOUT IT. NEW YORK, NY: BASIC BOOKS.

STUART, M., & STAINTHORP, R. (2015). READING DEVELOPMENT AND TEACHING. THOUSAND OAKS, CA: SAGE.

WILLINGHAM, D. (2017). THE READING MIND: A COGNITIVE APPROACH TO UNDERSTANDING HOW THE MIND READS. SAN FRANCISCO, CA: JOSSEY-BASS

INTERVIEW WITH THE AUTHORS:

 WWW.SEEHEARSPEAKPODCAST.COM/EPISODE-1/
EPISODE-1-THE-READING-WARS-WITH-ANNE-CASTLES-AND-KATE-NATION

 BLOG BY PAUL KIRSCHNER AND MIRJAM NEELEN: ARE COMPREHENSIVE READING ASSESSMENTS UNFAIR? NO COMPREHENSION WITHOUT PRIOR KNOWLEDGE

AVAILABLE VIA HTTPS://TINYURL.COM/X22AY9HW

21 WHY TECHNOLOGY SHOULD BE THE SERVANT NOT THE MASTER

MATTHEW KOEHLER AND PUNYA MISHRA ON PCK AND TECHNOLOGY

DOI: 10.4324/9781003228165-25

21 WHY TECHNOLOGY SHOULD BE THE SERVANT NOT THE MASTER

ARTICLE What is technological pedagogical content knowledge?[1]

QUOTE *"Teachers need to master more than the subject matter they teach; they must also have a deep understanding of the manner in which the subject matter (or the kinds of representations that can be constructed) can be changed by the application of particular technologies."*[2]

Why You Should Read This Article

The invention of the X-ray

On November 8, 1895, Wilhelm Conrad Roentgen made a startling discovery. While testing whether cathode rays could pass through glass he noticed a strange green light on a screen nine feet away. This was hard to explain as the cathode tube was wrapped in thick black paper. He discovered that this strange light would pass through most substances but leave impressions of more solid objects. One of his early experiment was on his wife's hand, with her wedding ring clearly visible. He referred to these rays as "X" as they were unknown and thus the "X-ray" was born. Within a year this new technology was being used to *see* items within the human body such as bullets, kidney stones and broken bones resulting in a complete revolution in healthcare. In 1901, Roentgen was awarded the first Nobel Prize in physics and when asked what his thoughts were at the moment of his discovery he replied "I didn't think, I investigated". Spoke like a true scientist.

---

[1] KOEHLER, M. J., & MISHRA, P. (2009). WHAT IS TECHNOLOGICAL PEDAGOGICAL CONTE KNOWLEDGE? *CONTEMPORARY ISSUES IN TECHNOLOGY AND TEACHER EDUCATION*, 9(1), 60– REPRODUCED BY PERMISSION OF THE PUBLISHER, © 2012 BY TPACK.ORG.

[2] IBID., P. 65

However, what made this so effective was not the technology itself but rather the ways in which it could be used in conjunction with knowledge about human anatomy. This intersection between technology and content knowledge is what the authors of this paper call *Technology Knowledge* (TK) where specific domain knowledge used in conjunction with rapidly developing technology can have transformative effects. This element is just one part of a broader construct they term TPACK where knowledge of technology, pedagogy and subject content are vital interleaving elements of teacher effectiveness. They claim that "understanding the impact of technology on the practices and knowledge of a given discipline is critical to developing appropriate technological tools for educational purposes" (p. 65). In other words, teachers need to not only know the content they are teaching, how they should teach it but also how technology can change the ways in which their subject matter is represented or understood.

Abstract of the Article

This paper describes a framework for teacher knowledge for technology integration called technological pedagogical content knowledge (originally TPCK, now known as TPACK, or technology, pedagogy, and content knowledge). This framework builds on Lee Shulman's construct of pedagogical content knowledge (PCK) to include technology knowledge. The development of TPACK by teachers is critical to effective teaching with technology. The paper begins with a brief introduction to the complex, ill-structured nature of teaching. The nature of technologies (both analogue and digital) is considered, as well as how the inclusion of technology in pedagogy further complicates teaching. The TPACK framework for teacher knowledge is described in detail as a complex interaction among three bodies of knowledge: content, pedagogy, and technology. The interaction of these bodies of knowledge, both theoretically and in practice, produces the types of flexible knowledge needed to successfully integrate technology use into teaching.

TPACK: Technology, pedagogy and content knowledge

The Article

As should be obvious by now, teaching is a messy business. Not only do teachers need to have a strong knowledge of *what* they're teaching and *how* to teach it but they also need to know how students *learn* it. Indeed, the authors in this article describe teaching as "an ill structured discipline" (p. 61) which requires teachers to apply varying structures of knowledge across a range of radically different contexts. Much of this is covered in Lee Shulman's work on PCK covered in Chapters 2 and 16, and in this article Matthew Koehler and Punya Mishra offer a framework to include technology knowledge within that construct.

The word *technology* covers many things, even just in an educational context. For example, a pencil is a form of technology but unlike modern technology, a pencil has a fairly obvious and straightforward application: you write with it. In contrast to this, digital technologies such as computers, handheld devices, and phones are "protean (usable in many different ways; (Papert, 1980); unstable (rapidly changing); and opaque (the inner workings are hidden from users" (p. 61). As is the case with all technology,[3] digital technology is neither neutral nor unbiased but can offer radically different possibilities depending, among other things, on th medium. For example, video calling offers synchronous communication where tone and expression can play a key role whereas the medium of email or discussion forums do not. In addition, the technological conditions under which different teachers work are very different as is the teacher's own knowledge and training in how to incorporate technology.

The authors claim that teaching should be seen as an "interaction between what teachers know and how they apply what they know in the unique circumstances or contexts within their classrooms" (p. 61) where there are three core components; technology, pedagogy, and content knowledge which form the basis of the (TPACK) framework. Of vital importance is not just these different elements as discrete elements but also the intersections between them (see Figure 21.1).

Technology isn't neutral

FIGURE 21.1
THE TPACK FRAMEWORK AND ITS KNOWLEDGE COMPONENTS. (FROM KOEHLER & MISHRA, 2009, P. 63. REPRODUCED BY PERMISSION OF THE PUBLISHER, © 2012 BY TPACK.ORG). THE INTERSECTING ELEMENTS ARE PCK (PEDAGOGICAL CONTENT KNOWLEDGE), TCK (TECHNOLOGICAL CONTENT KNOWLEDGE), AND TPK (TECHNOLOGICAL PEDAGOGICAL KNOWLEDGE).

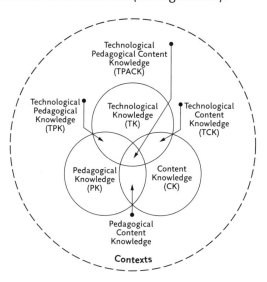

3   IF YOU'RE INTERESTED IN READING MORE ABOUT THIS WE CAN OFFER YOU TWO READI SUGGESTIONS NAMELY:

A CLASSIC ARTICLE BASED ON A VIADUCT IN NEW YORK: WINNER, L. (1980). ARTIFACTS HAVE POLITICS? *DAEDALUS, 109*(1), 121–36. AVAILABLE VIA WWW.CC.GATE EDU/~BEKI/CS4001/WINNER.PDF OR THE BOOK "WEAPONS OF MATH DESTRUCTIC BY CATHY O'NEIL

The TPACK
framework

Content Knowledge (CK) refers to the subject specific knowledge teachers need to know to teach what they are teaching. However, it's not enough just to know the material to be taught, content knowledge as understood within Shulman's paradigm, also includes "knowledge of concepts, theories, ideas, organizational frameworks, knowledge of evidence and proof, as well as established practices and approaches toward developing such knowledge" (p. 63). For example, to teach Shakespeare effectively, an English teacher needs to know not only the play they're teaching but also something of the history of the time in which the play was written, possibly the changing meaning of specific words through time and, some knowledge of the life of the writer themself. To make this more complicated, all of this of course is also under debate within a broader curricular context in almost all domains where the question of whether a curriculum should be knowledge rich or general skill directed is being hotly debated. At any rate, as we claimed in Chapter 2, *those who understand teach* and those who do not understand what they are teaching can do great harm causing students to develop deep misunderstandings about the material they are being taught which can affect future learning (National Research Council, 2000; Pfundt & Duit, 2000).

The importance
of knowing how
learning happens

Pedagogical Knowledge (PK) refers to what we might more commonly term "teaching" where teachers have a sound knowledge of classroom management, lesson planning assessment but should also include broader educational purposes, values, and aims. This means teachers should have a good knowledge of how learning happens (see our first book) and a real understanding of "cognitive, social, and developmental theories of learning" (p. 64). Closely related to this is the notion of PCK which really refers to the specific kind of alchemy that teachers use when transforming the base metals of content into the gold of student understanding. More specifically, this transformation occurs when the teacher "interprets the subject matter, finds multiple ways to represent it, and adapts and tailors the instructional materials to alternative conceptions and students' prior knowledge (p. 64). This also means that teachers not only need to know one way of teaching content but also several ways of teaching it. For example, the ways in which students learn on a Monday morning can be very different to how they learn on a Friday evening and can be very different at different times of the year. To make it even more complicated, each student has a different set of psychological and emotional factors which can affect their learning and having a sophisticated working knowledge of different techniques to help them is a key characteristic of the effective teacher.

Technology Knowledge (TK) is inherently different than the other elements in this framework in the sense that it is in a constant state of flux. If you want a clear (and sometimes funny) example of this, look at how to use examples of technology in the classroom from 20 or even 10 years ago. Tips on how to use technology don't always age well, for example it was fairly *de rigeur* post 2000 for classes to use Google to "research" a domain of knowledge such as a certain historical figure but this has been proved to be largely a fruitless exercise. (See Chapter 29 from HLH on why you can't "just Google it".) However, the authors stress that there are some general principles that are useful and that the teacher who's effectively able to incorporate technology into their practice will "understand information technology broadly enough to apply it productively at work and in their everyday lives, to recognize when information technology can assist or impede the achievement of a goal, and to continually adapt to changes in information technology" (p. 64).

Knowing where to use technology

Technology and Content Knowledge (TCK) have a long and synergistic relationship in fields as diverse as physics, medicine, psychology, and archaeology where technological developments when used in conjunction with specific knowledge can have a huge impact, for example Roentgen's aforementioned discovery of X-rays or the ways in which the calculator has transformed humankind's ability to manipulate and understand data. TCK refers to the ways in which technology can not only assist instruction but also the ways in which it can constrain it. For example, using an interactive map of the world can be a very useful tool for a Geography teacher but perhaps not as useful in other subjects. Knowing how content and technology intersect is vital.

In contrast, *Technological Pedagogical Knowledge* (TPK) refers to the ways in which technology can offer new ways of *how* content can be taught. More specifically it means knowing the "pedagogical affordance and constraints of a range of technological tools as they relate to disciplinarily and developmentally appropriate pedagogical designs and strategies" (p. 65). The authors note that TPK becomes particularly important as most popular software programmes such as Microsoft Office are not designed with education in mind and so teachers need to look past their "functional fixedness" (Duncker, 1945) and consider new ways of using them. We would add however that many software programmes have changed since the writing of this article in 2009 and there are now many more bespoke educational functions in software programmes today.

TEXT PROCESSOR OR TECHNOLOGICAL PEDAGOGICAL TOOL?

MILOU DE SMET ET AL. (2011, 2014) studied how using the outline function of Microsoft Word (we assume that most of you don't know of this functionality and if you do, that you've never used it yourself or with your students) affects learning, argumentative writing performance products, and mental effort. The function allows students to first write an outline of an essay or report, fold and unfold the different heading levels, move them around, and so forth. This can then be sent to the teacher who can comment on the form, structure, and proposed content. The teacher can at this point make suggestions and/or changes before the essay/report has been written thus helping the student avoid major mistakes and helping them gather their thoughts and structure the final product. This saves time and effort for the student who doesn't hear afterwards that the whole essay needs to be restructured and rewritten and for the teacher when assessing the final product as they've received a well-structured product. And it also leads to better argumentative essays and better learning!

Technology, Pedagogy, and Content Knowledge (TPACK; also called Technological Pedagogical Content Knowledge) is what the authors refer to as an emergent form of knowledge that transcends the three "core" components (content, pedagogy, and technology). In order for teachers to be able to assimilate all these strands into effective teaching practice they need to be open to the following:

1. Concepts from the content being taught can be represented using technology
2. Pedagogical techniques can communicate content in different ways using technology
3. Different content concepts require different skill levels from students, and edtech can help address some of these requirements
4. Students come into the classroom with different backgrounds – including prior educational experience and exposure to technology – and lessons utilising edtech should account for this possibility
5. Educational technology can be used in tandem with students' existing knowledge, helping them either strengthen prior epistemologies or develop new ones (Kurt, 2018)

All of this requires that teachers are able to "flexibly navigate the spaces" (p. 66) of the three elements of content, pedagogy, and technology. Once again, this highlights a common theme in this book: the notion that creativity and what appears like *effortless* capability is usually characterised by a deep body of domain specific knowledge. As the authors point out in a previous article, the process of incorporating these separate knowledge strands is an

> analytic act and one that is difficult to tease out in practice. In actuality, these components exist in a state of dynamic equilibrium or, as the philosopher Kuhn (1977) said in a different context, in a state of 'essential tension' . . . . Viewing any of these components in isolation from the others represents a real disservice to good teaching.
>
> (Mishra & Koehler, 2006, p. 102)

Conclusions

Teaching is messy. Teachers need "flexible access to rich, well-organized and integrated knowledge from different domains" (p. 61). In effect, TPACK represents the culmination of three core forms of knowledge around using technology and a close examination of how "technology-related professional knowledge is implemented and instantiated in practice" (p. 67). It's an important approach because too often in the classroom technology is the cart before the horse and school leaders can ask the wrong question such as "how can we use technology in the classroom?" whereas this framework grounds the adoption of knowledge within the more important aspects of knowledge and asks "how do technology, content, and pedagogy work together to improve student outcomes?"

One of the central problems with technology in education is the use of technology for technology's sake. This leads to often gimmicky approaches which might look impressive but not very effective for student learning. Bells and whistles might look fancy but without a solid understanding of *what* is being taught and the ways in which technology can be harnessed in *how* to teach that content, then it's likely to be a waste of time. For example, take the well-meaning history teacher who gets his class to use the Internet to research the French Revolution and create presentations using PowerPoint. What often ends up happening is that students spend more time on the superficial aspects of the task such as what font/colour/PowerPoint design they will use rather than thinking the content and how that relates to what they already know. Additionally they will often copy and paste dates, facts, and pictures from their research and create what, on the surface, looks like an impressive presentation but in actuality is merely an assemblage of information not an assimilation knowledge. As the saying goes, "all the gear but no idea".

Content, pedagogy and technology knowledge need to work in tandem

Using technology for technology's sake is unlikely to be effective

Takeaways

- Content should inform what technology should be used, not the other way round.
- Technology can be useful in representing subject content in novel ways.
- Different forms of technology should be used with different subjects.
- Knowledge of content, pedagogy and technology should be considered together.
- Using technology for technology's sake is unlikely to be effective.

References

C3 TEACHERS. (2021, SEPTEMBER 29). *DID THE PRINTING PRESS PRESERVE THE PAST OR INVENT THE FUTURE?* [SAMPLE LESSON PLAN]. AVAILABLE VIA HTTPS://C3TEACHERS.ORG/WP-CONTENT/UPLOADS/2015/09/NEWYORK_9_PRINTING_PRESS.PDF

DE SMET, M. J. R., BRAND-GRUWEL, S., LEIJTEN, M., & KIRSCHNER, P. A. (2014). ELECTRONIC OUTLINING AS A WRITING STRATEGY: EFFECTS ON STUDENTS' WRITING PRODUCTS, MENTAL EFFORT AND WRITING PROCESS. *COMPUTERS & EDUCATION, 78*, 352–366.

DE SMET, M. J. R., BROEKKAMP, H., BRAND-GRUWEL, S., & KIRSCHNER, P. A. (2011). EFFECTS OF ELECTRONIC OUTLINING ON STUDENTS'' ARGUMENTATIVE WRITING PERFORMANCE. *JOURNAL OF COMPUTER ASSISTED LEARNING, 27*, 557–574.

DUNCKER, K. (1945). ON PROBLEM SOLVING. *PSYCHOLOGICAL MONOGRAPHS, 58*(5), 1–110.

KOEHLER, M. J., & MISHRA, P. (2009). WHAT IS TECHNOLOGICAL PEDAGOGICAL CONTENT KNOWLEDGE? *CONTEMPORARY ISSUES IN TECHNOLOGY AND TEACHER EDUCATION, 9*(1), 60–70.

KUHN, T. (1977). *THE ESSENTIAL TENSION.* THE UNIVERSITY OF CHICAGO PRESS.

KURT, S. (2018, MAY 12). *TPACK: TECHNOLOGICAL PEDAGOGICAL CONTENT KNOWLEDGE FRAMEWORK WEBSITE.* AVAILABLE VIA HTTPS://EDUCATIONALTECHNOLOGY.NET/TECHNOLOGICAL-PEDAGOGICAL-CONTENT-KNOWLEDGE-TPACK-FRAMEWORK/

MISHRA, P., & KOEHLER, M. J. (2006). TECHNOLOGICAL PEDAGOGICAL CONTENT KNOWLEDGE: A FRAMEWORK FOR INTEGRATING TECHNOLOGY IN TEACHER KNOWLEDGE. *TEACHERS COLLEGE RECORD, 108*(6), 1017–1054.

NATIONAL RESEARCH COUNCIL. (2000). *HOW PEOPLE LEARN: BRAIN, MIND, EXPERIENCE, AND SCHOOL.* NATIONAL ACADEMY PRESS.

PAPERT, S. (1980). *MINDSTORMS: CHILDREN, COMPUTERS AND POWERFUL IDEAS.* BASIC BOOKS.

PFUNDT, H., & DUIT, R. (2000). *BIBLIOGRAPHY: STUDENT'S ALTERNATIVE FRAMEWORKS AND SCIENCE EDUCATION* (5TH ED.). UNIVERSITY OF KIEL.

Suggested Readings and Links

CLARK, R. E. (1983). RECONSIDERING RESEARCH ON LEARNING FROM MEDIA. *REVIEW OF EDUCATIONAL RESEARCH, 53*, 445–459. AVAILABLE VIA WWW.UKY.EDU/~GMSWAN3/609/CLARK_1983.PDF

GLASER. R. (1984). EDUCATION AND THINKING: THE ROLE OF KNOWLEDGE. *AMERICAN PSYCHOLOGY, 39*(2), 93–104.

KOEHLER, M. J., & MISHRA, P. (2008). INTRODUCING TPCK. IN AACTE COMMITTEE ON INNOVATION AND TECHNOLOGY (ED.), *THE HANDBOOK OF TECHNOLOGICAL PEDAGOGICAL CONTENT KNOWLEDGE FOR EDUCATORS* (PP. 3–29). LAWRENCE ERLBAUM ASSOCIATES.

MISHRA, P., & KOEHLER, M. J. (2006). TECHNOLOGICAL PEDAGOGICAL CONTENT KNOWLEDGE: A FRAMEWORK FOR TEACHER KNOWLEDGE. *TEACHERS COLLEGE RECORD, 108*(6), 1017–1054.

VIDEOS

"TPACK IN TWO MINUTES"

THIS IS A QUICK INTRODUCTION TO THE DYNAMIC FRAMEWORK, TPACK (MISHRA & KOEHLER, 2006). IT IS NOT MEANT TO BE AN IN-DEPTH VIEW OF THE FRAMEWORK.

AVAILABLE VIA HTTPS://YOUTU.BE/FAGVSQLZELY

TO DIG A LITTLE BIT DEEPER, YOU CAN VIEW THIS VIDEO FEATURING ONE OF THE TPACK FOUNDERS, DR PUNYA MISHRA

AVAILABLE VIA HTTPS://YOUTU.BE/WN4ELDEZQEM

A USEFUL WEBSITE CREATED BY THE AUTHORS DETAILING MANY OF THE CONCEPTS THEY'VE OUTLINED IN THE ORIGINAL PAPER:

AVAILABLE VIA HTTP://TPACK.ORG/

WEBSITES

PUNYA MISHRA'S WEB: TPACK NEWSLETTER ARCHIVE, TPACK VIDEOS, SILLY TPACK IMAGES (OVER THE YEARS), AND TPACK FUN

AVAILABLE VIA HTTPS://PUNYAMISHRA.COM/RESEARCH/TPACK/

INTERESTING ARTICLE ON THE NEUTRALITY OF TECHNOLOGY AND INANIMATE OBJECTS: "DO ARTIFACTS HAVE POLITICS?"

AVAILABLE VIA WWW.CC.GATECH.EDU/~BEKI/CS4001/WINNER.PDF

SECTION 5

IN THE CLASSROOM

There have been many memorable fictional educators down the years, but ask a teacher whether they recognise these characters as realistic depictions of what it means to teach and you'll likely get a "mixed" response.

This is because depictions of teachers in film and fiction tend to exaggerate, compartmentalise, or thinly represent the real stuff of teaching. If the world of make-believe was to be believed, we would be forgiven for thinking that the world is full of teachers who are effortlessly inspirational (John Keating from *Dead Poets Society*); who break all the rules but somehow make it work (Dewey Finn from *School of Rock*); who are boring, ineffective, and largely ignored (The Economics teacher from *Ferris Bueller's Day Off*); or whose sole purpose in life is to make their students' lives a living hell (Miss Trunchbull from *Matilda*).

In reality, the persona of the teacher and the dynamic they create with the students in their charge goes well beyond such shallow caricatures. The world of the classroom is complex and nuanced in ways that are easy to gloss over. Indeed, it's even tempting for teachers to assume something closer to a caricatured version of themselves because more nuanced approaches are harder to understand and enact.

Thankfully, there are ways in which we have come to understand how teachers and students come together to create productive working relationships defined by mutual respect; just as we have come to understand what tends to go wrong when the opposite is the case.

In this section of the book, we'll step inside the classroom by asking the following questions: What does it mean to be an authentic teacher? How do teacher-student relationships effect student outcomes? and How do effective teachers manage their classrooms?

DI: 10.4324/9781003228165-26

22 "TO THINE OWN SELF BE TRUE"[1]

THE AUTHENTIC TEACHER: PEDRO DE BRUYCKERE & PAUL A. KIRSCHNER ON TEACHER AUTHENTICITY

---

[1] SHAKESPEARE, W. (1992). HAMLET, PRINCE OF DENMARK (C. WATTS & K. CARABINE, EDS.). WORDSWORTH EDITIONS. (ORIGINAL WORK PUBLISHED 1599) (1.3.84–86)

22 "TO THINE OWN SELF BE TRUE"

ARTICLE Authentic teachers: Student criteria perceiving authenticity of teachers[2]

QUOTE *"It is striking how little the students are interested in teaching methods or other pedagogic principles."*[3]

Why You Should Read This Article

The authentic self

In Shakespeare's play *Hamlet*, the farcical character of Polonius is giving advice to his son Laertes who is about to leave for Paris when he offers advice which has become a well-worn cliché over the last 500 years: "to thine own self be true". However, he meant this in a much more Elizabethan context where being "true" to yourself means acting in accordance with your own best interests. In a modern context this phrase has come to embody the rather more Southern Californian interpretation where an individual may "find themselves" through looking inward towards some kind of *true* or *real* self. This notion of authenticity has perhaps come to mean something we usually see on inspirational posters but this concept has an important resonance for the classroom.

We all remember one teacher who had a real impact on us. A teacher who made us see the world differently, who showed us what it meant to be passionate about Shakespeare or Newton or teaching in a way we never thought possible. But what was it about that teacher that was so memorable? For many pupils it's the about the quality of authenticity which the respondents in this article characterise as having four specifi elements.

---

2 DE BRUYCKERE, P., & KIRSCHNER, P. A. (2016). *AUTHENTIC TEACHERS: STUDENT CRITERIA PERCEIV AUTHENTICITY OF TEACHERS.COGENT EDUCATION, 3*, 1247609. HTTP://DX.DOI.ORG/10.1080/23 86X.2016.1247609

3 IBID., P. 8.

Subject knowledge, passion, uniqueness, being caring (but distant) are all hallmarks of effective teachers but what's particularly useful in terms of classroom practice and what's unique about the research done here is that the researchers did not try and define what authentic means, which is a very slippery concept, but rather they attempted to identify what authenticity means *in the eyes of students themselves*. In essence, it's not even about how students perceive authenticity in a teacher, but rather their conception of what authenticity is as it relates to teachers. This is extremely useful for teachers to know as so much research focuses on how teachers view themselves or other teachers, but this article by Pedro De Bruyckere and Paul A. Kirschner focuses on how students view specific aspects of an effective teacher.

Abstract of the Article

Authenticity is seen by many as a key for good learning and education. There is talk of authentic instruction, authentic learning, authentic problems, authentic assessment, authentic tools, and authentic teachers. The problem is that while authenticity is an often-used adjective describing almost all aspects of teaching and learning, the concept itself is not very well researched. This qualitative study examines – based on data collected via interviews and focus groups – which criteria students in secondary education use when determining if their teachers are authentic. It yielded four criteria learners use: expertise, passion, unicity, and distance.

The Article

The word *authentic* may be one of the most overused words that we come across. Politicians need to be seen as authentic in order to get elected (i.e., they need to be seen as real people and, thus, to be trusted), products need to be seen as authentic in order to be bought and sold (i.e., either "Coke: It's the real thing" or "Just like grandma made") and even in the arts (i.e., music as well as painting should convey genuinely feelings for and experiences in what you write and/or sing about or paint). And, of course, education is inundated with authenticity as De Bruyckere and Kirschner note: "In education, researchers stress the importance of authenticity for optimal learning, assessment and even teacher-student relationships. In teacher training programmes . . . the student is often advised to 'just be yourself' " (p. 1–2). But what does that mean? What is "being yourself"?

Broadly speaking, there are two different types of research on authenticity as it relates to teaching and/or education. The first is related to research that tries to describe what a "good teacher" is or should be

The concept of authenticity is both empirical and philosophical in nature

and how authenticity (whatever that may be) plays a role there or that tries to determine how authentic a teacher should be or how an authentic teacher should act. The second type of research on authenticity in education is philosophical in nature, something which is very valuable in its own right, but doesn't bring us much further than conjectures as to what it is. This research starts "from the premise that authenticity is important for the relation between students and teachers" (p. 2) and attempts to gain a more empirical view on what teacher authenticity means through the eyes of students.

The researchers here used semi-structured interviews to ask students for the elements which would make them view a teacher as being authentic or fake, within a formal learning context. Based upon a two-step analysis of the statements made by the students who were interviewed (N = 42), four criteria were determined with respect to whether students saw their teachers as authentic or not: expertise, passion, unicity, and distance.

Authenticity Is Expertise

The value of teacher subject knowledge

Respondents said that they expected to learn something in a lesson and that they mainly look to the teacher in that respect. A hugely important part of expertise is "topical knowledge" which was also part of the statement in the interviews. Interestingly, the students were aware that enjoyment did not necessarily lead to learning stating that "the lessons might be pleasant and even fun, but that is not the most important thing" (p. 7). In addition, there was a feeling that clear and varied explanation of a topic was a key part of expertise with one student claiming "it's only expertise if it's also explained in different ways" (p. 7).

Although much discussion around teaching involves pedagogy, it's clear that these discussions can mean very little in a context where there is a poor learning atmosphere or where students feel their teacher doesn't care about their progress. De Bruyckere and Kirschner note that the students who were interviewed "felt that a teacher attempts to involve them/rouse their interest/motivate them for the subject matter, and together with them strive to get a good result" (p. 7).

> Not really the way they taught but more the way they cared about us, . . . They wanted us to get good marks, wanted us to get our diploma because they know how important that is and if you have a problem then they always make that extra effort to help you, that's for sure. (p. 7)

In other words: If the teacher doesn't care about their learning then why should they? Of course, the notion of caring for someone is clearly a very difficult thing to define and looks very different with different students. As every good football coach knows, some players respond well to an arm around the shoulder while others respond better to a stern talking to. But what other elements of authenticity were important to students?

Authenticity Is Passion

A hugely important aspect of authentic teaching is passion for subject. For the students surveyed in this study, it was not enough simply to know a lot about their subject, what was important was to make it *come alive*, indeed as one student put it, what was really important was to see that the teacher "lives for his[4] subject" (p. 7). For example, many students will have never seen anyone being passionate about Shelley or Newton or Pythagoras or even someone using an expansive vocabulary in an impressive way. Hearing someone talk and model what it means to *truly* love something can be life changing for an impressionable young mind and there are countless examples of highly accomplished people whose understanding of the world were transformed by a passionate teacher.

And this idea of passion relating to authenticity goes beyond simple subject knowledge and exposition. On the one hand it means that students perceive a passionate teacher as someone who invests "time and effort in preparing lessons, who looks for creative ways and methods to bring across the subject matter, and who sees to it that students hold their attention" (p. 8). On the other hand, the passionate teacher not only loves their subject but also wants their students to love it:

> "I find this one much more authentic because she really wants to do something. For instance, if you take football, the coach is simply so passionate about it that he's going to do everything he can to see that you win. That's great to know that they're never going to give up. . . . I think it's great to be among people like that." (p. 8)

Authenticity Is Unicity

A third element is what the authors call *unicity* or how unique the lessons were. Students felt that teachers who followed a similar lesson plan over and over again were less authentic. This is directly linked to the quality of passion for subject in the sense that the more passionate and specific

---

4 IN THE QUOTES OF WHAT STUDENTS SAID, WE RETAIN THEIR PRONOUN USE.

a teacher is, the more likely the lessons are to be different. This is a lovely example from a student talking about an economics teacher:

> the teacher would not only discuss the subject matter but also things from his own experience, what he knows, things that have a lot to do with it but that in fact aren't directly linked to the subject matter. (p. 9)

The value of digression

So digression and embellishment is good right? Well again, this is a delicate thing and contains a huge variance in terms of quality and effect. Certainly there are teachers who can spend an entire lesson going off topic and students can learn nothing and can even be irritated but teachers who see the *subject itself* as more important than the lesson plan and are not afraid to follow an interesting line of enquiry wherever it may lead, are seen as more authentic. Another aspect of unicity that respondents valued was that the teacher was in some sense being themselves as in "putting your 'own personal stamp' on the teacher role" (p. 9). Again this is hard to define in a general sense but teachers who were able to bring as aspect of their own lives to their teaching whether i* be sharing an appropriate anecdote or story were appreciated by student*

Authenticity Is Not Too Near and Not Too Far (Distance)

Authenticity and distance

The last criterion is perhaps the most counterintuitive and seems contradictory within the context of the last criterion. Respondents also stated that they valued a teacher who kept clear boundaries between themselves and their students. Although they were passionate about their subject and the wellbeing and progress of their students, they weren't trying to be their best friend. In other words, they were liked because they were not *trying* to be liked. As one student noted: "when there was something wrong he comes over to you but still kept his distance to an extent" (p. 10). This is again a very nuanced quality to have and probably one that is to a certain extent, a natural aptitude that certain personality types have.

There is also a constant friction between nearness and distance. The authentic teacher knows that some areas of students' social lives, for example their social media, are out of bounds and that during the lesso* they are in a position of authority but after the lesson they're the same a* anyone else.

Furthermore, authentic teachers are able to spot if something is wrong with their students and adjust accordingly. As the researchers so aptly put it: "A positive relationship between teacher and student requires (limited) 'active' involvement from the teacher. Teachers have to have 'antennae' to pick up things that are part of their students' lives; repressed tension that might be present, etc." (p. 10).

We will all have experienced people in our lives who have this kind of "antennae", who are instinctively able to respond to people's needs whether they express them or not. We can talk about lesson objectives, dual coding or cognitive load all we want but if a teacher does not have this instinctive ability to empathise with another human being then they are missing huge part of what makes an authentic teacher.

Conclusions

The difference between knowing something and being able to explain it

As previous research has shown, there's no direct link between subject knowledge and great teaching (Hattie, 2003, 2012). It's not enough to know your subject well, you have to be able to *explain* it well. Furthermore, you need to be seen as an expert in your field and have the ability to communicate that expertise. As the authors put it "one could say that the teacher needs to be an expert in the eyes of the students and (s)he shows this by translating the to-be-learnt content to the level of the learner" (p. 11).

Part of the ability to explain something well is having a passion for what you're explaining. Listening to a teacher who isn't only very knowledgeable about what they're teaching but can communicate their own passion for what they are teaching can have a "contagious" effect on the pupils. It's difficult to be interesting if you're not interested in what you're talking about.

For the students surveyed, the lessons of an authentic teacher are always different. There's a unique aspect to their lessons where they're not afraid to go off the prescribed topic of a lesson if it furthers some tangential aspect of the knowledge surrounding the lesson. The authentic teacher is led by the topic itself, not the bureaucracy of the topic.

Again, a paradox is evident here which is outlined by the authors: "this gives a strong focus on a teacher who takes the lead in the education process, but not as a contradiction of not being student-centred. It is taking the lead to put the student in the centre" (p. 12). In other words, student-centred teaching doesn't mean following the passions of the student as Rousseau would have us do, but rather it means showing them what it means to be passionate. It means introducing them to brave new worlds beyond the often narrow confines of their own and broadening their horizons the transformative power of human intellectual achievement.

An important distinction to be made is between the teacher feeling they are being authentic and whether or not their students *perceive* them as authentic or "true to themselves". For example, a teacher might feel they are a diligent, empathetic teacher but their students may have a different view (Van Petegem, 2008).

Takeaways

- Authenticity as teacher quality is a unique combination of expertise, passion, unicity, and distance.
- It's not enough to know something well, you have to be able to *explain* it well.
- It's OK to stray from the lesson plan if an interesting path emerges.
- Authentic teachers can spot a problem where the student *themselves* might not have spotted a problem.
- Truly authentic teachers have a good blend of expertise in their subject, passion for their subject and teaching it, unicity in their approach to teaching and interacting with students, and balancing distance from and nearness to their students.

References

DE BRUYCKERE, P., & KIRSCHNER, P.A. (2016). AUTHENTIC TEACHERS: STUDENT CRITERIA PERCEIVING AUTHENTICITY OF TEACHERS. *COGENT EDUCATION, 3,* 1247609. AVAILABLE VIA HTTP:// DX.DOI.ORG/10.1080/2331186X.2016.1247609

HATTIE, J. (2003, OCTOBER). *TEACHERS MAKE A DIFFERENCE: WHAT IS THE RESEARCH EVIDENCE?* PAPER PRESENTED AT THE AUSTRALIAN COUNCIL FOR EDUCATIONAL RESEARCH ANNUAL CONFERENCE ON BUILDING TEACHER QUALITY, MELBOURNE, AUSTRALIA.

HATTIE, J. (2012). *VISIBLE LEARNING FOR TEACHERS: MAXIMIZING IMPACT ON LEARNING.* ROUTLEDG

SHAKESPEARE, W. (1992). *HAMLET, PRINCE OF DENMARK* (C. WATTS & K. CARABINE, EDS.). WORDSWORTH EDITIONS. (ORIGINAL WORK PUBLISHED 1599)

VAN PETEGEM, K. (2008). *RELATIONSHIP BETWEEN STUDENT, TEACHER, CLASSROOM CHARACTERIST AND STUDENTS' SCHOOL WELLBEING.* UNPUBLISHED DOCTORAL DISSERTATION, GHENT UNIVERSI

Suggested Readings and Links

BREKELMANS, J. M. G., WUBBELS, T., & CRETON, H.A. (1989). A TYPOLOGY OF STUDENT PERCEPTIONS OF TEACHER BEHAVIOUR. *PEDAGOGISCHE STUDIEN, 66,* 315–326.

AVAILABLE VI HTTPS://ONLINELIBRARY.WILEY.COM/DOI/ABS/10.1002/ TEA.3660270405

DECI, E. L., & RYAN, R. M. (2000). THE "WHAT" AND "WHY" OF GOAL PURSUITS: HUMAN NEEDS AND THE SELF-DETERMINATION OF BEHAVIOR. *PSYCHOLOGICAL INQUIRY, 11,* 227–268.

AVAILABLE VIA HTTP://DX.DOI.ORG/10.1207/S15327965PLI1104_01

INTERESTING DISCUSSION OF A STUDY WHERE RESEARCHERS QUESTIONE TEACHERS AND STUDENTS ON THEIR INTERESTS AND THEN SELECTIVELY SHARED EXAMPLES FROM THE SURVEY RESULTS WITH TEACHERS AND STUDENTS TO SHOW THEM THAT THEY HAD THINGS IN.

AVAILABLE VIA WWW.NPR.ORG/2015/10/13/444446708/ IN-THE-CLASSROOM-COMMON-GROUND-CAN-TRANSFORM-GPAS

STUDY IN WHICH KATJA UPADYAYA AND JACQUELYNNE S. ECCLES FOUND THAT TEACHERS' EXPECTATIONS ABOUT WHETHER A STUDENT IS GOING TO SUCCEED CAN AFFECT STUDENT ACADEMIC OUTCOMES.

AVAILABLE VIA HTTPS://DIGITALCOMMONS.WAYNE.EDU/MPQ/VOL60/ISS4/3/

23

RELATIONSHIPS MATTER

THEO WUBBELS & MIEKE BREKELMANS ON THE
IMPORTANCE OF RELATIONSHIPS

OI: 10.4324/9781003228165-28

23 RELATIONSHIPS MATTER

ARTICLE Two decades of research on teacher-student relationships in class[1]

QUOTE *"One cannot not communicate when in the presence of someone else."*[2]

Why You Should Read This Article

At the beginning of F. Scott Fitzgerald's *The Great Gatsby* we're introduced to the novel's eponymous character by narrator Nick Carraway, who says of Gatsby, "If personality is an unbroken series of successful gestures, then there was something gorgeous about him" (Fitzgerald, 2019, p. 2). Putting aside Nick's unreasonable admiration of Gatsby, there's nevertheless an intriguing idea bound up within his observation: the perceptions people have of us are the result of the accumulated impact of all the gestures we have ever made in their presence.

This concept is perhaps truer for teaching than many professions, since the net effect of the innumerable gestures and behaviours demonstrated by a teacher over time serve as *the* influencing factor in how students will perceive them and, by extension, the learning environment more broadly. The question of how teachers should "present" to their students is what gives rise to the "Don't smile 'til Christmas" brand of advice that has long been offered to those new to the profession. These words ring true because they're rooted in the same direct-line relationship between teacher behaviours, student perception and resulting teacher-student relationships, as well as the innumerable knock-on effects borne of that relational dynamic.

Compelling as this idea is, there's little more to be said about the specificity of its application to teaching, unless we understand the relational dynamics of the classroom in greater detail. To get at that level of nuance, we might ask this: What would be revealed if we could map the

---

[1] WUBBELS, T., & BREKELMANS, M. (2005). TWO DECADES OF RESEARCH ON TEACHER-STUDENT RELATIONSHIPS IN CLASS. *INTERNATIONAL JOURNAL OF EDUCATIONAL RESEARCH, 43,* 6–24.

[2] IBID., P. 7.

modes of communication employed by teachers, understand their effect on the teacher-student relationship, and demonstrate the impact all that can have on student outcomes? That was the tall-order question Theo Wubbels and Mieke Brekelmans set about answering in their fascinating paper: two decades of research on teacher-student relationships in class.

Synopsis of the Article

Based on a 25-year program of study, this paper describes the nature of teacher-student relationships in terms of teacher behaviour. Student and teacher perceptions on teacher-student relationships are explored through data collected using the Questionnaire on Teacher Interaction (QTI). The paper reviews studies showing that high degrees of teacher influence and proximity towards students are conducive with high student outcomes. The paper also draws conclusions about non-verbal behaviour and spatial positioning of teachers, recommending that beginning teachers communicate the persona of an experienced teacher when addressing whole-class groups.

The Article

As Teachers, We Cannot Not Communicate

Communicative systems approach

Theo Wubbels and Mieke Brekelmans begin their paper by laying out the "communicative systems approach" that informs their study. They draw on the work of Watzlawick et al. (1967) in assuming that "every behavior that someone displays in the presence of someone else is communication" and since "teaching is a form of communication" (p. 7) it, too, is ripe for a "systems approach" in which all teacher behaviours, regardless of their intent, should be seen as subject to inference by students, impactful on the relational dynamic, and therefore open to systematic analysis.

Teaching is communication

So, what does a systematised, analytical approach for understanding the complex relational dynamics of classrooms look like in practice? To answer this, we must first ground some terms that define the parameters of Wubbels and Brekelmans' investigation. The authors delineate two aspects of communication: a *content* aspect (what is said/done by a teacher) and a *relation* aspect (how it is said/done by a teacher). They then distinguish between two levels of communication: a *message* level (individual instances of communication) and a *pattern* level (those habits of communication that forge the relational dynamic over time). The pattern level is what we mean by the aggregated impact of all the gestures and behaviours enacted by a teacher and the general perception that forms in the eyes of their students.

Two aspects of communication: content & relation

Two levels of communication: message & pattern

	Content aspect (What is said/done)	Relation aspect (How it is said/done)
Message level	Your answer is wrong; it should be . . . That's not the answer I expected. Try to solve it this way. How did you come to that answer? Can you think of a different approach?	Disapproving/Strict Directive/Didactic Encouraging/ Empathetic
Pattern level	Continual critical or disapproving comments about student(s). Caring that the student(s) didn't understand a concept, leading to new explanations or tutoring of specific students. Challenging comments to the students or class where they're encouraged to think differently or more deeply.	Deprecatory Understanding/Patient Metacognitive/ Encouraging

A Model for Mapping Teacher-Student Relationships

Model for Interpersonal Teacher Behavior

The teacher actions and resultant student perceptions described above can be mapped and represented within a *Model for Interpersonal Teacher Behavior (MITB)*, (Wubbels et al., 1985). The model relies on two dimensions: *Influence* (expressed on a continuum from Dominance to Submission) and *Proximity* (expressed on a continuum from Opposition to Cooperation). These axes can be seen in Figure 23.1.

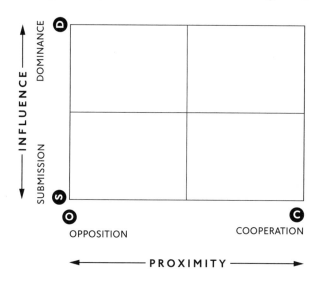

FIGURE 23.1
TWO-DIMENSIONAL COORDINATE SYSTEM OF THE MODEL FOR INTERPERSONAL TEACHER BEHAVIOUR. ADAPTED FROM WUBBELS AND BREKELMANS (2005).

Typical questions to map student perceptions of a teacher can be found below. Here, a 5-point Likert scale is used to capture from the students' perspective where their teacher lands on the dominance-to-submission and cooperation-to-opposition axes.

Dominance (D)

The teacher determines the student's activities

5-4-3-2-1

Submission (S)

The students' can determine their own activities

Cooperation (C)

The teacher shows approval of the students and their behaviour

5-4-3-2-1

Opposition (O)

The teacher shows disapproval of the students and their behaviour

These questions and how they map patterns of student perceptions over time allow for the categorising of typical teacher behaviours that flesh out the model (see Figure 23.2).

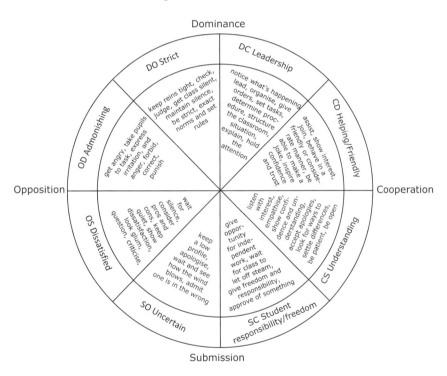

FIGURE 23.2
MODEL FOR INTERPERSONAL TEACHER BEHAVIOUR.

ools: Questionnaire on Teacher Interaction

As you can see, a seemingly simple set of axes describing student perceptions of teacher behaviours quickly becomes a more comprehensive model for mapping teacher-student relational types, once you begin asking the right kinds of questions. In this case, Wubbels and Brekelmans call on the *Questionnaire on Teacher Interaction* (QTI; Wubbels et al., 1985), a 77-item scale subdivided according to the eight teacher behaviour types in Figure 23.2. Though the authors point out that less research has been carried out on student perceptions at the *message* level (capturing individual instances of communication), the extent of the research base at the *pattern* level (capturing mutual perceptions of the relational dynamic developed over time) is more extensive, allowing for an even more nuanced understanding of teacher-student dynamics.

Building Teacher-Student Relationship Profiles

Wubbels and Brekelmans explore this nuance by identifying relational profiles, essentially categorical teacher types identified by noting patterns in the QTI which can be mapped onto the *Model for Interpersonal Teacher Behavior*. The authors describe how, "a profile is the particular combination of eight scale scores resulting from the administration of the QTI" (p. 11) and offer eight pattern types within the MITB model: Authoritative, Directive, Drudging, Tolerant, Repressive, Tolerant/Authoritative, Uncertain/Aggressive, and Uncertain/Tolerant. For instance, a Tolerant/Authoritative profile would come from students perceiving a teacher as relatively high on both the cooperation and dominance scales, while an Uncertain/Aggressive profile would land instead within the opposition and submission quadrant of the model (see Figure 23.3).

Teacher-Student Relationship Profiles with eight pattern types

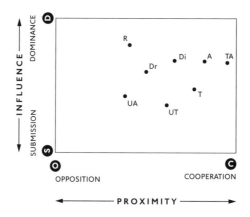

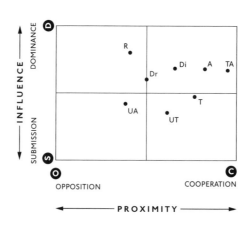

FIGURE 23.3
MAIN POINTS OF THE EIGHT TYPES OF PATTERNS OF INTERPERSONAL RELATIONSHIPS. A= AUTHORITATIVE, DI=DIRECTIVE, DR=DRUDGING, T=TOLERANT, R=REPRESSIVE, TA=TOLERANT/ AUTHORITATIVE, UA=UNCERTAIN/ AGGRESSIVE, UT=UNCERTAIN TOLERANT. ADAPTED FROM WUBBELS AND BREKELMANS (2005)

The Link Between Teacher-Student Relationships and Student Outcomes

Why does it matter that we can map the relational dynamic between teachers and students? What difference does it make without a connection to what this actually means for student outcomes?

To address these questions, the authors refer to a study of Physics teachers (Brekelmans, 1989) that uses the identified relationship patterns in Figure 23.3, to investigate "the relationship between student outcomes and students' perceptions of teacher-student relationships". That study draws the following "on average" conclusions:

- Teachers seen as *Repressive* have the highest student achievement outcomes.
- In disorderly classrooms, the *Uncertain/Tolerant*, *Uncertain/Aggressive*, and *Drudging* teachers reflect relatively low student achievement outcomes, whereas *Directive*, *Authoritative*, and *Tolerant* teachers have relatively high outcomes.
- *Authoritative* and *Directive* teachers have the highest student attitude scores.
- Students of *Drudging*, *Uncertain/Aggressive*, and *Repressive* teachers have the worst attitudes toward their subject.

The effect of Influence

This study offers a telling insight into the impact of teacher-student relational dynamics, with Wubbels and Brekelmans pointing out how, "teacher influence was the most important variable at the class level" and that "the higher a teacher was perceived in the Influence dimension, the higher the outcomes of students on a Physics test" (p. 13).

The effect of proximity

They identify similar trends in the *Proximity* dimension as those seen in *Influence*, citing another study in which "the more teachers were perceived as cooperative, the higher students' scores on cognitive tests" (p. 41). An example of what this looks like at the level of individual teachers can be seen in Figure 23.4.

FIGURE 23.4
INTERPERSONAL PROFILES OF TEACHERS WITH RELATIVELY HIGH AND LOW STUDENT OUTCOMES.

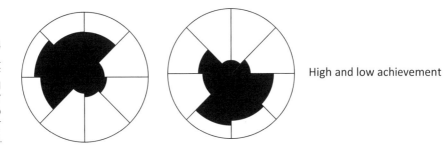

High and low achievement

On the affective dimension, they note and even more consistent pattern connecting teacher-student relationships to student affect.

FIGURE 23.5
INTERPERSONAL
PROFILES OF
TEACHERS WITH
RELATIVELY
HIGH AND
LOW STUDENT
ATTITUDES
TOWARDS
THE LEARNING
ENVIRONMENT.
NOTE: HIGH
STUDENT
ATTITUDES
EQUATE TO HIGH
MOTIVATION
FOR LEARNING
A GIVEN SUBJECT
WHILE LOW
STUDENT
ATTITUDES
EQUATE TO
LOW STUDENT
MOTIVATION FOR
LEARNING THAT
SUBJECT.

Their investigation shows that "all studies find a positive relationship of both influence and proximity with affective outcome measures, usually measured in terms of subject-specific motivation" and that "generally, effects of proximity are somewhat stronger than effects of influence". The headline conclusion here is that "the higher the perception of proximity, the higher the motivation of the students is" (p. 14) as seen in Figure 23.5.

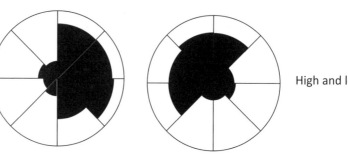

High and low attitudes

These conclusions are significant because they draw that all-important connection between teacher-student relations and student performance. Even though positive teacher-student relationships are an absolute good in their own right, understanding how they impact learning adds an even more consequential dimension to that dynamic. By breaking down the factors influencing teacher-student relations in the ways described, Wubbels and Brekelmans shed light on the all-too-often a black box of classroom practice: the effect of teacher behaviour on the teacher-student dynamic and its impact on students' learning experiences and outcomes.

Comparing Teachers' and Students' Perceptions

As well as capturing student perceptions, the *Questionnaire on Teacher Interaction (QTI)* can also be taken by teachers to rate themselves, as well as to capture their ideal perception – that is to say, how a teacher would *like* to be perceived. Measuring gaps between the teacher ideal, teacher self-perception, and student perception sheds important light on the overlapping interpretations of classroom dynamics.

Comparing teachers'
and students'
perceptions

Barring a few exceptions, most studies on *Influence* and *Proximity* find important differences between how teachers see themselves and how students see them. Wubbels and Brekelmans note that, "on average, teachers reported higher ratings of their own leading, helpful/friendly and understanding behaviour than did their students, whereas they reported lower perceptions of their own uncertain, dissatisfied and admonishing behaviour on their students" and other studies which reported, "higher teacher than student perceptions of strict and lower teacher than student perceptions of student freedom and responsibility" (p. 19). Clearly students often see their teachers differently than teachers see themselves

They go on to note an important connection between these disparities of teacher-student perception and student outcomes. Teacher behaviours scoring higher in self-perception than student perception (e.g., teachers who see themselves as more helpful/friendly, or understanding than their students do) are positively related to student achievement and motivation; whereas behaviours scoring higher in student perception than teacher self-perception (e.g., teachers whose students see them as more uncertain or admonishing than they see themselves) are negatively associated to student achievement and motivation.

In other words, teachers tend to judge the learning environments they create more favourably than their students. This may help explain why reflecting on practice, watching back over their own instruction, or reacting to student climate surveys can be particularly difficult for teachers. After all, holding a mirror up to classroom dynamics from the students' perspective appears to highlight a gap between what teachers think is happening and what students actually experience.

Comparing Teachers' Perceptions With Their "Ideal"

When considering differences between the teacher ideal, teacher self-perception, and student perceptions along the eight scales as Wubbels et al. (1992) did in a subsequent study, we see the widest gap between the teacher ideal and student perceptions. For what it's worth, there's also a gap between teachers' self-perception and their ideal but it isn't as wide.

In the same study, they categorised two types of teachers: the first, visible in two-thirds of the teachers sampled, found teacher self-perception to occupy "a position between the teacher's ideal about the teacher-student relationship and the students' perceptions" (p. 19). An example of what this looks like can be found in Figure 23.6.

FIGURE 23.6
TEACHER IDEAL, SELF-REPORT AND STUDENTS' PERCEPTIONS OF ONE TEACHER. THE SELF-REPORT OCCUPIES A POSITION BETWEEN STUDENTS' PERCEPTIONS AND IDEAL.

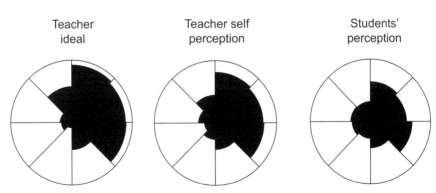

Teacher ideal · Teacher self perception · Students' perception

Wubbels et al. refer to this as the "wishful thinking" example, since "these teachers see their behaviour more like their ideal than their students". Drawing on the work of Leon Festinger (1957), they suggest that such wishful thinking "may function to reduce cognitive dissonance" (p. 20). In other words, some teachers may unwittingly immunise themselves against confronting the competing perceptions of classroom dynamics by assuming that things are better than they really are.

COGNITIVE DISSONANCE

Cognitive dissonance

LEON FESTINGER posited in his Theory of Cognitive Dissonance (1957), that we strive for internal psychological consistency to function in the real world. When we experience inconsistency between our perception of something and reality, we tend to become psychologically uncomfortable and are motivated to reduce the ensuing cognitive dissonance. In other words, when two actions or ideas aren't psychologically consistent with each other, we do all that we can do to change them until they become consistent.

For example, though we know that smoking is unhealthy, many people who've tried and failed to quit (in other words, there's a dissonance between what they know they should do and what they do) rationalise their failure by adjusting either their functional beliefs (e.g., "Smoking calms me down", "Smoking helps me concentrate") or their risk-minimising beliefs (e.g., "The medical evidence is exaggerated" or "Smoking is no more risky than many other things we do") to better correspond with their actions and reduce their dissonance (Fotuhi et al., 2013).

Another segment of teachers, constituting one-third of the sample, are referred to as the "protection against disappointment" group (see Figure 23.7) since "the self-report is lower than the students' perceptions of the actual behaviour, whereas the ideal is higher than both actual behaviour and self-report" (p. 20).

FIGURE 23.7
TEACHER IDEAL, SELF-REPORT AND STUDENTS' PERCEPTIONS OF ONE TEACHER. THE TEACHER'S SELF-PERCEPTION IS FURTHER AWAY FROM THE IDEAL THAN THE STUDENTS' PERCEPTIONS.

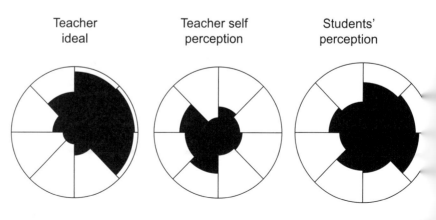

Teacher ideal   Teacher self perception   Students' perception

Here, the immunisation is even more prominent. Something Wubbels points out when he suggests that such a configuration would "protect the teacher against potential disappointment resulting from confrontation with more negative students' perceptions" (p. 20).

Teacher-student Relationships and Students' Learning Activities

One of the more interesting findings of the research into student perceptions of the teacher-student relationship is that it even extends to the perception students have of the tasks and activities in which they engage. A study by Brekelmans et al. (2001) examined how students perceived those moments when teachers invited them to initiate learning by themselves. The authors found that students reacted more positively to an invitation to own their learning when their overall perception of the teacher was higher on the *Influence* scale. Wubbels and Brekelmans note how this dynamic might seem surprising at first glance but conclude that, "To give students appropriate freedom and responsibility during group and independent work, it appeared to be important for a teacher to be a strong leader in central lesson segments. The learning environment they create in central moments extends to individual work" (p. 15).

This is a telling finding which calls into question the "student-centred learning" narratives that have become widespread over the last few decades. Rather than seeing student ownership of learning in absolute terms, it seems students respond better to opportunities for independent learning when the teacher has first established their influence as the principal leader of learning in the classroom (an idea we discuss in Chapter 22 of this book on teacher authenticity). Indeed, the higher this perceived influence is, the more positively students react when their teacher affords them greater autonomy in their learning.

Conclusion

The concepts explored in this chapter reinforce the idea that perceptions and relationships matter in teaching and learning. Specifically, the way students and teachers perceive patterns of communication are significant in shaping their experience of the student-teacher relationship – all of which have important implications for classroom dynamics and the learning that follows. Understanding how classroom dynamics are formed is important because it allows teachers to shed light on the difference between "how things are going" from their perspective and "how things are *really* going" for their students.

This is not to say that student perceptions should serve as the solitary driver for the choices teachers make; nor should we infer that there exists a mystical "sweet-spot" on the *Model for Interpersonal Teacher Behavior* towards which every teacher should aspire, or else. Rather, this paper reminds us that teachers have agency and can make thoughtful choices about how they come across to their students. Wubbels and Brekelmans' term for engaging in these ideas is "meta-communication". That is to say, "communication about how teacher and students communicate with each other" (p. 20). Their work offers a useful pathway towards this meta-communicative approach and helps us better understand the impact teacher behaviours have on student perceptions, classroom dynamics, and what students learn and do as a result.

Takeaways

- All teaching is communication of one form or another.
- By exploring the communication patterns in classrooms across teacher self-report, the teacher ideal and student perceptions, we can arrive at a picture of teacher-student relationships and connect those dynamics to student outcomes.
- Even though there is no hard-and-fast rule for how a teacher should present to their students, teachers who score higher on the influence and proximity metrics on the QTI tend to cultivate teacher-student relationships that are relatively more conducive for high student outcomes.
- Students respond better to opportunities for independent learning when the teacher has first established influence as the principal leader of learning within the relational dynamic.
- Since novice teachers are less likely to engage in behaviours that promote perceptions of influence and dominance than more experienced teacher there is scope for mentorship that concentrates on how such behaviours can be incorporated into novice teachers' classroom practice.
- Students often see their teachers differently than teachers see themselve
- The higher the students' perception of proximity, the higher their motivation.
- Engaging in a meta-communicative approach (communicating about communication) helps teachers better understand how certain classroom dynamics are created and maintained.

References

BREKELMANS, M. (1989). *INTERPERSONAL TEACHER BEHAVIOUR IN THE CLASSROOM*. W.C.C. (IN DUTCH).

BREKELMANS, M., SLEEGERS, P., & FRASER, B. (2001). TEACHING FOR ACTIVE LEARNING. IN J. SIMONS, J. VAN DER LINDEN, & T. DUFFY (EDS.), *NEW LEARNING* (PP. 227–242). KLUWER ACADEMIC PUBLISHERS.

FESTINGER, L. (1957). *A THEORY OF COGNITIVE DISSONANCE*. ROW, PETERSON.

FITZGERALD, F. S. (2019). *THE GREAT GATSBY.* WORDSWORTH EDITIONS.

FOTUHI, O., FONG, G. T., ZANNA, M. P., BORLAND, R., YONG, H. H., & CUMMINGS, K. M. (2013). PATTERNS OF COGNITIVE DISSONANCE-REDUCING BELIEFS AMONG SMOKERS: A LONGITUDINAL ANALYSIS FROM THE INTERNATIONAL TOBACCO CONTROL (ITC) FOUR COUNTRY SURVEY. *TOBACCO CONTROL, 22(1),* 52–58.

WATZLAWICK, P., BEAVIN, J. H., & JACKSON, D. (1967). *THE PRAGMATICS OF HUMAN COMMUNICATION.* NORTON.

WUBBELS, T., & BREKELMANS, M. (2005). TWO DECADES OF RESEARCH ON TEACHER-STUDENT RELATIONSHIPS IN CLASS. *INTERNATIONAL JOURNAL OF EDUCATIONAL RESEARCH, 43,* 6–24.

WUBBELS, T., BREKELMANS, M., & HOOYMAYERS, H. P. (1992). DO TEACHER IDEALS DISTORT THE SELF-REPORTS OF THEIR INTERPERSONAL BEHAVIOR? *TEACHING AND TEACHER EDUCATION, 8,* 47–58.

WUBBELS, T., CRÉTON, H. A., & HOOYMAYERS, H. P. (1985). DISCIPLINE PROBLEMS OF BEGINNING TEACHERS, INTERACTIONAL TEACHER BEHAVIOR MAPPED OUT. *ABSTRACTED IN RESOURCES IN EDUCATION, 20(12),* 153. ERIC DOCUMENT 260040.

Suggested Readings and Links

WUBBELS, T., DEN BROK, P., VAN TARTWIJK, J., & LEVY, J. (2012). *INTERPERSONAL RELATIONSHIPS IN EDUCATION AN OVERVIEW OF CONTEMPORARY RESEARCH.* SENSE PUBLISHERS.

AVAILABLE VIA HTTPS://TINYURL.COM/WVWPP3W7

WUBBELS, T., LEVY, J., & BREKELMANS, M. (1997, APRIL). PAYING ATTENTION TO RELATIONSHIPS. *EDUCATIONAL LEADERSHIP, 54(1),* 82–86.

TEACHERS' INTERPERSONAL SKILLS ARE ESSENTIAL TO CREATING A POSITIVE CLASSROOM CLIMATE. THE QUESTIONNAIRE FOR TEACHER INTERACTION – DEVELOPED IN THE NETHERLANDS, THE U.S., AND AUSTRALIA – PROVIDES A ROADMAP FOR PROFESSIONAL IMPROVEMENT.

AVAILABLE VIA HTTPS://TINYURL.COM/4DC3HNVR

WUBBELS, T., BREKELMANS, M., DEN BROK, P., LEVY, J., MAINHARD, T., & VAN TARTWIJK, J. (2012). LET'S MAKE THINGS BETTER: DEVELOPMENTS IN RESEARCH ON INTERPERSONAL RELATIONSHIPS IN EDUCATION. IN T. WUBBELS, P. DEN BROK, J. VAN TARTWIJK, & J. LEVY (EDS.), *INTERPERSONAL RELATIONSHIPS IN EDUCATION* (PP. 225–250). SENSE PUBLISHERS.

AVAILABLE VIA HTTPS://TINYURL.COM/58PW9VS7

VIDEOS

THIS IS PART OF THE VODCAST SERIES PRODUCED BY PROF. SUSAN RODRIGUES. IN THIS VODCAST PROF THEO WUBBELS (PHD) TALKS ABOUT HIS RESEARCH ON INTERPERSONAL INTERACTIONS BETWEEN THE STUDENT AND TEACHERS AND THE IMPACT IN HAS ON BEHAVIOUR IN THE CLASSROOM.

AVAILABLE VIA WWW.YOUTUBE.COM/WATCH?V=XW2-UK9G0JS&T=7S

INSTITUTE OF EDUCATION SCIENCES: STRENGTHENING RELATIONSHIPS WITH STUDENTS FROM DIVERSE BACKGROUNDS.

AVAILABLE VIA WWW.YOUTUBE.COM/WATCH?V=2HW0DBXOMJQ

WEBSITES

EDUCATION NORTHWEST: RESOURCES FOR BUILDING TEACHER-STUDENT RELATIONSHIPS.

AVAILABLE VIA HTTPS://EDUCATIONNORTHWEST.ORG/RESOURCES/
RESOURCES-BUILDING-TEACHER-STUDENT-RELATIONSHIPS

THE NATIONAL CENTER ON SAFE SUPPORTIVE LEARNING ENVIRONMENTS (NCSSLE): INFORMATION AND TECHNICAL ASSISTANCE FOR STATES, DISTRICTS, SCHOOLS, INSTITUTIONS OF HIGHER LEARNING, AND COMMUNITIES FOCUSED ON IMPROVING SCHOOL CLIMATE AND CONDITIONS FOR LEARNING

AVAILABLE VIA HTTPS://SAFESUPPORTIVELEARNING.ED.GOV/

24 WHY RELATIONSHIPS MATTER

ROBERT MARZANO ON CLASSROOM MANAGEMENT

24 WHY RELATIONSHIPS MATTER

ARTICLE The Key To Classroom Management[1]

QUOTE *"The interaction of these two dynamics – dominance and cooperation – is a central force in effective teacher-student relationships."*[2]

Why You Should Read This Article

On the 3rd May 2015, Chelsea won the Premier League title with three games to spare. For manager Jose Mourinho, it was his 21st trophy, marking him out as the most decorated manager in recent club football history. In August he was rewarded with a multi-million-pound contract that would see him at the club until 2019. By December he was sacked.

The club had inexplicably nosedived in the new season with reports of "palpable discord" in the dressing room exacerbated by his public admonishment and subsequent ostracism of team doctor and well-respected member of the group, Eva Carnerio. One of the major question that emerged from Mourinho's "annus horribilis" is how did a group of players who won the league at a canter a matter of months earlier, capitulate in such a dramatic fashion?

In direct contrast to this, in 2016 we witnessed possibly the greatest sporting phenomenon in English football history with Leicester City winning the Premier League, a feat made all the more remarkable by the fact that at the same time the previous year they were bottom of the league and fighting for their lives to even stay in it (older Americans can liken this to what the "Amazing Mets" did in 1969). The difference appears to be their new manager, the genial Claudio Ranieri who elevate a disparate band of largely unknown players to the pinnacle of football history within less than a year by fostering an indomitable team spirit that has seen each and every player performing well beyond their limits

1   MARZANO, R. J., & MARZANO, J. S. (2003). THE KEY TO CLASSROOM MANAGEMENT. *EDUCATIO LEADERSHIP*, 61(1), 6–13. AVAILABLE VIA HTTPS://TINYURL.COM/3X5VFH3T.
2   IBID., P. X.

Great teachers have much in common with great coaches. They have a dizzying knowledge of their field with an infectious passion for it, and they can communicate that passion clearly and in ways that inspire as we have seen in Chapter 22. They have an unquestionable authority, the total respect of the players in their charge and crucially, they can engender trust and belief in their team to the extent that they will walk through walls for them. Conversely, if that relationship breaks down, players can be shadows of their former selves: aimless, lacking in confidence and self-belief and playing "within themselves".

Many of us will remember a teacher who seemed to command such unwavering respect from even the most challenging of classes. They could walk into a room and establish silence with a mere glance or the raising of a hand. In contrast we'll also remember that teacher whose classroom can only be described as a scene from "Lord of the Flies". In some cases the second type of teacher is given the "lateral arabesque"[3]: a phrase coined by Laurence Peter which is essentially a horizontal promotion where that person is given a longer title, a remote office and a vague set of responsibilities to keep them away from combustible material so to speak.

Lateral arabesque: a sideways promotion used with ineffective employees

But what is it that distinguishes those two? For many teachers, explicit training is an incidental part of becoming a teacher based on the odd tip from the old, wizened pro in the staffroom who had honed their craft over many years. As a result, many teachers find themselves facing a class for the first time with some knowledge of learning theories but little in the way of practical techniques they can use to establish an effective working atmosphere. Despite the fact that effective classroom management can look to the novice like some form of sorcery, there are a range of tools and techniques that can be learned to create a healthy atmosphere and establish positive working relationships between teacher and student. This article is one of the most comprehensive reviews on the kinds of approaches effective teachers use when managing a classroom.

Abstract of the Article

In a recent meta-analysis of more than 100 studies, the authors found that the quality of teacher-student relationships is the keystone for all other aspects of classroom management. The characteristics of effective teacher-relationships have nothing to do with the teacher's personality or even whether the students view the teacher as a friend, they assert. Instead, the most effective teacher-student relationships are characterised by specific teacher behaviours: exhibiting appropriate

---

3   PETER, L. J., & HULL, R. (1970). *THE PETER PRINCIPLE* (P. 34). BANTAM.

levels of dominance, exhibiting appropriate levels of cooperation, and addressing the problems of high-needs students. The article describes teacher strategies for shaping the dynamics of the classroom through the balance of these three types of behaviour.

The Article

Robert and Jana Marzano begin their article by stating that a comprehensive literature review (Wang et al., 1993) shows that effective classroom management had the largest effect on student achievement, something that anyone who has taught in classroom will instinctively know. As we have shown before, any kind of drain on working memory and attention can have disastrous effects on learning and there is nothing more draining for students than a chaotic classroom (see Chapter 2 from *HLH*). The authors also note that their own research indicates that the quality of teacher-student relationships is the "keystone for all other aspects of classroom management" (p. 6). As we have seen in Chapter 23, positive teacher-student relationships in this sense does not mean being friends with the students or even that it is dependent on the personality of the teacher but rather a particular kind of dynamic where the teacher is "exhibiting appropriate levels of dominance; exhibiting appropriate levels of cooperation; and being aware of high-needs students" (p. 6).

Appropriate Levels of Dominance

The word *dominance* is perhaps a problematic one in terms of defining teacher-student relationships and certainly one you would never hear in a school today (see also Chapter 23) but according to research in this area *appropriate* dominance is defined as "the teacher's ability to provide clear purpose and strong guidance regarding both academics and student behavior" (p. 8).

Appropriate dominance in the classroom

There is the view that the stricter the teacher, the more disliked they are but this is not borne out by this research surveyed here which shows that students prefer a teacher who can control a class and provide a safe, collegial working atmosphere. For example, one study they cite by Chiu and Tulley (1997) that involved 700 students in grades 4–7 showed that students voiced a clear desire for "strong teacher guidance and control rather than more permissive types of teacher behaviour" (p. 2). Additionally, they note that important research from the 1980s by Edmund Emmer and his colleagues in secondary schools shows that establishing clear rules and procedures with consequences for infringement is key to effective classroom management. Setting ground rules for group work, using equipment, transitions, and the beginnings and endings of lessons can create a positive habit loop in which poor behaviour doesn't even arise.

The authors also claim it's also a good idea to involve students as much as possible in establishing of these ground rules, however this is probably less about students actually creating the rules but rather the teacher persuading the students that having a clear set of established routines is a good thing not just for their learning but also their mental health and wellbeing.

The importance of physical cues

Based upon research by Stage and Quiroz (1997) the authors note that it's helpful in defining specifically what strategies help create a positive working environment:

- Using a wide repertoire of verbal and physical cues to react to students' misbehaviour, such as raising a hand or putting fingers to lips.
- Giving clear recognition of appropriate behaviour and even providing rewards such as tokens.
- Holding the entire group accountable for behaviour.
- Keeping contact with home and informing parents/guardians of rewards and sanctions.

Furthermore, the Marzanos recommend providing clear goals at the outset of a unit or lesson in terms of what's to be learned along with rubrics such as what students will achieve by the end of that unit or lesson. As any teacher will tell you, one of the quickest ways to create a volatile atmosphere is to have a roomful of pupils who don't know what they're meant to be learning or how they're meant to do it. There's a fine line however between being dominant in a positive way and dominant in a negative way. Perhaps a better word is assertive, and the authors suggest the following approaches:

- Using assertive body language by maintaining an erect posture, facing the offending student but keeping enough distance so as not to appear threatening and matching the facial expression with the content of the message being presented to students.
- Using an appropriate tone of voice, speaking clearly and deliberately in a pitch that is slightly but not greatly elevated from normal classroom speech, avoiding any display of emotions in the voice.
- Persisting until students respond with the appropriate behaviour. Don't ignore an inappropriate behaviour; don't be diverted by a student denying, arguing, or blaming, but listen to legitimate explanations.

Appropriate Levels of Cooperation

In addition to an environment where the driving force is the teacher, an additional tool is to establish a concurrent mode of working where the pupils are functioning in tandem with the teacher and each other to further their own learning. After all, pupils who are merely passively following orders and not using their own agency and autonomy to learn are unlikely to learn the kinds of behaviours that they will need outside the classroom in their own independent study. This is where perhaps having a positive bond with students is most important. They conclude that taking a personal interest in students' lives and concerns beyond merely their academic progress can have a very positive impact.

Equitable and Positive Classroom Behaviours

Another important tool is to not only be consistent but also equitable an positive in how teachers relate to their students. This can be achieved by maintaining eye contact with all students, moving freely around the room, acknowledging/commending class contributions through physic gestures, linking one students ideas to another for example "Cecilia just added to Aida's idea by saying that . . ." (p. 5) drawing in all students not just the ones who always put their hand up and providing an appropriat "wait time" for students to reflect and answer questions. The important point here is that all students feel included in the classroom activities and that their contributions feel just as valued as any other member of the class.

Every student needs
to feel included

Awareness of High-Needs Students

According to the authors, some 12–22% of students suffer from mental, emotional, or behavioural disorders with many of these not receiving adequate support. Although the majority of classroom teacher are not trained in special education needs, it's important that they're aware of all students' needs and to foster specific strategies to attend to them (Marzano, 2003). Drawing on their own previous research, the authors categorise five elements of high needs students and strategies to deal with them, namely passive students, aggressive students, students with attention problems, perfectionists, and students who are socially inept (see Table 24.1).

TABLE 24.1
CATEGORIES OF HIGH NEEDS STUDENTS[4]

Category	Definitions & Source	Characteristics	Suggestions
Passive	Behaviour that avoids the domination of others or the pain of negative experiences. The child attempts to protect self from criticism, ridicule, or rejection, possibly reacting to abuse and neglect. Can have a biochemical basis, such as anxiety.	**Fear of relationships:** Avoids connection with others, is shy, doesn't initiate conversations, attempts to be invisible. **Fear of failure:** Gives up easily, is convinced he or she can't succeed, is easily frustrated, uses negative self-talk.	Provide safe adult and peer interactions and protection from aggressive people. Provide assertiveness and positive self-talk training. Reward small successes quickly. Withhold criticism.
Aggressive	Behaviour that overpowers, dominates, harms, or controls others without regard for their well-being. The child has often taken aggressive people as role models. Has had minimal or ineffective limits set on behaviour. Is possibly reacting to abuse and neglect. Condition may have a biochemical basis, such as depression.	**Hostile:** Rages, threatens, or intimidates others. Can be verbally or physically abusive to people, animals, or objects. **Oppositional:** Does opposite of what is asked. Demands that others agree or give in. Resists verbally or nonverbally. **Covert:** Appears to agree but then does the opposite of what is asked. Often acts innocent while setting up problems for others.	Describe the student's behaviour clearly. Contract with the student to reward corrected behaviour and set up consequences for uncorrected behaviour. Be consistent and provide immediate rewards and consequences. Encourage and acknowledge extracurricular activities in and out of school. Give student responsibilities to help teacher or other students to foster successful experiences.

(Continued)

---

4   MARZANO, R. J. (2003). *WHAT WORKS IN SCHOOLS: TRANSLATING RESEARCH INTO ACTION* (PP. 104–105). ASSOCIATION FOR SUPERVISION AND CURRICULUM DEVELOPMENT.

Category	Definitions & Source	Characteristics	Suggestions
Attention problems	Behaviour that demonstrates either motor or attentional difficulties resulting from a neurological disorder. The child's symptoms may be exacerbated by family or social stressors or biochemical conditions, such as anxiety, depression, or bipolar disorders.	**Hyperactive:** Has difficulty with motor control, both physically and verbally. Fidgets, leaves seat frequently, interrupts, talks excessively. **Inattentive:** Has difficulty staying focused and following through on projects. Has difficulty with listening, remembering, and organising.	Contract with the student to manage behaviours. Teach basic concentration, study, and thinking skills. Separate student in a quiet work area. Help the student list each step of a task. Reward successes; assign a peer tutor.
Perfectionist	Behaviour that is geared toward avoiding the embarrassment and assumed shame of making mistakes. The child fears what will happen if errors are discovered. Has unrealistically high expectations of self. Has possibly received criticism or lack of acceptance while making mistakes during the process of learning.	Tends to focus too much on the small details of projects. Will avoid projects if unsure of outcome. Focuses on results and not relationships. Is self-critical.	Ask the student to make mistakes on purpose, then show acceptance. Have the student tutor other students.
Socially inept	Behaviour that is based on the misinterpretation of nonverbal signals of others. The child misunderstands facial expressions and body language. Hasn't received adequate training in these areas and has poor role modelling.	Attempts to make friends but is inept and unsuccessful. Is forced to be alone. Is often teased for unusual behaviour, appearance, or lack of social skills.	Teach the student to keep the appropriate physical distance from others. Teach the meaning of facial expressions such as anger and hurt. Make suggestions regarding hygiene, dress, mannerisms, and posture.

SHOULD WE TREAT ALL STUDENTS THE SAME?

Treating students as individuals

People are often complimented on their capacity to "treat everyone the same" regardless of who they are dealing with but is this an effective approach in the classroom? Not according to some research which claims that teachers who do not vary their approach with different students are likely to fail (see Brophy, 1996; Brophy & McCaslin, 1992):

> "The study found that the most effective classroom managers did not treat all students the same; they tended to employ different strategies with different types of students. In contrast, ineffective classroom managers did not appear sensitive to the diverse needs of students". (p. 9)

Of course this doesn't mean that teachers shouldn't be consistent with how they deal with a class. One way resentment is formed in a class is if students feel that there's any kind of favouritism going on. However it should be fairly uncontentious that when dealing with a demotivated student who's suffering from mental health problems the teacher must vary their approach than when dealing with a confident and independent student.

Conclusions

One of the difficult things about effective classroom management is that so much of it appears on the surface to be tied to a certain kind of personality defined by confidence and charisma and it's impossible to "teach" someone that. However, there are many observable characteristics of teachers who are effective managers of behaviour. And more than that, those teachers are not just merely managing a room but are creating a productive atmosphere in which students can not only flourish academically but also feel safe and validated in their own classroom. This review shows that beyond teacher personality and charisma, there are routines, techniques and processes that most teachers can learn which can affect that productive atmosphere. These approaches are based on the teacher being an authority in the classroom (see also Chapter 22,) but them at the same time, creating a classroom culture where students are empowered and actively involved in their own progress.

Takeaways

- State clearly what's to be learned and how students will learn it.
- Use eye contact to establish rapport and acknowledge student behaviour.
- You don't need to be liked by a class but you do need to be respected.
- Students don't like teachers who cannot control a class.
- Be aware of high-needs students and how to attend to those needs.
- Don't treat every student the same.
- Establish a positive line of communication with parents and guardians.
- Communicate clearly and often with your students; they need to know you and you them.

References

BROPHY, J. E. (1996). *TEACHING PROBLEM STUDENTS.* GUILFORD.

BROPHY, J. E., & MCCASLIN, N. (1992). TEACHERS' REPORTS OF HOW THEY PERCEIVE AND COPE WITH PROBLEM STUDENTS. *ELEMENTARY SCHOOL JOURNAL, 93,* 3–68.

CHIU, L. H., & TULLEY, M. (1997). STUDENT PREFERENCES OF TEACHER DISCIPLINE STYLES. *JOURNAL OF INSTRUCTIONAL PSYCHOLOGY, 24*(3), 168–175.

MARZANO, R. J. (2003). *WHAT WORKS IN SCHOOLS.* ASCD.

MARZANO, R. J., & MARZANO, J. S. (2003). THE KEY TO CLASSROOM MANAGEMENT. *EDUCATIONAL LEADERSHIP, 61*(1), 6–13. AVAILABLE VIA HTTPS://TINYURL.COM/3X5VFH3T

PETER, L. J., & HULL, R. (1970). *THE PETER PRINCIPLE.* BANTAM.

STAGE, S. A., & QUIROZ, D. R. (1997). A META-ANALYSIS OF INTERVENTIONS TO DECREASE DISRUPTIVE CLASSROOM BEHAVIOR IN PUBLIC EDUCATION SETTINGS. *SCHOOL PSYCHOLOGY REVIEW, 26*(3), 333–368.

WANG, M. C., HAERTEL, G. D., & WALBERG, H. J. (1993). TOWARD A KNOWLEDGE BASE FOR SCHOOL LEARNING. *REVIEW OF EDUCATIONAL RESEARCH, 63*(3), 249–294.

Suggested Readings and Links

A COMPREHENSIVE BOOK ON CLASSROOM MANAGEMENT FROM THE DFE BEHAVIOUR TSAR AND FOUNDER OF RESEARCHED, TOM BENNETT:

BENNETT, T. (2020). *RUNNING THE ROOM.* JOHN CATT EDUCATIONAL LTD.

A SEMINAL AND WILDLY POPULAR BOOK ON CLASSROOM MANAGEMENT THAT HAS PROVED VERY EFFECTIVE IN THE U.S.:

LEMOV, D. (2014). *TEACH LIKE A CHAMPION 2.0.* JOHN WILEY & SONS.

VIDEOS

SHORT VIDEO WITH ROBERT MARZANO GIVING A BRIEF OVERVIEW OF CLASSROOM MANAGEMENT STRATEGIES:

AVAILABLE VIA HTTPS://YOUTU.BE/_BDDWIGN6MK

DOUG LEMOV TALKING THROUGH SOME OF HIS "TEACH LIKE A CHAMPION" STRATEGIES:

HTTPS://YOUTU.BE/AR-31JYGTAK

25 TEACHERS AS INTELLIGENT CONSUMERS

BERLINER ON CLASSROOM MANAGEMENT

I: 10.4324/9781003228165-30

25 TEACHERS AS INTELLIGENT CONSUMERS

CHAPTER Effective classroom management and instruction:
A knowledge base for consultation[1]

QUOTE *"To be knowledgeable means to have learned a body of findings,
to have understood a set of concepts, to have gained experience
in using new technology, and to have assimilated certain theories
to guide classroom observation."*[2]

Why You Should Read This Chapter

In 2012, a team of Harvard Business School researchers introduced
us to the "IKEA effect": the idea that consumers place more value on
products they self-assemble (such as a night table or cabinet bought
from the famous Swedish store) when compared to similar products
that they didn't have a hand in constructing. In a similar phenomenon,
the researchers pointed out that when instant cake mixes were first
introduced into American homes in the 1950s, manufacturers were
disappointed in the slow uptake of sales. It was only when marketeers
realised that they had made baking feel too easy and that an egg should
be added to the process that sales skyrocketed. The fact that an egg plays
almost no part in the baking or flavour of an instant cake is beside the
point. Much more important is an enduring truth illustrated by this
research: when you play a part in making something, you're more likely
to think it's great.

This is all well and good when it comes to furniture and cake mix
but there's a downside to the phenomenon which adversely affects the
teaching profession. Teachers spend a lot of their time either creating or
inheriting instructional materials and approaches. This means they

---

[1] BERLINER, D. C. (1988). EFFECTIVE CLASSROOM MANAGEMENT AND INSTRUCTION: A KNOWLEDGE BASE FOR CONSULTATION. IN J. L. GRADEN, J. E. ZINS, & M. J. CURTIS (EDS.), *ALTERNATIVE EDUCATIONAL DELIVERY SYSTEMS: ENHANCING INSTRUCTIONAL OPTIONS FOR ALL STUDENTS* (PP. 309–325). NATIONAL ASSOCIATION OF SCHOOL PSYCHOLOGISTS.
[2] IBID., P. 323.

not only have to contend with understanding, internalising, and readying those things for use in the classroom, they also have the important responsibility of deciding whether a chosen course of action is valid and appropriate in the first place. The challenge of interrogating your own approaches becomes more problematic when sentiments such as, "We spent the whole summer building these resources" or "We've always used the same lesson plans for this unit" come into play. This is because the IKEA effect can blind us to the inadequacies of our own creations. It's only when we learn how to break down an approach, to understand and internalise exactly how it works, that we can know if it's as good as it purports to be. Just ask anyone who has had to disassemble a piece of IKEA furniture, only to realise at that point how cheaply it had been made all along.

Like any thoughtful consumer, teachers need ways to make sense of the instructional possibilities on offer so that they can make good choices. The alternative is tantamount to falling for an approach not because it works but because it has the allure of familiarity and ease. In his seminal work, *Effective Classroom Management and Instruction: A Knowledge Base for Consultation*, David C. Berliner summarises a host of evidence-informed approaches for effective classroom management that have been shown to work time and again. Just as significantly, perhaps, he offers teachers a lens for consuming and interrogating research so that they're less likely to fall foul of the IKEA effect in their own practice.

Abstract of the Chapter

In the business world there are various professionals who regard the discovery that a major system is not working well, as a great opportunity. Trouble-shooters, problem solvers, creative entrepreneurs – consultants of all kinds – try to identify problems and then attempt to ameliorate them. In the process, of course, they create a market for themselves. It is my contention that problems exist in our system of education that can be ameliorated through the services of school psychologists. New roles, new markets if you will, exist for school psychologists if they choose to pursue them. And a new knowledge base for school psychologists to use their work also exists, giving them an advantage over less qualified professionals who might see the same educational problems as signs of opportunity for promoting their services. Throughout this chapter these two themes will recur: that a need exists for a special kind of consultant in the classroom and that school psychologists, if they learn a new body of scientific knowledge, are uniquely qualified to take on that role.

The Chapter

When it comes to classroom management, Berliner reminds us that one of the most important tools at a teacher's disposal is their pedagogical knowledge. Despite this understanding, he points out that "because of the public's belief that pedagogical knowledge was scanty and that whatever knowledge did exist was of little value" teacher preparation programs ended up cutting back on the extent to which new teachers were trained in pedagogical approaches. Even more tragic (and in no small way ironic) is that the same period of cutbacks "coincided with a great burst of productivity from the educational research community" and "now that considerable amounts of scientifically based pedagogical information is available there is almost no time left in teacher education programs to communicate this information" (p. 310).

Novice teachers are underprepared

Though Berliner wrote this in 1988, so much of what he said is still true today. Many novice teachers still find themselves underprepared, especially in terms of practical approaches to classroom management. To survive, they're forced to either build the plane while they're flying it or to rely on received wisdom and hand-me-downs from colleagues, mentors, or frenzied internet searches. While these approaches *appear to* suffice, the teacher has no way of knowing for sure whether there exists better way than the one they are cobbling together, and so the IKEA effec takes hold.

In response to this, Berliner structures his article according to the developments in classroom organisation and management made during the aforementioned burst of productivity, effectively presenting the case for infusing these and other parts of research into our teaching practice. He breaks these developments down into four main categories, referring to them as "Our *findings*, our *concepts*, our *technology* and our *theory*", an argues that each "can help teachers solve many of their problems" (p. 314 in their own way. As you'll see, he presents these not just as categories o knowledge making up the research base for classroom management bu also as ways of seeing, understanding, and interrogating what works in classrooms and why.

Findings

Findings: what works without adverse effects

Berliner defines "findings" as those "isolated bits of information that every science accumulates" (p. 314). These are the empirical observatior shown to have positive effects on student learning, with little-to-no adverse side effects, and which are highly replicable in study after study

Wait time

He offers *wait time* (Rowe, 1974) as an archetypal example of such a finding, showing that when the time between a teacher asking a questic and a student responding extends from 0.8 seconds (the average) to 3 seconds, the following things happen (p. 314):

- The length of student responses increases.
- The number of alternative explanations given by students increases.
- The number of students who fail to respond decreases.
- The complexity and cognitive level of student responses increase.
- The number of unsolicited but appropriate student responses increases.
- The number of student-to-student interactions increases.
- Student achievement (in mathematics and science) goes up.

Berliner refers to this as a "simple, scientifically derived, and well-validated teaching technique" that has "powerful main effects, with no harmful side effects". Yet, regardless of such compelling selling points, Berliner is quick to remind us that wait time *still* hasn't found its way into common enough usage in classrooms. This, he argues, is down to a problem of false choices. For instance, he points out how many teachers who try out wait time as a technique, "often realize that a slowdown in the pace of instructional activities may take place" meaning that "many are likely to abandon it" (p. 314).

False choices

Such false choices are problematic because they rest on the misguided notion that the benefits of one approach (wait time) will cost you the benefits of another (a purposeful pace to the lesson). As you can see from the effects listed, it's clear that a lesson can employ wait time *and* still can move along in a purposeful and productive manner. Berliner's case for research applied in this way is simple: being armed with an understanding of robust and replicable findings such as these can clear up harmful misconceptions and, if adopted and applied smartly, provide the evidence-informed version of a "quick and easy win" for teachers.

Concepts

Concepts: developing a common language

Beyond empirical findings, Berliner points to "concepts" as those ways of seeing classroom practice that "help us to organize our world better . . . by allowing us to name things, by giving us a technical vocabulary that we can then use with colleagues as we describe classroom phenomena" (p. 315). This is an important component of what it means to apply research because it involves teachers and schools naming and owning practices rather than them remaining "out there" in the further reaches of academia, cognitive science, or educational psychology. For something to work in the day-to-day of school life, we must find a way to talk about, internalise, and normalise the approach – all of which Berliner bounds up in this principle of conceptualisation.

One such example is that of Academic Learning Time (ALT; Fisher et al., 1980) which he describes as, "that part of classroom time that is allocated to a curriculum content area in which students are *engaged* and *successful*, and during which the *activities or materials they are involved with are related to outcomes that are valued*" (p. 317). The idea that we would have to name that the amount of time students spend engaged in meaningful work as having an impact on their learning seems so obvious as to be moot – but he shows through his own research (Berliner, 1979) that even when you control for contextual factors, there's "enormous between-classroom variation in rates of engagement" with "40–50% time-on-task level in one classroom while next door . . . we may see a 90% time-on-task level" (p. 316).

So, what makes expert teachers stand apart from novice ones when it comes to maximising ALT? For this, Berliner again turns to the research and points out that *routines* are a tried and tested way for teachers to cut through the impediments that all-too-often prevent engaged learning from taking place. In one study cited by Berliner (Brooks & Hawke, 1988) experienced/effective teachers were compared with inexperienced/ineffective 7th grade math teachers. The following represents the feature they saw playing out time and time again in either case:

Experienced/Effective Teachers:	Inexperienced/Ineffective Teachers
■ develop a routine opening that features visual scanning ■ use a quick call to order in a business-like tone of voice ■ have a method of roll taking that is time efficient ■ use an opening verbal sequence that includes behavioural and academic expectations ■ anticipate areas of confusion in explanations ■ call for questions before signalling the beginning of the first activity	■ don't have an effective day-to-day behavioural routine ■ don't use visual scanning ■ use a slower call to order in a non-business-like tone of voice ■ have a procedure for taking roll that's time consuming ■ aren't able to anticipate confusion ■ don't make use of or even have advanced organisation

So, it seems reinforcing a fundamental aspect of classroom management at the conceptual level (variability in the amount of ALT) so that tried and tested approaches for maximising learning time (employing effective routines at the beginnings of lessons) is a challenge that can be named, normalised and applied.

What's more, we now understand that focusing student attention on the meaning of content through, among other things, effective questioning is a highly effective way to ensure that information is processed more deeply and retained more durably (Graesser & Olde, 2003). In other words, we might hold onto two truths that justify the absolute importance of a concept like ALT: (1) the more time students spend paying attention to the things you want them to learn, the more likely they'll be to learn that content, (2) the more deeply students are invited to think about the things you want them to learn, the more lasting their memory of that content will be.

Importance of the concept Academic Learning Time

Technology

Technology: tools for teaching and learning

Berliner refers to "technology" not in the broadest sense that we have come to know it but rather as "the scientifically derived tools for teaching and learning that we have invented" and which can solve problems for teachers if applied successfully. To illustrate effective technology at work, Berliner cites a whole host of applications, including some that (once again) might strike us as disarmingly straightforward at first glance. For instance, he turns to Good et al. (1983) and their finding that if, in a mathematics class, "[y]ou first start with review, second present new material, third do guided practice, fourth provide corrections and feedback, fifth give independent practice, and six provide for weekly and monthly review sessions, then your students are likely to achieve well" (p. 321). This is exactly what Barak Rosenshine calls explicit instruction (see Chapter 12) and what many "progressive" educators dismiss as something close to an algorithmic or "painting-by-numbers" approach to teaching – but Berliner's argument is that when something has been shown to work so robustly it is at least worth paying attention to and experimented with as a part of one's own practice.

Behaviour management

In another example, in ways similar to how one might describe the advent of a new technology as it is developed and then "taken to market", Berliner tells the story of how specific classroom behaviour practices, first conceived by Jacob Kounin (1970) rose to prevalence and then entered widespread use. He describes how "the recommendations for teachers were as simple as 'Stand at your door on opening day because . . .' and as complex as deciding when to intervene in a behavior problem" (p. 321). These practices were first built out at the theoretical level, then turned into teacher-training materials at the University of Texas and Utah State University (Borg & Ascione, 1982) before finally being field-tested by the American Federation of Teachers in classrooms around the country.

What unified these behaviour management practices was the confidence with which they could be employed because of the robustness of the process that brought them into the field in the first place. This, for Berliner, is one way to see the technology of classroom practice being put through its paces: first as a finding, then as an adopted concept that continues to show its worth through use, so that eventually it begins to feel like a trusted tool.

Theory

Theory: pulling together Findings, Concepts, and Technologies

Berliner describes "theory" as what happens when we pull together the various strands of knowledge from *Findings*, *Concepts*, and *Technologies* into an integrated and coherent approach to teaching and learning. This integrated structure has a two-fold advantage: first, it enables us to combine previously disparate phenomena around the stuff of teaching and learning in an effort to better understand how and why they occur. Second, it provides the means by which to understand, hypothesise, test, and apply certain approaches – such that they can be honed for their most effective use.

Evidence-informed approach to teaching

Berliner illustrates what this might look like by taking the classroom management concept of "pacing" (i.e., the effective rate at which a teacher is able to cover content meaningfully in a given period of time) and presenting how we might work through a logical, evidence-informed application of the approach into our own practice (pp. 322–323):

- **Identifying a problem area** – Berliner's research into pacing shows that "with students of approximately equal ability we have recorded differences across classrooms in the amount of instruction covered per unit of time in ratios of 10 to 1". Clearly, if pacing is a consequential component of effective classroom management, a wide degree of variability such as this presents an area in which significant improvement could well occur.
- **Controlling for the variable** – Since we have findings that tell us with replicable certainty that "pacing is causally related to achievement" we can "demonstrate our ability to *control*" for that variable. In other words, we can say with certainty that pacing is a validated approach, supported by robust evidence, that has the potential to address the problem.
- **Predicting outcomes** – Through observation of instruction and the application of concepts such as ALT, we're able to "demonstrate that more-effective teachers are likely to maintain a faster pace through the curriculum than their colleagues". This essentially means that we can now more safely say that (all other things being equal) the more effective a teacher is, the more likely they'll be to employ effective pacing, which itself is something we now know to be effective.
- **Arriving at an understanding** – Now we can hang all this information together into a coherent theory about pacing and its effects under certain conditions. Namely, we can hypothesise that "the reason the variable called pacing is a consistent predictor of achievement is that it regulates the amount of opportunity students are provided for learning the things that they are to be held responsible for learning".

Based on our understanding of the above, we can now say that pacing helps students achieve, that it is a trait of effective teachers, and that it corresponds with other findings about time engaged in meaningful content. Or to put it another way: effective pacing works.

Conclusions

We have mentioned this caveat many times in this book but it bears restating here: context is everything and just because something works and is highly replicable doesn't mean that it will work everywhere, all of the time. Berliner acknowledges this on numerous occasions, including during his exploration of new educational technologies, when he makes it clear that "[t]aking on the risk of technological change requires a safe and supportive environment" (p. 322).

Nevertheless, the research Berliner cites throughout his article offers us insights into those approaches to classroom management that are more likely to help than others. Just as important as the content of his advice, however, is the attention he pays to the rigorous manner in which these theories were developed – all of which shows us how we should interrogate any approaches that come our way with a keen eye. He takes the time to examine how empirical, conceptual, technologically applicable, and theoretically sound approaches to teaching and learning can be arrived at – all of which help when considering what is or is not worth adopting in our own classrooms, and all of which serves as an effective immunisation against the IKEA effect.

Takeaways

- Teachers are often underprepared for the classroom because they don't always receive the necessary pedagogical knowledge required for effective classroom management.
- This results in them crafting or adopting approaches to teaching and learning, absent the means to differentiate between gradations of quality.
- Berliner offers four ways of addressing the problem and of interacting with research more broadly:
  - *Findings* – Empirical observations shown to have positive effects on student learning (e.g., wait time).
  - *Concepts* – Shared ways of seeing and describing classroom phenomena (e.g., Academic Learning Time).
  - *Technology* – Scientifically derived tools for teaching and learning (e.g., effective structures for mathematics instruction).
  - *Theory* – An integrated and coherent approach to teaching and learning, grounded in the above components (e.g., an evidence-informed understanding of pacing and its application in practice).

References

BERLINER, D. C. (1979). TEMPUS EDUCARE. IN P. L. PETERSON & H. L. WALBERG (EDS.), *RESEARCH ON TEACHING: CONCEPTS, FINDINGS, AND IMPLICATIONS.* MCCUTCHEN.

BORG, W. R., & ASCIONE, F. R. (1982). CLASSROOM MANAGEMENT IN ELEMENTARY MAINSTREAMING CLASSROOMS. *JOURNAL OF EDUCATIONAL PSYCHOLOGY, 74,* 85–95.

BROOKS, D. M., & HAWKE, G. (1988). EFFECTIVE AND INEFFECTIVE SESSION OPENING TEACHER ACTIVITY AND TASK STRUCTURES. *JOURNAL OF CLASSROOM INTERACTION, 23*(1), 1–4.

FISHER, C., BERLINER, D. C., FILBY, N., MARLIARE, R., CAHEN, L. S., & DISHAW, M. (1980). TEACHING BEHAVIORS, ACADEMIC LEARNING TIME, AND STUDENT ACHIEVEMENT: AN OVERVIEW IN C. DENHAM & A. LIEBERMAN (EDS.), *TIME TO LEARN.* NATIONAL INSTITUTE OF EDUCATION, EDUCATION DEPARTMENT.

GOOD, T., GROUWS, D., & EBMEIR, M. (1983). *ACTIVE MATHEMATICS TEACHING.* LONGMAN.

GRAESSER, A. C., & OLDE, B. A. (2003). HOW DOES ONE KNOW WHETHER A PERSON UNDERSTANDS A DEVICE? THE QUALITY OF THE QUESTIONS THE PERSON ASKS WHEN THE DEVICE BREAKS DOWN. *JOURNAL OF EDUCATIONAL PSYCHOLOGY, 95,* 524–536.

KOUNIN, J. (1970). *DISCIPLINE AND GROUP MANAGEMENT IN CLASSROOMS.* BASIC BOOKS.

ROWE, M. B. (1974). WAIT-TIME AND REWARDS AS INSTRUCTIONAL VARIABLES, THEIR INFLUENCE ON LANGUAGE, LOGIC, AND FATE CONTROL: PT. 1. WAIT-TIME. *JOURNAL OF RESEARCH IN SCIENCE TEACHING, 11, 81–94.*

Suggested Readings and Links

BERLINER, D. C. (1985). EFFECTIVE CLASSROOM TEACHING: THE NECESSARY BUT NOT SUFFICIENT CONDITION FOR DEVELOPING EXEMPLARY SCHOOLS IN G. AUSTIN & H. GARBER (EDS.), *RESEARCH ON EXEMPLARY SCHOOLS.* ACADEMIC PRESS.

DENHAM, C., & LIEBERMAN, A. (EDS.). (1980). *TIME TO LEARN.* NATIONAL INSTITUTE OF EDUCATION.

GAGE, N. L., BERLINER, D. C., & ROSENSHINE, B. (1987). *TALKS TO TEACHERS: A FESTSCHRIFT FOR N.L. GAGE* (PP. 93–110). RANDOM HOUSE.

VIDEOS

IN THIS VIDEO, DAVID BERLINER TALKS ABOUT THE ROLE OF RESEARCH IN EDUCATION – AND HOW WE GO ABOUT MAKING SENSE OF THE COMPLEXITY THAT LIES THEREIN.

AVAILABLE VIA WWW.YOUTUBE.COM/WATCH?V=PJ6SGCB5PRC&T=567S

IN THIS VIDEO, RICHARD FEYNMAN (WHOM BERLINER HAS OFTEN CITED IN HIS OWN WORK) TALKS ABOUT THE RELATIONSHIP BETWEEN OBSERVING AND UNDERSTANDING – WHICH WE THINK SERVES AS AN ELEGANT METAPHOR FOR HOW WE MIGHT VIEW TEACHING PRACTICE.

AVAILABLE VIA WWW.YOUTUBE.COM/WATCH?V=ZBFM3RN4LDO

WEBSITES

OXFORD HANDBOOKS ONLINE: A COMPREHENSIVE REVIEW OF THE OPPORTUNITY TO LEARN (OTL) LITERATURE, OF WHICH ACADEMIC LEARNING TIME IS A PART.

AVAILABLE VIA HTTPS://TINYURL.COM/P94EJWS

SECTION 6

ASSESSMENT

In his book *How Not To Be Wrong*, Jordan Ellenberg tells the story of Abraham Wald – the pioneering mathematician whose grasp of statistics was instrumental in saving the lives of World War II fighter pilots.

Wald spent much of the war working with the Statistical Research Group, which Ellenberg describes as "something like the Manhattan Project, except the weapons being developed were equations, not explosives". In addition to calculating the ideal trajectory an airplane could adopt to avoid an arc of enemy fire, Wald and his team were tasked with working out the best places to fit reinforcing armour onto allied planes so that they could withstand a direct hit.

When the US military approached Wald and his colleagues with this challenge, they brought with them a data set. These data explained the extent of the damage incurred when American planes returned from dog fights over Europe, as well as the distribution of bullet holes over their surface:

Plan Section	Bullet Holes per Square Foot
Engine	1.11
Fuselage	1.73
Fuel system	1.55
Rest of plane	1.8

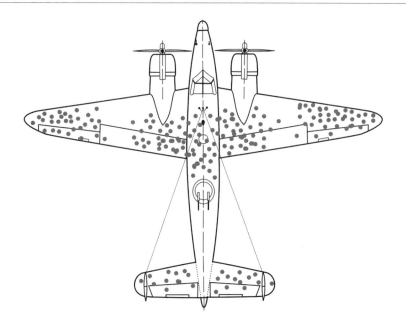

What do you notice when you see these statistics and the accompanying image? If you were on Wald's team, what part of the plane would you recommend be prioritised for additional armoured plating: the engine, the fuselage or the fuel system?

If your response was "the fuselage", you're not alone. Indeed, many of Wald's contemporaries drew similar conclusions and made the same recommendation. Nevertheless, if you *had* made such a suggestion, you would have been wrong – and Abraham Wald would have put you right.

Wald's genius was to see not what the data showed but what it didn't. This is because the above data was collected from those planes that had successfully *returned* from battle, and not from the planes that had been shot down over Europe.[1] Armed with this revelation, Wald famously said that the armour shouldn't go where the bullet holes are, it should go where the bullet holes *aren't*. In other words: protect the engines first.

Wald's example reminds us how important it is to approach the collection, interpretation, and analysis of data with critical consideration. This phenomenon is equally true of teaching – since what we choose to assess, how we choose to assess it, and what we do with the results is so influential in shaping student outcomes.

In this chapter, we explore the functions of assessment by addressing the following questions: What's the difference between formative and summative assessment? Does giving a right answer mean they understand it? and Why is teaching to the test so bad?

---

1 THIS IS WHAT IS KNOWN AS SURVIVORSHIP BIAS: THE LOGICAL ERROR OF CONCENTRATING ON THE PEOPLE OR THINGS THAT MADE IT PAST SOME SELECTION PROCESS AND OVERLOOKING THOSE THAT DID NOT, TYPICALLY BECAUSE OF THEIR LACK OF VISIBILITY.

26 THE MANY FACES AND USES OF ASSESSMENT

BENJAMIN BLOOM AND COLLEAGUES ON DIFFERENT TYPES OF
EVALUATION

DOI: 10.4324/9781003228165-32

26 THE MANY FACES AND USES OF ASSESSMENT

BOOK   Handbook on formative and summative evaluation of student learning[2]

QUOTE   *"Properly used, evaluation should enable teachers to make marked improvements in their students' learning."* [3]

Why You Should Read This Book

On August 17, 1960, five unknown musicians from Liverpool arrived in Hamburg to begin a 48-night gig at the Indra club, near the city's Reeperbahn red-light district. The quintet – Pete Best, George Harrison, John Lennon, Paul McCartney, and Stuart Sutcliffe – were known as the Silver Beatles. They were contracted to play for four and a half hours each weekday night and for six hours on weekend nights for practically nothing.[4] After the Indira closed (because of complaints about the noise), they moved to the Kaiserkeller and then continued to other clubs in the ensuing months. Their performance skills, to put it mildly, were rudimentary and their performances weren't always met by positive reactions from the audience which at the beginning was primarily prostitutes and their clients, underworld types, and the people who inhabited the harbour city's red light district. At one point, the club's owner had to hire protection for the group on stage. Not only were their performance skills lacking, their repertoire was also minimal. According to John Lennon, to fill the sets songs lasted twenty minutes and had twenty solos in them. The crowd liked it as long as it was loud. The band and its members were being tested nightly and they were getting strong feedback. The owner would yell at them not to just stand there but give the customers a performance, and I don't think it would be proper to

---

2   BLOOM, B. S., HASTINGS, J. T., & MADAUS, G. F. (1971). *HANDBOOK ON FORMATIVE AND SUMMAT. EVALUATION OF STUDENT LEARNING.* MCGRAW-HILL.
3   IBID., P.V.
4   DM 30 ($7.19, £2.56 IN 1960) PER PERSON PER DAY.

repeat what the customers said. And these daily evaluations went a long way towards forming the band. Paul McCartney once said that time in Hamburg was 800 hours in the rehearsal room which allowed the Beatles' sound to develop.

The harshness of the Hamburg music scene could have indicated to the Fab Four that they were bad and had failed as musicians . . . instead, it turns out that those conditions provided all-important feedback that helped shape them as a band. Had they seen it as the former, the world might never have known them (and with them the rest of the bands in the so-called British Invasion), heard their music, and experienced the revolution that they brought about in the music scene. Instead, the fab four saw their time in Hamburg as something they could use to help them develop. Benjamin Bloom, J. Thomas Hastings, and George Madaus would label the former (i.e., proof that they were bad) as summative and the latter (i.e., an impetus to get better) as formative evaluation. Just as John, Paul, George, and Ringo were a powerful force in changing music, Ben, Tom, and George with their *Handbook on Formative and Summative Evaluation of Student Learning* were a powerful force in changing our thinking about evaluation and assessment.

Abstract of the Book

This is a book about the "state of the art" of evaluating student learning. It is intended primarily for present and future classroom teachers. Properly used, evaluation should enable teachers to make marked improvements in their students' learning. It is the improvement of student learning which is the central concern of this book.

The busy teacher, responsible for large classes with a great variety of students, has been so concerned with the instructional process that he [sic] has given little time or attention to the evaluation process. Furthermore he has not been able to keep abreast of the growing literature on the art and science of evaluation. This handbook, by bringing together the best of evaluation techniques in general as well as in each of the major subject disciplines and levels of education, is intended to help the teacher use evaluation to improve both the teaching process and the learning process.

The Book

The year 1971 can be seen as a watershed moment in education. In that year, Benjamin Bloom, J. Thomas Hastings, and George Maddaus published their *Handbook on Formative and Summative Evaluation of Student Learning*. Of course, there were things leading up to this like Bloom's 1956 the *Taxonomy of Educational Objectives: The Classification of*

Taxonomies of educational objectives

Educational Goals in the cognitive domain, followed by David Krathwol et al. in the affective domain (1964) and Elizabeth Simpson in the psychomotor domain (1966) or Robert Mager's *Preparing objectives for Programmed Instruction* (1962).

It's impossible to go into detail for the rest of the book. We have about 4,000 words per chapter and this handbook is 923 pages long! To this end we'll just go into a few key points that we feel need to be emphasised. The first is that this handbook isn't meant for linear reading (i.e., from cover to cover) and should be read when and where necessary. Of course, it's a good idea to familiarise yourself with the basis in Part I.

Second, the book is divided into two parts. Part I, divided into four sections, deals with the procedures just described in a general way and which all teachers are likely to encounter. The first section is on education and evaluation where the authors relate their philosophy of the shift of education from gatekeeper to developer of the individual. The second deals with using evaluation for making instructional decisions where the teacher is made aware of the different purposes of evaluation and how different types of evaluation instruments can be developed for and used in the classroom. Section 3 deals specifically with evaluation of cognitive and affective objectives and is organised around Bloom et al.'s (1956) and Krathwohl et al.'s (1964) taxonomies. The final section, evaluation systems, apprises the reader of how they can collaborate with specialists to reduce the work involved in all of this evaluation and improve the effectiveness of evaluation in the school.

Part II provides readers – teachers of specific subject domains at specific levels – with illustrations of the procedures and techniques "which are likely to have the greatest practical value in each subject field or program" (p. 15). The second part wasn't written by them, but rather by specialists from the different fields. The areas handled are *preschool education* with respect to socio-emotional, perceptual-motor, and cognitive development in one chapter and early language development in another and *specific subject domains* at the elementary and secondary school levels. The domains handled are language arts, social studies, art, science, mathematics, literature, writing, second language learning, and industrial education.

Until this book, schools were primarily used for "selection purposes" while in Bloom et al.'s eyes, the primary function of the school was "the development of the individual" (p. 6). In their view, "the central task of the schools is to develop those characteristics in students that will enabl them to live effectively in a complex society" (p. 6). Sound familiar? This is exactly what so-called progressive educators and 21st-century skills adepts are saying today, but Bloom and colleagues posed that the way to do this was to define the objectives clearly and behaviourally and then to

Evaluation for selection

rigorously use two types of assessment (i.e., formative and summative) to achieve this. Quite a difference!

Formative and
summative
evaluation

Summative evaluation is a form of assessment where the focus is on the outcome of a programme. The goal of this type of assessment is the evaluation of student learning at the end of a lesson, series of lessons, or a course or curriculum by comparing the students" results to a standard or benchmark.

Formative evaluation encompasses a broad range of assessment procedures with the goal of allowing teachers to frequently assess both their learners' progress and the effectiveness of their own practice. Teachers can and should use this during the learning process to modify their teaching and student learning activities to improve student learning.

The authors note that education has for centuries been seen as a pyramid or ladder where few reach the top. As such, examinations were used as a way to make decisions about who is allowed to proceed to the next level. "As part of the process, the results of the examinations and teacher judgements have been turned into a grading system" with a "fixed curriculum, a graded set of learning tasks, and a mixed group of learners to be classified at each major time unit in the system . . . to make critical and often irreversible decisions about each student's worth and his [sic] future in the education system" (p. 7) and entire career.

Five functions of
evaluation

With their book, the authors wanted to present a broader view of evaluation and of its place in education. They saw evaluation as a:

1. *method* to acquire and process data needed to improve student learning and teacher teaching including evidence beyond the final examination for a course;
2. way to *clarify goals/objectives* of teaching/learning/education;
3. *process* for determining how students are developing towards the stated goals/objectives;
4. *system of quality control* to see if the teaching-learning process is or isn't effective, and if it isn't to help determine how it can be changed to make it effective before it's too late; and
5. *tool* to ascertain if other procedures are equally effective (or not) to achieve the goals/objectives.

analysis of learners,
instruction, and
outcome

In the book, the authors make clear the relation between (1) evaluation, (2) instructional decisions taken, and (3) the analysis of learners, instruction, and learning outcomes. With respect to the *analysis of* learners, instruction, and learning outcomes it's imperative to diagnose the relevant learner characteristics. At the beginning of a learning unit (this could be a single lesson, a part of a course, a whole course, or the curriculum as a whole), the teacher attempts to determine what the learner brings to the learning task. They also ascertain whether there are special problems for individual students or the class as a whole. Are they old enough, do they have the requisite prior knowledge, what has their prior experience within the subject been, and so further. The crux here is the interaction between learners, material, and instruction (i.e., the instructional process).

Instructional decisions

With respect to *instructional decisions*, the teacher must, on the one hand, determine the state of the learner, their readiness for the tasks and objectives, and aspects of possible special preparation and orientation of the learners. On the other hand, they must decide on the structure and organisation of each learning unit or task, how best to sequence it, on the feedback on the learner's progress at each step, and on a "prescription of alternative learning approaches and tasks as they are found necessary" (p. 14). Finally, the teacher must, keeping the objectives in mind, ascertain whether, and to what extent, the intended learning has taken place, whether the instructional process has been effective, and what changes are needed.

Three types of evaluation: Initial, Formative, Summative

For all of this, *evaluation* is essential! The authors distinguish between initial evaluation, formative evaluation, and summative evaluation. *Initial evaluation*, is based upon the students' record of previous relevant achievement, diagnostic and placement testing, and aptitude tests relevant for making instructional choices. *Formative evaluation* encompasses "tests relevant to the structure of each learning unit or task analysis and diagnosis of what still must be learned, [and] prescription of alternative learning materials and approaches needed" for mastery (p. 14). Finally, *summative evaluation* encompasses testing a sample of attainment the objectives/goals, analysis and diagnosis of the attainment of various parts of the intended learning, all of this with the aid of what they call a *table of specifications*.

		Objectives				
		A	B	C	D	E
Content	1					
	2					
	3					
	4					
	5					
	6					

FIGURE 26.1 TABLE OF SPECIFICATIONS FOR MODEL OF OUTCOMES (ADAPTED FROM *BLOOM ET AL.*, 1971, P. 14).

While the book is titled *Handbook on Formative and Summative Evaluation* . . ., the authors constantly warn the reader that the

> distinction between a formative and a summative unit is not clear-cut. The major difference lies not in the amount of content covered . . . but rather in the purpose. . . . If the evaluation is performed to determine how well students have mastered various elements in a postulated hierarchy so that decisions can be made on how instruction should best proceed, then it is formative in nature. However, given the same amount of content material, if the purpose is simply to grade the student at the end of one unit before proceeding to the next, then the evaluation is summative. (p. 28)

Mastery

Grading on the curve

As their words clearly show, the goal is mastery (see also Chapter 13 in *HLH*). The authors devote a whole chapter to learning for mastery. Grading is often based upon the normal curve (see Figure 26.2). This is in line with the pyramid or ladder function often found in education. Also, if "too many" students get an A, the teacher is seen as being too easy or if there are too many Fs the teacher is too hard. The authors posit a different approach. Teaching and grading on the curve effectively convinces students that it's normal and that they "can only do C or D work" (p. 44). For Bloom and his colleagues, "[E]ducation is a purposeful activity, and we seek to have the students learn what we have to teach. If we are effective in our instruction, the distribution of achievement should be very different from the normal curve. In fact, we may even insist that our educational efforts have been unsuccessful to the extent that the distribution of achievement approximates the normal distribution" (p. 45).

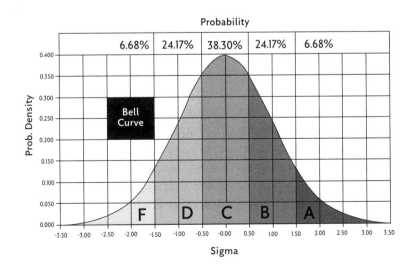

FIGURE 26.2
GRADING ON THE CURVE.

Teaching for mastery

In line with this view, they propose teaching for mastery which requires taking heed of the variables that play a role in mastery learning strategies. They base this on John Carroll's model of school learning (1963). Carroll made clear that if students' aptitudes are normally distributed, then giving all students the same instruction will lead to exam results along the curve. Carroll, however, saw aptitude, and with it the variables for achieving mastery as (1) the amount of time that the learner needs to attain mastery of a learning task, (2) the quality of instruction as the "degree to which the presentation, explanation, and ordering the elements of the task to be learned approach the optimum for a given learner" (p. 47), and (3) the ability to understand instruction in terms of understanding the nature of the task and procedures that need to be followed in learning the task. Hence, if the kind and quality of instruction along with the amount of time available for learning are made appropriate to the characteristics and needs of each student, then the majority of students should achieve mastery.

Aptitude

To this end, formative evaluation is a part of the learning process to achieve mastery. Frequent formative evaluation helps pace the instruction and motivates learners to persevere and put forth the necessary effort at the proper time. It ensures that the student who has mastered the learning is reinforced in their view that their way of studying is adequate (i.e., it provides them with metacognitive knowledge about their study approach). For the student who doesn't achieve mastery, the frequent formative evaluation will reveal specific points of difficulty. This diagnosis, as they call it, should be accompanied by very specific prescriptions of what can be done about the difficulty. In other words, "[F]ormative evaluation tests should be regarded as part of the learning process, and should in no way be confused with the judgement of the student's capabilities or included in the grading process" (p. 54).

They conclude that

> If the system of formative evaluation (diagnostic-progress tests) and the summative evaluation (achievement examinations) informs the student of his [sic] mastery of the subject, he will come to believe in his own mastery and competence. He may be informed by the grading system as well as by the discovery that he can adequately cope with the variety of tasks and problems in the evaluation instrument
>
> When the student has mastered a subject and when he receives both objective and subjective evidence of the mastery, there are profound changes in his view of himself and of the outer world.

Perhaps the clearest evidence of affective change is the interest the student develops for the subject he has mastered. He begins to "like" the subject and to desire more of it. . . . Motivation for further learning is one of the more important consequences of mastery. *(p. 56)*

Conclusions

Before this book, assessment and evaluation was primarily, if not exclusively, used for making low- and high-stakes decisions as to the qualifications of the person being assessed. It was used as a gateway to further study and determined what secondary school you might go to, what college, and what graduate school. If you passed the exam or got the right grade, then you were blessed with options for the future. If you failed, or if your grade was not up to snuff, then profitable paths disappeared and the educational journey ended. Bloom, Hastings, and Madaus showed us that assessment can stand for more than a means of determining a person's future; they showed us that it can be used to help learners learn better and help teachers teach better. Just like the fab four had done for music, this was assessment's *Love me do* moment, and it opened up an entirely new way of seeing and using evaluation as a force for good; for helping learners learn better and teachers teach better. Chapter 29 takes the use of assessment one step further, namely as a tool for learning (assessment as learning strategy).

Takeaways

- There are two types of assessment. Summative evaluation focuses on the outcome of a programme while formative assessment allows teachers to assess both learners progress and the effectiveness of their own practice.
- The primary function of the school is to develop the individual and those characteristics in students that will enable them to live effectively in a complex society.
- The teacher needs to be aware of the relation between (1) evaluation, (2) instructional decisions taken, and (3) the analysis of learners, instruction, and learning outcomes.
- Our educational efforts have been unsuccessful to the extent that the distribution of achievement approximates the normal distribution; they've been successful when all those who can master what we teach do so.

References

BLOOM, B. S., ENGELHART, M. D., FURST, E. J., HILL, W. H., & KRATHWOHL, D. R. (1956). *TAXONOMY OF EDUCATIONAL OBJECTIVES. THE CLASSIFICATION OF EDUCATIONAL GOALS, HANDBOOK I: COGNITIVE DOMAIN.* DAVID MCKAY COMPANY, INC.

BLOOM, B. S., HASTINGS, J. T., & MADAUS, G. F. (1971). *HANDBOOK ON FORMATIVE AND SUMMATIVE EVALUATION OF STUDENT LEARNING.* MCGRAW-HILL.

CARROLL, J. (1963). A MODEL OF SCHOOL LEARNING. *TEACHERS COLLEGE RECORD, 64,* 723–733.

KRATHWOHL, D. R., BLOOM, B. S., & MASIA, B. B. (1964). *TAXONOMY OF EDUCATIONAL OBJECTIVES. THE CLASSIFICATION OF EDUCATIONAL GOALS, HANDBOOK II: AFFECTIVE DOMAIN.* DAVID MCKAY COMPANY, INC.

MAGER, R. F. (1962). *PREPARING OBJECTIVES FOR PROGRAMMED INSTRUCTION.* FEARON PUBLISHERS.

SIMPSON, E. J. (1966). THE CLASSIFICATION OF EDUCATIONAL OBJECTIVES: PSYCHOMOTOR DOMAIN. *ILLINOIS JOURNAL OF HOME ECONOMICS, 10*(4), 110–144.

Suggested Readings and Links

BLACK, P. (1993). FORMATIVE AND SUMMATIVE ASSESSMENT BY TEACHERS. *STUDIES IN SCIENCE EDUCATION, 21,* 49–97.

BLACK, P., & WILIAM, D. (1998). ASSESSMENT AND CLASSROOM LEARNING *ASSESSMENT IN EDUCATION: PRINCIPLES, POLICY & PRACTICE, 5*(1), 7–74.

AVAILABLE VIA HTTPS://TINYURL.COM/BB8PSNU5

BLACK, P., & WILIAM, D. (2010). INSIDE THE BLACK BOX: RAISING STANDARDS THROUGH CLASSROOM ASSESSMENT. *PHI DELTA KAPPAN, 92*(1), 81–90.

AVAILABLE AT HTTPS://TINYURL.COM/6PB9M8VA

DIXSON, D. D., & WORRELL, F. C. (2016). FORMATIVE AND SUMMATIVE ASSESSMENT IN THE CLASSROOM. *THEORY INTO PRACTICE, 55*(2), 153–159.

AVAILABLE VIA HTTPS://TINYURL.COM/44ZEJAHP

SHUTE, V. J. (2008). FOCUS ON FORMATIVE EVALUATION. *REVIEW OF EDUCATIONAL RESEARCH, 78*(1), 153–189.

AVAILABLE VIA HTTPS://TINYURL.COM/4UAKS4UV

VIDEOS

WATCH AS DYLAN WILIAM REVIEWS THE NATURE OF FORMATIVE ASSESSMENT AND HOW TEACHERS CAN USE IT TO GAIN BETTER INSIGHTS INTO STUDENT LEARNING AND ACHIEVEMENT.

AVAILABLE VIA WWW.YOUTUBE.COM/WATCH?V=SYDVE5O7KBE

IN THIS VIDEO, DYLAN WILIAM PROVIDES BOTH AN INTUITIVE AND AN EMPIRICAL RATIONALE FOR FORMATIVE ASSESSMENT, DISCUSSES WHAT IT AND WHAT IT ISN'T, AND OUTLINES THE FIVE KEY STRATEGIES OF FORMAT ASSESSMENT: CLARIFYING, SHARING AND UNDERSTANDING LEARNING INTENTIONS; PROVIDING FEEDBACK THAT MOVES LEARNING FORWARD; ACTIVATING LEARNERS AS LEARNING RESOURCES FOR ONE ANOTHER; AN ACTIVATING LEARNERS AS OWNERS OF THEIR OWN LEARNING.

AVAILABLE VIA WWW.YOUTUBE.COM/WATCH?V=ZZL6ZF5LMVW

WEBSITES/BLOGS

 TOM SHERRINGTON'S BLOG *TEACHERHEAD* **DISCUSSES DYLAN WILIAM'S FIVE "KEY STRATEGIES" THAT SUPPORT THE IMPLEMENTATION OF EFFECTIVE FORMATIVE ASSESSMENT.**

AVAILABLE VIA HTTPS://TINYURL.COM/KD39DFD

27 WHEN TESTING KILLS LEARNING

JOHN BIGGS ON CONSTRUCTIVE ALIGNMENT

I: 10.4324/9781003228165-33

27 WHEN TESTING KILLS LEARNING

ARTICLE Assessing for learning: Some dimensions underlying new approaches to educational assessment[1]

QUOTE *"Educational considerations should drive testing, not psychometric or political ones."*[2]

Why You Should Read This Article

Robert McNamara was, by any standards, a wildly successful man. Harvard graduate, president of Ford motors, then rising to the heights a U.S. Secretary of Defence in the 1960s. McNamara epitomised American élan, one of the men characterised by David Halberstam as "The Best and the Brightest"[3] that America had to offer. But he had one major flaw – he saw the world in numbers. During the Vietnam War, McNama employed a strategic method he had successfully used during his days a Ford where he created data points for every element of production and quantified everything in a ruthless fashion to improve efficiency and production. One of the main metrics he used as Defence Secretary was evaluate progress and inform strategy was body counts. "Things you ca count, you ought to count", claimed McNamara, "loss of life is one".[4]

The McNamara Fallacy and the problem with numbers

The problem with this was that the Vietnam war was characterised b the unmeasurable chaos of human conflict, not the definable productic of parts on a factory assembly line. Things spun out of control as McNamara's statistical method failed to take into account numerous unseen variables and the public turned against American involvement in the war through a cultural outcry that would change the country.

---

1 BIGGS, J. (1995). ASSESSING FOR LEARNING: SOME DIMENSIONS UNDERLYING NEW APPROACHE EDUCATIONAL ASSESSMENT. *ALBERTA JOURNAL OF EDUCATIONAL RESEARCH*, 41(1), 1–17. REPRIN BY PERMISSION FROM SPRINGER NATURE.
2 IBID., P. 1.
3 HTTPS://EN.WIKIPEDIA.ORG/WIKI/THE_BEST_AND_THE_BRIGHTEST
4 MCNAMARA, R. *MCNAMARA: VIETNAM WAR A MISTAKE*. UPI ARCHIVES. AVAILABLE VIA WWW.UPI.C ARCHIVES/1995/04/09/MCNAMARA-VIETNAM-WAR-A-MISTAKE/6984797400000/

Although on paper America was "winning" the war, ultimately they lost it. As the war became more and more untenable, McNamara had to increasingly justify his methods. Far from providing an objective clarity, his algorithmic approach gave a misleading picture of what was becoming an unfathomably complex situation. While there is some merit to this approach in certain situations, there is a deep arrogance in the reduction of complex human processes to statistics, an aberration which led the sociologist Daniel Yankelovitch coining the term the "McNamara fallacy":

1. Measure whatever can be easily measured.
2. Disregard that which cannot be measured easily.
3. Presume that which cannot be measured easily is not important.
4. Presume that which cannot be measured easily does not exist.[5]

These principles will be recognisable to many of us in education – certainly the first two are consistent with some aspects of standardised testing, inspections and graded lesson observations and this is just one approach that John Biggs criticises in this paper. A central theme in this article and indeed in his broader body of work is that testing should be guided by educational aims and purposes not by the mechanism of measurement itself.

Abstract of the Article

The theory and practice of assessing learning are currently undergoing a paradigm shift. The critical realisation in producing this change is that educational considerations should drive testing, not psychometric or political ones. Three dimensions interact to yield different modes of assessment, including different kinds of performance assessment: the measurement vs. the standards model of testing, quantitative and qualitative assumptions as to the nature of what is learned, and whether the learning and testing is situated or decontextualised. The modes of assessment so generated are suited for different educational aims, but the most appropriate modes are under-represented in current practice, with quantitative and decontextualised modes being greatly over-represented, resulting in backwash often deleterious to teaching and learning. Conceptual and structural difficulties in implementing qualitative and situated modes of assessment are discussed.

---

5 YANKELOVICH, CITED IN O'MAHONY, 2017, PP. 281–282

The Article

For the last 100 years, the assessment of education achievement has been dominated by what Biggs calls the *measurement model* in which test item scores are deemed to be consistent with each other and thus align along a single dimension. From this assumption, the technologies of test construction, which items were selected, and the reliability and validity of tests followed. This watered-down model of testing was then applied in the classroom in the belief that traits are normally distributed across a range which must mean that test scores are too (see *HLH*, Chapter 13). In other words, very few students are high ability, most are of average ability and a few are low ability such as what you'd expect on a classic bell curve.

The problem with this is that there is very little alignment between the aspired outcomes, what is taught, and what is assessed. So, for example, one page of writing in which a student writes a speech or a letter is then subjectively assessed by one person, given a percentage number, and used to create a rank order of student ability in a class. Worse still, this number is seen to be stable across domains of knowledge, so a 60% score in English is seen as "equal" to a 60% score in Biology so that an average across all subjects can be determined. The central argument here is that using this form of measurement in the classroom to assess student ability makes no sense because there are simply too many unseen variables. Biggs claims, however, that the problem here is not that teachers are incompetent but rather that the "technology of assessment that grew out of test theory . . . lacked a basis in psychological theory" (Wilson & Kirby, 1994, p. 107).

In contrast, *criterion reference testing* is what Taylor (1994) calls the *standards model* of assessment, which is based on such assumptions as "public standards can be set; they can be reached by most students, albeit by different kinds of performance; and fair and consistent judgments are possible to determine whether the standards have been met or not" (p. 2). In this model, a performance is "assessed" against a rubric or set of criteria and it doesn't matter what the rest of the class got: if this student wrote a speech which fulfils the A criteria as defined in the rubric, then scored an A. If all the students in the class wrote speeches which fit with the criteria of an A, then the whole class gets an A. This is completely different to the measurement model which asserts that there must be a distribution of ability (see also Chapter 26). The problem with this model is that the criteria used aren't related to what was taught. This will be familiar to many teachers in the humanities who have to interpret the vaguest set of assessment criteria to mark a piece of work. For example, what exactly distinguishes an "accomplished" piece or writing from a "sophisticated" piece of writing? These are the kind of debates English teachers have all the time.

The Quantitative and Qualitative Traditions

The quantitative and qualitative traditions of assessment

According to Biggs, there are, broadly speaking, two views of assessment: quantitative and qualitative. The quantitative view is really the McNamara fallacy in action where numbers give a false view of the thing to be measured. For example, Lohman (1993) give the example of a multiple-choice test based on the 200th anniversary of the U.S. Constitution. There was only one question on the test referring to Thomas Jefferson which was: "Who was the signer of the constitution who had six children?" The issue here for Biggs is that this tells the child that every item on the test is equally important and that the task should be to get 10/10 as opposed to thinking about how discrete elements of knowledge interact and lead to greater understanding. Lohman recounts that, after a year, he asked a student what they remembered of Jefferson to which the child said "he has six children" but remembered nothing of his role in the constitution. Such a form of testing sends out the message that:

> There is no need to separate main ideas from details; all are worth one point. And there is no need to assemble these ideas into a coherent summary or to integrate them with anything else because that is not required. (Lohman, 1993, p. 19)

In contrast, the qualitative tradition is rooted in nineteenth century phenomenology and later Gestalt psychology. Within this paradigm, the dominant approach is constructivism which Biggs explains is a "family of theories rather than any one, according to which students are assumed to learn cumulatively, actively interpreting and incorporating new material with what they already know" in which "an active learner seeking meaning by constructing knowledge rather than by receiving and storing knowledge" (p. 4). However, Biggs' own view and that contained in this article is one informed by cognitive psychology in which comprehension of a topic "evolves cumulatively over the long haul, having 'horizontal' interconnections with other topics and subjects, and 'vertical' interconnections with previous and subsequent learnings in the same topic" (p. 4).

Situated and Decontextualised Assessment

Situated cognition

In recent years assessment has incorporated a range of ecological approaches such as "authentic" assessment which claims that children should be tested on material that can be applied in the "real world". This is related to the notion of *situated cognition* where for Brown et al. (1989; see Chapter 23 in *HLH*), learning needs to take place in a context where knowledge is not a disembodied series of items but rather used within a context which is in some way "authentic". In other words, instead of teaching students how to solve mathematical problems, they should be taught how to solve real world problems (such as managing a business budget, dividing up pizza, or interior design geometrical problems) *using* mathematical principles.

However, for Biggs this approach "grabs the moral high ground" (p. 5) and a central problem with this view for him is that if schools were only to teach kids to discover knowledge for themselves in an authentic or *real-world* setting, then humankind would not have progressed as much as we have. He writes: "If knowing and doing were inseparable, there could be a problem in accounting for civilization; to know only through doing virtually requires each generation to reinvent the wheel" (p. 5). Indeed, the purpose of schools is to enable children to learn knowledge in a decontextualised fashion and so there must be a way of assessing that declarative and procedural knowledge in a meaningful way. If everything we had to teach children was done in a *real-world* way, then what is the point of school? Also, is school not the *real world* for a 14-year-old?

SOLO taxonomy

Biggs is probably most well-known for his work on SOLO taxonomy in the 80s, which he describes as a "systematic way of describing how a learner's performance grows in complexity when mastering many tasks, particularly the sort of tasks undertaken in school" (p. 6). This approach is really his way of reconciling the quantitative and qualitative traditions, and it has gained a lot of popularity; however, it is not without its problems.

BACKWASH: PROBLEM OR SOLUTION?

Backwash: the tail wagging the dog

Backwash refers to the idea that instead of designing a broad a balanced curriculum, then considering methods of teaching it and finally a valid and reliable way of assessing progress, what actually happens is the reverse: testing drives what is on the curriculum and how it is taught (see also Chapter 7 on the tail wagging the dog). The most egregious example of this is teaching to the test. One of the central problems of backwash is that it rewards the wrong thing in a test where "those who typically focus on and reproduce detail (a 'surface' approach to learning) like the strategy and do well, but those who adopt a more academic or 'deep' approach, originally better than surface learners, become frustrated and do progressively worse" (p. 9).

It can be very difficult to assess this difference. A fascinating example of this is a study (Wong, 1994) in which a parallel test

(Continued)

(Continued)
was set on a Maths topic where students answered questions both quantitatively and qualitatively. The difference between the students was really between novices and experts where novices are characterised by solving problems correctly but in a very algorithmic way and experts solving the same problems in an original way based on first principles. Surprisingly, it was the *same* student who was both novice and expert, with the variable being the test item type. What is important then is to "think in *increasingly complex* ways about a topic, not to obtain a certain number of correct items" (p. 9).

Conclusions

As any teacher working in a school or university will know, there is an "almost irresistible pressure on teachers to use quantitative marking schemes, because marks are easily added up and averaged, and make discrimination between students extremely easy" (p. 14). This is the McNamara fallacy in action where we measure what can easily be measured and disregard what cannot be. This mode of assessment which is now dominant (writing this in 1995 but which has undoubtedly become more widespread since) is one which is informed by "political and utilitarian administrative ends rather than educational ones" (p. 12).

The function and context of testing

Arising from this then are three questions or "dimensions" as Biggs puts it. Firstly, what's the *function* of testing: "is it to rank individuals along some assumed trait, as in Taylor's measurement model, or to refer an individual's performance to a standard?" (p. 10). Secondly, what's the *nature* of what it is that is to be assessed? Is it performance or the development of understanding? And lastly, what's the *context* in which the test item is placed? is it in a real-world context or is it abstract and decontextualised? From here, Biggs makes a key statement:

> We then need to distinguish between testing the student's developing understanding of a concept, particularly but not essentially of declarative knowledge, and the student's ability to involve that knowledge in a task that has ecological validity with respect to the learning goals. (p. 10)

This is easier said that done of course. All major stakeholders appear to prefer the illusory certainty of a number over the ambiguity of what learning looks like in actuality. After all, two things can be true at the same time: a student can be working at both an A grade and a D grade within the same domain. So, in order to assess more effectively what students have learned, we probably need to give up the idea that we can represent learning in a number. The signal to noise ratio is often so low that we should accept that assessment is really just a messy *indicator* or learning rather than an accurate measurement of it.

Takeaways

- Performance in the form of numbers can give a false picture of progress
- The curriculum should determine the test not the other way around.
- Authentic or *real-world* tasks/assessment would require each generation to reinvent the wheel.
- Teaching to the test is bad for long term learning.
- Constructive alignment means linking aspired outcomes, what is taught and what is assessed.

References

BIGGS, J. B., & COLLIS, K. F. (1982). *EVALUATING THE QUALITY OF LEARNING: THE SOLO TAXONOMY.* ACADEMIC PRESS. AVAILABLE VIA HTTP://UDPRISM01.UCD.IE/TALISPRISM/DOOPENURLSEARCH.DO?SID=TALIS:PROD_TALIS&PID=KEY%3A64921%3BARTIFACTTYPE%3AMARC21SLIM%3BSEARCHLOCATION%3ATALISLM

BROWN, J. S., COLLINS, A., & DUGUID, P. (1989). SITUATED COGNITION AND THE CULTURE OF LEARNING. *EDUCATIONAL RESEARCHER, 18*(1), 32–41.

LOHMAN, D. F. (1993). TEACHING AND TESTING TO DEVELOP FLUID ABILITIES. *EDUCATIONAL RESEARCHER, 22*(7), 12–23.

O'MAHONY S. (2017). MEDICINE AND THE MCNAMARA FALLACY. *THE JOURNAL OF THE ROYAL COLLEGE OF PHYSICIANS OF EDINBURGH, 47*(3), 281–287.

WILSON, R. J., & KIRBY, J. R. (1944). INTRODUCTION: SPECIAL ISSUE ON COGNITION AND ASSESSMENT. *THE ALBERTA JOURNAL OF EDUCATIONAL RESEARCH, 40,* 105–108.

WONG, C. S. (1994). *USING A COGNITIVE APPROACH TO ASSESS ACHIEVEMENT IN SECONDARY SCHOOL MATHEMATICS.* UNPUBLISHED M.ED. DISSERTATION, UNIVERSITY OF HONG KONG.

Suggested Readings and Links

BIGGS, J. B. (2003). *TEACHING FOR QUALITY LEARNING AT UNIVERSITY.* THE OPEN UNIVERSITY PRESS.

RAMSDEN, P. (1984). THE CONTEXT OF LEARNING. IN F. MARTON, D. HOUNSELL, & N. ENTWISTLE, N. (EDS.), *THE EXPERIENCE OF LEARNING.* SCOTTISH ACADEMIC PRESS.

TAYLOR, C. (1994). ASSESSMENT FOR MEASUREMENT OR STANDARDS: THE PERIL AND PROMISE OF LARGE SCALE ASSESSMENT REFORM. *AMERICAN EDUCATIONAL RESEARCH JOURNAL, 31,* 231–262.

WEBSITES

BLOG BY DAVID DIDAU RE-EVALUATING THE EFFECTIVENESS OF SOLO TAXONOMY: HTTPS://LEARNINGSPY.CO.UK/LEARNING/CHANGED-MIND-SOLO-TAXONOMY/

PIECE IN THE MIT REVIEW ON THE PROBLEMS WITH A DATA DRIVEN APPROACH BY KENNETH CUKIER AND VIKTOR MAYER-SCHÖNBERGERARCHIVE

AVAILABLE VIA WWW.TECHNOLOGYREVIEW.COM/2013/05/31/178263/ THE-DICTATORSHIP-OF-DATA/

BLOG BY DAISY CHRISTODOULOU IN WHICH SHE ARGUES THAT TEACHING KNOWLEDGE AND TEACHING TO THE TEST ARE VERY DIFFERENT THINGS.

AVAILABLE VIA HTTPS://DAISYCHRISTODOULOU.COM/2017/01/ TEACHING-KNOWLEDGE-OR-TEACHING-TO-THE-TEST/

BLOG BY CARL HENDRICK ON THE MCNAMARA FALLACY AND THE PROBLEM WITH USING NUMBERS TO EVALUATE PERFORMANCE AND PROGRESS IN EDUCATION:

AVAILABLE VIA HTTPS://CHRONOTOPEBLOG.COM/2015/04/04/THE-MCNAMARA-FALLACY-AND-THE-PROBLEM-WITH-NUMBERS-IN-EDUCATION/

VIDEO

DYLAN WILIAM, A LEADING AUTHORITY ON ASSESSMENT ON WHAT DO WE MEAN BY ASSESSMENT FOR LEARNING?

HTTPS://YOUTU.BE/Q-MYBW36_DA

DON'T ASK QUESTIONS THAT DON'T REQUIRE UNDERSTANDING TO ANSWER

28

RICHARD ANDERSON ON TEST DESIGN

DOI: 10.4324/9781003228165-34

28 DON'T ASK QUESTIONS THAT DON'T REQUIRE UNDERSTANDING TO ANSWER

ARTICLE How to construct achievement tests to assess comprehension[1]

QUOTE *"Whether a test item measures comprehension depends upon the relationship of the wording of the test item to the wording of the instruction."*[2]

Why You Should Read This Article

After teaching something, how do you know that your students have learned anything? This is a lot more difficult than it seems as Richard Anderson illustrates in this chapter. Normally we might ask students to recall some word, term, or concept we've taught them but being able to recall it doesn't mean they *understand* it. This is a bit like when you're given directions to a particular destination that seem relatively simple such as "go straight on, turn left after half a mile, then take the next right and the next left and then it's the last turn on the right". "Got it" you might say, but after following those instructions to the letter, you find yourself lost. Why is this? Well slight variations in conditions where left means not a right angle left or where certain turnings are not obvious mean that what's clear and obvious to the person giving the directions is radically different in the mind of the person following them. In other words, one person knows the way and the other person doesn't. A fundamental question of teaching is this: How do *we* know that *they* know it?

1   ANDERSON, R. C. (1972). HOW TO CONSTRUCT ACHIEVEMENT TESTS TO ASSESS COMPREHENSIC
    REVIEW OF EDUCATIONAL RESEARCH. 42(2), 145–170. DOI:10.3102/00346543042002145.
2   IBID., P. 167.

The right answer doesn't always indicate understanding

Richard C. Anderson makes the claim that if the questions students are asked in a test are sufficiently similar to the original instruction, then this is a bad measure of whether they have learned anything. On a simple level, if a teacher says "five times three is fifteen. What does five times three equal?" The class parrot back "fifteen" and the impression of learning occurs but in reality little learning is actually happening. Now this approach might be useful as a behaviour management tool or as a broader set of questions which lead to a bigger question or task where the students will have to generate an answer themselves by applying new knowledge to what they already know, but by itself it is a relatively superficial enterprise. As Anderson shows, testing students on what they've truly learned is a very difficult thing to get right and requires an often stealthy approach.

Abstract of the Article

The thesis of this paper is that educational research workers have not yet learned how to develop achievement tests that meet the primitive first requirement for a system of measurement, namely that there is a clear and consistent definition of the things being counted. By "achievement test" I mean a set of questions asked to ascertain what a person has learned from exposure to instruction. There will be in the following a tacit restriction to paper-and-pencil test questions expressed in a natural language, though much of the discussion can be interpreted more broadly. The purpose of this paper is to propose the distinctions necessary to determine whether a person has comprehended an instructional communication, to outline procedures for constructing test questions based on these distinctions, and to show that test questions derived according to the procedures give rise to orderly, sensible data. The starting point for the analysis will be the now-classic Taxonomy of Educational Objectives (Bloom et al., 1956), and I shall rely on the important recent work of Bormuth (1970) and Hively (1970). Finally, a number of articles in the recent literature will be reviewed to determine how investigators currently construct tests and what they report about these tests.

The Article

Three levels of encoding: orthographic, phonological, and semantic

Anderson begins by attempting to define in clear terms what comprehension means and he does this in relation to printed matter only. Firstly, we perceive what is written down, engaging in a process called *orthographic encoding*; in other words the rules by which something is written such as spelling, punctuation, or syntax. The next level of processing probably involves how what's written down sounds, which he terms *phonological encoding* where the written word is rendered into speech, either implicitly (in your head) or explicitly (out loud). Lastly there's *semantic encoding* where a person "may bring to mind meaningful representation based on the words he [sic] sees, or hears himself saying" (p. 146).

This last distinction is important and one that characterises one of the most important findings in education psychology. Indeed, Anderson draws upon a long tradition in memory research to claim that if something is to be truly remembered (encoded into long-term memory) then what's most important is the fundamental *meaning* (semantic encoding) of the material. When we remember something, we don't remember it word for word or letter by letter but rather "store meanings rather than strings of symbols or speech sounds" (p. 146). Put simply, we don't remember letters and words, we remember the underlying *meanings* of those letters and words.

Despite this, mature readers (those who have cracked the alphabetic code – see Chapter 20) don't always make sense of what they're reading. For example, someone with no knowledge of football might read the following sentence and recognise every single word and even *understand* every single word but not understand the words used together in this context:

The Striker Was Caught Offside by the Last Defender Stepping Up

To understand this, the reader needs to know the offside rule in footba and the use of particular phrases in discussing that. In contrast, children can learn something by rote but not understand anything of what they have "learned". For example, a three-year-old can recognise a word such as "world" (as in *the best girl in the world*) yet their actual understanding of what the world is, is probably very shallow. So, the key point here is that understanding is a difficult thing to understand and thus, a difficult thing to assess for. As Anderson puts it "We do no yet have a complete and consistent model of what a person has in his head when he comprehends a communication" (p. 147).

While there's evidence that we can remember a lot using imagery (Paivio & Yuille, 1967), this mainly works for relatively simple paired associations such as numbers or simple words. Remembering abstract nouns such as "justice" or "truth" is much more difficult if not impossib to remember in visual form and that's before we get to complex concept and ideas. Furthermore, those more complex terms and ideas have no agreed form and will look radically different to different people. For example, the number 72 looks the same to everybody and so is relatively easy to test for whereas the word "intelligence" is much harder to define and can often lead to heated debate (and that's just in the field of education). So again, trying to assess what has been learned using that approach is futile.

In order to assess comprehension then, Anderson draws on Bloom's work in the 1950s and his distinction between knowledge, comprehension, and application where memorising words is very different to being able to then apply that knowledge in a new or novel situation using an "abstraction" where the situation is different than the original context of what was learned. In other words, someone might be able to memorise a speech about a particular historical event and *appear* very knowledgeable about it but when questioned about a tangential aspect of the topic they are completely lost. (A very good example of this is a politician being asked about anything.) Many History teachers will be familiar with the student who gives a very impressive presentation on World War II using dates, facts, and images but then when asked a question at end about the possible causes of the war stares at the teacher with incredulity.

So another way of thinking about this is: Do students have to struggle or *think hard* to answer the questions they are being asked? Are they merely repeating back something or offering a slightly reconfigured version of what they have been taught? If so, they are probably answering questions which require no understanding.

WHAT KINDS OF QUESTIONS REQUIRE NO UNDERSTANDING?

Verbatim questions: repeating word for word what has been asked.

Transformed verbatim questions: meaning can be rearranged in a slightly different form and may look like an application of knowledge but again, might not be evidence of comprehension. Being able to deal with transformed statements is a necessary but not sufficient condition for comprehension. For example:

"Suppose the nonsense sentence, *The sleg juped the horm*, were presented. A person competent in the language could answer, *Who juped the horm?*, and could also answer, *By whom was the horm juped?*, but he wouldn't comprehend the message" (p. 150).

Bloom's model is more famously known as "Bloom's Taxonomy"[3] which Anderson spotted was a problem even back then noting that the categories overlap and the taxonomy doesn't lead to operational definitions. Anderson then calls for a new form of assessment where what is required is a "system of explicit definitions and rules to derive test items from instructional statements such that a person can answer the items correctly if, and only if, he comprehends the statements" (p. 149). In other words, we shouldn't ask students questions which require no understanding to answer them.

WHAT KINDS OF QUESTIONS REQUIRE UNDERSTANDING?

Paraphrase questions: understanding a question that is qualitatively different in form than the original is likely to be a better indicator or comprehension that a student parroting back something they have learned. Paraphrased questions (1) have no substantive words (nouns, verbs, modifiers) in common and (2) are equivalent in meaning.

Transformed paraphrase questions: further rearrangement or transformation of paraphrased questions.

In other words, if you want to test whether a student understands photosynthesis, try to ask them in a way that is very different to the original form but where the *meaning* is the same. (See the end of this chapter for more examples of this.)

Based on this, Anderson makes the following recommendations:

"There are at least two ways to assess comprehension of concepts. The first involves paraphrase of the concept definition. Given the name of the concept the student selects the paraphrased definition, or given the paraphrased definition he selects or supplies the concept name". (p. 152)

So, Anderson suggests that there are two types of questions we should ask if we want to test for understanding of a principle. Firstly, questions using paraphrases of the principle itself using sufficiently different

Paraphrasing

---

3   FOR MORE ON THIS, READ DE BRUYCKERE, P., KIRSCHNER, P.A., & HULSHOF, C. D. (2015). *URBAN MYTH ABOUT LEARNING AND EDUCATION.* ELSEVIER ACADEMIC PRESS.

language or in the case of concepts, the principle may be referred to and the student required to give a new example of that principle. But what if there is a concept which is not so cut and dry, what if there is significant debate around a particular topic? Anderson offers the following advice: "One solution is to qualify the items (e.g., "Answer this question under the assumption that the principle of intermittent reinforcement is applicable") (p. 158).

Substitution

Another approach is to substitute general terms for particular terms and then require the student to "induce" the principle, that is, to say in a general way what the instruction has stated in particular way. Take for example a study (Barrett & Otto, 1968) featuring the following task where children were asked to summarise the "main idea" in the following passage:

> Robins may build nests under a roof. Bluejays like nests in trees. Ducks make nests in tall grass. Woodpeckers build nests inside wood fence posts.

The general principle or "answer" here is that birds build their nests in different places. That general principle has been swapped for specific examples and requires an abstraction to arrive at the general principle or "main idea".

Of course, the central question facing any teacher assessing student knowledge is "Of all the stuff I've taught them, what should they be tested on?" There's a real danger here that thinking about this before instruction can lead to a narrow type of instruction which "may lead to a trivial sort of teaching to the test" (p. 161). This is a serious unintended consequence of assessment where the means can defeat the ultimate goal, which is to give students the kind of knowledge which will allow them to become confident, autonomous thinkers. This is a good example of *Goodhart's Law*. Anderson spells out how this works in practice:

> Performance is poor on a test item, so the author or programmer includes statements within the instruction which give the answer to the question; or perhaps he [sic] asks the question during the course of instruction in a context in which the student cannot fail to answer correctly. Performance on the offending test item is bound to improve. But the question of what has been learned must be asked. It may well be that students have only learned to repeat or recognize strings of words. (Anderson, 1969, p. 16)

GOODHART'S LAW AND TEACHING TO THE TEST

GOODHART'S LAW is a principle named after economist Charles Goodhart who in a 1975 article on monetary policy wrote that "any observed statistical regularity will tend to collapse once pressure is placed upon it for control purposes".[4] This was brilliantly summarised by Marilyn Strathern as "When a measure becomes a target, it ceases to be a good measure".[5]

In other words, if a school sets a target of say 70% of students in a cohort getting a C grade or above, then the focus becomes merely getting the grade rather than acquiring the knowledge needed in that particular domain. This can have disastrous consequences for education where nefarious approaches are incentivised such as in the Atlanta Public Schools Cheating Scandal where teachers and administrators "gave children answers, erased incorrect answers, hid and altered documents, offered monetary incentives to encourage the cheating, and punished employees who refused to cheat".[6]

One way of alleviating this is to create a "universe" of test items in a field of knowledge (Hively et al., 1968). Assessment would then be based on a random set of questions from that "universe" where teaching to the test as it were would be a largely useless enterprise.

Conclusions

The central idea in this paper is that in order to accurately test comprehension, we need to ask questions that show *actual comprehension* not a mere memorisation of relatively superficial elements such as dates, terms, or definitions. Of course, all of these elements are an important part of comprehension but there must be an assimilation and synthesis of these variables into a broader understanding and subsequent application. If a test item or question, has a particular kind of wording that is very similar to the original instruction then what you are testing could well be memorisation not comprehension.

It can be easy for teachers and administrators to forget that the whole point of testing is to enhance student learning and as Anderson points out "answering test questions during or shortly after instruction has a

4   GOODHART, C. (1975). PROBLEMS OF MONETARY MANAGEMENT: THE U.K. EXPERIENCE. IN PAP IN MONETARY ECONOMICS (VOL. 1). RESERVE BANK OF AUSTRALIA.
5   STRATHERN, M. (1997). IMPROVING RATINGS': AUDIT IN THE BRITISH UNIVERSITY SYSTEM. EUROP. REVIEW, 5(3), 305–321.
6   THE ATLANTA PUBLIC SCHOOLS CHEATING SCANDAL. AVAILABLE VIA WWW.GEORGIAPOLICY.ORG/ISS THE-ATLANTA-PUBLIC-SCHOOLS-CHEATING-SCANDAL/ (WEBSITE ACCESSED AUGUST 9, 2021)

pronounced effect on learning and retention" (p. 163). Indeed there's a large body of evidence that asking students comprehension questions say at the end of a chapter or section can have a much enhanced effect on long term retention and learning. This is a form of what is now called retrieval practice. So regular questioning of material during rather than at the end of instruction can have profound effects. All of this has serious implications for teaching and learning. After all, if we don't have a reliable way of knowing what students know or don't know then where are we?

Takeaways

- Teaching should be geared towards comprehension, not the *testing* of comprehension.
- Recall is not the same as understanding.
- If the test question uses the same language as the instruction, you may not be testing comprehension.
- Tests which assess the "main idea" around a concept are better than asking for mere definitions of the concept.
- Questions using the paraphrasing of a taught concept or idea are better for assessing learning than mere rote recall.
- Don't instantiate Goodhart's Law. Don't make measurement the target of your teaching, but rather the measure of understanding.

References

ANDERSON, R. C. (1969). THE COMPARATIVE FIELD EXPERIMENT: AN ILLUSTRATION FROM HIGH SCHOOL BIOLOGY. IN *PROCEEDINGS OF THE 1968 INVITATIONAL CONFERENCE ON TESTING PROBLEMS.* EDUCATIONAL TESTING SERVICE

THE ATLANTA PUBLIC SCHOOLS CHEATING SCANDAL. AVAILABLE VIA WWW.GEORGIAPOLICY.ORG/ISSUE/THE-ATLANTA-PUBLIC-SCHOOLS-CHEATING-SCANDAL/ (WEBSITE ACCESSED AUGUST 9, 2021)

BARRETT, T., & OTTO, W. (1968). *ELEMENTARY PUPILS" ABILITY TO CONCEPTUALIZE THE MAIN IDEA IN READING.* PAPER PRESENTED AT THE ANNUAL CONVENTION OF THE AMERICAN EDUCATIONAL RESEARCH ASSOCIATION, CHICAGO, FEBRUARY.

BLOOM, B. S., HASTINGS, J. T., & MADAUS, T. (1956). *TAXONOMY OF EDUCATIONAL OBJECTIVES.* DAVID MCKAY COMPANY.

BORMUTH, J. R. (1970). *ON THE THEORY OF ACHIEVEMENT TEST ITEMS.* UNIVERSITY OF CHICAGO PRESS.

GOODHART, C. (1975). PROBLEMS OF MONETARY MANAGEMENT: THE U.K. EXPERIENCE. IN *PAPERS IN MONETARY ECONOMICS* (VOL. 1). RESERVE BANK OF AUSTRALIA.

HIVELY, W. (1970). *DOMAIN-REFERENCED ACHIEVEMENT TESTING: THEORY AND PRACTICE.* UNPUBLISHED MANUSCRIPT.

HIVELY, W., PATTERSON, H. L., & PAGE, S. H. (1968). *GENERALIZABILITY OF PERFORMANCE BY JOB CORP TRAINEES ON A UNIVERSE-DEFINED SYSTEM OF ACHIEVEMENT TESTS IN ELEMENTARY MATHEMATICAL CALCULATION.* MINNESOTA NATIONAL LABORATORY.

PAIVIO, A., & YUILLE, J. C. (1967). MEDIATION INSTRUCTIONS AND WORD ATTRIBUTES IN PAIRED-ASSOCIATE LEARNING. *PSYCHONOMIC SCIENCE, 8,* 65–66.

STRATHERN, M. (1997). IMPROVING RATINGS': AUDIT IN THE BRITISH UNIVERSITY SYSTEM. *EUROPEAN REVIEW, 5*(3), 305–321.

Suggested Readings and Links

BLOG BY CHRISTODOULOU, D. ASKING THE IMPORTANT QUESTION "HOW USEFUL ARE TESTS?"

HTTPS://DAISYCHRISTODOULOU.COM/2013/12/HOW-USEFUL-ARE-TESTS/

COMPREHENSIVE BOOK ON EDU-MYTHS AND FADS: DE BRUYCKERE, P., KIRSCHNER, P.A., & HULSHOF, C. D. (2015). *URBAN MYTHS ABOUT LEARNING AND EDUCATION.* ELSEVIER ACADEMIC PRESS.

GUEST POST BY KATHY RASTLE ON TDT BLOG LOOKING AT THE VALUE OF TESTING FOR LONG-TERM LEARNING:

HTTPS://TDTRUST.ORG/2016/05/23/TESTING-IS-KEY-TO-LONG-TERM-LEARNIN

AUTHORITATIVE PIECE BY ONE OF THE LEADING FIGURES IN ASSESSMENT DYLAN WILIAM ARGUING THAT "THERE IS NO SUCH THING AS A VALID TEST"

WWW.DYLANWILIAMCENTER.COM/2018/05/11/THERE-IS-NO-SUCH-THING-AS-A-VALID-TEST/

29 WHY TEACHING TO THE TEST IS SO BAD

DANIEL KORETZ ON GRADE INFLATION

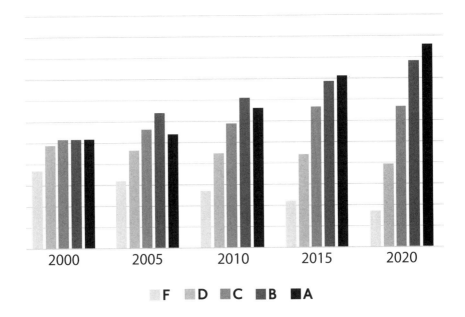

DI: 10.4324/9781003228165-35

29 WHY TEACHING TO THE TEST IS SO BAD

ARTICLE Alignment, high stakes, and the inflation of test scores[1]

QUOTE *"If the system measures what is valuable and rewards and punishes educators, and sometimes students, for their degree of success in producing it, students and teachers will be motivated to produce more."*[2]

Why You Should Read This Article

The Lake Wobegon Effect

In the 1980s Garrison Keillor created a fictional town called Lake Wobegon (pronounced Woe Be Gone) for his much-lauded radio programme *A Prairie Home Companion*. The location, a small rural town in central Minnesota, served as a backdrop for a cast of local characters who Keillor used to tell touching and often humorous stories of human struggle in a rapidly changing America. The residents were marked out by a strange collective delusion however where "all the women are strong, all the men are good-looking, and all the children are above average" (Garrison Keillor in Phelps, 2005, p. 2). Around the same time in 1987, a physician called John Cannell published the results of a study looking at national test scores in elementary schools. He noticed that West Virginia students kept scoring above the national average on a norm-referenced standardised test. He found this quite strange considering the fact that West Virginia students scored much lower on other measures of academic performance. He subsequently then looked at other states' performance and noticed that they too reported that their students were above the national average which led him to dub this phenomenon the *Lake Wobegon Effect*.

---

[1] KORETZ, D. (2005). ALIGNMENT, HIGH STAKES, AND THE INFLATION OF TEST SCORES. IN J. HERMAN E. HAERTEL (EDS.), *USES AND MISUSES OF DATA IN ACCOUNTABILITY TESTING. YEARBOOK OF THE NATION SOCIETY FOR THE STUDY OF EDUCATION* (VOLUME 104, PART 2, P. 99–118). BLACKWELL PUBLISHING.

[2] IBID., P. 17.

The Lake Wobegon effect would have serious implications, most alarmingly the conclusion that "half the school superintendents in the country were lying about their schools" academic achievement. It further implied that, with poorer results, the other half might lie, too" (Phelps, 2005, p. 3). This phenomenon is a stunning example of Campbell's law which states: "The more any quantitative social indicator is used for social decision-making, the more subject it will be to corruption pressures and the more apt it will be to distort and corrupt the social processes it is intended to monitor" (Campbell, 1979, p. 87). In other words, the perverse incentives of this system led to teachers teaching to the test which then inflated test scores.

In this article, Daniel Koretz explores how high stakes assessment can lead to some quite nefarious practices where learning comes second to scoring a grade and worse still, the whole enterprise creates an inaccurate picture of achievement in the form of grade inflation which Koretz neatly defines as "a gain in scores that substantially overstates the improvement in learning it implies" (p. 1). Koretz looks at three specific aspects of teaching to the test which he calls reallocation, alignment, and coaching.

Abstract of the Article

There are many reasons to align tests with curricular standards, but this alignment is not sufficient to protect against score inflation. This report explains the relationship between alignment and score inflation by clarifying what is meant by inappropriate test preparation. It provides a concrete, hypothetical example that illustrates a process by which scores become inflated and follows this with more complete discussion of the mechanisms of score inflation and their link to teachers' responses to high-stakes testing. Policymakers embarking on an effort to create a more effective system less prone to the drawbacks of simple test-based accountability cannot rely solely on alignment and should consider several additional steps: redesigning external tests in other ways to minimise inflation, setting attainable performance targets, relying on multiple measures, and re-establishing a role for professional judgment. Developing more effective alternatives will take us beyond what is well established and will require innovation, experimentation, and rigorous evaluation.

The Article

eaching to the test   Koretz defines *inappropriate test preparation* as essentially teaching to the test. This is a problem which has two aspects. First, it leads to the inflation of test scores and the second is what he calls "undesirable pedagogy" where the lessons are exclusively focused on what might turn up in the test and negates content not likely to be tested. The former is also known as intentional learning and the latter incidental learning. Of course, these two elements are inextricably linked: if a teacher teaches to the test focusing not on mastering a domain of knowledge but rather mastering a one-hour exam, then grades for the class will most likely be inflated. By measuring the wrong thing, policymakers and school leaders risk creating a set of perverse incentives which may lead to short term gains but ultimately result in long term problems. This is a good example of the *Cobra Effect*.

THE COBRA EFFECT

During Colonial rule of India, governors within the British Empire were very concerned about the number of venomous cobras in Delhi and decided to offer a bounty for every dead cobra handed into authorities. Initially this scheme seemed to work very well with record numbers of dead cobras being culled but some enterprising locals realised they could make a lot more by breeding cobras rather than hunting them so there began to be several cobra farms around the city. When the authorities were alerted to this fact, they scrapped the bounty scheme and as a result, the cobra farmers released all the snakes back into the wild. So, by the end of this intervention there were actually more dangerous snakes in the city than before.

The Cobra Effect

This anecdote by Horst Siebert is the basis for the *Cobra effect* where perverse incentives can lead to unintended consequences. The story may well be apocryphal but it illustrates very nicely a key point about incentives or rather incentivising the *wrong thing* and this is the key point made by Harvard professor Daniel Koretz in this article. As we have seen elsewhere in this section, assessment in the form of standardised testing can have the veneer of certainty, after all what can be more certain than numbers? But often those "certainties" can mask some serious deficiencies.

Tests are essentially a sample of performance in order to make judgements about a student's proficiency in a broad domain of knowledge. However we should make a distinction between performanc and learning (see Chapter 14 on *desirable difficulties*). Some domains are so large that if we were to assess them in all areas of knowledge, students would be doing a 12-hour test. So, we use a small sample and then generalise from that regarding their relative proficiency. The relative quality of that inference is what is meant by *validity*. Koretz gives a neat example to illustrate some of these issues in Figure 29.1. Let's say you wanted to test a range of graduate students who have applied to work on a new journal and you decide that their vocabularies are a good way to differentiate between them. So, you choose a range of 40 words with which to do this and create three lists (A, B, and C). With list A the words are highly specialised and so very few students would know them, meaning you'd get very few right answers and thus this would be a poor way of measuring their relative vocabulary. In contrast list B is made up of very simple words and so you'd have the same problem in reverse: they would know all the words this time so again, you'd have no way of differentiating their relative strengths. List C has a group of words that are not too difficult but not easy either, so list C is the best option because it allows you to more accurately gauge how good their vocabulary is.

FIGURE 29.1 AN EXAMPLE FROM KORETZ, D. (2005). ALIGNMENT, HIGH STAKES, AND THE INFLATION OF TEST SCORES. IN J. HERMAN AND E. HAERTEL (EDS.), USES AND MISUSES OF DATA IN ACCOUNTABILITY TESTING. YEARBOOK OF THE NATIONAL SOCIETY FOR THE STUDY OF EDUCATION (VOLUME 104, PART 2, PP. 99–118). BLACKWELL PUBLISHING.

A	B	C
siliculose	bath	feckless
vilipend	travel	disparage
epimysium	carpet	miniscule

Now let's say that on the way to the test, someone told the students all the words that would come up. Again, this would ruin the validity of the test because you would have a group of candidates who have perfect or near perfect scores and so are indistinguishable. This is a form of teaching to the test which would *appear* to improve performance but if we say that the average candidate roughly knows 20 out of 40 words and then learned the other 20 that would be on the test through cheating. So they may score very highly on that one test but in real terms, this would have improved their vocabularies by a tenth of one percent which is a trivial amount. It would thus be very misleading to claim that these students had dramatically improved vocabularies and so the test would not be representative of the domain of words which the test was supposed to be testing. In other words, this test would give a hugely false impression of the relative ability of the people taking it.

Grade inflation

This is a hypothetical example of the problem with grade inflation but Koretz then gives examples in real life where a school district in 1986 used a multiple-choice achievement test. During the years up to 1986 scores on this test had increased substantially however in 1987, the district changed to a competing test by another provider and the scores dropped by half an academic year (average grade equivalent). However, over the next three years, the average score on the same test increased to the same level of the test originally taken in 1986. This is an example of the sawtooth effect as when viewed on a graph, the data takes on a shape similar to the teeth on a saw.

The Sawtooth effect

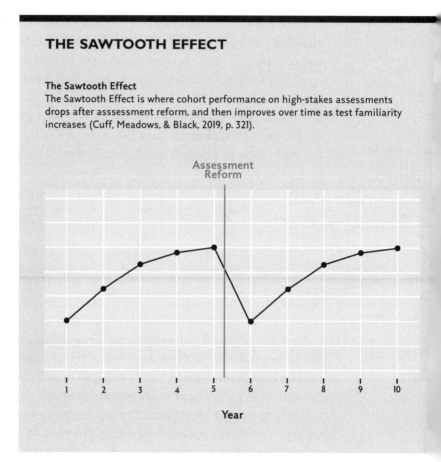

THE SAWTOOTH EFFECT

The Sawtooth Effect
The Sawtooth Effect is where cohort performance on high-stakes assessments drops after asssessment reform, and then improves over time as test familiarity increases (Cuff, Meadows, & Black, 2019, p. 321).

Assessment Reform

Year

FIGURE 29.2 *THE SAWTOOTH EFFECT (CUFF, 2016).*

Forms of Test Preparation

Test preparation

Koretz then examines how some of these considerations play out in practice. Some forms of test preparation may result in "unambiguous, meaningful gains in performance. Teachers may work harder, for example, or they may find ways to teach more effectively. They may also teach more by providing remedial instruction outside of regular school hours" (p. 12). These sorts of outcomes are seen as desirable but at the other end of the spectrum, teachers or students (or both) may cheat where teachers give advance access to test material, change wrong answers after the test or provide assistance during the test. Whatever the method, we cannot call the gains made here in any sense *meaningful*.

Reallocation

Reallocation

Reallocation refers to a change in instructional resources where teachers focus more on material expected to be covered on the test than the whole domain of knowledge. Reallocation is seen as one of the most important factors in causing the sawtooth pattern seen in Figure 29.2. As Koretz puts it "when reallocation inflates scores, it does so by making the score created from the tested elements unrepresentative of the domain about which inferences are drawn" (p. 13). For example, let's say a class is taking a unit on the second World War. There's a broad domain of knowledge that needs to be mastered to understand, for example, the causes of the war but a teacher might know from experience that the test doesn't require students to explicitly know this and so doesn't cover this crucial aspect in as much detail as the area they're expecting to come up in the test. The class may then perform very well on the test but if they have a shallow knowledge of the causes of World War II, then in what meaningful sense could we say they are knowledgeable about it?

Alignment

Alignment

Content and standards are essentially things that someone has considered to be important enough to test someone on. *Alignment* refers to the correlation between tests and standards so that a teacher will align their instruction to meet those standards. This is different from what Biggs calls *constructive alignment* (see Chapter 7). No tests, no matter how well aligned, can produce more than a small sample of the material implied by the standards and so a key problem here is that "alignment of instruction with the test is likely to produce incomplete alignment of instruction with the standards, even if the test is aligned with the standards" (p. 14). In other words, if the performance on the emphasised elements of their course increases then scores will become inflated and it will be merely the scores that improve, not "actual mastery of the content standards" (p. 14).

Coaching

Coaching

Coaching here refers to instruction that is focused on the "narrow, substantive aspects of a test" (p. 15). For example, on certain test questions a particular kind of phrasing is used to ask certain questions. Over a number of years teachers become familiar with these kinds of questions and will coach students to respond to the question in certain ways in order to achieve higher marks. The worst example of this would be where a teacher sets a mock exam or test with a question phrased one way and then the real test is phrased in an almost identical way but with the content slightly changed. In this case the question is different but also exactly the same. See Figure 29.3

> The question on the review sheet for . . . [the] exam . . . reads in part:
>   The average amount that each band member must raise is a function of the number of band members, b, with the rule $f(b)=12000/b$.
>   The question on the actual test reads in part:
>   The average amount each cheerleader must pay is a function of the number of cheerleaders, n, with the rule $f(n)=420/n$.

We all want pupils to not only be knowledgeable about certain domains but we want them to be able to transfer that knowledge to novel situations and to be able to make new connections and ways of understanding the world. If we focus however on test scores, we risk sending the message that the only reason to know this stuff is to score a certain grade. As every teacher can attest, the most dispiriting thing a teacher can hear when discussing some aspect of their subject they are passionate about is "but will this be in the exam?" This may not be a deficiency in the pupil either because, as Baker reminds us, high stakes testing can "lead teachers, school personnel, parents, and students to focus on just one thing: raising the test score by any means necessary" (Baker, 2000, p. 18).

Will this be in the exam?

Conclusions/Implications of the Work for Educational Practice

What do tests actually measure?

It's important for educators to consider carefully what tests *actually* measure. As Koretz notes, test scores "do not provide a direct and complete measure of educational achievement. Rather, they are incomplete measures, proxies for the more comprehensive measures that we would ideally use, but that are almost always unavailable to us" (Koretz, 2008, p. 25). If we want to test a cohort of students' proficiency in a particular domain, such as say English literature, we need to review what we consider to be the benchmarks of that proficiency. If we take something like Shakespeare for example, which play? Which part of that play? Do we focus on language, structure, or themes? Now an exam board/school/teacher might consider all of these things important but the next question is how we measure these things and if there's an excessive focus at a school and teacher level to achieve a certain standard of test scores then we risk the cobra effect where schools are likely instead to "produce substantial inflation of scores and a variety of undesirable changes in instruction, such as excessive focus on old tests, inappropriate narrowing of instruction, and a reliance on test-taking tricks" (Koretz, 2008, p. 25).

Of course there needs to be a way of differentiating students through performance for a range of purposes, but a system where schools are teaching to the test and coaching students on test techniques rather than the broader domain of knowledge and how to make connections to other domains of knowledge then to what extent are we preparing them for the world of university and beyond?

The dubious validity of test score gains

A central claim in this article and indeed in Koretz's work overall is that we should closely look at the validity of score gains. Almost every year we see news reports about end of school test scores being "higher than ever" or achievement gaps between ethnic groups narrowing but what does this actually mean and can it be trusted? Not according to Koretz who claims that what we call academic progress is often just a form of inflation which "creates an illusion of overall progress and can be misleading in other ways as well. For example, variations in the amount of inflation can incorrectly suggest that some programs or schools are more effective than others" (p. 16).

At a whole school, district, or policy level there needs to be an evaluation of what's important. If teachers are spending the majority of their time preparing for tests, marking tests, and directing their instruction *towards* tests then something is seriously wrong. If the system rewards students for the wrong thing such as knowing how to pass a test and punishes them for less *testable* things such as knowing a lot about a domain then we should be looking at the incentives we are giving. In other words, if students are using *techniques* to pass an exam rather than their own knowledge and understanding then this represents a debased form of teaching where the primacy of the subject comes second to a test score.

Takeaways

- High stakes testing can create perverse incentives which diminish what they're trying to test.
- Direct students to the domain of knowledge to be mastered not "techniques" for the test.
- Don't focus on a narrow part of the curriculum just because it might come up on the exam.
- Mock exams which are almost identical to the real exam are not really a test.
- Redesign tests where adding tests items that are sufficiently different to alleviate the danger of coaching and large-scale evaluations.

References

BAKER, E. L. (2000). UNDERSTANDING EDUCATIONAL QUALITY: WHERE VALIDITY MEETS TECHNOLOGY. IN *WILLIAM H. ANGOFF MEMORIAL LECTURE. EDUCATIONAL TESTING SERVICE.* POLICY INFORMATION CENTER.

BJORK, E. L., & BJORK, R. A. (2011). MAKING THINGS HARD ON YOURSELF, BUT IN A GOOD WA
CREATING DESIRABLE DIFFICULTIES TO ENHANCE LEARNING. IN M. A. GERNSBACHER, R. W. PEW, L. M. HOUGH, & J. R. POMERANTZ (EDS.), *PSYCHOLOGY AND THE REAL WORLD: ESSAYS ILLUSTRATING FUNDAMENTAL CONTRIBUTIONS TO SOCIETY* (PP. 56–64). WORTH.

CAMPBELL, D. T. (1979). ASSESSING THE IMPACT OF PLANNED SOCIAL CHANGE. *EVALUATION AN PROGRAM PLANNING, 2,* 67–90.

CANNELL, J. J. (1987). NATIONALLY NORMED ELEMENTARY ACHIEVEMENT TESTING. IN *AMERICA PUBLIC SCHOOLS: HOW ALL 50 STATES ARE ABOVE THE NATIONAL AVERAGE* (2ND ED.). FRIENDS OF EDUCATION.

CUFF, B. M. P. (2016). *AN INVESTIGATION INTO THE 'SAWTOOTH EFFECT' IN GCSE AND AS/A LEVEL ASSESSMENTS.* OFFICE OF QUALIFICATIONS AND EXAMS REGULATION.

KORETZ, D. M. (2005). ALIGNMENT, HIGH STAKES, AND THE INFLATION OF TEST SCORES. IN J. HERMAN & E. HAERTEL (EDS.), *USES AND MISUSES OF DATA IN ACCOUNTABILITY TESTING. YEARBOOK O THE NATIONAL SOCIETY FOR THE STUDY OF EDUCATION* (VOL. 104, PART 2, PP. 99–118). BLACKWELL PUBLISHING.

KORETZ, D. M. (2008). A MEASURED APPROACH: VALUE-ADDED MODELS ARE A PROMISING IMPROVEMENT, BUT NO ONE MEASURE CAN EVALUATE TEACHER PERFORMANCE. *AMERICAN EDUCATOR, 3*(2), 18–39. AVAILABLE VIA WWW.AFT.ORG/SITES/DEFAULT/FILES/PERIODICALS/KORETZ PDF

KORETZ, D. M. (2009). HOW DO AMERICAN STUDENTS MEASURE UP? MAKING SENSE OF INTERNATIONAL COMPARISONS. *FUTURE OF CHILDREN, 19*(1), 37–51.

Suggested Readings and Links

KORETZ, D. M. (2008). *MEASURING UP: WHAT EDUCATIONAL TESTING REALLY TELLS US.* HARVARD UNIVERSITY PRESS.

PHELPS, R. P. (1999). EDUCATION ESTABLISHMENT BIAS? A LOOK AT THE NATIONAL RESEARCH COUNCIL'S CRITIQUE OF TEST UTILITY STUDIES. *THE INDUSTRIAL-ORGANIZATIONAL PSYCHOLOGIST, 36*(4), 37–49.

PHELPS, R. P. (2005). THE SOURCE OF LAKE WOBEGON. *NONPARTISAN EDUCATION REVIEW, 1*(2). AVAILABLE VIA HTTPS://FILES.ERIC.ED.GOV/FULLTEX ED499390.PDF

WEB

ENGAGING AND INSIGHTFUL INTERVIEW WITH DANIEL KORET WHEN TESTING TAKES OVER

AVAILABLE VIA WWW.GSE.HARVARD.EDU/NEWS/UK/17/11/WHEN-TESTI TAKES-OVER

VERY USEFUL BLOG BY DAISY CHRISTODOULOU: HOW USEFU ARE TESTS?

AVAILABLE VIA HTTPS://DAISYCHRISTODOULOU.COM/2013/12/HOW-USEFUL-ARE-TESTS/

VIDEO

WIDE RANGING DISCUSSION WITH DANIEL KORETZ AND RICK HESS ON WHY TESTING HAS LED TO CHEATING AND POOR INSTRUCTION: HTTPS://YOUTU.BE/T4G7-NCTRLI

30 HOCUS-POCUS TEACHER EDUCATION

NCTQ ON WHAT TEACHERS DON'T LEARN IN SCHOOL

I: 10.4324/9781003228165-36

30 HOCUS-POCUS TEACHER EDUCATION

REPORT   Learning about Learning: What every new teacher needs to know[1]

QUOTE   *"The transfer of knowledge – from researchers to publishers to teacher educators to aspiring teachers – is not happening while the need to impart it has never been more urgent."*[2]

Why You Should Read This Report

Imagine, if you will, a world where doctors go to school for a number of years, taught by academics and other doctors, to learn their craft. In those years at school they learn and receive training in the laying of hands, homeopathy, the hidden medicinal qualities of semi-precious stones, and astrological healing. In the course of their study, they don't however receive any information or training about anatomy, physiology, pathology, surgery and/or antibiotics and antivirals. At the end of their schooling, they receive a diploma and can start their own practice or work in a hospital, taking "care" of patients, diagnosing illnesses, prescribing medications, and even operating on them. Sounds farfetched or even ludicrous doesn't it? Yes it does, but luckily, in most countries, this isn't the case.

But what if we were to tell you that studies have shown that many teachers complete their education and training taking courses that teach them about the learning pyramid, learning styles, multiple intelligences, 21st-century skills, and digital natives (all of which we discussed in the final chapter of *HLH*, *The ten deadly sins*). In the course of their study, they don't however, receive any information or training in human cognitive architecture, cognitive psychology, spaced practice, retrieval practice, interleaving, elaboration, or other evidence-informed study or teaching

1   POMERANCE, L., GREENBERG, J., & WALSH, K. (2016, JANUARY). *LEARNING ABOUT LEARNING: WHAT EVERY NEW TEACHER NEEDS TO KNOW*. NATIONAL COUNCIL ON TEACHER QUALITY. AVAILABLE VIA WWW. NCTQ.ORG/DMSVIEW/LEARNING_ABOUT_LEARNING_REPORT.
2   IBID., P. V.

strategies. Sounds farfetched or even ludicrous doesn't it? Yes it does, but unfortunately this is actually the case in many countries.

Laura Pomerance et al. (2016) carried out a study for the National Council on Teacher Quality (NCTQ) entitled *Learning About Learning: What Every New Teacher Needs to Know*. In that report they showed the sorry state of teacher training in the United States with respect to the teaching future teachers about evidence-informed teaching and learning strategies and practices.

Abstract of the Report

Every year about 190,000 teacher candidates graduate from traditional teacher preparation programs believing they are ready to begin the relentlessly demanding career of teaching. Each of these aspiring teachers will have taken at least one education psychology course or instructional methods course (usually both) designed to teach them how children learn and how to create lessons whose content their students will remember. These topics then will be revisited in much of their other coursework. No other subjects will receive as much attention during teacher training as those that purportedly focus on how students learn.

This report contends that textbooks used in this coursework neglect to teach what we know about how students learn despite its central importance in training. Compelling cognitive research that meets scientific standards about how to teach for understanding and retention barely gets a mention in many texts, while anecdotal information is dressed up as science. Theories du jour and debunked notions are being passed on to new teachers as knowledge and best practice.

To write this report, we combed through thousands of pages of teacher education textbooks for discussion of research-based strategies that every teacher candidate should learn in order to promote student learning and retention. What few references we found were buried among pages discussing teaching strategies with much less – often no – scientific merit. This report asserts that textbook publishers and authors are failing the teaching profession, students, and the public by neglecting to provide our next generation of teachers with the fundamental knowledge they need to make learning "stick". The transfer of knowledge – from researchers to publishers to teacher educators to aspiring teachers – is not happening while the need to impart it has never been more urgent.

The Report

Learning About Learning: What Every New Teacher Needs to Know, published in January 2016 by the National Council on Teacher Quality (NCTQ), is an incredibly important document for both the teaching profession in general and for teacher training specifically. To show both the quality and the gravity of the study, it begins with a prominent "Letter of support" from seven of the world's most renowned educational cognitive psychologists, such as Richard Mayer (Cognitive Theory of Multimedia Learning. *HLH* Chapter 5), John Dunlosky (Improving Students' Learning With Effective Learning Techniques, *HLH* Chapter 21 Katherine Rawson (same), Daniel Robinson (one of the founders of Deans for Impact), and Hal Pashler (Organizing Instruction and Study to Improve Student Learning), most of whom are discussed in *HLH*.

Pomerance, Greenberg, and Walsh analysed 48 textbooks[3] – thousand of pages – used in a representative group of 219 American teaching preparation programs. They looked for information and explanations or evidence-based (or better, evidence-informed if you ask us) strategies th every new teacher should know and be able to apply. The reason for doir the study was because, in their opinion, it's an imperative that future teachers are taught how children learn and how to create lessons whose content their students will learn and remember.

What Are These Evidence-Based Strategies?

Using the report *Organizing Instruction and Study to Improve Student Learning: A Practice Guide* (Pashler et al., 2007) from the Institute of Education Sciences, the research institute from the U.S. Department of Education, the researchers identified a series of proven general approaches to improve student learning, regardless of age/year or lesson content. Even better, these strategies work exceptionally well for "struggling students' as well. Six learning strategies stood way out abov the pack because they're underpinned by an extremely large amount of high-quality research.

Taking in information

Connecting information

Remembering information

Two of the six strategies are focused on *taking in information*; that is (1) pairing graphics with words and (2) linking abstract concepts with concrete representations. Two others guarantee that learners *connect information to deepen their understanding* (or pre-existing knowledge); that is (3) posing probing questions (or epistemic questions) on the how, why, what if, and how do you know? as well as (4) repeatedly alternating problems with their solutions provided and problems that students mus solve. Finally, there were two strategies *on helping students remember wha they learned* through (5) distributing practice, meaning that learners sho practice material several times after initial learning instead of practicing hours and hours on end, and (6) formative and summative assessment o what has been learned versus what should have been learned.

---

3   HERE IS A LINK TO THOSE TEXTBOOKS: WWW.NCTQ.ORG/DMSVIEW/APPENDIX_A_557078

Textbooks drive
instruction

The premise behind their study was that *textbooks drive instruction*. They write, "Examination of course materials from teacher preparation programs in the sample testifies to the importance of textbooks in disseminating knowledge and training teachers. Textbooks are the backbone of coursework and a critical resource for the teaching profession" (p. 3). Though not all of the 219 courses in general methods, educational psychology, and subject-specific methods courses used a textbook, they found that more than 85% required a textbook to support instruction. They didn't stop there and also examined lecture and discussion topics, assignments, and assigned readings (i.e., course syllabi) of the courses that didn't use a textbook and found that those courses "typically address the same topics as courses with textbooks" (p. 3). In other words, you could say that while what was in the textbooks isn't exactly what was taught in the courses and that it's possible that things were taught outside of the materials the researchers studied, it seems fair to say that if the textbooks and syllabi didn't discuss something, then it probably wasn't taught. Their analysis confirms "common sense [that]: Textbooks both capture and reinforce the consensus of the field as to what future teachers need to know about instructional strategies. What these textbooks fail to cover is by no means inconsequential" (p. 3).

Were These Strategies Part of the Textbooks and if So, to What Extent?

Needles in a
haystack

According to the authors, looking for the six strategies was like looking "for six needles in a haystack. Even a sentence dedicated to one of the research-based strategies is infrequent" (p. 6), and they conclude that it's highly unlikely that any of the strategies would make an impression on the students, let alone be remembered. Even if the bar was incredibly low and the criterion was simply mentioning the six strategies, you would expect in the 48 textbooks that there would be 288 references (6 strategies x 48 textbooks). In reality there were just 118 mentions total.

They also found that none of the textbooks outlined all six strategies specifically. At best, they discussed two out of six. Of the textbooks, 10% that discuss the proven effective learning strategies only spent 1–2 sentences on them (see Figure 30.1 for a distribution of the amount of space dedicated to the six strategies). Not unimportant is to realise that each book has over 100 pages and in total there were more than 14,000 pages.

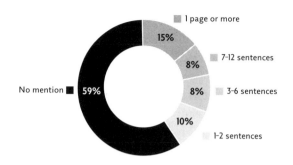

FIGURE 30.1
FREQUENCY
AND LENGTH OF
MENTIONS OF
ANY OF THE SIX
FUNDAMENTAL
INSTRUCTIONAL
STRATEGIES
(*POMERANCE
ET AL., 2016*).

To try to get a handle on whether the students would learn the strategies, they looked at how often textbooks "adequately" covered, and not just mentioned, a strategy. They defined adequately as follows:

Key concepts discussed

1. The *key concepts* necessary to understand the strategy are present. For example if the textbook talks about combining text and images, concepts such as cognitive architecture, dual coding, memory stores and so forth had to be used.

Consistency

2. The message was *consistent*. A textbook couldn't, for example, say on one page that distributing practice is most productive immediately following instruction and somewhere else say that practice should be spaced at greater intervals.

Universality

3. Each strategy was presented such that it conveys *universality*. "In referring to any of the six strategies, texts had to make it clear that the strategy could be applied no matter what the approach to instruction (i.e., teacher-directed instruction or cooperative learning)" (p. 7).

The conclusion: no single textbook covered more than two strategies, while almost half didn't even cover a single strategy! Looking at what was covered and what wasn't, two of the strategies, namely *repeatedly alternating solved and unsolved problems* (interleaving) and *assessing to boost retention* (retrieval practice) weren't covered in any textbook. In total, of 14,000 pages of textbook, less than 1% of the content was related to discussing the six strategies.

But if those six strategies weren't covered, what was? The study revealed that, in general, most textbooks focused on the following (p. 12):

- How teachers and students should organise themselves.
- The importance of student engagement.
- The benefits of cooperative learning.
- The merits and/or pitfalls of homework.
- How to activate prior knowledge (e.g., KWL or know/want to know/learned charts).

Criteria for rigour

Pomerance and her colleagues also looked at the hundreds of studies cited in the textbooks to determine the scientific rigour of the cited studies. The criteria that they used were based on standards of the Institute of Education Sciences (IES; the "research arm" of the U.S. Department of Education). These standards include, among other things, adequate sample size, internal and external validity, use of a treatment and a control group either randomly selected or equivalent in composition, whether learning/achievement was actually measured, and whether or not an impact on actual learning was found. Here we see the same sorrowful results. Only 7% of the sampled citations satisfied these standards (see Figure 30.2).

FIGURE 30.2
SCIENTIFIC
RIGOUR BEHIND
TEXTBOOK
REFERENCES
(*POMERANCE
ET AL., 2016*).
NO = DOESN'T
MEET THE IES
STANDARDS;
YES = MEETS THE
IES STANDARDS
TO A CERTAIN
EXTENT.

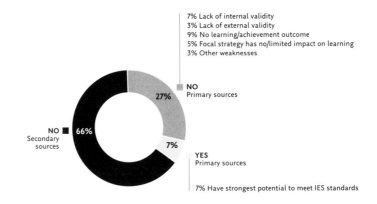

The researchers also looked at 48 elementary and secondary teacher preparation programmes that use the reviewed textbooks. However, also within these programmes, the six strategies were virtually non-existent during lessons. And if they were discussed, they were hardly practiced, except for posing probing questions (see Figure 30.3) though this was primarily a strategy their teachers used.

FIGURE 30.3
COMPARISON OF
THE COVERAGE
STRATEGIES IN
TEXTBOOKS AND
PREPARATION IN
COURSEWORK
(*POMERANCE
ET AL., 2016*).

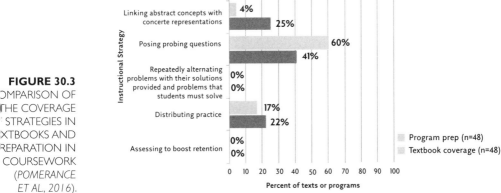

We'd like to close this section with two disheartening results:

- The average textbook or syllabus is more likely to encourage future teachers to adapt their instruction to students' *learning styles* – which is a myth with no empirical support whatsoever – than to explain the information processing model, which explains our learning processes
- Even if one or more of the six strategies are mentioned, they almost never include details needed for effective classroom use (e.g., the delay between sessions of distributing practice should be weeks and months and not a day or two). This means that a future teacher might have heard of a strategy but has no idea how to use it in the class.

Recommendations of the Report

Pomerance and colleagues close their report with a few recommendations for authors and publishers. Their first recommendation is that textbooks should be a "how to" guide for teachers, presenting them with what they need to know about effectively implementing fundamental instructional strategies in the classroom. Also, at a minimum, textbooks "should present the six fundamental instructional strategies as the cognitive bedrock of effective instructional design. The strategies should be presented in depth, and their universal applicability should be clear" (p. 27).

In addition, they recommend that publishers should insist/require that most if not all references be primary sources that satisfy the criteria for well-designed studies according to IES standards. Finally, if there is a valid reason to include discussions of instructional topics that have little to no support, these must be clearly set apart from well-designed studies.

Conclusions

There are staggeringly few references to evidence-based strategies in the textbooks and syllabi being used to teach and train future teachers. And this while

> [t]extbooks are a critical and indispensable means for applying the best work by education researchers to teacher training, and for preparing those on whom we depend to educate our children. It is beyond disheartening that there is not a closer examination of textbook content along with higher standards around the science and knowledge textbooks are pushing into the field. In fact, we might go so far as to suggest that pushing weak, even junk science on aspiring teachers is educational malpractice. (p. 27)

And the fault doesn't lie only in the teacher training institutions. Textbook publishers and authors also fail terribly because they ignore the fundamental knowledge necessary for good teaching and learning and this is by no means inconsequential. After all, the next generation teachers are being disadvantaged and even worse, their students will be suffering because of it. And it's not just the textbook authors who are responsible; the teacher prep programmes aren't any better. Cognitive research that meets scientific standards about how to teach for understanding and retention is sorely lacking in textbooks, syllabi, and programmes. This stands in stark contrast with the enormous amount of anecdotal evidence on teaching strategies and classroom management there, all dressed up as solid science.

Addressing These Challenges

Rather than providing a representative example of how the lessons of the report might play out in a classroom, we end this final chapter with two real-world examples of how the field is beginning to address these challenges – both of which we think provide reasons to be hopeful.

Deans for Impact

The first is *Deans for Impact* (DfI), founded in large part as a response to the damning conclusions of such reports on the state of Educator Preparation. As such, DfI works with Educator Preparation programmes across the U.S. to improve the ways teacher candidates are readied for the profession.

Central to their work is the belief that understanding evidence-informed approaches (what DfI refers to as "learning science") and being able to apply this understanding in instructional contexts should be a foundational component of any effective teacher training experience.

Collaboration with cognitive scientists and educational psychologists

To underpin this commitment, DfI collaborated with leading cognitive scientist Dan Willingham to create *The Science of Learning* (Deans for Impact, 2016) a cornerstone paper naming those high-leverage, evidence-informed practices a teacher could employ – along with specific illustrations of what that might look like in the form of teacher actions (see Figure 30.4).

They then created learning experiences and assessments that mapped onto the cornerstone principles and associated teacher actions, such that trainee teachers' knowledge and application of learning science could be captured and their growth over time could be determined.

Learning by Scientific Design

The reason for hope in DfI's model is that it shows how evidence-informed approaches to instruction can be infused into the programmatic and practical experiences trainee teachers receive in systematic ways. Through their time working with Schools of Education and the candidates who pass through them, DfI has come to

1 | How Do Students Understand New Ideas?

Cognitive Principles	Practical Implications for the Classroom
Students learn new ideas by reference to ideas they already know.	■ A well-sequenced curriculum is important to ensure that students have the prior knowledge they need to master new ideas.
	■ Teachers use analogies because they map a new idea onto one that students already know. But analogies are effective only if teachers elaborate on them, and direct student attention to the crucial similarities between existing knowledge and what is to be learned.

FIGURE 30.4 ONE EXAMPLE COGNITIVE PRINCIPLE AND ITS APPLICATION TO THE CLASSROOM IN THE FORM OF SUGGESTED TEACHER ACTIONS.

learn where and how evidence-informed approaches have traditionally shown up in the teacher trainees' experience. In their report, *Learning by Scientific Design* (LbSD; Deans for Impact, 2020), they describe conversations with teacher-candidates "who have described taking a single course on learning science (often labeled "education psychology"), usually at the beginning of their teacher preparation, that is otherwise disconnected to the rest of their coursework and clinical experiences" (p. 17). Rather than seeing learning science as an add-on to the candidate experience, DfI instead envisioned a fully integrated approach, including the following (p. 20):

- Developing and administering the LbSD [Learning Science] Assessment
- Identifying strengths and growth areas within their programs.
- Building faculty knowledge of learning science.
- Observing teacher-candidates to explore how knowledge of learning science can impact pedagogical practice.
- Examining coursework structure and field placements to determine how they might align with learning science as a focus.

Efforts such as these address the very concerns outlined in the NCQT report by placing the applied science of learning at the heart of an emerging teacher's experience rather than tangential to it. Indeed, in their follow-up report, *Deepening Meaning and Learning* (Deans for Impact, 2021) DfI was able to demonstrate through subsequent administration of the same learning science assessment, "sizable differences between the scores of teacher-candidates who had access to learning-science-focused learning opportunities, and those who did no (p. 4) after just one year of implementing the above practices. In other words, providing focused attention to the role learning science plays in classroom practice and using that to redesign the teacher training experiences *actually works*.

The second example comes from the world of education policy at the national level: England's Department for Education (DfE) and their *Early Career Framework* (ECF; Department for Education, 2021). This framework, developed with the Chartered College for Teaching and the Educational Endowment Foundation (amongst others), is meant to support the professional development of novice teachers.

The ECF connects to the arc of a teacher's career (the DfE refers to this as the *Golden Thread*) with evidence-informed practice underpinning expectations for early career teachers, middle/senior leaders, headship, and executive headship. Significantly, the ECF emphasises what beginning teachers are *entitled to* and provides a fully sponsored two-year package of structured training and support, which has been built on the best available evidence from learning and teaching research. The support includes funding and guaranteeing 5% off-timetable in the second year of teaching for all early career teachers; early career teachers will continue to have a 10% timetable reduction in their first year of induction; creating high quality, freely available ECF curricula and training materials; establishing full, high quality ECF training programmes; funding time for mentors to support early career teachers; and fully funded mentor training.

The DfE also designed a *Core Content Framework* as a basis for teacher education and training. This framework defines the standards that each teacher minimally needs to meet in their teacher education drawing on the best available evidence. It consists of eight standards:

1. Set high expectations.
2. Promote good progress.
3. Demonstrate good subject and curriculum knowledge.
4. Plan and teach well-structured lessons.
5. Adapt teaching.
6. Make accurate and productive use of assessment.
7. Manage behaviour effectively.
8. Fulfil wider professional responsibilities.

Each of these standards begins (see left-hand column in Figure 30.5) with what the teacher-in-training should know at the completion of the curriculum (Learn that . . .) based on the best available educational research. The right-hand column contains a list of things that the teacher-in-training should be able to do upon completion of the curriculum (*Learn how to . . .*), explaining how the teacher can accomplish the given goal and what it looks like in practice, again based on research-based knowledge, as well as conversations with

Margin notes:

Early Career Framework

Golden Thread

Core Content Framework

professionals, such as scholars, pedagogical centres, and of course teachers (DfE, 2019).

How Pupils Learn (Standard 2 | Promote good progress)

Learn that . . .	Learn how to . . .
1 | Learning involves a lasting change in pupils' capabilities or understanding. 2 | Prior knowledge plays an important role in how pupils learn; committing some key facts to their long-term memory is likely to help pupils learn more complex ideas. 3 | An important factor in learning is memory, which can be thought of as comprising two elements: working memory and long-term memory. 4 | Working memory is where information that is being actively processed is held, but its capacity is limited and can be overloaded. 5 | Long-term memory can be considered as a store of knowledge that changes as pupils learn by integrating new ideas with existing knowledge. 6 | Where prior knowledge is weak, pupils are more likely to develop misconceptions, particularly if new ideas are introduced too quickly.	Avoid overloading working memory, by: ■ Receiving clear, consistent, and effective mentoring in how to take into account pupils' prior knowledge when planning how much new information to introduce. ■ Discussing and analysing with expert colleagues how to reduce distractions that take attention away from what is being taught (e.g., keeping the complexity of a task to the minimum, so that attention is focused on the content). And – following expert input – by taking opportunities to practise, receive feedback and improve at: ■ Breaking complex material into smaller steps (e.g., using partially completed examples to focus pupils on the specific steps). Build on pupils' prior knowledge, by: ■ Discussing and analysing with expert colleagues how to sequence lessons to that pupils' secure foundational knowledge before encountering more complex content. ■ Discussing and analysing with expert colleagues how to identify possible misconceptions and plan how to prevent these forming. And – following expert input – by taking opportunities to practise, receive feedback and improve at: ■ Encouraging pupils to share emerging understanding and points of confusion so that misconceptions can be addressed.

FIGURE 30.5 ANOTHER EXAMPLE OF LEVERAGING COGNITIVE SCIENCE FOR TEACHER PRACTICE FROM THE ITT CORE CONTENT FRAMEWORK (DFE).

In a separate initiative, the Education Endowment Foundation create toolkits discussing more than 40 different approaches to improve teaching and learning, and which demonstrate efficacy according to the average impact on learning, cost of implementing the approach and strength of supporting evidence. In the EEF's own words: "The Toolkits not make definitive claims as to what *will* work to improve outcomes in given school. Rather they provide high quality information about what *likely to be beneficial* based on existing evidence".

All of which feels like a fitting place to draw our exploration of effective teaching to an end. If there's a theme to this book, perhaps it's, as Dylan Wiliam has said, "everything works somewhere and nothing works everywhere". However, just because the contextually dependent nature of teaching demands that we remain cognisant of our setting, that doesn't mean we cannot make best bets around what is more or less likely to be beneficial for the students in our charge.

That was our hope in writing this book: not to offer a panacea for teaching, but rather to articulate and exemplify a series of best bets around what works and why that teachers can pick up, internalise, adapt, and apply to their own contexts and approaches.

The field of education and the evidence that underpins it will continue to evolve and there will no doubt be the odd mutation along the way. For now at least, we hope you have enjoyed exploring with us some of the seminal works and telling moments in its evolution to date, and that you gained something useful from our snapshot of this unimaginably complex and wonderful practice we call teaching.

Takeaways

- What works as a teaching or study strategy is often/usually not included in textbooks for future teachers.
- Textbooks used in training future teachers neglect to teach what we know about how students learn despite its central importance in training.
- When a textbook cites research, the research of often secondary (someone writing about someone else's study) and not primary (the actual study) and in 93% of the cases fails to meet the minimal criteria for scientific rigour.
- Many textbooks focused on more nebulous areas such as engagement and co-operative learning.
- Many misconceptions which are learned in initial teacher training can endure for years without being challenged.

References

DEANS FOR IMPACT. (2016). *THE SCIENCE OF LEARNING.* AVAILABLE VIA HTTPS:// DEANSFORIMPACT.ORG/WP-CONTENT/UPLOADS/2016/12/THE_SCIENCE_OF_LEARNING.PDF

DEANS FOR IMPACT. (2020). *LEARNING BY SCIENTIFIC DESIGN: EARLY INSIGHTS FROM A NETWORK TRANSFORMING TEACHER PREPARATION.* AVAILABLE VIA HTTPS://DEANSFORIMPACT.ORG/ WP-CONTENT/UPLOADS/2020/03/DEANS_FOR_IMPACT_LBSD_REPORT_FINAL-1.PDF

DEANS FOR IMPACT. (2021). *DEEPENING MEANING AND LEARNING: HOW FUTURE TEACHERS ARE PUTTING LEARNING SCIENCE INTO ACTION TO SUPPORT ALL STUDENTS.* AVAILABLE VIA HTTPS:// DEANSFORIMPACT.ORG/WP-CONTENT/UPLOADS/2021/06/DFI_DEEPENING-MEANING-AND-LEARNING.PDF

DEPARTMENT FOR EDUCATION. (2019). *ITT CORE CONTENT FRAMEWORK.* AVAILABLE VIA HTTPS://ASSETS.PUBLISHING.SERVICE.GOV.UK/GOVERNMENT/UPLOADS/SYSTEM/UPLOADS/

ATTACHMENT_DATA/FILE/843676/INITIAL_TEACHER_TRAINING_CORE_CONTENT_FRAMEWORK.
PDF

DEPARTMENT FOR EDUCATION. (2021). *EARLY CAREER FRAMEWORK.* AVAILABLE VIA WWW.
GOV.UK/GOVERNMENT/PUBLICATIONS/EARLY-CAREER-FRAMEWORK-REFORMS-OVERVIEW/
EARLY-CAREER-FRAMEWORK-REFORMS-OVERVIEW

Education Endowment Foundation. Teaching and Learning Toolkit: An accessible summary of
education evidence. Available via https://educationendowmentfoundation.org.uk/education-evidence/
teaching-learning-toolkit

**PASHLER, H., BAIN, P., BOTTGE, B., GRAESSER, A., KOEDINGER, K., MCDANIEL, M.,
ET AL.** (2007). *ORGANIZING INSTRUCTION AND STUDY TO IMPROVE STUDENT LEARNING* (NCER 2007–
2004). NATIONAL CENTER FOR EDUCATION RESEARCH, INSTITUTE OF EDUCATION SCIENCES, U.S.
DEPARTMENT OF EDUCATION. AVAILABLE VIA HTTPS://FILES.ERIC.ED.GOV/FULLTEXT/ED498555.PDF

POMERANCE, L., GREENBERG, J., & WALSH, K. (2016, JANUARY). *LEARNING ABOUT LEARNING:
WHAT EVERY NEW TEACHER NEEDS TO KNOW.* NATIONAL COUNCIL ON TEACHER QUALITY.
AVAILABLE VIA WWW.NCTQ.ORG/DMSVIEW/LEARNING_ABOUT_LEARNING_REPORT.

Suggested Readings and Links

APPENDICES TO POMERANCE, L., GREENBERG, J., & WALSH, K. (2016,
JANUARY). *LEARNING ABOUT LEARNING: WHAT EVERY NEW TEACHER NEEDS TO
KNOW.* NATIONAL COUNCIL ON TEACHER QUALITY.

AVAILABLE VIA WWW.NCTQ.ORG/DMSVIEW/ALL_APPENDICES

IES STANDARDS FOR EXCELLENCE IN EDUCATIONAL RESEARCH

AVAILABLE VIA HTTPS://IES.ED.GOV/SEER/INDEX.ASP

SURMA, T., VANHOYWEGHEN, K, CAMP, G., & KIRSCHNER, P.A. (2018).
DISTRIBUTED PRACTICE AND RETRIEVAL PRACTICE: THE COVERAGE OF
LEARNING STRATEGIES IN FLEMISH AND DUTCH TEACHER EDUCATION
TEXTBOOKS. *TEACHING AND TEACHER EDUCATION, 74,* 229–237.

AVAILABLE VIA WWW.SCIENCEDIRECT.COM/SCIENCE/ARTICLE/PII/S07420
51X17320656

Glossary

Aptitude   Usually seen as a component of a competence to do a certain kind of work at a certain level. For Bloom it's the amount of time required by the learner to attain mastery of a learning task.

Assessment for learning   The use of low-stakes or no-stakes assessment as a learning or study strategy.

Assessment of learning   The use of assessment to determine what has been learnt.

Authenticity   An authentic teacher has subject matter expertise, passion and enthusiasm for their subject, is unique and maintains the necessary distance or proximity to their students.

Backwash   When testing drives what is on the curriculum and how it is taught.

Behavioural objective   A desired learning outcome that is stated in measurable terms (e.g., apply in a specific situation vs. understand), which gives direction to the learner's study and forms the basis for assessment.

Cognitive dissonance   We seek consistency in our attitudes and perceptions. If the two conflict, this leads to feelings of unease or discomfort. When these things aren't cognitively consistent, we do all we can to change them until they become consistent.

Cognitive load   The amount of information that working memory can hold at one time.

Cognitive schema   A pattern of thought or behaviour that organises different categories of information and the relationships between them. And which guides our cognitive processes and behaviours.

Communicative systems approach   A "systems approach" to communication that assumes that one cannot not communicate when in the presence of someone else. Whatever a person's intentions are, others will infer meaning from this behaviour.

Constructive alignment   A systems-based approach to teaching and learning where (1) the intended or desired learning outcomes are defined before teaching takes place, (2) the chosen instructional approaches are well-suited for achieving the intended or desired outcomes, and (3) the assessment methods used are designed to reliably assess whether the intended or desired learning outcomes have been achieved.

Contextual interference   Similar to interleaving, but here you make the task environment – not the task – more variable or unpredictable in a way that creates, at least temporarily, interference for the learner.

Curricular knowledge   Knowledge of the full range of how to teach the content at a certain level, the instructional materials available, and when, why, and how to use or not use certain things in certain circumstances.

Curse of knowledge/Curse of expertise   A cognitive bias that arises when a person who's communicating with others, incorrectly assumes that everyone knows as much about a subject as they do. This not only makes it hard to imagine what it's like not knowing what they know, but it also makes it difficult to share their knowledge, because they can't understand the other's state of mind.

Desirable difficulties   The counterintuitive concept that there are ways of learning that may feel less effective and lead to more errors during the learning process, but that lead to better performance in the long term. Examples are retrieval practice, spaced practice, and interleaving.

Direct Instruction (DI)   An explicit, carefully sequenced, and scripted model of instruction as prescribed by Engelmann. It's a collection of formal, highly scripted, and formatted curricula in the form of lessons, textbooks, and sequencing.

direct instruction (di)   A term that Barak Rosenshine gave to a set of variables found to be significantly related to student achievement. It is an instruction strategy, not a curriculum. In his original work, he referred to it as "explicit instruction".

Distributed practice   A study or learning strategy, where practice is split into a number of short sessions over a longer period of time instead of fewer, longer training sessions. Often called spaced practice.

Eduquack   An Eduquack (neologism made up by Paul years ago; portmanteau word combining education + quackery) is the educational variant of what is commonly known as a quackademic: an academic with little or no real knowledge of what they're talking about but who has no problem venting that ignorance. The Urban Dictionary calls them fraudulent or ignorant pretenders; a quackish or pseudoscientific academic.

Enactive representation   A representation showing the actions appropriate for achieving a set result.

Encoding   Transforming the information coming from sensory input into a form so it can be stored in the brain; changing internal thoughts and external events into short term and long-term memory.

Episodic memory   A type long-term memory that involves the recollection of specific events, situations, and experiences that we have encountered (i.e., episodes in our lives).

External validity   How well the outcome of a study can be expected to also be expected in other settings. In other words, how generalisable the findings are across grade levels or subject areas. We see this in research that focuses on a highly specific student group such as middle school students struggling with basic arithmetic.

Extraneous cognitive load   The mental effort needed to carry out a task caused by the instructional approach used to teach/carry out the learning task.

Formative assessment/evaluation   A broad range of assessment procedures which allows teachers to frequently assess both their learners' progress and the effectiveness of their own practice. Teachers can and should use this during the learning process to modify their teaching and student learning activities to improve student learning.

Generative learning activities   Learning strategies or activities intended to improve students' learning by prompting them to actively make sense of the material to be learned.

Gestalt Psychology   A school of psychology founded in the 20th century looking at the human mind and behaviour as a whole.

Grading on a curve   Adjusting student grades to ensure that the student scores are "properly" distributed (e.g., 20% receive As, 30% Bs, etc.), as well as a desired total average (e.g., a C grade average for a given test).

Iconic representation   A representation showing the summary images or graphics that stand for a concept without defining it fully.

Interleaving   A study or teaching strategy where variation and/or unpredictability in the training environment is introduced by mixing multiple subjects or topics during study and practice. The opposite is blocked practice where one topic is studied or practiced to mastery before moving on.

Internal validity   The extent to which observed results represent the truth in the population being studied and, thus, are not due to methodological errors. Lack of internal validity makes it difficult if not impossible to infer causal relationships. Examples are these: all teachers at each participating school are assigned to the same condition, making it unclear whether treatment or school variables are responsible for the outcomes, or that there is no evidence of pre-test equivalence for groups in a quasi-experiment.

Intrinsic cognitive load   The mental effort needed to carry out a task caused by the task's inherent complexity which is determined by the amount of information that needs to be processed (i.e., the number of new information elements in the task) and the task's complexity which is determined by the interactivity of the elements.

Learning   Relatively long-lasting/permanent changes in our long-term memory or behaviour.

Learning task (in 4C/ID)   Authentic, whole-task experiences based on real tasks that integrate the necessary skills, knowledge, and attitudes organised in stages, with each stage having diminished learner support.

Likert scale   A psychometric (psychological measurement) scale often used in questionnaires to measure perceptions, feeling, attitudes, etc. It assumes that the strength or intensity of an attitude is linear (e.g., a continuum from strongly agree to strongly disagree or very dull to very interesting), and also assumes that such attitudes can be measured. The scale usually has an odd number of choices (most typically 5, 7, or 9) with the centre-point being neutral.

Mastery learning   A set of group-based, individualised, teaching and learning strategies based on the premise that students will achieve a high level of understanding in a given domain if they are given enough time.

Mastery-based learning   An approach to learning and instruction where students must demonstrate their understanding of a topic or subject area before going on to another topic or subject area.

Matthew effect   A social phenomenon where those with the most skills and/or resources are able to increase their position in society whereas those with the least are left behind.

Metacognition   Called metamemory by Robert Bjork, the extent to which learners can validly and reliably judge their own learning or competence.

Missing paradigm   Introduced by Lee Shulman, the missing paradigm relating to research on and requirements for teaching is the absence of content area knowledge in relation to teaching.

Modality principle   Replacing information presented in one modality (e.g., a written explanation) coupled on another (e.g., a diagram) with information in two modalities such as a spoken explanatory text and a visual source of information (e.g., using visual and auditory modalities) has a positive effect on learning and transfer.

Oracy   Similar to numeracy in mathematics or literacy in reading and writing, oracy is the fluent, confident, and correct use of the standard spoken form of one's native language. It's a person's ability to express themself well; having the vocabulary to say what they want to say and the ability to structure their thoughts to make sense to others.

Orthographic encoding   Understanding the rules by which something is written such as spelling, punctuation, or syntax.

Part-task practice   Here students perform/practice routine activities to develop a high level of automaticity. Part-task practice requires huge amounts of repetition and should only start after the routine has been introduced within a whole, meaningful learning task.

Pedagogical Content Knowledge   Knowing and understanding the subject matter for teaching. This includes understanding what makes certain things easy or difficult to learn, knowing the conceptions, preconceptions and even misconceptions that different learners bring with them to the lessons.

Performance   Temporary changes or variations in our knowledge or behaviour that is usually determined during or directly after the learning experience. This is usually what we see at the time of testing.

Phenomenography   A qualitative research methodology that investigates the qualitatively different ways in which people experience something or think about something.

Phonics   Reading instruction strategy where the focus is on the matching of sounds of spoken English with individual letters or groups of letters.

Phonological encoding   Where the written word is rendered into speech, either implicitly (in your head) or explicitly (out loud).

Procedural information   Tells learners how to perform routine aspects of learning tasks (how-to instructions). It's best presented to them just-in-time, precisely when they need it during their work on learning tasks.

Reflection-in-action   Unlike traditional perceptions of reflection which assume its taking place "after the fact" this is reflection that takes place in the midst of action and informs that action.

Reliability   The overall consistency of a measure. A measure has high reliability if it produces similar results under consistent conditions. A reliable bathroom scale should give approximately the same weight every time you stand on it.

Retrieval   The process of remembering information stored in long-term memory. This can be via recall or recognition. In recall, the information must be retrieved from memory. In recognition, a familiar outside stimulus provides a cue that the information was seen earlier.

Retrieval practice   A learning or study strategy where the learner must retrieve information stored in long term memory. This recalling of information forces the learner to pull stored knowledge "out" and examine what they know.

Seductive detail   A text, animation, photo, illustration, sound or music used in instruction which are interesting but not directed toward the learning objectives of a lesson and which distract the learner leading to poorer learning.

Self-concept   How you perceive your own behaviour, abilities, and unique characteristics. Deals with questions like these: "Who am I?", "What can and can't I do?", "What do I want to be able to do?".

Select–Organise–Integrate (SOI) Framework   Learning is knowledge construction through the cognitive process of (a) selecting relevant information, (b) organising incoming information, and (c) integrating incoming information with exist knowledge.

Self-esteem   The individual's subjective evaluation of their own value or worth, encompassing beliefs about themself (e.g., "I'm smart", "I'm important") as well as their emotional states (e.g., feelings of despair, pride, shame).

Self-explanation effect   Self-explanation improves acquiring problem-solving skills when studying worked-out examples as students become aware of the actual level of their understanding and may receive key information about areas of confusion and/or understanding.

Semantic encoding   Processing and understanding the underlying meaning of something.

Semantic memory   The knowledge that we have accumulated in our long-term memories about what we know of the world around us. It consists of facts, ideas, and concepts and is entwined in our experiences and is dependent on our culture.

Sigma (σ)   Sigma (σ) is the symbol for the standard deviation in statistics; 2σ means two standard deviations away from the mean in a normal distribution or "statistically significantly better" with a confidence of 95%.

SOLO Taxonomy   A systematic way of describing how a learner's performance grows in complexity when mastering many tasks, particularly the sort of tasks undertaken in school.

Spaced practice   A study or learning strategy, where practice is split into a number of short sessions over a longer period of time instead of fewer, longer training sessions. Often called distributed practice.

Spatial Split-Attention Principle   Replacing multiple sources of information (e.g., frequently visual representations and accompanyi prose text) with a single, integrated source of information (e.g., text in the visual representation). Eliminating spatial split-attention has a positive effect on rule formation and transfer.

Split-Attention Effect   The phenomenon that learning is hampered when learners must integrate information sources split either in time (temporal split-attention) or space (spatial split-attention) to fully understand something.

Subject matter content knowledge   The amount and organisation of knowledge in the mind of the teacher in their domain of teaching.

Summative assessment/evaluation   A form of assessment where the focus is on the outcome of a programme. Its goal is the evaluation of student learning at the end of a lesson, series of lessons, or a course or curriculum by comparing the students' results to a standard or benchmark.

Supportive information   Helps learners perform non-routine aspects (problem solving, reasoning, decision making) of learning tasks. It is presented to them before they start working on learning tasks and/or made available to them while they are working on these tasks.

Symbolic representation   A representation showing the symbolic or logical propositions drawn from a symbolic system governed by rules for forming and transforming propositions

Synform   Pairs or groups of words that are similar in form.

Systematic   Something – an action or set of actions – that's done according to some plan, system, or organised method.

Systemic   Something that happens inside a system and that, when it happens, affects all other parts of a system.

Task analysis   A process of learning about what people do by observing them in action to understand in detail how they perform their tasks and achieve their intended goals, including the mistakes that they make.
A specific type of task analysis is cognitive task analysis where we attempt to gain information about the knowledge, thought processes and goal structures that underlie observable task performance.

Taxonomy of educational objectives   A framework to classify statements of what we expect or intend students to learn through our instruction, providing us with a common language with which to discuss educational goals.

Teaching effectiveness studies   A way of studying classroom instruction, looking at the relationship between forms of teaching practice/instruction and student learning/academic achievement.

Temporal split-attention effect   Presenting multiple sources of information (e.g., mutually referring pictures and text) at the same time, instead of one by one. Eliminating temporal split attention has a positive effect on rule formation and transfer.

TPACK   Technology, pedagogy, and content knowledge or Technological Pedagogical Content Knowledge.

Unicity   The fact of being or consisting of one, or of being united as a whole.

Validity   The degree to which something measures what it is supposed to measure. A bathroom scale should measure your weight and a yardstick your height.

Worked example   An instructional approach that consists of the given of a problem, the solution steps for the problem, and the final solution itself.

Index

4C/ID (Four Component Instructural Design) 82–83, 119

achievement: measure of (testing) 302, 310–311, 321, 323, 335; as teacher expertise 8, 10, 28, 293
ACT-R model (Adaptive Control of Thought-Rational model) 167–168
affective models 122, 124
aptitude 9, 182, 246, 294
aptitude test (teacher) 15–16, 181, 292
assessment: of learning 79, 158, 332; for learning 147
authentic: knowledge 304; meaning of 243; teacher 7, 239, 242, 244, 246–247
authenticity 244–247 see also teacher

backwash 75, 301, 304
basic-skills models 122, 124
Beatles 288–289
behaviour management 291, 311
biologically primary 124, 290, 295
biologically secondary 27, 341

case knowledge 20
chalk and talk 115, 118
classroom: behaviours 270, 281; differences 280; disorderly 254; dominance (appropriate level of) 268–269; dynamics 66, 258–262; management 29, 37, 190, 233, 266–269, 276–278, 280, 282; routines 280; teaching 17, 182
cognitive: architecture (human) 144, 208, 330; dissonance 260; load theory 97, 132, 168, 170, 247; schema 153
Cognitive-Conceptual Models 122, 124
common content knowledge 190–191, 193
communication conventions 120–121

communicative systems approach 253
compartmentalisation 84
competence 17–18, 84–85, 157, 294
constructive alignment: assessment/learning objectives 73–74, 325; benefits of 75, 306
content aspect of communication 253–254
content knowledge (CK) 232, 233
context 38–39, 41, 50
Core Content Framework 339, 340
covert performance 108–109
culture 6, 10, 38, 154, 182
curricular knowledge 19, 179, 191
curriculum development 21, 69, 73, 75, 89
curse of expertise 172
curse of knowledge 211–212

Deans for Impact (DfI) 337
desirable difficulties: learning skills 152–153; unpredictability training 155–156, 159–160
direct instruction (di): instruction strategy 120, 132
Direct Instruction (DI): key features 123; theory (of instruction) 118–120, 124
distributed practice 27, 155–156
domain knowledge 202, 231, 234, 236, 322, 325, 327
drawing: as generative learning 143, 145, 147–148; as symbolic representation 96–97, 108
Dynamic Model of Educational Effectiveness 50

Early Career Framework (ECF) 339
education policy 25–26, 30, 339
Educational Endowment Foundation 339–340

Eduquacks 164
effect-heavy practices 38
elaboration theory 90, 119, 133, 135, 330
enacting 62, 70, 143, 145, 147, 149
enactive representation 96–97, 101
encoding 154, 311–312
episodic memory 154
experienced teachers 6, 201–202, 262
experiments 66, 199, 203, 221, 230, 321
expert teachers 5–6, 8–10, 202, 280
expertise: person/environment 6, 9–10; prototypic features 8; subject specific 181; in teaching 5, 9, 28, 172, 180
explicit instruction: differs from chalk and talk 115, 120, 130–132, 138; requires active participation 135, 218, 281
extraneous cognitive load 132

formative evaluation (assessment) 289, 291–292, 294
Four Component Instructural Design (4C/ID) 82–83, 119
fragmentation 84–85

generative learning activities 133, 143
Gestalt psychology 303
grading on the curve 293

iconic representation 96–97
imagining 143, 145, 147–148
influence 257, 261
instructional objectives: criterion 105, 110; preparing 104; quality 111; speed and accuracy 110–111
interleaving 155, 169, 231, 330, 334
intrinsic cognitive load 132

knowledge: in action 64; building foundations of 99; common content 190–191, 193; constructing 303; in action 64; of content and curriculum 181, 192, 193, 194; of content and students (KCS) 189–192, 193, 194; of content and teaching 190, 192, 193, 194; curse of 211–212; explicit versus tacit 107, 178, 184, 211–212, 215; flow of 62; mathematical 191–192, 193, 194; at the mathematical horizon 192; pedagogical 19, 180, 201–202, 212, 232, 233, 278; propositional 20; sharing 99; subject matter 26, 175, 193, 200, 204

learning: environment 51, 132, 252, 261 from examples 164; independent 261–262; and performance 156, 159; to read/write 218–221, 226; strategie 136, 143, 144, 294, 331–333; student (improving) 36–38, 41, 49, 52, 194, 291, 331–332
literacy 97, 209, 220, 224
literature: appreciation versus teachin 213; English 183, 209, 211, 224, 326; for teaching 53, 73, 164–165, 183

mapping 143, 145, 148, 254
mastery: approaches to (teaching) 292–295; student (of curricula) 37, 43, 123, 126, 134
mathematical knowledge for teachin (MKT) 188–191, 194
Matthew effect 224
McNamara Fallacy 300–301, 303, 305
mental model 39–40, 53–55, 65, 212–213
metacognition 157, 160
missing paradigm 18, 20, 176, 190
Model for Interpersonal Teacher Behavior (MITB) 254, 256

novice teachers 180, 262, 278, 339

orthographic encoding 311
orthographic learning 223
overt performance 108

pedagogical content knowledge (PCK lack of 176; research on 199; teache readiness 190–191; traditional knowledge 192–194, 200–202
performance: academic 320; covert 108–109; Lake Wobegon Effect 320–321; learner/student 17, 25, 73 121, 159, 190, 258; versus learning 1 overt 108; post training 153, 155–1! short-term 156–157; teacher 26
phonics 217, 219–220, **222–223**, 226–: phonological encoding 312
Project Follow Through 122, 124
propositional knowledge 20, **21**
proximity: effects of 257–258, 262; t matched problems 165, 172, 173; teacher/student perceptions 254, !

qualitative and qualitative assessme 25, 303–304
Questionnaire on Teacher Interactio (QTI) 253, 255–256, 258

reading: learning to read 221; linguistic comprehension 225; morphological instruction 223–224; phonics-based instruction 219, **222**; simple view of 224; tier two words 226; what it is 220–221; writing systems 226

reading wars 218

reflection in action 64, 66–67

reliability 203

retrieval 154

retrieval (practice) 27, 132, **134**, 147, 156, 317, 330, 334

rote learning 77, 79, 313

schema/schemata: cognitive 153; sophisticated knowledge 2, 143, 233

science of learning 143, 199, 204, 219, 338

seductive details **134**

select-organise-integrate (SOI) framework 143–144, 144

self-explaining 143, 145, 147–148

self-explanation 171, 172, 173

self-perception 258–259, 260

self-testing 143, 145, 147–148

semantic encoding 212

sematic memory 154

SOLO taxonomy (Structure of the Observed Learning Outcome) 76, 304

split attention effect 168

strategic knowledge 20

subject matter content knowledge 18–20, **21**, 26, 31, 175, 191, 214

summarising 143, 145, 148

summative evaluation (assessment) 291–292, 294–295

symbolic representation talent 96, 98–99

tacit knowledge 107, 178, 184, 212

task analysis 122, 292

Taxonomy of Educational Objectives (Bloom) 289, 311

teacher behaviour: appropriate levels of 267–268; defining 17, 35, 37, 44; interpersonal model of 254–255; physical ques 269; positive and equitable 270; practice 243

teacher expertise: automaticity (ease of sharing old knowledge in new ways) 214, 221; content knowledge 18–19, 184, 211; effectiveness 26–29, 49–50; good *versus* successful 5–9; requires

flexibility 83, 106, 154, 180–181, 214, 231; subject specific 8, 14, 26, 181, 213–214, 233, 333

teacher preparation: characteristics 5, 27–28; effectiveness 24–29, 37, 48, 52, 120; policy and procedures 30–31; standards 29–30, 180–181; student learning outcomes 31–32

teacher-student relationship profiles 256–257

teaching: culture 6–7; effectiveness studies 49, 120, 133; standards 8, 15, 26, 29, 180

teaching context: education policy 6, 25–26, 30–31; policymakers 54, 125, 321; working conditions 5, 54, 267–269

technical rationality: the illusion of order 61–63, 66; problem solving 63, 66–67

Technological Pedagogical Content Knowledge (TPACK) 176; components of knowledge 232–233; emergent form of knowledge 235; technology knowledge 231

Technological Pedagogical Knowledge (TPK) 232, 234

Technology and Content Knowledge (TCK) 232, 234

Ten Steps to Complex Learning 86

testing: experiments 66; placement testing 292; practice testing 148; student testing 31

testing, criterion-referenced 302

textbooks 333–337

textbooks drive instruction 333–334

TPACK: technical, pedagogy and content knowledge 176, 231–232, 235–236

transfer of knowledge 330–331

transfer paradox 84–85

unicity 7, 245–246, 248

unified model of professional development 52–53

validity (external/internal) 335

validity (of tests) 302, 322–323, 327

wait time 37, 270, 278–279

worked example 166, 168–169, 171

worked-out example 165

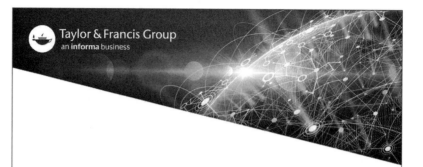